Royal Air Force
COASTAL COMM.
LOSSES
of the Second World War

Volume 1
Aircraft and Crew Losses
1939 - 1941

MIDLAND
An imprint of
Ian Allan Publishing

Royal Air Force
COASTAL COMMAND
LOSSES
of the Second World War

Volume 1
Aircraft and Crew Losses
1939 - 1941

ROSS McNEILL

Royal Air Force
Coastal Command Losses of the Second World War
1939-1941

First published in 2003 by
Midland Publishing
4 Watling Drive, Hinckley
LE10 3EY, England
Tel: 01455 254 490 Fax: 01455 254 495
E-mail: midlandbooks@compuserve.com

Midland Publishing is an imprint of
Ian Allan Publishing Ltd.

Worldwide distribution (except North America):
Midland Counties Publications
4 Watling Drive, Hinckley
LE10 3EY, England
Tel: 01455 254 450 Fax: 01455 233 737
E-mail: midlandbooks@compuserve.com
www.midlandcountiessuperstore.com

North American trade distribution:
Specialty Press Publishers & Wholesalers Inc
39966 Grand Avenue, North Branch, MN 55056, USA
Telephone: 651 277 1400 Fax: 651 277 1203
Toll free telephone: 800 895 4585
www.specialtypress.com

Printed in Great Britain by Ian Allan Printing Ltd
Riverdene Business Park, Molesey Road
Hersham, Surrey, KT12 4RG

Front cover illustration:
**Saro A27 London Mk.II K5910, 'BN-L' of 240 Squadron,
was photographed over the North Sea in mid-May 1940.
Londons remained in front-line use with 202 Squadron,
in Gibraltar, until mid-1941.** *P.H.T.Green collection*

Illustration on the half-title page:
**A formation of Bristol 149 Blenheim IVFs
from 254 Squadron, photographed sometime in 1941.
This unit was engaged in shipping protection duties,**
P.H.T. Green collection

Contents

Acknowledgements

I wish to acknowledge the immense assistance given by fellow researchers and enthusiasts in providing information from their files.

Countries and Regions
My thanks to Eric R Schwarz for information relating to the Norwegian Campaign, and to Ragnar J Ragnarsson on all items Icelandic.

Also to both Henk Welting (for helping to check the entire loss data) and Hans Nauta for details of the Netherlands.

Losses in Northumbria were examined and corrected by Jim Corbett.

Squadrons and Units
Andy Bird assisted with 235 Squadron and Ron Bramley with 22 Squadron.

General
The Royal National Lifeboat Institute for permission to use extracts from the Records of Service. Staff at the RAF Air Historical Branch and RAF Museum, Hendon, for answering many letters, and the Commonwealth War Graves Commission for allowing the use of casualty information.

Finally, but not at all least, the staff at the Public Record Office, Kew, for making my visits to the archives as painless and productive as possible.

Sources and Select Bibliography

SOURCES
Commonwealth War Graves Commission:
  Cemetery Registers.
Air Historical Branch:
  Aircraft Accident Cards; Aircraft Movement cards.
Public Record Office:
  Squadron Operational Record Books;
  Station Operational Record Books; Prisoner of War File.

FURTHER READING
Aircraft of the Royal Air Force since 1918 (9th edition):
  Owen Thetford; Putnam, 1996
Allied Convoy System 1939-1945, The: Arnold Hague;
  Vanwell Publishing, St Catharines, Ontario, 2000
Beaufort File: Roger Hayward; Air-Britain (Historians)
  Limited, Tunbridge Wells, 1990.
Blenheim Strike: Theo Boiten; Air Research Publications,
  Walton-on-Thames, 1995.
British Military Aircraft Serials 1878-1987:
  Bruce Robertson; Midland Counties Publcns, 1987.
Canadian Squadrons in Coastal Command: A Hendrie;
  Vanwell Publishing, St Catharines, Ontario, 1997.
Fledgling Eagles: Christopher Shores et al;
  Grub Street, London, 1991.
Flying Units of the RAF: Alan Lake;
  Airlife Publishing, Shrewsbury, 2001.
Hell on High Ground – Vols 1 & 2: David W Earl;
  Airlife Publishing Limited, Shrewsbury, 1989.
JG26 War Diary, The – Vol.1: Donald Caldwell;
  Grub Street, London, 1996.
K File, The Royal Air Force of the 1930s, The:
  James J Halley MBE; Air-Britain (Historians) Ltd,
  Tunbridge Wells, 1995.
Lockheed Hudson in World War II: Andrew Hendrie;
  Airlife Publishing Limited, Shrewsbury, 1999.
Northumberland Aviation Diary 1790-1999:
  Derek Walton, Norav Publications, Seahouses, 1999.
RAF Coastal Command 1936-1969: Chris Ashworth,
  Patrick Stephens Limited, Yeovil, 1992.
RAF Squadrons: Wing Commander C G Jefford MBE RAF;
  Airlife Publishing Limited,Shrewsbury, 1988.
RNLI Records of Service 1939 to 1946 – Supplement:
  Royal National Lifeboat Institute, 1947.
Royal Air Force Bomber Command Losses of the
  Second World War – Vol.1 - 1939-1940; Vol.2 - 1941:
  W R Chorley; Midland Counties Publications,
  Leicester, 1992 (Vol.1) and 1993 (Vol.2).
Short Sunderland in World War II: Andrew Hendrie;
  Airlife Publishing Limited, Shrewsbury, 1994.
Sopwiths to Sunderlands – 210 Squadron 1917 to 1941:
  John Evans; Paterchurch Publications, Pembs, 1999.
Squadron Codes 1937-56: Michael J F Bowyer and
  John D R Rawlings; Patrick Stephens Limited, 1979.
Squadrons of the Royal Air Force and Commonwealth
  1918-1988, The: James J Halley MBE;
  Air-Britain (Historians) Limited, Tonbridge, 1988.

The following, all edited by James J Halley MBE, were published by Air-Britain (Historians) Ltd, 1976-2000:
Royal Air Force Aircraft (series) – L1000 to N9999;
P1000 to R9999; T1000 to V9999; W1000 to Z9999;
AA100 to AZ999; BA100 to BZ999. (Some as 2nd edns).

Introduction

This book lists the aircraft losses suffered by Royal Air Force coastal squadrons operating from United Kingdom bases. The coastal units that are considered within the scope of this book are those operating under the control of Coastal Command as either full units or as detachments from other RAF Commands.

Aircraft have been listed where the loss is due to flying accident, enemy action, ground accident or damaged beyond economic repair. In all these cases the aircraft has been lost to unit use before being declared surplus to requirements and so falls within the scope of this book.

It should be considered that aircraft are just machines and for each loss in this book, a human crew was also involved in the eventual end of the airframe. This book will show the scale of sacrifice by the crews who flew on operations during the period covered by this volume. Due to the unforgiving nature of the seas the ratio of crews killed to those Safe or PoW is much higher than that of other commands. Also noticeable from the casualty lists are the large numbers who have no known grave and their only commemoration is an inscription on the Runnymede Memorial to the missing. Not included among the casualty lists are those airmen killed in the air whose aircraft have made safe returns or those of groundcrew of the coastal squadrons killed as a result of air-raids.

To put the individual operations into context I have included a brief description of the coastal campaign for the period covered by each chapter. The reader is encouraged to consult other published works for full details of the actions during this time period.

The loss lists have been collated from five primary sources: the unit Operations Record Books (ORBs) and the official air forces' Prisoner of War file held by the National Archives Public Record Office (PRO) at Kew; the Aircraft Accident and Movement Cards retained by the RAF Museum at Hendon and the Cemetery Registers published by the Commonwealth War Graves Commission (CWGC).

Each aircraft delivered to the RAF was assigned an Aircraft Movement Card, Form 78, which listed, in date order, movements from unit to unit during its service life. Where the aircraft was involved in an accident then an Aircraft Accident Card, Form 1180, was raised giving details on the loss and its suspected cause. Nearly all of the losses can be identified from these two sources. To add the crew and operation details requires the use of the ORBs.

The unit ORBs are normally split into two sections, Form 540 and Form 541. These are the daily and monthly summaries of all operational flying carried out by the unit. The detail varies from unit to unit and from recording clerk to recording clerk. Despite the variations in accuracy these records remain the most important source of loss details.

In the early stages of the war and for all non-operational losses the ORBs list only the aircraft captain and seldom give any further details of the crew. The Cemetery Registers and the Prisoner of War file provide the best mechanism for identifying crew names and ranks.

As in companion volumes from this publisher the sequence of reporting is in date chronological order, thereafter by squadron, aircraft type and serial number. The aircraft code letters, the type of duty or operation, the base, time of day, crew list and service numbers, brief description of loss and, where a fatality occurs, details of commemoration, are added where known. The meanings of most of the terms used are described in the Glossary of Terms section. In the case of a loss attributed to a *Luftwaffe* pilot then the word 'believed' should be firmly held in mind.

Where possible I have tried to list the crew in order of Captain, pilot, observer/navigator, WOp and AGs but due to the incomplete nature of the records consulted I cannot be certain of the exact crew functions.

Following the name or names of the aircrew, a '+' indicates a life lost. DoW or DoI means died of wounds or injuries). 'Wounded' denotes physical harm suffered in battle while 'Injured' is used to denote post-battle or accidental harm. PoW indicates prisoner of war status, while 'Evaded' means just that and usually implies a return to Britain. A crash-landing implies that the pilot had lost control of his machine, whereas a forced-landing suggests a landing with some degree of control (even if without power). The use of one (or more) asterisk after a decoration is an indication that a person has won that award more than once. For example DFC** indicates three awards of the DFC, and is usually quoted as a 'DFC and two Bars'.

All times quoted are in 24-hour clock and are shown exactly as given in the RAF and *Luftwaffe* records. See page 9 for additional notes on this subject and on the presentation of global positioning within this work.

Question marks used in the serial number or crew columns are either used to cast doubt on an identity or to show that the identity is not known.

Where a member of the Royal Canadian Air Force (say) was serving with a RCAF squadron, or a RAAF pilot with an Australian squadron, etc., such entries have *not* been afforded a RCAF or RAAF suffix, but their names have been suffixed appropriately if they were serving with a unit of another air arm, as have RAF personnel serving with non-RAF units.

Where I have introduced an error, or additional information comes to light, I would welcome such information, via the publisher, for inclusion in a future volume.

Ross McNeill
Bewdley, Worcs.   July 2003

Abbreviations

DECORATIONS

AFC	Air Force Cross
AFM	Air Force Medal
BEM	British Empire Medal
CBE	Commander of the Order of the British Empire
CGM	Conspicuous Gallantry Medal
DCM	Distinguished Conduct Medal
DFC	Distinguished Flying Cross
DFM	Distinguished Flying Medal
DSC	Distinguished Service Cross
DSO	Distinguished Service Order
EGM	Empire Gallantry Medal
GC	George Cross
GM	George Medal
KCB	Knight Commander of the Bath
KCMG	Knight Commander of the Order of St Michael and St George
KBE	Knight of the British Empire
MBE	Member of the Order of the British Empire
MiD	Mentioned in Dispatches
OBE	Officer of the Order of the British Empire
VC	Victoria Cross

RANKS

AC1	Aircraftman First Class
AC2	Aircraftman Second Class
AOC	Air Officer Commanding
C-in-C	Commander-in-Chief
CO	Commanding Officer
Cpl	Corporal
Ens	Ensign (American)
F/Lt	Flight Lieutenant
F/O	Flying Officer
F/Sgt	Flight Sergeant
Fw	*Feldwebel*
G/C	Group Captain
Hptm	*Hauptmann*
LAC	Leading Aircraftman
Lt	Lieutenant
Lt/Cdr	Lieutenant Commander
Ltn	*Leutnant*
NCO	Non-Commissioned Officer
Oblt	*Oberleutnant*
Ofw	*Oberfeldwebel*
P/O	Pilot Officer
Pte	Private
Sgt	Sergeant
S/Ldr	Squadron Leader
S/Lt(A)	Sub Lieutenant (Air) – Fleet Air Arm
Uffz	*Unteroffizier*
W/C	Wing Commander
W/O	Warrant Officer

ARMED SERVICES

AuxAF	Auxiliary Air Force (British)
FAA	Fleet Air Arm (British)
FAFL	Free French Air Force
KM	Royal Netherlands Navy
RAAF	Royal Australian Air Force
RAF	Royal Air Force (British)
RCAF	Royal Canadian Air Force
RN	Royal Navy (British)
RNorAF	Royal Norwegian Air Force
RNethAF	Royal Netherlands Air Force
RNNAS	Royal Netherlands Naval Air Service
RNZAF	Royal New Zealand Air Force
USN	United States Navy
WAAF	Women's Auxiliary Air Force

OTHERS

AA	Anti-Aircraft (fire, from the ground)
A-S or A/S	Anti-Submarine (or Anti-Shipping)
ASI	Air Speed Indicator
ASV	Aircraft to Surface Vessel
Bv	Blohm und Voss (with numerical suffix)
CWGC	Commonwealth War Graves Commission
Do	Dornier (with numerical suffix)
DoI	Died of Injuries (eg. in accidents)
DoW	Died of Wounds (post aerial combat etc.)
ETA	Estimated Time of Arrival
Fw	Focke-Wulf (with numerical suffix)
GP	General Purpose
GR	General Reconnaissance
He	Heinkel (with numerical suffix)
HMS	His Majesty's Ship
HSL	High Speed Launch (Air sea rescue)
IFF	Identification Friend or Foe
JG	*Jagdgeschwader*
Ju	Junkers (with numerical suffix)
KG	*Kampfgeschwader*
Me	Messerschmitt (with numerical suffix)
MTB	Motor Torpedo Boat
MU	Maintenance Unit
MV	Motor Vessel
NJG	*Nachtjagdgeschwader*
ORB	Operational Record Book
OTU	Operational Training Unit
PoW	Prisoner of War
RNLI	Royal National Lifeboat Institute
RP	Rocket Projectile (munition)
SoC	Struck off Charge
SOS	Save our souls (distress message)
SS	Steam-ship
SSQ	Station Sick Quarters
WOp	Wireless Operator
ZG	*Zerstörergeschwader*

Glossary

OPERATION CODE NAMES

Archery	Convoy Escort.
Bert	Bergen to Stavanger (patrol).
Bust	Boulogne to Ushant (patrol).
Dundee	Dunkirk to Dieppe (patrol).
Emro	Emden to Rotterdam, in darkness (patrol).
Focher	Photographic sortie to Cherbourg.
Gardening	Air dropping of sea mines.
Habo	Le Havre to Boulogne (patrol).
Hach	Le Havre to Cherbourg (patrol).
Hookos	Hook of Holland to Oostende (patrol).
Hornli	Horns Reef to Lister (patrol).
Intruder	Day or night sortie to attack German aircraft, or ground targets of opportunity.
Moon	English Channel (line patrol).
Nomad	Offensive shipping patrol, Oostende to Borkum.
Pirbo	Norfolk to Dutch Coast (line patrol).
Roadstead	Low level attack on coastal shipping
Rover	Offensive shipping patrol of the southern North Sea.
Stab	Standlandet to Bergen (patrol).
Stand	Stavanger to Kristiansand (patrol).
Sweep	Offensive shipping patrol, Horns Reef to Heligoland.

OTHER TERMS

AA	Anti-aircraft artillery fire from the ground; sometimes termed as Ack-Ack or 'flak'.
A/c	Aircraft
Det	Part of a unit, detached to another base for operations in another area.
D/F	Direction Finding (station)
E/A	Enemy Aircraft
Flak	Anti-aircraft fire; acronym from the German Fliegerabwehrkanone.
Flight	Subdivision of a squadron - usually 2 or 3 flights ('A', 'B' and 'C') per squadron.
kts	Knots (nautical miles per hour)
lb	Pound (weight)
Op	Operational task (abbreviation)
Recce	Reconnaissance
R/T	Radio telegraphy
Scramble	General term for aircraft being given the order to get airborne urgently.
Section	Subdivision of a Flight; usually 2 to 4 a/c and defined by a colour, e.g. 'Red Section'.
Sortie	Individual operation by an aircraft. Six a/c on a Sweep would constitute 6 sorties.
Sqn	Squadron
T/o	Took off or Take-off
U/c	Undercarriage (aircraft landing wheels)
W/T	Wireless telegraphy

REPORTING OF TIME

All times quoted are in the 24-hour clock mode and are shown exactly as given in RAF and *Luftwaffe* records. No attempt has be made to reduce allied and axis times to a common base.

RAF flying control recorded take-off in local time: this may or may not have been adjusted to GMT from the Observer/Navigator logs. Times of crashes may be in local or GMT. It should be borne in mind that 'double summer time' was in use in the UK at times.

The Royal Navy used GMT (or 'Z' time) for reports and signals, ie. the four-figure time group suffixed by a letter 'Z'.

The *Luftwaffe* and German Navy used Central European Time for signalling and reporting purposes. CET was two hours in advance of GMT.

During research for this work, there were several instances where the recorded time standard for a loss was at variance with other records.

CONVOY CODE PREFIXES

The following code prefixes have been identified in relation to convoys mentioned within the main text.

EC	Southend to Clyde, Loch Ewe or Oban, via Firth of Forth (in 1941).
EN	Methil (Fife) to Oban via Loch Ewe.
FS	Forth South (Firth of Forth to Thames).
HG	Homeward from Gibraltar.
HX	Halifax to UK; later New York to UK.
OA	Thames to Liverpool (1939-40); Methil to Liverpool to disperse in N.Atlantic (from July 1940).
OB	Liverpool outward; often joined up by the OA of the same number.
ON	Outward North, Liverpool to North America.
SC	Sydney (Cape Breton) or Halifax or New York to United Kingdom.
SL	Freetown to United Kingdom.
WS	UK to Suez and Bombay (troop convoys).

Notes

PR SPITFIRES – THE EARLY YEARS

In 1939 every Spitfire was needed to defend the UK, but permission was eventually granted to convert two for PR duties. Immediately successful, more were modified. These varied in camera, fuel, engine and armament fit, depending on their rôle, therefore a unique designation system was introduced, retrospectively. The original two PR Spitfires were deemed Type A, and subsequent variants, all of which included conversions in small numbers from Mk.I fighters, continued the series through to Type H. A production version of the Type D (based on the Mk.V fighter) was designated PR.IV – the 'PR' prefix being used well ahead of the official introduction of such rôle prefixes. Identification of some PR Mk.Is remains obscure. The Types A and B did not serve with Coastal Command.

A brief summary of the Royal Air Force PR variants that served prior to the end of 1941, follows:

Type A – Two Mk.Is (N3069, N3071) for the Heston Special Flight (later No 2 Camouflage Unit and PDU), no armament, one F.24 (5in) vertical camera in each wing. First op 18 Nov 39; both lost on ops Mar/Apr 40.

Type B – Eight to ten Mk.Is with F.24 (8in) camera in wings and extra 29 Imp gall fuel tank in rear fuselage. Operational with 212 Sqn in France, Feb 40.

Type C – Up to 20 converted from Mk.Is with an F8 camera in rear fuselage, and two F.24 cameras in blister under one wing and 30 Imp gall tank in blister under other wing, plus rear fuselage tank as Type B. Operational with 212 Sqn and PDU, Apr 40.

Type D – Two prototypes, first one flown 15 Sep 40; then twelve Mk.Is with Merlin 45 engines delivered from mid-41. Two x 66½ Imp gall fuel tanks in wings; two cameras in rear fuselage; extra oil in port wing.

PR.IV – Production version of Type D but based on Mk.V fighter airframe; 217 with Merlin 45 or 46 engines. First optnl sortie 5 Apr 41; all delivered by Mar 43.

Type E – Low-altitude PR variant; featured oblique F24 camera in blister under each wing, also fuselage tank. Conversions from Type C or Mk.V fighter airframe. In service with the PDU from Apr 40.

Type F – Interim long-range variant, prior to delivery of PR.IVs. Some converted from Type C, also 15 from Mk.V; all with two F24 or F8 cameras behind cockpit, Merlin 45 engine, blister wing tanks, deepened nose.

Type G – First armed PR version with 29 Imp gall fuselage tank, three F24 cameras, Merlin 45. Approx 24 conversions; in service from at least May 41.

Sometime after 1941 the Types A to H were redefined as Spitfire PR Mk.I to PR Mk.VIII respectively, even though by then no Type A or B remained in service, and the Type H (a proposed Mk.I PR variant with the Merlin 32) was not produced. Many early PR Spitfires were colloquially termed PR Mk.IIIs, seemingly to differentiate between them and the Mk.I & II fighters.

REPORTING OF POSITION

Global position indications within this work are quoted in one of the three forms to be found in official documents of the period, namely –
Conventional latitude and longitude;
Admiralty letter-number codes;
Bearing-feature-distance.
Although reference can be made to the ADM class of records held at the PRO for conversion between conventional and letter/number schemes, it is recognised that such positions are difficult to visualise, therefore it is intended to include a decoder for Coastal position codes covering 1939 to 1945 in a projected later volume in this series.

United Kingdom county titles quoted in this work are intended to be appropriate for the period.

PATROL CODE NAMES

Although a number of the code names for the anti-submarine and anti-shipping patrols and operations are provided under a sub-heading in the Glossary, it is openly acknowledged that many more code names listed within the main text defied explanation while this subject was being researched.

Just as we were about to go to press, an extensive document that goes a long way towards de-coding the patrol names and the areas and/or boundaries covered by the patrols, has been unearthed, albeit by accident, from an unexpected source within the PRO. Although an important find, time and space have colluded to prevented its inclusion within this volume.

However, it is intended that 'Coastal Command Anti-Submarine Patrol Areas' will form an Appendix in a future Volume in this series.

MESSERSCHMITT Bf or Me ?

The question as to whether 'Bf' or 'Me' should be used as the prefix for the Messerschmitt 109 and 110 fighters has generally settled upon them being *Bayrische Flugzeugwerke* (ie 'Bf') designs. The German Air Ministry (*Reichsluftfahrtministerium* or *RLM*) marks the transition from 'Bf' to 'Me' between the unsuccessful Bf162 Jaguar (whose number was subsequently allocated to the He162 Volksjäger) and the Me163 Komet.

However, all of this was unknown to those serving in the British and Allied armed forces and the aircraft were universally regarded (and written up as such in the Operations Record Books) as 'MEs' and for this series these types will be recorded in that vein, ie as Me109s or Me110s, rather than the more technically correct Bf109 or Bf110.

Chapter 1

Pre-War

Coastal Command was formed on the 13th July 1936 by the reorganisation of the existing fighting, bombing and coastal areas into commands based on function rather than geographical location. The new Commands of Fighter, Bomber and Coastal created under Expansion Scheme 'F', approved in February of 1936, allowed for a doubling of the size of the entire RAF by March 1939 but had very little effect on the new Coastal Command.

The establishment of Coastal Command remained at seven General Reconnaissance (GR) land based squadrons (126 aircraft), six flying-boat squadrons (36 aircraft) and one torpedo-bomber wing (30 aircraft).

Proposed as part of Expansion Scheme 'F' was a large increase in FAA fleet aircraft numbers for embarking on the new aircraft carriers expected to enter service. This led to a question about the role of the RAF in maritime operations with the Admiralty lobbying to take over both the FAA and Coastal Command establishment. In July of 1937 the government announced that although the FAA was to be transferred to Admiralty control, the RAF component was to remain under the control of Coastal Command.

It was not until the end of 1937 that the Air Ministry provided a directive on the tasks and estimated establishment for Coastal Command. The proposed tasks in descending order of importance were: protection of trade and trade routes by 213 aircraft, support of Fleet by 84 reconnaissance aircraft and Royal Navy co-operation by 42 aircraft.

After the Munich Crisis in 1938 the transfer of four Auxiliary Air Force squadrons boosted Coastal Command but their operational use was delayed until they had exchanged their current aircraft for more suitable types. Clarification of the functions and task order of Coastal Command were also declared as: reconnaissance in home waters; Royal Navy co-operation in trade route protection; and offensive action in defence of trade.

In August 1939, on the eve of war, Coastal Command assets were just 19 squadrons equipped with a total of six front-line aircraft types to fulfil those allotted tasks: the Avro Anson (equipping 9½ squadrons), Lockheed Hudson (1½), Saro London (2), Supermarine Stranraer (1), Short Sunderland (3) and Vickers Vildebeest (2). Typically, each GR squadron had 24 aircraft, flying-boat squadrons had 6 aircraft and the torpedo-bomber squadrons 15 aircraft giving an actual strength of 298 aircraft but only 171 were available for operations.

These 19 squadrons were controlled and divided between three operational groups, 15, 16 and 18. Coastal training assets were vested in 17 Group, which was headquartered at Gosport and had control over such diverse constituent units as the Torpedo Training School, the School of General Reconnaissance and the Seaplane Training Squadron. The losses incurred by these training units, and the soon to be established Coastal OTUs etc., are intended to be detailed in a later volume of Coastal Command losses.

In addition to the above types, the Saro Lerwick (after the Sunderland, the second of the monoplane flying-boats to be ordered for the RAF) had undergone three months of service trials with 240 Squadron from June 1939. It was not a success, only 21 were built and further production cancelled but due to an acute shortage of maritime aircraft, an operational squadron, 209, was formed at Calshot in the December and flew the Lerwicks until they were replaced by the Consolidated PBY-5 (known as the Catalina in the RAF) from April 1941 onwards. The Lerwicks passed into a training role with 4 (Coastal) OTU and those that survived the OTU helped work up 422 (RCAF) Squadron, from July to October 1942.

Reconnaissance patrols were started on the 24th of August, just missing the main German Naval deployment into the Atlantic of U-boats and cruiser forces (*Graf Spee* and *Deutschland*) on the 19th and 22nd of August.

So at the start of the war Coastal Command was under strength, with only the Sunderland and Hudson capable of carrying an adequate bomb-load with reasonable range. Available armament was the general-purpose bomb and an anti-submarine bomb that had proved ineffective in trials.. Hardly an ideal platform from which to start to fight a war !

Chapter 2

4th September 1939 to 31st December 1939

The August deployment of the German surface and submarine forces into the Atlantic led to very few Coastal Command crews reporting any contacts or action during the long patrols. The bulk of the aircraft losses during this period were due to weather or mechanical failure. Pre-war planning had been based on the premise that the greatest threat to the trade routes was from surface raiders in the North Atlantic. The expected route of Hitler's three heavy cruisers and three Hipper-class cruisers was from their bases in Northern Germany, through the Norwegian Sea and North Sea into the Atlantic.

From the 24th August 1939 Coastal Command carried out an 'Endless Chain' patrol between Wick in Scotland and territorial waters at the south-western tip of Norway. The Ansons that were allocated for this task were too short in range to cover the entire patrol area and the remaining gap of about 50 miles had to be covered by Admiralty submarines. It was not until the end of the year that Hudsons had been delivered in sufficient numbers to allow the whole patrol area to be covered by air and so release the submarines for other tasks.

Initially the 'Endless Chain' patrol could only be maintained in daylight so with the longer winter nights this was augmented by Dawn and Dusk patrols. The patrols were carried out by Sunderlands based at Sullom Voe/Invergordon to the north and Hudsons from Leuchars to the south.

Further south, on the 5th September, off the Dutch coast, 206 Squadron sighted a U-boat and attacked but their damage claim was not accepted. Also on that day an Anson of the same squadron was involved in the first air-to-air combat of Coastal Command, being shot down by two Blohm und Voss Bv138 flying-boats.
Coastal Command would need to wait until the 8th of October before 224 Squadron shot down a Dornier Do18 flying-boat: this proved to be the first confirmed RAF claim of the War.

The scale of U-boat victims (48 ships, 178,621 tons) in the first month of the war led to Armstrong Whitworth Whitley IIIs of 58 Squadron being detached from Bomber Command from the end of September and used for anti-submarine patrols over the English Channel until early 1940. Few U-boat sightings were reported by Coastal Command patrols because the Germans were air-dropping magnetic mines to occupy the resources of the Royal Navy in home waters and had deployed the U-boats into the Atlantic trade routes.

In November, N9025, a Sunderland of 228 Squadron on reconnaissance off Norway, sighted the *City of Flint*, which had been captured by the *Deutschland* and manned by a German prize crew. The German crew took the *City of Flint* into Bergen and surrendered before the Royal Navy reached them. The *Deutschland* slipped back into the Baltic later in the month having evaded all patrols.

Coastal Command also received its first Bristol Beaufort aircraft in November, when deliveries were made to 22 Squadron at Thorney Island. The Beaufort was a four-place torpedo-bomber and general reconnaissance version of the sprightly Bristol Blenheim GR coastal-bomber that had served with the RAF since 1937. The Beaufort working-up period was a prolonged and problematical affair and the unit suffered several losses prior to mounting its first operational sorties on 15th April 1940. Ironically, the first of 22's accidental losses (on 22nd December) involved a Blenheim that presumably was on strength to assist in the task of pilot conversion.

The first attack by Coastal Command on an enemy ship took place in December off the coast of Denmark but resulted in little damage to the four destroyers involved.

4th September 1939

48 Sqn	Anson I		K8704	OY-E	Op:	Patrol
	Sgt	R E Williams	580037	Safe	Base:	Thorney Island
	Sgt	F Burton	563612	Safe	T/o time:	04:15
	LAC	J Meek	526257	Safe		
	AC	D Hider	552077	Safe		

Suffered an engine failure while overshooting in ground fog. Sgt Williams then tried to go around again and restart the engine but the Anson would not maintain height and was eventually ditched into Thorney creek some 200 yards from the airfield perimeter.
The aircraft sank immediately injuring two of the crew in the process.

233 Sqn	Hudson I	N7239	ZS-	Duty:	Training
	F/Lt G P Robinson	33282	+	Base:	Leuchars
	F/O E D Godfrey	39167	+	T/o time:	15:45

Failed to set tail trimming gear to the correct position for take-off. Climbed steeply, stalled, the Hudson turned onto its back and spun into the River Eden before being burned out. F/O Godfrey was buried in Leuchars Cemetery while F/Lt Robinson rests in St Peter Churchyard, Duddon.

5th September 1939

206 Sqn	Anson I	K6183	VX-B	Op:	Patrol
	P/O L H Edwards	31687	PoW	Base:	Bircham Newton
	Sgt A O Heslop	566050	+	T/o time:	05:25
	AC1 G Sheffield	552231	+		
	LAC J Quilter	524808	+		

Twelve aircraft took off for a parallel line search of the North Sea. P/O Edwards was at 300 feet when he sighted and attacked a German float-plane off the Freisians. Early in the 15 min dogfight LAC Quilter was hit, rendering the Anson virtually defenceless. P/O Edwards tried to bring down the enemy with his fixed forward firing gun but eventually he was shot down into the sea and blew up due to return fire from the Heinkel He115, M2+FH of I/KuFlGr 160. The German crew circled the crash site then landed to pick up two men in the water but they could only find the badly injured P/O Edwards. Those who died are commemorated on the Runnymede Memorial.

233 Sqn	Anson I	K8845	ZS-N	Op:	Anti-Submarine Patrol
	P/O G J D Yorke	36185	Safe	Base:	Leuchars
	Sgt D J Muir	580184	Safe	T/o time:	16:00

On the return from patrol P/O Yorke sighted a submarine submerging in position ZGCB 4000 and attacked, dropping his entire bomb-load. The submarine was logged as damaged at 20:05 hrs in the attack and the Anson set course for base. On the return leg fuel was draining away through shrapnel holes in the wing tanks and resulted in a forced landing into the River Eden estuary off Shelly Point. All of the crew escaped by dinghy and were quickly rescued. Mess celebrations were short lived when they were informed by Admiralty that they had attacked HMS *Seahorse* and that the well placed bomb-load had caused no appreciable damage.

7th September 1939

224 Sqn	Hudson I	N7247	QX-G	Op:	Search
	F/O H D Green	39155	+	Base:	Leuchars
	P/O C N Whittington	36184	+	T/o time:	17:10
	LAC J L Calpin	531154	+		
	AC1 A McR Rodger	543962	+		

Dived into the North Sea at 22:10 hrs, 4 miles NNE of the North Carr Light Vessel. Despite a long search by the Broughty Ferry lifeboat and Ansons of 233 Squadron, nothing was found of the crew. Two months later a cowling panel from the Hudson was recovered from the sea in the crash area. The navigator, P/O Whittington, from New Zealand, and the other members of the crew are commemorated on the Runnymede Memorial.

8th September 1939

224 Sqn	Hudson I	N7210	QX-	Duty:	Training
	Sgt F A E Cramp	562618	Safe	Base:	Leuchars
				T/o time:	?

Due to construction activities on the aerodrome Sgt Cramp carried out a night landing on bad ground. Shortly after touch down the Hudson started a violent turn to port and the brakes were applied to correct the slew. The undercarriage collapsed and Sgt Cramp was thrown out of his seat by the force of the impact but escaped without injury.

9th September 1939

48 Sqn	Anson I	K8707	OY-K	Op:	Reconnaissance
	F/Lt G E Ford	. . . . .	Safe	Base:	Detling
	Sgt F M Pennell	580304	Safe	T/o time:	17:54
	Cpl Parkinson	575887	Safe		
	LAC A G Willis	568341	Safe		

Crashed into the Channel at 20:30 hrs off Hastings, Sussex, on the return leg. At 21:29 hrs the coastguard at Fairlight reported that an aeroplane had come down in the sea 1 mile to the east. The weather was clear and the sea was calm. At 21:35 hrs the Dungeness lifeboat station was told by the observer post at Dungeness that an aeroplane had come down in the sea about 7 miles WSW of Dungeness. At 21:40 hrs Mr R Cooke, volunteer-in-charge of the life-saving corps at Pett, was told that an aeroplane had come down about 1½ miles south of Pett. The Hastings lifeboat, *Cyril and Lillian Bishop*, was launched at 21:47 hrs; the Dungeness motor lifeboat, *Charles Cooper Henderson*, at 21:45 hrs. Mr Cooke called for a crew to man his motor boat, and put out with three men. He was the first to find the aeroplane. Her crew of four, were on the top of the machine. Mr Cooke landed them at Pett. At 22:40 hrs the Hastings lifeboat found the aeroplane, abandoned by her crew, and towed it into Hastings, arriving at 01:30 hrs. The Dungeness lifeboat cruised about, using her searchlight, for an hour and a half, but found no trace of the aircraft. Later she learned from a destroyer that the crew had been saved, and returned to their station, arriving at 01:00 hrs.

48 Sqn

		Anson I	L7058	OY-J	Op:	Reconnaissance
Sgt	G N Wilkinson		580240	Injured	Base:	Detling
P/O	J J Drummond		41267	+	T/o time:	18:06
AC1	Clarke		551551	Injured		

Took off for an operation to the southern part of the North Sea. Became lost in bad weather, ran out of fuel and tried to carry out a forced landing in a field on the summit of Cap Gris Nez, France, but crashed when the starboard engine cut during a right hand turn on the approach. P/O Drummond, from Hawkes Bay, New Zealand, is buried in Terlincthun British Cemetery, Wimille, Pas de Calais.

206 Sqn

		Anson I	K6187	VX-E	Op:	Patrol
P/O	R T Kean		41295	Safe	Base:	Bircham Newton
P/O	H M F Barnitt		.....	Safe	T/o time:	17:55
AC	Caulfield		......	Safe		
LAC	Thompson		......	Safe		

Took off tasked with a parallel track search of the North Sea. On the return from patrol the Anson missed the aerodrome in the blackout and continued on a southern course until an engine cut due to lack of fuel. The New Zealand pilot, P/O Kean, was unable to maintain height and the aircraft was finally ditched into the Channel off the Dyck lightship. The crew were rescued and returned to base.

500 Sqn

		Anson I	N5066	MK-	Op:	Reconnaissance
P/O	Lane		.....	Safe	Base:	Detling
P/O	E N Harris		.....	Safe	T/o time:	17:43
AC2	R H Coomber		812107	Safe		
AC2	W J Smith		812204	Safe		

Ran out of fuel on a search sortie in fog over the North Sea and ditched at 22:45 hrs off Seasalter, Kent. A number of small boats including the Margate and Southend-on-Sea lifeboats carried out a search for the crew who were safely recovered.

500 Sqn

		Anson I	N5052	MK-	Op:	Reconnaissance
F/O	R E Jay		90011	Injured	Base:	Detling
LAC	J H Baldry		812099	Injured	T/o time:	17:49
AC2	S F C Cunningham		812142	Safe		
AC2	H G Ridley		812197	Safe		

Ran out of fuel and abandoned by parachute from 4,000 feet on a night search in bad weather over North Sea. F/O Jay and LAC Baldry were injured when the crew abandoned the aircraft near Polegate, Sussex. The Anson crashed at 22:30 hrs near Wilmington Sussex.

10th September 1939

228 Sqn

	Sunderland I	N6135	DQ-U	Duty:	Ferry Flight
S/Ldr G L Menzies		32061	Safe	Base:	Kalafrana, Malta
				T/o time:	05:30

At approximately 18:30 hrs S/Ldr Menzies landed downwind due to bad weather and tore both wing tip floats off after ferry flight to Pembroke Dock. During subsequent salvage operations the Sunderland capsized and was finally beached in that condition. There were no reported injuries to the crew.

17th September 1939

210 Sqn	Sunderland I	L2165	DA-B	Op:	Anti-Submarine Patrol
	F/Lt T I Davies	34103	+	Base:	Pembroke Dock
	P/O G W Sutton	40647	+	T/o time:	11:30
	P/O G W Brant	40598	+		
	Cpl R W Ewens	563456	+		
	AC1 M Murphy	518041	+		
	AC1 F J Soffe	566819	+		
	AC1 W A Soanes	521516	+		
	AC1 F E Hudson	529152	+		
	AC2 J Moss	570205	+		
	AC2 W A O'Brien	552026	+		

Returning at night the aircraft failed to find Pembroke Dock and D/F bearings were requested and obtained. The bearings given indicated that the Sunderland was over the Irish Sea and when St Ann's lighthouse was found the petrol supply was exhausted, and the aircraft crashed in the sea at the entrance to Milford Haven in Dale Roads at 00:30 hrs on the morning of the 18th. The Angle lifeboat carried out a search of the area but found only wreckage. F/Lt Davies, P/O Sutton, a New Zealander from Auckland, P/O Brant, a Canadian from Saskatchewan, Cpl Ewens, AC1 Murphy, from Eire, and AC2 Moss all rest locally in Llanion Cemetery, Pembroke Dock. AC1 Soffe and AC1 Hudson are commemorated on the Runnymede Memorial while AC1 Soanes is buried in St John the Baptist Churchyard, Newton Nottage, Glamorganshire, and AC2 O'Brien, from Eire, rests in Ballon Catholic Churchyard, County Carlow, Eire.

25th September 1939

220 Sqn	Anson I	K6202	NR-E	Op:	Convoy Escort FN10
	P/O G W McNeill	41043	Safe	Base:	Thornaby
	F/O C W Wright	39427	Safe	T/o time:	16:20

At 19:45 hrs on the return from the operation the Anson overshot during landing and damaged the undercarriage. Struck off charge on 22nd November 1939.

30th September 1939

224 Sqn	Hudson I	N7216	QX-D	Op:	Reconnaissance
	F/O J R Hollington MiD	37881	+	Base:	Leuchars
	Sgt R S Pitts	565342	+	T/o time:	?
	AC1 G Rout	550531	+		
	AC1 A Bathgate	567441	+		

Sent on a photo operation to Brunsbuttel/Wilhelmshaven and failed to return. The Hudson was claimed as shot down by Ltn Heinz Demes of 4./JG77 flying an Me109 at Brunsbuttel. F/O Hollington was recovered from the sea on the 27th November west of Tammwarft, Pellworm, was initially buried at Husum but now rests in Kiel War Cemetery. Sgt Pitts was washed ashore on the 17th November and rests in Klitmoller Churchyard, Denmark, while AC1 Rout and AC1 Bathgate are commemorated on the Runnymede Memorial.

224 Sqn	Hudson I	N7219	QX-V	Op:	Reconnaissance
	P/O D G Heaton-Nichols	27275	PoW	Base:	Leuchars
	Sgt J Pearce	564932	+	T/o time:	?
	AC1 A Sill	520315	+		
	AC1 A Thomason	530618	+		

Sent on photo operation to the island of Sylt but shot down by flak from Marineflakabteilung 264 and crashed 300 yards from the beach. The flak battery reported two parachutes. Those killed were initially buried at List, Sylt on the 2nd October 1939 but now rest in Kiel War Cemetery.

2nd October 1939

48 Sqn	Anson I	K6234	OY-T	Op:	Air Striking Force
	P/O M V Hunter	.....	Safe	Base:	Thorney Island
	Sgt R A Bate	564536	Injured	T/o time:	19:05
	AC1 S McCracken	535633	Safe		
	AC Hills	......	Safe		

Force-landed at 20:30 hrs into the sea just to the south of East Stoke, Hayling Island, Sussex, when returning from an unsuccessful striking force. The forced landing was apparently due to an engine failure from unknown cause. Superficial cuts and bruises were received by the crew, while the aircraft became a complete loss.

4th October 1939

224 Sqn	Hudson I	N7214	QX-T	Duty:	Transit Flight
	F/O D G Perry	37899	+	Base:	Thornaby
	P/O J W C McFarlane	39638	+	T/o time:	?
	Sgt H Letchford	580247	+		
	P/O R A Barker	40199	+		
	AC1 F H May	521784	+		
	AC1 C A Bates	511737	+		

Delivered a relief aircraft to the detached flight and returned with relieved crew and kit. Dived into the ground from 300 feet, half a mile N of Leuchars, Fife, after a presumed loss of control due to unbalanced load. Sgt Letchford, P/O McFarlane, P/O Barker and AC1 Bates rest locally in Leuchars Cemetery. F/O Perry is buried in Longparish Cemetery, Hampshire and AC1 May in St John's Westgate Cemetery, Newcastle-upon-Tyne.

7th October 1939

500 Sqn	Anson I	N5233	MK-Q	Op:	Convoy
	F/O D G Mabey	90008	+	Base:	Detling
	P/O A MacD Paterson	90572	+	T/o time:	15:57
	Cpl J F Drew	812045	+		
	LAC F Messent	812073	Safe		

Took off to escort convoy OA16 from North Foreland. Control was lost after an engine failure in bad weather and the Anson crash-landed near Cranbrook Road, Benenden, Kent at 20:40 hrs. LAC Messent abandoned by parachute before the crash. F/O Mabey rests in Tonbridge Cemetery, P/O Paterson in St Martin Churchyard Extension, Detling and Cpl Drew in Canterbury Cemetery.

10th October 1939

233 Sqn	Hudson I	N7227	ZS-Y	Op:	Patrol
	F/O C H C Clark	39272	+	Base:	Leuchars
	P/O W E Lockley	41436	+	T/o time:	14:20
	AC1 B N Blades	550711	+		
	AC2 W M Cochrane	620399	+		

The Hudson was flying very low as the visibility was poor with a low cloud base and it struck high ground at 19:40 hrs, 1½ miles S of Freuchie, Fife, when returning from patrol. Fire broke out immediately and the wreckage was distributed over a large area. The crew of four were killed instantly. F/O Clark, a New Zealander from Wellington City, and P/O Lockley are buried in Leuchars Cemetery while AC1 Blades was taken to St Mary Churchyard, Wath, Yorkshire and AC2 Cochrane rests in Ryden Mains Cemetery, New Monkland, Lanarkshire.

13th October 1939

204 Sqn	Sunderland I	N9045	KG-	Op:	Anti-Submarine Search
	F/Lt E L Hyde	37179	Safe	Base:	Mount Batten
	P/O W H Tremar	.....	Safe	T/o time:	10:20
	W/O Castle	.....	Safe		
	AC Stringer	......	Safe		
	AC Dark	......	Safe		
	AC Perry	......	Safe		
	AC D S Lloyd	547593	Safe		
	AC Hosking	......	Safe		
	AC Athins	......	Safe		
	AC Arundell	......	Safe		
	AC Marles	......	Safe		
	Lt Carron	......	Safe		
	W/O Haley	......	Safe		

Took off for an anti-submarine search in position 48 42N 15 55W. At 18:40 hrs, in position 257 Scillies 18, the aircraft was force-landed owing to lack of fuel. Two engines were used to approach a ship seen nearby before all four engines cut. There was a 50 ft sea and wind at gale force which caused the port float to be carried away on landing. Six of the crew were immediately sent onto the starboard wing and SOS signals were made to the ship by W/T and visual signal. Nine of the crew then left in rubber dinghies and were subsequently picked up by the ship's lifeboat which was lowered when the flying-boat was half a mile from the ship. The aircraft then took up an angle of 45° to normal and the crew had considerable difficulty in maintaining their position on the starboard wing. Three flares were lit but only one went off, indicating to the ship's captain the fact that all the crew had not been taken off. As the Dutch Merchant Vessel *Bilderdijk* moved around the Sunderland they collided and the aircraft sank immediately. The rescued airmen were transferred to HMS *Icarus* and landed at Plymouth after the destroyer had completed its task. The court of inquiry found that the petrol consumption of the Sunderland had been abnormal and thought that flying in cloud with the carburettor shutters closed may have been the cause.

14th October 1939

48 Sqn	Anson I		K8711	OY-E	Op:	Anti-Sub Convoy Patrol
	Sgt	Bodien	. . . . . .	Safe	Base:	Thorney Island
	Sgt	Williams	. . . . . .	Safe	T/o time:	16:30
	AC	D Hider	552077	Safe		
	AC	Fog	. . . . . .	Safe		

Became lost and was forced to ditch at 20:30 hrs due to lack of fuel. At 21:20 hrs the coastguard reported that the Shambles Lightship had fired guns and rockets. A strong east wind was blowing, with a moderate sea and rain. At 22:00 hrs the motor lifeboat *William and Clara Ryland* was launched, and learnt from the lightship that an aeroplane had come down 2 miles to the NE. The lightship's boat had already put off to the rescue, manned by four men. The lifeboat found this boat 2 miles away. She had already succeeded in rescuing the crew of four of the aeroplane a very fine piece of work in the darkness and rain with a strong wind blowing and was putting them aboard a destroyer. She was herself waterlogged, so the lifeboat took on board the four men and brought them back to the lightship, returning to her station at 02:15 hrs. A destroyer tried to salvage the floating Anson but tore the tail off causing the aircraft to sink.

15th October 1939

204 Sqn	Sunderland I		N9030	KG-B	Op:	Patrol
	F/Lt	H B Johnson	. . . . .	Injured	Base:	Mount Batten
	F/O	D Ford	37631	+	T/o time:	11:45
	Sgt	Watkins	. . . . . .	Injured		
	AC2	J D Whitford	552435	+		
	AC2	W H Fiddock	619855	+		
	AC2	J H Hayward	621542	+		

Took off for a patrol to a position off Vermout. On landing at 21:15 hrs the Sunderland flew into the water in bad visibility outside the breakwater killing four and injuring seven of the crew. Three engines of the aircraft were later salvaged. F/O Ford rests in St John Churchyard Extension, Hooe, Devon, both AC2 Hayward and AC2 Whitford in S.S. Macra, Mary and Julian Churchyard, Maker, Cornwall, while AC2 Fiddock is commemorated on the Runnymede Memorial.

18th October 1939

233 Sqn	Anson I	K6268	ZS-G		Ground Loss
				Base:	Leuchars
				Time:	?

Hit by Hudson N7271 while picketed at dispersal.

233 Sqn	Hudson I		N7271	ZS-R	Op:	Patrol
	F/O	G Edwards	39309	Safe	Base:	Leuchars
	Sgt	F F Hallam	564213	Safe	Time:	?

Swung badly on take-off and crashed into Anson K6268 which was picketed at a dispersal point. The Hudson continued to crash over the edge of the aerodrome into the River Eden. Both aircraft were wrecked. The crew were uninjured except for shock and slight cuts. Hoar frost was suspected as the cause of the accident.

27th October 1939

608 Sqn	Anson I	N5204	UL-N	Op:	Convoy Patrol
	P/O A D Baird	91062	+	Base:	Thornaby
	F/Lt G W Garnett	90302	+	T/o time:	11:00
	Cpl R A Wilson	808180	+		
	AC2 Smith	. . . . . .	Wounded		

Failed to return from escort duties. Later information was received that aircraft had been shot down in vicinity of Humber Lightship by a Hurricane. HMS *Stork* picked up two of the crew at about 12:00 hrs. Cpl Wilson rests in Oxbridge Lane Cemetery, Stockton-on-Tees, County Durham and AC2 Smith who was wounded was admitted to HMS *Ganges*, Harwich. P/O Baird and F/Lt Garnett are commemorated on the Runnymede Memorial.

3rd November 1939

209 Sqn	Stranraer I	K7294	WQ-	Duty:	Training
	Sgt Harrold	563890	Injured	Base:	Falmouth
	Cpl J W Jay	347747	Injured	T/o time:	?
	LAC G Peterson	520852	Injured		
	LAC G W Bowman	520242	+		
	AC1 S C Colbridge	570418	+		

Took off for local flying training but hit a swell, bounced, stalled and hit the water. The wreck of the aircraft was later salvaged and the bodies of the two crewmen killed were recovered. LAC Bowman rests in Eastcote Lane Cemetery, Harrow, Middlesex, and AC1 Colbridge in St Mary Magdalene Churchyard, Great Burstead, Essex.

240 Sqn	London II	K9686	BN-K	Op:	Reconnaissance
	F/Lt J MacL H Sinclair MiD	37428	+	Base:	Sullom Voe
	Sgt T E Page	565335	+	T/o time:	?
	AC1 J C Lewis	519767	+		
	LAC A J Saffin	534026	+		
	AC1 C Wilson	538736	+		
	Cpl D D Kane	543862	+		

Failed to return from an operation to the Norwegian coast. AC1 Wilson rests in Stavne Cemetery, Trondheim, Norway while the rest of the crew are commemorated on the Runnymede Memorial to the missing.

5th November 1939

48 Sqn	Anson I	K8781	OY-Y	Duty:	Transit Flight
	Sgt R A Bate	564536	Safe	Base:	Thorney Island
	P/O M J Hunter	. . . . .	Safe	T/o time:	14:15
	AC McIlvenny	. . . . . .	Safe		
	AC Leigh	. . . . . .	Safe		

Landed out of wind in gusting winds and rain then skidded into a hedge at Guernsey Airport, Channel Islands 15:45 hrs. The Anson was considered to have been damaged beyond economic repair.

6th November 1939

269 Sqn	Anson I	N4961	UA-S	Op:	Parallel Track Search
	F/Lt H G Mossford	. . . . .	Safe	Base:	Wick
	P/O Brinsden	. . . . .	Safe	T/o time:	14:45

Forced landing in Cullen Bay, Banffshire at 18:30 due to fuel shortage. Four men at once put out to the rescue in the motor boat *Quest*. A light SW wind was blowing, with a slight swell, but the aircraft was near the rocks and the rescuers ran great risk of having their boat washed on to them. The work of rescue was made still more dangerous by the fact that the Anson was carrying live bombs, but the four men were successful in rescuing the crew of four without mishap. The Fraserburgh lifeboat also took part in a search for the aircraft.

8th November 1939

220 Sqn	Hudson I	N7290	NR-	Duty:	Training
	P/O A H J Ryan	41324	+	Base:	Thornaby
	P/O D H Robertson	41469	+	T/o time:	?
	Sgt R Mitchell	580183	+		
	AC1 A Wade	534389	+		

Stalled on the approach and then crashed into a house in Cambridge Road, Middlesborough, North Yorkshire. P/O Ryan, a New Zealander from Canterbury, rests in Hartshill Cemetery, Stoke-on-Trent, P/O Robertson, a New Zealander from Nelson, in Thornaby-on-Tees Cemetery, AC1 Wade in St Mary Church Cemetery, Burley-in-Wharfedale, Yorkshire; and Sgt Mitchell in Byker and Heaton Cemetery, Newcastle-upon-Tyne.

14th November 1939

201 Sqn	London II	K5912	ZM-	Op:	North Sea Patrol
	F/O J D Middleton	33326	Safe	Base:	Sullom Voe
	P/O Lindsay	.....	Safe	T/o time:	08:50

Took off on Track A to Norway but force-landed in the North Sea 80 miles from Shetland at 13:45 hrs. The crew were picked up 18:20 hrs by HMS *Imperial* and landed at Methil. HMS *Imperial* later sank the aircraft by gunfire. See loss of F/Lt Middleton on Sunderland N6133, 9th July 1940.

19th November 1939

220 Sqn	Hudson I	N7284	NR-	Duty:	Training
	P/O H J Keller	36173	+	Base:	Thornaby
	P/O J W C Robertson	41533	+	T/o time:	?

Crashed into the North Sea 4½ miles E of Seaham, Co Durham, after air gunnery practice on sea markers and was seen to sink by HMS *Dalmarron* in position 5450N 0110W, 4½ miles 090° from Seaham Harbour. A search by the Seaham lifeboat failed to find any trace and later it was reported that the aircraft had been located by a trawler but no sign of the crew. Both crew members are commemorated on the Runnymede Memorial. P/O Keller was a New Zealander from Taranaki.

224 Sqn	Hudson I	N7213	QX-L	Op:	Patrol L.1
	F/Lt A E Williamson	37370	Safe	Base:	Leuchars
				T/o time:	11:10

The starboard wing dropped on take-off causing the Hudson to swing and crash.

20th November 1939

48 Sqn	Anson I	(K8833 ?)	OY-A	Op:	Dutch Patrol
	P/O Allsopp	.....	Safe	Base:	Detling
	P/O Collins	.....	Safe	T/o time:	13:48
	LAC Crawford	......	Safe		
	LAC Smith	......	Safe		

Landed in the sea due fuel shortage at c.19:00 hrs. The crew were picked up by HMS *Greyhound*.

22nd November 1939

201 Sqn	London II	L7042	ZM-		Ground Loss
				Base:	Lerwick
				Time:	?

Attacked by an He111 of II/KG26 and destroyed by fire at its moorings in Lerwick Harbour, Shetland, while undergoing engine change. A few days later the wreckage was towed into deep water and sunk.

28th November 1939

269 Sqn	Anson I	K8744	UA-Y	Op:	Anti-Submarine Patrol
	P/O P N Trolove	36183	Safe	Base:	Wick
	P/O Brinsden	.....	Safe	T/o time:	07:50

Crashed on landing.

6th December 1939

206 Sqn	Anson I	K6189	VX-R	Op:	Reconnaissance
	P/O J H Grimes	41237	+	Base:	Bircham Newton
	Sgt V D MacMillan	526547	+	T/o time:	09:25
	Cpl H J Cockayne	550939	+		
	AC1 J C Bagley	528459	+		

Took off tasked with an operation to the Maas and Haaks Light-vessels. Collided with an Me110 from II/ZG26, which also crashed killing its crew, during combat 70 miles N of Texel, Holland, while on North Sea patrol. All are commemorated on the Runnymede Memorial.

10th December 1939

500 Sqn	Anson I	N5231	MK-P	Op:	Dover Patrol
	P/O B H Arkell	40498	Injured	Base:	Detling
	LAC J Walton	812061	Injured	T/o time:	07:41
	LAC H J Le Gassick	551562	Injured		
	Sgt Braybrooks	580240	Injured		

Flew into trees in low cloud just after take-off. LAC Le Gassick of 48 Sqn died later in West Kent General Hospital and is buried in Palmerston Road Cemetery, Chatham, Kent.

22nd December 1939

22 Sqn	Blenheim I	L1531	OA-	Duty:	Training
	P/O A G Rigg	41067	Safe	Base:	Thorney Island
				T/o time:	?

Took off for circuits and landings. Tried to retract the u/c before becoming fully airborne but the Blenheim struck a rise in the ground before the wheels were fully up and locked. P/O Rigg found that he could not raise or lower the u/c from its jammed mid-travel position so he finished the circuit and carried out a belly-landing.

27th December 1939

269 Sqn	Anson I	K6286	UA-E	Op:	Patrol
	P/O A J MacDonald	36176	+	Base:	Wick
	P/O J B Beer	41364	+	T/o time:	10:26
	AC1 T Finnigan	547574	+		
	AC2 W T Lowey	619235	+		

Failed to return owing to an irregular mechanical failure over the sea and was ditched east of Orkney. P/O MacDonald and his crew are commemorated on the Runnymede Memorial.

29th December 1939

502 Sqn	Anson I	N5063	YG-N	Op:	Convoy Escort
	F/O Bell	. . . . .	Safe	Base:	West Freugh
	P/O Egerton	. . . . .	Safe	T/o time:	12:10
	Cpl Evans	. . . . . .	Safe		
	Sgt Mason	. . . . . .	Safe		

Landed at West Freugh at 12:10 hrs then, owing to a temporary improvement in the weather, took off again for Aldergrove but force-landed at 13:15 hrs near Elliotts Farm, 2 miles E of Aldergrove, County Antrim.

Chapter 3

1st January 1940 to 7th April 1940

Magnetic mines were deployed around British coastal waters by the Germans late in 1939 and proved to be a formidable weapon. De-gaussing of ship's hulls helped in reducing the losses but the harbour approaches still required clearing. No 1 General Reconnaissance Unit was formed on the 5th December 1939 with specially adapted Wellingtons and flew its first sortie over the Thames Estuary on the 8th January 1940. The large rings on these aircraft generated a strong magnetic field, which triggered the mine detonator without damage to the aircraft and allowed large sea areas to be swept clear.

ASV radar and IFF was now being fitted to the Hudsons. Although incapable of detecting a submerged U-boat the primitive radar could locate a vessel running on the surface in good conditions. The increased use of ASV radar and the convoy routing system caused mounting U-boat losses and limited the numbers of Merchant Vessels sunk.

Increased commitments prompted four squadrons of Blenheim fighters to be transferred over from Fighter Command. No 254 Squadron arrived at the end of January; the other three squadrons, 235, 236 and 248 followed a month later, although the latter two were very soon to return to their former masters before a more permanent spell with Coastal Command. No 10 (RAAF) Squadron was officially transferred to Coastal Command on 10th February 1940, bringing the number of operational Sunderland units to four. Short Brothers had completed the initial Sunderland order and started to dismantle the construction jigs to concentrate on development of the Stirling four-engined bomber. This action delayed any new production of Sunderlands.

Following the scuttling of the *Graf Spee* off Montevideo, her supply ship the *Altmark,* tried to break through the North Sea blockade back to German home waters. On board the *Altmark* were 299 British Merchant Navy seamen from the five vessels sunk by the *Graf Spee.* Coastal Command searched the Norwegian coast and on 16th February, 220 Squadron sent a sighting report to the Admiralty. In an attempt to repeat the November 1939 success with the *City of Flint* a naval force was sent to the reported position but nothing was found. More reconnaissance was ordered and a Hudson of 233 Squadron finally found the *Altmark* in Norwegian waters. In a breach of neutrality HMS *Cossack* entered Jossing Fjord and, after a brief fight, captured the vessel and released the prisoners. This act triggered Hitler to order the invasion of Norway to protect his shipments of ore from Sweden through Narvik. The U-boats were recalled to Norwegian waters and a task force prepared to seize Trondheim and Narvik. Coastal Command Hudsons sighted the task force including *Scharnhorst* and *Gneisenau* at sea on the 7th April 1940 but its implications for Norway were mistaken.

1st January 1940

220 Sqn	Hudson I	N7232	NR-T	Op:	Search
	F/Lt T H Clarke	37960	+	Base:	Thornaby
	Sgt R J Peacock	562854	+	T/o time:	08:35
	LAC C F Hudson	524576	+		
	LAC D M Rowson MiD	550760	+		

Crashed into the North Sea in the vicinity of ZGSE 0227 and ZGSE 1634, some 20 miles E of St Abbs Head, Berwickshire, following an attack on a Ju88 of I/KG30. From 11:04 hrs to 11:41 hrs a number of bearings were given by both RAF Thornaby and RAF Leuchars D/F stations to the aircraft. All are commemorated on the Runnymede Memorial.

3rd January 1940

502 Sqn	Anson I	N5234	YG-H	Op:	Convoy Escort
	F/Lt R T Corry	90034	Safe	Base:	Hooton Park
	Cpl H C Moorby	816074	Safe	T/o time:	07:25
	AC1 R Beattie	521868	Safe		
	LAC Robinson	......	Safe		

Stalled on a night take-off and crashed into a field adjoining the aerodrome, possibly due to frost on the wings

5th January 1940

224 Sqn	Hudson I	N7229	QX-T	**Duty:**	**Transit Flight**
	P/O A P Davis	41261	Safe	Base:	St Athan
	Forced landing at Prestwick, Ayrshire.			T/o time:	?

224 Sqn	Hudson I	N7250	QX-X	**Duty:**	**Transit Flight**
	P/O A P Davis	41261	Injured	Base:	St Athan
	Sgt T Gosling	566256	Injured	T/o time:	?
		. . . . . .	Injured		
		. . . . . .	Injured		

Overshot on landing, opened the throttle with flaps fully extended, stalled and hit the ground at 15:05 hrs at Prestwick, Ayrshire. Also see Hudson T9272 accident on 5th August 1940.

6th January 1940

48 Sqn	Anson I	K6246	OY-N	**Op:**	**Anti-Sub Convoy Patrol**
	F/O H B M Pearson	37983	+	Base:	Thorney Island
	Sgt F M Pennell	580304	+	T/o time:	09:00
	LAC C Ritter	535157	Injured		
	AC1 F H Rook	527377	+		

Struck trees on high ground and flew into a hill at approximately 11:45 hrs when returning from convoy patrol in low cloud at Niton, near Ventnor, Isle of Wight. LAC Ritter was admitted to Royal County Hospital, Ryde. F/O Pearson, from Eire, and the other crewmen were taken for burial in St Nicholas Churchyard, West Thorney.

7th January 1940

233 Sqn	Hudson I	N7256	ZS-L	**Duty:**	**Air Test**
	Sgt F F Bousfield	565845	+	Base:	St Athan
	Sgt F F Hallam	564213	+	T/o time:	?
	LAC A W Smith	550814	+		
	Mr R K Beattie	–	+		
	?	–	+		

During a flight test after installation of ASV radar, strayed off course into the cloud covered Mynydd Maendy, near Nant-y-Moel, Glamorgan. Sgt Bousfield is buried in Hollinwood Cemetery, Oldham, Lancs; Sgt Hallam and LAC Smith are buried in Yorkshire, in Loxley United Reformed Chapelyard and Hessle Cemetery, Haltemprice, respectively. Two civilian contractors were killed in the crash.

8th January 1940

22 Sqn	Beaufort I	L4447	OA-E	**Duty:**	**Training**
	F/O T J Gascoigne	. . . . .	Safe	Base:	Thorney Island
				Time:	?

On take-off for practice circuits the aircraft started a swing which was not immediately corrected. It then struck a hedge before the pilot throttled back and unsuccessfully used the rudder.

10th January 1940

42 Sqn	Vildebeest IV	K6411	AW-D	**Duty:**	**Training**
	P/O K J Masters	41941	Safe	Base:	Bircham Newton
				T/o time:	?

P/O Masters took off for local flying training in his first flight on the type. On landing he held off too high and stalled the aircraft from 25 feet above the runway, landing heavily.

11th January 1940

224 Sqn	Hudson I	N7262	QX-W	**Op:**	**Patrol L1**
	P/O A Barkley	41246	+	Base:	Leuchars
	P/O R C Lloyd	41594	+	T/o time:	08:05
	Cpl D Turner	526986	+		
	AC1 R S Morton	551834	+		

Shot down by anti-aircraft fire from three destroyers of the 4th Zerstörer Flotilla near Horns Reef in position XGCT1626 at 10:15 hrs. P/O Barkley and his crew are commemorated on the Runnymede Memorial.

12th January 1940

269 Sqn	Anson I		K6317	UA-V	Op:	Reconnaissance
	F/O	Haley-Bell	. . . . .	Safe	Base:	Wick
	Sgt	Reen	. . . . . .	Safe	T/o time:	08:15

After action against enemy flying-boat ,overshot, hit a wall on landing and damaged beyond repair.

14th January 1940

612 Sqn	Anson I		N5270	WL-D	Op:	Anti-Submarine Patrol
	P/O	Stephen	. . . . .	Safe	Base:	Dyce
	Sgt	Griffin	. . . . . .	Safe	T/o time:	11:37
	LAC	Erskine	. . . . . .	Safe		
	AC	Gillespie	. . . . . .	Safe		

The navigator plotted the position of the Danish freighter *Paris* as off Newburgh. The Anson flew to the head of four ships in line astern, the first of which was the *Paris*. While doing this a photograph was taken of the ship and the aircraft lost height rapidly during a turn at low altitude and struck the water at 12:30 hrs. The perspex panels immediately burst and water entered the fuselage in large quantities causing the aircraft to sink within a few minutes. The captain and crew abandoned the Anson and entered or hung onto the rubber boat until picked up by a lifeboat from the *Paris* from which they were later transferred to a lifeboat from SS *Highlander* which landed P/O Stephen and his crew at Aberdeen Harbour at 14:00 hrs.

15th January 1940

233 Sqn	Hudson I		N7245	ZS-F	Op:	Patrol L1
	F/O	A H McLaren DFC	39019	Safe	Base:	Leuchars
	P/O	A E Evans	41162	Safe	Time:	08:20

When taking off the pilot raised the undercarriage too soon. The Hudson stalled and ran into an electric transformer in a wood then caught fire, the crew of four escaping through the cabin door. The fire increased causing the bombs to explode, the whole aircraft, except engines, being blown into small fragments about four minutes after the crash.

500 Sqn	Avro Tutor	K3422	MK-	Duty:	Ferry Flight
	?	. . . . . .	Safe	Base:	Linton-on-Ouse
				T/o time:	?

Flying in company with Tutor K4820 but became lost in fog near Alston, Cumberland. The pilot of K4820 made an emergency landing while the pilot of K3422 baled out safely leaving his aircraft to crash near the top of Green Hill, Northumberland.

16th January 1940

22 Sqn	Beaufort I		L4446	OA-K	Duty:	Training
	Sgt	J Hammond	550321	Safe	Base:	Thorney Island
					T/o time:	?

Suffered an engine failure due to mishandling. The pilot ditched into the English Channel some 50 yards off Fort Blockhouse, Gosport; the crew all safely abandoning before the Beaufort sank.

48 Sqn	Anson I	K8833	OY-	Op:	?
	?			Base:	?
	?			T/o time:	?

Lost at sea by enemy action. No further details.

19th January 1940

502 Sqn	Anson I		N5050	YG-B	Op:	Convoy Escort
	F/O	Garrett	. . . . .	Injured	Base:	Hooton Park

Sgt	H C Moorby	816074	+	T/o time: 08:00
AC1	R Beattie	521868	Injured	
LAC	T C McClure	816021	Injured	

Control was lost in a snow storm and the Anson spun onto the foreshore at 09:00 hrs some 4 miles east of Rhyl. Sgt Moorby rests in Knockbreda Church of Ireland Churchyard, County Down and both AC1 Beattie and LAC McClure died from their injuries and are buried in Kirkmaiden Cemetery, Wigtownshire and Belfast City Cemetery respectively.

23rd January 1940

58 Sqn	Whitley III		K8964	GE-R	Op:	Patrol
	F/O	Bintley	.....	Safe	Base:	Boscombe Down
	P/O	McPherson	.....	Safe	T/o time:	06:50
	Sgt	Dent	......	Safe		
	LAC	Lemmon	......	Safe		
	AC	Hill	......	Safe		

Engine cut after take-off. The Whitley was force-landed at 07:00 hrs with wheels up near the aerodrome. This was the first loss of a Whitley while in the service of Coastal Command.

2nd February 1940

608 Sqn	Anson I		N5199	UL-M	Op:	M/T Convoy Patrol
	F/O	Johnson	.....	Safe	Base:	Thornaby
	P/O	Lambert	.....	Safe	T/o time:	10:45
	AC2	Lumley	......	Injured		
	Cpl	Young	......	Safe		

Forced to land into the sea due to engine failure and sank after 45 minutes. The crew were picked up by minesweeper 6 miles off Blyth, Northumberland. Only AC2 Lumley had superficial injuries.

4th February 1940

240 Sqn	London II		K6927	BN-	Duty:	Transit Flight
	P/O	Willis	.....	Safe	Base:	Oban
	P/O	H A B Porteous	.....	Safe	T/o time:	?

During a transit flight from Oban to Calshot the weather deteriorated and P/O Porteous decided to land at Holyhead Harbour, Anglesey. Visibility was down to 200 yards or less and he had difficulty in deciding where to alight. While flying at about 50 feet over the harbour, he saw another London (of 201 Squadron) at moorings and flashing to him to indicate its position so he decided at once to land alongside this boat. This necessitated a very low right-hand turn over an almost glassy sea. The London's starboard wing-tip float touched the water while he was turning and the machine crashed, sinking about ten minutes later. The starboard wings had been torn off and the hull split open. Not one of the crew was seriously hurt and they were all picked up by a harbour motor boat.

6th February 1940

217 Sqn	Anson I		K8746	MW-O	Op:	Convoy Patrol
	F/O	J A C White	39406	+	Base:	St Eval
	P/O	A H M Wright	41643	+	T/o time:	07:40
	LAC	H J N Marsden	528828	+		
	?		......	Safe		

Set course to escort convoy OBM85G. Control was lost in a turn at 11:20 hrs and the Anson dived into the sea off Bishop's Rock. F/O White, a Canadian from Ontario, P/O Wright, a New Zealander from Wellington, and LAC Marsden are all commemorated on the Runnymede Memorial. A fourth member of the crew was rescued by HMS *Vimy*.

7th February 1940

48 Sqn	Anson I		K6224	OY-R	Op:	Special Cherbourg Convoy
	F/Lt	G E Ford	.....	Safe	Base:	Thorney Island
	P/O	H W Morton	.....	Injured	T/o time:	09:00

Cpl	Parkinson	. . . . . .	Safe	
AC	Spencer	. . . . . .	Safe	

Misjudged height due to rain on the windscreen and stalled into a ploughed field during a forced landing at 11:30 hrs near West Wittering, Sussex. P/O Morton was admitted to West Sussex General Hospital suffering from minor injuries.

10th February 1940

269 Sqn	**Anson I**		**N4959**	**UA-Z**	**Op:**	**Anti-Submarine Search**
	Sgt	Willitts	. . . . . .	Safe	**Base:**	Wick
	P/O	Ashby	. . . . .	Safe	**T/o time:**	12:30

Stalled in a forced landing at Stempster Farm, Caithness, while short of fuel at dusk on the return.

11th February 1940

220 Sqn	**Hudson I**		**N7294**	**NR-E**	**Op:**	**Patrol**
	F/O	T MacK Parker	39334	+	**Base:**	Thornaby
	Sgt	H F Bleksley	516366	+	**T/o time:**	04:10
	Cpl	N R Drury	537272	+		
	LAC	Barker	. . . . . .	Injured		

Windscreen iced up after take-off and the Hudson crashed a few minutes later almost at the summit of Cook Monument Hill near Great Ayton. LAC Barker was the only member of the crew not killed and escaped with concussion and severe cuts. He managed to scramble down the hill to a farmhouse which he reached at about 08:00 hrs. F/O Parker rests locally in Thornaby-on-Tees Cemetery, Sgt Bleksley in Canford Cemetery, Bristol, and Cpl Drury in North Walsham New Cemetery, Norfolk.

20th February 1940

209 Sqn	**Lerwick I**		**L7253**	**WQ-G**	**Op:**	**Escort**
	F/Sgt	G A Corby MiD**	561526	+	**Base:**	Oban
	P/O	W E Ogle-Skan	41609	Safe	**T/o time:**	11:30
	AC2	Taylor	. . . . . .	Safe		
	AC1	R J Webber	569704	+		
	AC2	L H Trumay	531133	+		
	LAC	G Peterson	520852	+		

Forced to return at 12:30 hrs due to bad weather. On reaching Oban the pilot decided to land well out in the Firth of Lorne due to poor visibility. Apparently owing to an error in judgement he stalled the aircraft onto the water causing it to bounce several times some 5 miles west of Oban off the lighthouse at the southern point of Lismore Island. In doing this the starboard wing tip float was knocked off and the aircraft heeled over causing water to enter through the windows. All the crew managed to get out into the water before the aircraft sank. F/Sgt Corby's body was recovered later and he now rests in St Mary & All Saints Old Churchyard, Langdon Hills, Essex. The others who died are commemorated on the Runnymede Memorial.

22nd February 1940

240 Sqn	**London II**	**L7040**	**BN-**		**Ground Loss**
				Base:	Sullom Voe
				Time:	?

Caught fire and sank at its moorings.

2nd March 1940

217 Sqn	**Anson I**		**K8766**	**MW-F**	**Duty:**	**Training**
	F/O	S E Bussey	. . . . .	Safe	**Base:**	St Eval
	P/O	S Livingstone	. . . . .	Safe	**T/o time:**	13:50

An engine appeared to catch fire on take-off and was shut down. Before reaching a safe height the aircraft turned downwind and crashed into a field 200 yards west of the aerodrome. The Court of Inquiry found that the heater had not been turned off and that smoke and fumes from a defective exhaust ring had caused the pilot to throttle back the healthy port engine.

8th March 1940

22 Sqn	Beaufort I	L4475	OA-E	Duty:	Training
	P/O J A Woollen	41238	+	Base:	Thorney Island
	LAC B Rees	611643	+	T/o time:	17:00

Stalled in the slipstream of another Beaufort while in formation and spun into the sea off Chichester Harbour, Sussex. Despite an extensive search by the Selsey lifeboat, only slicks of oil could be found, though the body of P/O Woollen was later recovered and taken for burial in the extension to St Nicholas' Churchyard in West Thorney. LAC Rees, who came from Wales, is commemorated on the Runnymede Memorial.

14th March 1940

224 Sqn	Hudson I	N7212	QX-H	Duty:	Training
	F/O J L Atkinson	37340	+	Base:	Leuchars
	P/O A A Greenberg	41919	+	T/o time:	?

Took off for dual instruction. Suffered an engine failure and spun into the ground 1 mile SW of Leuchars, Fife, and crashed near the railway signal box junction on the main St Andrews to Cupar line at 10:30 hrs. F/O Atkinson rests in Hampstead Cemetery, London, and P/O Greenberg was buried locally in Leuchars Cemetery, Fife.

20th March 1940

48 Sqn	Anson I	K8835	OY-		Ground Loss
				Base:	Tangmere
				Time:	?

Caught fire on the ground and burned out. The remains were reduced to produce.

254 Sqn	Blenheim IV	L8784	QY-	Duty:	Transit Flight
	Sgt G S Rose	565660	Safe	Base:	Dyce
	F/Sgt H H Brown	561051	Safe	T/o time:	10:15

Took off for formation training and transit to Lossiemouth due to the poor conditions at Dyce. Held off too high and the port oleo leg collapsed when landing at Lossiemouth at 10:30 hrs.

21st March 1940

269 Sqn	Anson I	N9673	UA-J	Op:	Anti-Submarine Patrol
	F/Lt C D W Price	37985	Safe	Base:	Wick
	?	. . . . . .		Time:	?

Wet conditions of the temporary runway hindered the take-off of the heavily laden aircraft. The end of the runway was blocked by a Hawker Hurricane and fuel bowser. Due to insufficient speed the take-off was aborted with the wings taking most of the landing shock. One crew member was admitted to the Station Sick Quarters (SSQ) and one to a local hospital.

30th March 1940

220 Sqn	Hudson I	N7237	NR-R	Duty:	Air Test
	P/O M C Petrie	40425	Safe	Base:	Thornaby
	P/O R O Lawry	41301	Safe	T/o time:	?
	S/Ldr Langford	. . . . .	Safe		
	F/O Barron	. . . . .	Safe		

While approaching the runway, a fire developed in the port engine. This was extinguished, but before the landing could be completed, flames again took hold and the Hudson crashed into a construction plant near the airfield perimeter and was totally destroyed. No serious injuries reported from either the crew, or the two passengers, S/Ldr Langford being the Padre and F/O Barron the Dentist.

Chapter 4

8th April 1940 to 15th May 1940

Reports of landings in Norway by German forces reached the Admiralty on the 8th of April 1940. A concentrated reconnaissance by units of Coastal Command over the next few days confirmed the occupation. The extreme range of the Norwegian coast limited the types of aircraft that Coastal Command could deploy to counter the German invasion and to protect the British invasion fleet. Anti-submarine operations were effective in preventing the U-boats taking advantage of the concentration of warships and transports in the Narvik area. Most of the Coastal Command effort during the period covered by this chapter was expended off the coast of Norway but the Command also provided air support for the British invasions of the Faeroe Islands on the 13th April and Iceland on the 10th May 1940.

Trials on air dropping of the magnetic mine were completed in March 1940 and 22 Squadron was tasked with carrying out the first operational drop on the night of 15th/16th April 1940. This went well with only one aircraft being lost and 815 Squadron FAA was moved to Bircham Newton to assist. The first FAA mine dropping operation, code named 'Bottle' was carried out by Swordfish aircraft off Schiermonnikoog on the night of 22nd/23rd April.

On 10th May the German attack on France and the Low Countries switched the British effort off the Dutch coast convoy protection duties to anti-shipping strikes and ground support. No 235 Squadron, operating a mix of Blenheim Is and IVs, had transferred from Fighter Command on 27th February and on 11th May found itself covering the troop landings at The Hague in an abortive attempt to help the Dutch halt the German advance.

8th April 1940

204 Sqn	**Sunderland I**	L5799	KG-D	Op:	Reconnaissance
	F/Lt R P A Harrison	37599	+	Base:	Sullom Voe
	P/O R F Hoskins	43152	+	T/o time:	10:30
	LAC A F Roberts	522093	+		
	LAC D S Lloyd	547593	+		
	AC1 B V H Bulmer	569834	+		
	AC1 C A Hughes	333908	+		
	AC1 L J Fowell	622095	+		
	AC2 H Harrott	618068	+		
	AC2 W H U Dolley	648552	+		

Took off tasked with a reconnaissance off the coast of Norway. The Sunderland failed to return after signalling an ETA 30 minutes before it was due to start the return leg and was shot down in a running dogfight with a Heinkel He111 of 1(F)./122 and crashed into the sea west of Bergen, Norway. F/Lt Harrison and his crew are commemorated on the Runnymede Memorial.

269 Sqn	**Anson I**	N9678	UA-Y	Op:	Patrol W.2
	P/O P D Aldous	40582	+	Base:	Wick
	Sgt G H Scott	566428	+	T/o time:	10:55
	Cpl G A Verlaque	525499	+		
	LAC N McReynolds	522965	+		

Believed crashed into the sea off Shetland. Wreckage and dinghy later found approximately 30 miles on homeward leg of patrol W.2. Three aircraft from the 224 Squadron detachment at Wick carried out a search for the Anson. P/O Aldous, a Canadian from Victoria, and his crew are commemorated on the Runnymede Memorial.

9th April 1940

210 Sqn	**Sunderland I**	L2167	DA-H	Op:	Reconnaissance
	F/Lt P W H Kite	40231	+	Base:	Invergordon
	Sgt J C Carpenter	745604	+	T/o time:	13:00
	P/O A F Le Maistre	41033	+		
	Sgt J A C Barter	751471	+		

LAC	D W B Upham	562805	+
LAC	F A Morrison	522580	+
AC1	G H Maile	543456	+
AC1	R L Millar	569861	+
AC2	G Eveson	635904	+
Sgt	O F George	619031	PoW

Took off to examine the Oslo area. Attacked by two Me110s of I/ZG76 over Fornebu at about 15:00 hrs and caught fire over Holsfjorden before finally exploding over Maidalen, Norway. The Sunderland was claimed by Oblt Hansen in Messerschmitt Me110 M8+JH but Ltn H Lent was also involved. Sgt George survived being blown out of the aircraft at 3,000 feet without a parachute and falling into deep snow. The remaining crewmen including Sgt Carpenter, an Australian from Sydney, and P/O Le Maistre, a Canadian from Winnipeg, rest in Sylling Churchyard, Norway.

12th April 1940

233 Sqn	Hudson I	N7258	ZS-J	Op:	Special
P/O	G J D Yorke	36185	+	Base:	Leuchars
F/Lt	A H McLaren DFC	39019	+	T/o time: 07:28	
Cpl	M Wilson MiD	522495	+		
LAC	J A Milne	610765	+		

Set out to intercept and shadow an enemy naval task force believed to include the *Scharnhorst* and two Hipper-class cruisers. Whilst shadowing *Scharnhorst* it is believed that the Hudson was shot down SW of Kristiansand by Oblt Carmann of II/JG77 at 13:55 hrs. P/O Yorke, a New Zealander from Wellington, who was involved in the first submarine attack of the war, and his crew, are commemorated on the Runnymede Memorial.

13th April 1940

233 Sqn	Hudson I	N7241	ZS-U	Op:	Stavanger
Sgt	J L Hawken DFM	564188	+	Base:	Leuchars
Sgt	S McCrossan	520724	+	T/o time: 09:20	
LAC	A R S Brown	531388	+		
AC1	T W Lerway	552657	+		

Shot down west of Hestholmen and claimed at 11:15 hrs by Unteroffizier Peter Lauffs in a Junkers Ju88C-2 from Zerstörerstaffel/KG30 at Sola. Sgt Hawken and his crew are commemorated on the Runnymede Memorial.

233 Sqn	Hudson I	N7323	ZS-Y	Op:	Stavanger
Sgt	R S Callinan	580171	+	Base:	Leuchars
Sgt	J S Scarffe	529786	+	T/o time: 13:42	
LAC	P Murray	524858	+		
LAC	T Liddle	568502	+		

Shot down off Stavanger, Norway, at 17:25 hrs by Unteroffizier Bruckner in a Messerschmitt Me110C-1 from 3./ZG76 based at Sola. Sgt Callinan, a New Zealander from Auckland City, and his crew are buried in Sola Churchyard, Norway.

14th April 1940

224 Sqn	Hudson I	N7306	QX-T	Op:	Stavanger
P/O	L G Nolan-Neylan	41455	+	Base:	Leuchars
Sgt	T Gosling	566256	+	T/o time: 21:25	
AC1	E G Newby	622865	+		
LAC	A Murcar DFM	532866	+		

Spotted by a Heinkel He115 from 3./KuFlGr506, two Messerschmitt Me109s were directed to intercept. An aerial victory was claimed by Oberleutnant Carmann of II/JG77. The Hudson crew are commemorated on the Runnymede Memorial.

15th April 1940

22 Sqn	Beaufort I	L4465	OA-G	Op:	Gardening
F/O	A R Fordham	70220	+	Base:	North Coates
Sgt	G Greenwood	566263	+	T/o time: 19:39	

AC1 J Wells   617573   +
LAC E W J Picot   364162   +
Ditched into the North Sea off Spurn Head with engine failure while on a mining operation off
the River Elbe. Two bodies were later recovered: Sgt Greenwood was taken to Donisthorpe
Cemetery, Leicestershire, and LAC Picot now rests in All Saints Churchyard, Easton-on-the-Hill,
Northants. F/O Fordham and AC1 Wells are listed on the Runnymede Memorial.

220 Sqn	Hudson I	N7289	NR-J	Op:	Patrol
	F/O C F Tulloch	39403	+	Base:	Thornaby
	F/O H O Thwaite	39399	+	T/o time:	12:45
	AC2 E B Summerfield	615808	+		
	AC1 G E Ridgeway	611142	+		

Took off and set course for a search on Track U. Shot down at 15:50 hrs into the western
Skaggerrak by Unteroffizier Helmut Enerlein in a Me110C-1 from 3./ZG1. F/O Tulloch and his
crew are commemorated on the Runnymede Memorial.

17th April 1940

22 Sqn	Beaufort I	L4517	OA-Q	Op:	Gardening
	P/O Willis	. . . . .	Safe	Base:	North Coates
	P/O J H T Foxton	. . . . .	Safe	T/o time:	19:09
	AC W J Davies	624095	Safe		
	AC Forrest	. . . . . .	Safe		

Tasked with a mining operation the crew were unable to ascertain the correct drop area and
returned with the mine still onboard. On the approach P/O Willis overshot and crashed at 23:07
hrs. All the crew were rescued from the wreckage without serious injury.

235 Sqn	Blenheim IV	P4836	LA-	Duty:	Training
	F/O J H Laughlin	39995	Safe	Base:	North Coates
				T/o time:	22:35

Took off for night flying and practice landings but overshot the flare-path in still wind conditions.
F/O Laughlin approached too fast, finally touched down at the number three flare and ran into a
ditch at the southern edge of the aerodrome. The u/c and airscrews of the a/c sustained damage.

18th April 1940

612 Sqn	Anson I	N5345	WL-N	Op:	Patrol
	P/O W J R Redman	. . . . .	Safe	Base:	Dyce

The Anson became bogged down taxying out for a patrol but was released by a combination of
engines and manual labour but later struck another bad patch and then the u/c collapsed.
The Anson was transferred to the RCAF as a ground instruction airframe on 17th July 1940.

23rd April 1940

224 Sqn	Hudson I	N7249	QX-	Op:	?
	P/O H G Webb	43154	+	Base:	Wick
	P/O A G J Pearson	. . . . .	Wounded	T/o time:	?

Shot down by AA fire from HMS *Curacoa* at Andalsnes. Loss blamed on the shore batteries not in
possession of recognition signals and had no advice of the intended operation. P/O Pearson
returned to the UK on HMS *Galatea*; P/O Webb is commemorated on the Runnymede Memorial.

24th April 1940

220 Sqn	Hudson I	N7285	NR-L	Op:	Escort
	Sgt E W A Peachey	566141	+	Base:	Leuchars
	P/O R H Sanders	41478	+	T/o time:	04:32
	AC1 R J Simpson	628649	+		
	LAC T Dobson	535582	+		

Escorted destroyers until 07:46 hrs when in position MBRU 3452 at 2,800 feet, sighted two Me109s
half a mile to starboard diving at 3,000 feet from the sun. On the first machine-gun burst the port
engine of the Hudson burst into flames. LAC Dobson was observed to continue firing, the aircraft
then attempted to land alongside a destroyer but lost control at 500 feet and turned over.

One crew member attempted to land by parachute but the canopy caught fire. The Hudson was claimed as shot down at 08:05 hrs by Ltn Demes and Ofw Arnoldy of 4./JG77. Sgt Peachey and his crew are all commemorated on the Runnymede Memorial.

220 Sqn	Hudson I	N7286	NR-Z	Op:	Escort
	P/O M C Petrie	40425	+	Base:	Leuchars
	P/O R O Lawry	41301	+	T/o time: 04:32	
	AC1 K C Merrick	624355	+		
	LAC P Wilson	514613	+		

Escorted destroyers until 07:46hrs when in position MBRU 3452 at 2,800 feet, sighted two Me109s half a mile to starboard diving at 3,000 feet from sun. P/O Petrie was attacked by the second Me109 and was seen to dive to sea level with black smoke issuing from an engine, followed by the enemy aircraft. The Hudson was claimed as shot down at 08:05 hrs by Ltn Demes and Ofw Arnoldy of 4./JG77. P/O Petrie from Wellington, a New Zealander, P/O Lawry, a New Zealander from Christchurch, AC1 Merrick (real name Maddocks) and LAC Wilson are all commemorated on the Runnymede Memorial.

224 Sqn	Hudson I	N7283	QX-S	Op:	Anti-Submarine Patrol
	F/O A A T Bulloch	33224	+	Base:	Leuchars
	P/O R G M Harmston	41845	+	T/o time: 05:04	
	LAC A W Hallam	534748	+		
	LAC S Lane	528628	+		

Shot down off Haakonshellen, Norway, at 07:30 hrs by either Fw Ertel or Oblt Pointner of 5./JG77. P/O Harmston rests in Mollendal Church Cemetery, Bergen, while the rest of the crew are commemorated on the Runnymede Memorial.

25th April 1940

206 Sqn	Hudson I	N7312	VX-	Op:	Reconnaissance
	Sgt E Abbott	564510	Safe	Base:	Bircham Newton
	F/Sgt G A Turner	564783	Safe	T/o time: 18:30	
	AC1 Tomlinson	550609	Safe		
	LAC Wilde	......	Safe		

Recce to Texel. Burst a tyre on landing at 21:00 hrs swinging the Hudson and collapsing the u/c.

29th April 1940

254 Sqn	Blenheim IV	R3628	QY-	Op:	Andalsnes
	?	......		Base:	Hatston (Orkneys)
				T/o time: 09:40	

In combat with a Junkers Ju88. The Blenheim's oil system in port engine was punctured so a course was set for Shetland. At 10:45 hrs they lost the port propeller and at 12:40 hrs a forced landing was carried out at Scatsta, Shetland.

1st May 1940

269 Sqn	Hudson I	N7278	UA-A	Op:	Bombing Sola
	Sgt K Bell	565626	+	Base:	Wick
	P/O A H Hayter	41289	+	T/o time: 05:59	
	Sgt G Kelly	522560	+		
	LAC G Welsh	617385	+		
	LAC J H MacKenzie	552160	PoW		

Took off tasked with a bombing attack on Sola Aerodrome. Shot down about 10 miles W of the coast of Norway at 08:23 hrs by Ltn G Schirmbock of 4./JG77. The crash was witnessed by HMS *Triton* but due to enemy air activity no investigation of the crash site was possible. Sgt Bell, from Greenwich, New South Wales, and his crew are commemorated on the Runnymede Memorial.

3rd May 1940

206 Sqn	Hudson I	N7319	VX-C	Op:	Reconnaissance
	P/O R T Kean DFC	41295	Wounded	Base:	Bircham Newton
	Sgt Deverill	......	Wounded	T/o time: 03:45	

	AC	Harrison	. . . . . .	Safe		
	LAC	E Townend	535545	+		

Damaged by Me109s of II(J)/TrGr186 off the Elbe Estuary and LAC Townend killed. The hydraulics were damaged by the machine-gun fire and the Hudson was belly-landed at 08:00 hrs on the return. LAC Townend is buried locally in St Mary's Churchyard, Great Bircham, Norfolk.

5th May 1940

SD Flight	Short S.30/M 'C' Class		V3137			Ground Loss
	F/Lt G Stone	. . . . .	Safe		Base:	Harstad

V3137 had just landed at Bodö from Harstad when it was spotted by Do17s from 1(F)./120. The pilot started the engines but ran aground while taxying. This was a former Imperial Airways 4-engined Empire flying-boat airliner, G-AFCU, named *Cabot*. After the attack, survivors from V3137 and V3138 (see below) used two motor boats to tow *Cabot* several miles along the coast to shelter near some steep cliffs, , but it was again spotted, bombed and destroyed by 1(F)./120.

SD Flight	Short S.30/M 'C' Class		V3138			Ground Loss
	F/Lt S G Long	. . . . .	Safe		Base:	Invergordon

Had just alighted at Bodö when spotted by Do17s from 1(F)./120, who promptly attacked, set her on fire, bombed and destroyed her where she lay. Five crew members were injured in the attack. V3138, a sister-ship to V3137 above, was the former G-AFCV, named *Caribou*.

Cabot was delivered to Imperial Airways (Atlantic) Ltd in March 1939 and took part in the second of that airline's trans-Atlantic experiments into air-to-air refuelling. On 5th and 6th August 1939, both flew from Southampton to New York, via Foynes, Botwood and Montreal. This was the first in a series of flights where Air-Mail was carried on scheduled flights and the aircraft were refuelled en-route by a Handley Page Harrow tanker aircraft.

The Short S.30/M 'C' Class flying-boats were strengthened versions of the S.23. Both Cabot and Caribou were impressed for wartime service in March 1940, along with their civilian crews, under the command of Captains G Store and S G Long respectively, and were delivered to RAF Invergordon where they were attached to the Special Duty Flight. Their conversion to military status included the fitting of seven Vickers K-type machine-guns. When the Germans invaded Norway Cabot and Caribou were tasked with taking an RAF radar unit to Bodö (V3137 flying via Harstad) and were destroyed as described above. The survivors from both crews were later evacuated to the UK along with other troops by a destroyer of the Royal Navy.

7th May 1940

22 Sqn	Beaufort I		L4472	OA-G	Op:	Shipping Strike
	F/O S P Woollatt	39451	+		Base:	North Coates
	F/O D J T Lusk	70413	+		T/o time: 14:52	
	AC1 S W Mills	623774	+			
	AC2 M J Delahunty	636904	+			

Formated with other squadron aircraft to bomb an enemy cruiser of the Nuremberg class which had been reported between Norderney/Juist. Claimed shot down by Uffz Kaiser of II(J)/TrGr186 into the North Sea off Norderney but may have been shot down by flak north of the Dutch Frisians. The body of F/O Lusk was washed ashore 6th August 1940 on the island of Ameland and was initially buried in the Nes Cemetery. F/O Lusk is now buried in Jonkerbos War Cemetery, Holland, but the others are commemorated on the Runnymede Memorial.

22 Sqn	Beaufort I		L4466	OA-U	Duty:	Training
	P/O J T Berryman	33506	+		Base:	North Coates
					T/o time: 15:00	

During the approach P/O Berryman decided to make another circuit and started to make a turn without retracting the flaps. The Beaufort stalled a wing and crashed onto the beach at 15:30 hrs just off the aerodrome. P/O Berryman, from Toronto, Canada, was taken to St Andrew Churchyard at Cranwell for burial.

22 Sqn	Beaufort I		L4464	OA-C	Op:	Shipping Strike
	W/C H M Mellor	16097	Safe		Base:	North Coates
	P/O I N M MacDonald	. . . . .	Safe		T/o time: 15:07	
	AC1 A D MacKenzie	623407	Safe			
	AC Traynor	. . . . . .	Wounded			

Took off in formation with other squadron aircraft to bomb an enemy cruiser of the Nuremberg class which had been reported between Norderney and Juist. The Beaufort was damaged by flak and by Ltn Schopper of II(J)/TrGr186 in the engagement; AC Traynor was wounded. The Hudson was eventually crash-landed by W/C Mellor back at base at 19:20 hrs. Both W/C Mellor and AC1 MacKenzie were to lose their lives on operations with the Squadron on 25th May 1940.

235 Sqn	Blenheim IV	P4844	LA-A	Duty:	Training
	Sgt V Allison	519436	+	Base:	Bircham Newton
	Sgt E O F Schmid	746761	+	T/o time:	?
	LAC V C E Neirynck	645692	+		

Lost height at night and dived into the ground about 2 miles from the aerodrome just after midnight. Sgt Allison rests in St Brandan Old Churchyard, Boyndie, Banffshire, LAC Neirynck was taken to North Road Cemetery, Southend-on-Sea, and Sgt Schmid was buried locally in St Mary's Churchyard, Great Bircham.

9th May 1940

22 Sqn	Beaufort I	L4453	OA-B	Op:	Gardening
	F/Lt C MacK Lester	37109	+	Base:	North Coates
	Sgt W Southward	565970	+	T/o time:	19:40
	LAC K P Turrell	531188	+		
	Cpl J W Maxey	506611	+		

Set course for the River Elbe but contact was lost after the Beaufort was fixed by D/F as 69 miles east of base. Aircraft of the squadron, an RAF HSL and trawlers all took part in an unsuccessful search. All the crew are commemorated on the Runnymede Memorial.

235 Sqn	Blenheim I	K7136	LA-	Duty:	Training
	P/O W F Smith	41958	+	Base:	Bircham Newton
				T/o time:	23:00

Took off for solo flying practice and suffered an engine failure, swung, stalled and crashed. P/O Smith was taken to St Mary's Churchyard, Hartlebury for burial.

254 Sqn	Blenheim IV	L9482	QY-	Op:	Escort Duty
	F/Lt A C Heath	37173	+	Base:	Hatston
	Sgt S A Nicholls	746976	+	T/o time:	16:20
	Lt R B Nuthall RN	.....	+		

Took off as fighter escort for eight FAA Skua aircraft tasked with attacking shipping in Bergen Harbour then independent light bombing. The Blenheim was hit by flak and was last seen spinning into the harbour. F/Lt Heath, from Cape Province, South Africa, is commemorated on the Runnymede Memorial while both Sgt Nicholls and Lt Nuthall, assigned to HMS *Sparrowhawk*, rest locally in Mollendal Church Cemetery, Bergen.

10th May 1940

235 Sqn	Blenheim IV	N6193	LA-N	Op:	Reconnaissance
	P/O R L Patterson	77529	Safe	Base:	Bircham Newton
	Lt Ogilvie RN	.....	Safe	T/o time:	19:30
	LAC A G Smith	552170	Safe		

Night reconnaissance sortie to the coast of Holland from Texel to Borkum. The accident was attributed to the pilot being short of stature, encumbered by his Mae West, being unable to operate the fuel cocks resulting in an engine failure. P/O Patterson believed that there was insufficient fuel in the tank of the live engine to remain airborne while he manually pumped down the u/c and flaps, so he belly-landed at 22:30 hrs, the aircraft catching fire in the crash after the u/c collapsed.

12th May 1940

206 Sqn	Hudson I	N7353	VX-	Op:	Reconnaissance
	P/O I L Gray	36188	+	Base:	Bircham Newton
	Sgt M Moore	565347	+	T/o time:	04:45
	AC1 B Gill	621946	+		
	LAC R J Sloan	517038	+		

Shot down north of Baltrum off the coast of Germany by Oblt Emmerich of II(J)/TrGr186. Sgt Moore rests in Sage War Cemetery while the other crewmen including P/O Gray, a New Zealander from Mount Eden, are commemorated on the Runnymede Memorial.

235 Sqn	**Blenheim IV**	**L9189**	**LA-O**	**Op:**	**Escort**
	P/O N A Savill	41956	PoW	Base:	Manston
	Sgt H R Sunderland	755141	+	T/o time:	05:00
	LAC R H Tyler	552475	+		

Took off in company with other aircraft of the squadron to cover troop landings at The Hague and was attacked by eight Me109s of II/JG27 at 07:55 hrs. Both the observer and the air gunner were killed in the attack and P/O Savill baled out of the burning aircraft at low altitude.
On landing on farmland along the Kloosterweg between Brielle and Oostvoorne, P/O Savill was captured by Dutch soldiers who were convinced that he was German and made preparations to shoot him. Despite being badly wounded and covered in burns he managed to convince them that he was an RAF officer and was taken to Vlaardingen hospital. Sgt Sunderland and LAC Tyler were both buried in field graves but now rest in Oostvoorne Protestant Cemetery, Zuid-Holland. The Blenheim wreckage was salvaged in 1967 by the RNethAF but only a few parts were found.

235 Sqn	**Blenheim IV**	**L9324**	**LA-P**	**Op:**	**Escort**
	P/O N A L Smith	40950	+	Base:	Manston
	Sgt J C Robertson	749443	+	T/o time:	05:00
	LAC T J Lowry	553205	+		

Took off in company with other aircraft of the squadron to cover troop landings at The Hague They were attacked by eight Me109s of II/JG26 at 07:55 hrs. The Blenheim was last seen with its starboard engine on fire. It crashed into a small field in the Nieuwlandse Polder near Hoek van Holland and close to two Junkers Ju52s which had landed there in the early morning of 10th May. P/O Smith rests in Westduin General Cemetery, The Hague, while the two other crew men are buried in the Hoek van Holland (Hook of Holland) General Cemetery.

Chapter 5

16th May 1940 to 31st July 1940

With the invasion of France and the Low Countries moving towards the coast with unbelievable speed the British/French activities in Norway were changed from bridgehead break-out to the defence of Narvik and denying the facilities to the Germans.

Permission was given to attack military targets in German ports/cities and on the 18th May Coastal Command carried out raids on oil installations at Hamburg and Bremen. The rest of the month was mostly devoted to attacks on E-boats off the Dutch coast with little or no effect on the battle taking place in Northern France.

On the evening of 26th May the evacuation of the BEF from Dunkirk started and Coastal Command carried out crossover patrols between the UK and Texel to protect the flank of the rescue fleet. As the evacuation continued standing patrols by Blenheim, Anson and Hudson aircraft provided daylight air cover.

The Anson units were used on strike operations to bomb enemy held harbours and were also expected to take on enemy fighters in dogfights. On the 1st June P/O Peters of 500 Squadron was involved in a mêlée of Me109s and succeeded in shooting down one enemy aircraft with his forward firing gun while his air gunner shot down another behind the Anson. Fighter tactics were not limited to the Ansons as a Hudson of 220 Squadron attacked forty Junkers Ju87s and shot down four before allied fighters arrived.

After the Dunkirk evacuation the *Scharnhorst* and *Gneisenau* arrived off Norway on the 8th June and sank HMS *Glorious* and her escorting destroyers, *Ardent* and *Acasta*. Damaged by a salvo of torpedos from the latter, the *Scharnhorst* put into Trondheim Fjord where over the next few days both Coastal Command and the FAA made numerous attempts to sink her. In company with the *Gneisenau* she left Trondheim for Kiel on the 20th June. The move was noted by the Royal Navy and a torpedo attack on the *Gneisenau* split the convoy. The *Scharnhorst* continued alone to Kiel, where it was located on the 21st by Hudsons and attacks launched by FAA Fairey Swordfish, Hudsons of 224, 233 and 269 Squadrons and Beauforts of 42 Squadron. All aircraft pressed home their attacks despite intense flak and large formations of Me109 and Me110 fighters but no appreciable damage was caused. With the capital ships now at anchorage, Coastal Command settled down to an armed reconnaissance role and whenever possible undertook offensive action by three-aircraft 'battle' flights on enemy shipping in the North Sea.

With the threat of invasion, 53 and 59 Squadrons were released from their army co-operation role and trans-ferred to coastal patrols. Nos 21 and 57 Squadrons of Bomber Command were detached to Lossiemouth to counter an invasion force launched from Norway. From Coastal Command bases on the Channel, offensive strikes were launched against enemy held harbours to slow the build-up of invasion barges and troop concen-trations. Selective strikes were also carried out to deter the U-boats from taking up bases on the French coast.

Importantly, the reconnaissance assets, (the Photographic Development Unit, Heston and the Interpretation Unit at Wembley), hitherto answering to various masters, were all placed under the control of HQ Coastal Command (but administered by 16 Group) with effect from 18th June. Shortly afterwards, on 8th July, the PDU was re-named the Photographic Reconnaissance Unit (PRU) to emphasise its operational role, and the aircraft were divided into five Flights and spread around the country.

17th May 1940

269 Sqn	Hudson I		N7365	UA-	Duty:	Training
	Sgt	Cotton	742495	Safe	Base:	Ringway
					T/o time:	

2nd pilot inadvertently let down the flaps fully and the aircraft undershot, crashing ¼ mile west of Ringway. Both crew escaped without injury.

18th May 1940

206 Sqn	Hudson I	N7329	VX-	Op:	Hamburg
	F/Sgt G A Turner	564783	+	Base:	Bircham Newton
	Sgt E Abbott	564510	+	T/o time: 20:25	
	AC1 W A Tomlinson	550609	+		
	P/O R J Lennox-French	77120	+		

Failed to return. F/Sgt Turner and his crew are commemorated on the Runnymede Memorial.

206 Sqn	Hudson I	N7400	VX-	Op:	Hamburg
	F/O G D O L Hutchesson	39283	+	Base:	Bircham Newton
	P/O A Bouwens	33420	+	T/o time: 23:00	
	Cpl R E Gumbrill	520854	+		
	AC1 J L Durant	627040	+		

Failed to return from Hamburg. All, including AC1 Durant from Regina, Saskatchewan, Canada, are commemorated on the Runnymede Memorial.

235 Sqn	Blenheim IV	L9395	LA-	Op:	Oostende
	P/O C S Robinson	41470	+	Base:	Bircham Newton
	Sgt D V Moseley	755471	+	T/o time: 17:50	
	LAC A E Waddington	638743	+		

Took off along with other squadron aircraft for trawler protection duties. Noticed as missing shortly after arrival off Oostende. Possibly shot down in error by Hurricanes who along with Spitfires attacked the formation. P/O Robinson, from Winnipeg, Manitoba, and his crew are commemorated on the Runnymede Memorial.

19th May 1940

206 Sqn	Hudson I	N7363	VX-	Op:	Photo-Reconnaissance
	Sgt E A Judge	565431	+	Base:	Bircham Newton
	Sgt W Jones	563455	+	T/o time: ?	
	Cpl A J Metcalfe	516026	+		
	AC1 H C Mewett	622864	+		

Shot down by Oblt Wulf of 6(J)./TrGr 186 some 50 km (c 31 miles) NW of Heligoland at 16:00 hrs. Sgt Judge and his crew are commemorated on the Runnymede Memorial.

20th May 1940

48 Sqn	Anson I	K8772	OY-G	Op:	Dutch Patrol
	F/Lt S Dodds MiD	37086	+	Base:	Detling
	P/O B S Booth	42045	+	T/o time: 17:10	
	LAC A H Gumbelton	538552	+		
	LAC N E Jacobs	526265	+		

Took off in company with two other Ansons to attack nine MTBs in position CPOX 2706. At 19:00 hrs, 35 km (c 21¾ miles) SW of Texel, they sighted eight or nine MTB's in convoy and attacked. F/Lt Dodds led the attack and was hit by flak from an E-boat in the starboard wing and was forced to ditch. All the crew are commemorated on the Runnymede Memorial.

206 Sqn	Anson I	N9897	VX-N		Ground Loss
				Base:	Bircham Newton
				Time:	?

While being refuelled, was hit by Blenheim L9256 of 235 Squadron, killing AC1 L G Curry.

235 Sqn	Blenheim IV	L9256	LA-	Op:	Escort
	Sgt Bessey	......	Safe	Base:	Bircham Newton
	Sgt Westcott	......	Safe	Time:	17:25
	LAC A G Smith	552170	Safe		

Engine failed on take-off and the Blenheim hit Anson N9897 (see above). Crew was not injured.

248 Sqn	Blenheim IV	P4837	WR-	Duty:	Training
	P/O A E Q Bourgeois	42100	+	Base:	Gosport
	P/O S G Tatar	42684	+	T/o time: ?	

Collided during a practice attack on 42 Squadron Beaufort L9455 and crashed into sea between Thorney Creek and Selsey Bill, Hampshire. Both P/O Bourgeois and P/O Tatar are commemorated on the Runnymede Memorial. P/O Bourgeois was a New Zealander, from Hawkes Bay.

22nd May 1940

22 Sqn	**Beaufort I**	**L4518**	**OA-S**	**Duty:**	**Training**
	P/O W D G McCaw	41397	Wounded	Base:	North Coates
				T/o time:	?

Crashed at base in a night forced landing after engine failure.

206 Sqn	**Hudson I**	**N7402**	**VX-**	**Op:**	**Reconnaissance**
	P/O M J Giles	41996	+	Base:	Bircham Newton
	P/O J A Clark	41986	+	T/o time:	11:30
	LAC L J Britton DFM	519168	+		
	AC1 J F Peel	623315	+		

Failed to return from off the German coast. Crew commemorated on the Runnymede Memorial.

24th May 1940

235 Sqn	**Blenheim IV**	**L9259**	**LA-**	**Op:**	**Escort**
	P/O M E Ryan	42154	+	Base:	Bircham Newton
	Sgt W Martin	748313	+	T/o time:	04:15
	LAC A G Smith	552170	+		

Took off to escort Hudsons of 206 Sqn from Borkum to the mouth of the Ems. P/O Ryan lagged behind the leader and was attacked by two Me109s and was shot down by Oblt Emmerich of II(J)/186 at 08:30 hrs. The Blenheim was seen to disappear into the sea off Schiermonnikoog by the air gunner of a Hudson. Both P/O Ryan and Sgt Martin are buried in Vredenhof Cemetery, Schiermonnikoog, but LAC Smith's body was not recovered and he is commemorated on the Runnymede Memorial.

25th May 1940

22 Sqn	**Beaufort I**	**L4450**	**OA-F**	**Op:**	**Gardening**
	W/C H M Mellor	16097	+	Base:	North Coates
	F/O F R Jamieson	37855	+	T/o time:	23:00
	LAC A D MacKenzie	623407	+		
	P/O H J Cook	77351	+		

Lost without trace into the North Sea, off Heligoland, Germany. W/C Mellor and his crew are commemorated on the Runnymede Memorial.

206 Sqn	**Hudson I**	**N7403**	**VX-N**	**Op:**	**Convoy**
	P/O H E M Featherstone	41275	Safe	Base:	Bircham Newton
	P/O C A S Greenhill	40906	Safe	T/o time:	08:40
	LAC R A Plowright	550840	Safe		
	LAC Keeper	......	Safe		

Crashed on landing at 12:40 hrs and blew up.

500 Sqn	**Anson I**	**N9731**	**MK-U**	**Op:**	**Dutch**
	P/O Grisenthwaite	.....	Safe	Base:	Detling
	P/O McLundie	.....	Safe	T/o time:	17:31
	LAC Bowers	......	Safe		
	AC H C R Hopwood	903368	Safe		

At 19:12 hrs carried out a dive-bombing attack on two enemy MTBs with two other squadron aircraft, but failed to sink them. The Flight then attacked using MG fire during which N9731 was hit in the port engine by the return fire from the MTBs. Height could not be maintained and the Anson was ditched on the return flight in position CPTS 4558, 15 miles off Texel, Holland. The crew were safely picked up by destroyer HMS *Javelin* F61 which was guided to the crash position.

26th May 1940

235 Sqn	**Blenheim IV**	**P6956**	**LA-**	**Op:**	**Reconnaissance**
	P/O C D Warde	.....	Safe	Base:	Bircham Newton
	P/O A H Murphy	78255	+	T/o time:	17:10
	LAC E P Armstrong	573130	+		

Took off for a reconnaissance of Zeebrugge area. Spun into ground out of cloud near Docking, Norfolk, at 17:15 hrs. The pilot P/O Warde abandoned by parachute. P/O Murphy is buried locally in St Mary's Churchyard, Great Bircham while the body of LAC Armstrong was returned to Durham Road Cemetery, Stockton-on-Tees.

27th May 1940

254 Sqn	Blenheim IV	R3624	QY-M	Op:	Stavanger
	P/O E H Alexander	41977	+	Base:	Sumburgh
	Sgt B A J Henrick	747704	+	T/o time: 05:30	
	Sgt T P N Hammond	625785	+		

Coastguards reported that an aircraft had crashed into the sea and the Thurso lifeboat was launched. Hmpt Lang of II/JG77 reported shooting a Blenheim down off Stavanger. All are commemorated on the Runnymede Memorial.

29th May 1940

235 Sqn	Blenheim IV	P6909	LA-	Op:	Patrol
	F/Lt R P Y Cross	40087	+	Base:	Detling
	Sgt A V Slocombe	744906	+	T/o time: 07:05	
	LAC J North	629429	DoI		

Took off in bad weather and circled to return to base then struck a tree while flying low over a thickly wooded hillock near Sittingbourne. F/Lt Cross and Sgt Slocombe were both buried locally in Herne Bay Cemetery and St Martin Churchyard Extension, Detling, respectively. LAC North died in hospital a few days later and is buried in Edgerton Cemetery, Huddersfield.

235 Sqn	Blenheim IV	L9260	LA-E	Op:	Goodwin Patrol
	P/O J R Cronan	42109	Safe	Base:	Detling
	Sgt A O Lancaster	755199	Safe	T/o time: 11:31	
	LAC Peebles	......	Safe		

Took off for a patrol of the Calais area. Shot down into Channel off Calais by six Me109s, after downing one. The crew were rescued from their dinghy.

235 Sqn	Blenheim IV	L9397	LA-	Op:	Patrol
	P/O A F Booth	42099	+	Base:	Detling
	Sgt D J Elliott	749407	+	T/o time: 11:31	
	LAC E R Scott	624256	+		

Shot down in flames into the sea off France. No trace of P/O Booth, from Selukwe, Southern Rhodesia, or his crew was found and they are all commemorated on the Runnymede Memorial.

235 Sqn	Blenheim IV	L9401	LA-	Op:	Patrol
	F/Lt G A P Manwaring	39156	+	Base:	Detling
	Sgt I MacPhail	581156	+	T/o time: 11:31	
	AC1 D B Murphy	629645	+		

Aircraft and crew lost in action. F/Lt Manwaring and AC Murphy are buried in Sage War Cemetery, Germany while Sgt MacPhail now rests in Ramsgate and St Lawrence Cemetery, Kent.

500 Sqn	Anson I	N5227	MK-L	Op:	Shamrock Patrol
	P/O I S Wheelwright	91003	+	Base:	Detling
	Sgt H W Johnson	521711	+	T/o time: 15:12	
	LAC F H Giles	812052	+		
	F/Sgt R G T Soper	903332	+		

Last seen on the surface of the sea in position VXWY 1357 near destroyer T61 at 18:00 hrs. The body of LAC Giles was washed ashore on the 30th of July and now rests in Nes General Cemetery on Ameland. The rest of the crew are commemorated on the Runnymede Memorial.

30th May 1940

48 Sqn	Anson I	N9919	OY-J	Op:	Thistle Patrol
	P/O Tilson	.....	Safe	Base:	Detling
	Sgt Cadenne	......	Safe	T/o time: 15:35	
	LAC O'Reilly	......	Injured		
	LAC Fish	......	Safe		

Damaged by friendly fire from a trawler at 20:20 hrs while trying to signal the position of shipping survivors. The port engine seized and height could not be maintained so the Anson was put down off Ramsgate, Kent, within sight of three ships and the crew was subsequently rescued by HMS *Vega*. The aircraft stayed afloat during the rescue and was later sunk by gunfire from another armed trawler. It was not until the next day that the crew was landed at Sheerness and LAC O'Reilly was admitted to RN Hospital, Gillingham.

48 Sqn	Anson I	K8773	OY-X	Op:	Shamrock Patrol
	F/O S Wherry	. . . . .	Safe	Base:	Detling
	P/O G Alington	. . . . .	Safe	T/o time:	14:50
	Cpl A D C Harding	568952	Safe		
	LAC L Dilnutt	523495	Wounded		

Attacked by three Me109s of JG26, 2 miles off Oostende, Belgium and suffered extensive damage to the wings and aileron controls. After beating off the attack an engine failed and a forced landing was made into the Channel off Deal at 18:30 hrs. The crew were rescued by a destroyer then transferred to a drifter before being landed at Ramsgate.

236 Sqn	Blenheim I	L8717	FA-	Duty:	Transit Flight
	F/O R M Power	39471	Safe	Base:	Filton
				T/o time:	?

Engine failed on the approach and the Blenheim was forced to land straight ahead in impossible country. They hit trees and landed in a small field on the hillside at 15:00 hrs some 1½ miles south of Colerne, Wiltshire. All the crew were safe.

269 Sqn	Hudson I	N7335	UA-F	Op:	Reconnaissance
	Sgt A A Townsend	580215	+	Base:	Wick
	F/O W N Hammond	43136	+	T/o time:	11:15
	P/O A V N Bartlett	78669	+		
	LAC S MacKenzie	524386	PoW		

Took off and set course for the Norwegian coast. Shot down at 14:30 hrs by Fw R Menge of 5./JG77 near the battery at Hellesto Island, off Stavanger, Norway. Those who died are commemorated on the Runnymede Memorial.

500 Sqn	Anson I	N5065	MK-N	Op:	?
	?	. . . . .		Base:	Detling
	?	. . . . . .		T/o time:	?

Shot down by Me109s of JG26 off Ramsgate, Kent, on the return from a raid.

31st May 1940

500 Sqn	Anson I	R3389	MK-W	Op:	Night Patrol
	F/O R D C Chambers MiD	39494	+	Base:	Detling
	P/O D E Bond	. . . . .	Injured	T/o time:	23:38
	Cpl Petts	. . . . . .	Safe		
	LAC Fish	. . . . . .	Safe		

Took off for a night Patrol off North Foreland, Kent. Undershot the landing and hit trees at 01:15 hrs before crashing into a field adjacent to the aerodrome. The Anson caught fire and one bomb exploded killing the navigator. The cause of the crash was blamed on lack of knowledge of the approach to the aerodrome for a night landing. F/O Chambers is buried in St Nicholas Churchyard, West Thorney, Sussex. Cpl Joan Pearson WAAF was awarded the George Cross for rescuing the Navigator; she went back for the pilot but found him dead.

1st June 1940

236 Sqn	Blenheim I	L6643	FA-	Duty:	Training
	F/O W S Moore	40007	Safe	Base:	Filton
				T/o time:	?

Engine failed in flight. Landed with u/c retracted at 16:25 hrs at Filton but the Blenheim was deemed to have been damaged beyond repair.

254 Sqn	Blenheim IV	L9481	QY-A	Op:	Goodwin
	F/O J W Baird	39408	+	Base:	Detling
	P/O G W Spiers	. . . . .	Safe	T/o time:	04:47
	Sgt R Roskrow	536061	+		

Jumped by 11 Me109s at 07:45 hrs whilst attacking Ju87s over the Goodwin Sands and was shot down into the Channel. F/O Baird is buried in Malo-les-Bains Communal Cemetery, France, while Sgt Roskrow, from 48 Sqn, is commemorated on the Runnymede Memorial.

254 Sqn	Blenheim IV	R3630	QY-Q	Op:	Goodwin
	Sgt R A Bate	564536	+	Base:	Detling
	Sgt J C Love	745109	+	T/o time:	05:00
	LAC W T Harrison	629949	+		

Jumped by 11 Me109s at 07:45 hrs whilst attacking Ju87s and was shot down into the Channel near the Goodwin Sands. All the crew are commemorated on the Runnymede Memorial.

3rd June 1940

48 Sqn	Anson I	L7047	OY-	Op:	Anti-Sub Convoy Patrol
	P/O C C Proby	. . . . .	Safe	Base:	Thorney Island
	?	. . . . . .	Safe	T/o time: 22:30	
	?	. . . . . .	Safe		
	?	. . . . . .	Injured		

Blinded by a searchlight on the approach to Thorney Island and ditched off Hayling Island, Sussex. Located by another 48 Squadron Anson, R3305, piloted by P/O P W Dunn, he returned to base and reported the position, returning again to the scene of the accident and remaining in the vicinity until the crew were rescued by the Hayling Lifeboat. R3305 used parachute flares to locate L7047. At 01:15 hrs a message was received at Bembridge from the Foreland coastguard, that an aeroplane had come down in the sea south-west of the coastguard hut at Hayling Island. A south-east wind was blowing, with a moderate sea. At 01:30 hrs the motor lifeboat *Jesse Lumb* was launched, and close inshore found four men in a rubber boat. One was injured. Their aeroplane had sunk. She took them on board, and after permission had been given by the examination vessel, landed them at Haslar Hospital, Gosport. She returned to her station at 05:45 hrs. At Selsey news was received from the coastguard at 01:20 hrs that the aeroplane was down. At 01:40 hrs the motor lifeboat *Canadian Pacific* was launched, but she was recalled when it was learned that the Bembridge lifeboat had rescued the men.

4th June 1940

42 Sqn	Beaufort I	L4483	AW-L	Duty:	Training
	F/Sgt R MacAskill	560677	Injured	Base:	St Eval
	F/Lt M R Baillon	37147	Safe	T/o time: 03:25	
	F/O Loyd				

Due to a fresher wind than usual F/Sgt MacAskill undershot the approach, struck the roof of a house and dived into a hay field 100 yards NW of the aerodrome.

5th June 1940

22 Sqn	Beaufort I	L9797	OA-F	Op:	Ghent
	P/O Westlake		Safe	Base:	North Coates
	Sgt S G Twitchen	590984	Safe	T/o time: 21:45	
	Sgt L E T Harris	623844	+		
	Sgt P O'Flaherty	637032	+		

While over Ashington, Northumberland, early in the morning of the 6th, the Beaufort collided with a barrage balloon cable when avoiding searchlights. Subsequently an engine failed and P/O Westlake and Sgt Twitchen baled out leaving the aircraft to crash into a terrace house at 77 Fifth Row killing the three residents. Sgt Harris is buried in Kingston Cemetery, Portsmouth and Sgt O'Flaherty, from Eire, is buried locally in Chevington Cemetery, Northumberland.

233 Sqn	Hudson I	N7255	ZS-S	Op:	Patrol S.A.2
	F/O J Dunn	39508	+	Base:	Leuchars
	P/O J L Piercey	44776	+	T/o time: 20:20	
	Cpl R Purves	549286	+		
	Sgt R C Dodd	530700	+		

Failed to return from patrol. The Hudson may have been shot down in error by an RAF fighter. The crew are commemorated on the Runnymede Memorial.

6th June 1940

220 Sqn	Hudson I	P5157	NR-		Ground Loss
220 Sqn	Hudson I	N7309	NR-		Ground Loss
				Base:	Thornaby
				Time:	00:15

Both aircraft were destroyed in an air raid.

11th June 1940

22 Sqn	**Beaufort I**	L4451	OA-J	**Duty:**	Training
	P/O Barrett	. . . . .	Safe	Base:	North Coates
	P/O Peters	. . . . .	Safe	Time:	12:00

Crashed after engine failure on take-off.

220 Sqn	**Hudson I**	P5127	NR-	**Op:**	?
	Sgt E Morgan	700305	+	Base:	Thornaby
	Sgt D R Holbeche	564819	+	T/o time:	?
	AC1 W C Irvine	625299	+		
	Sgt J R Butterworth	525413	+		

Swung after take-off and dived into the ground 1 mile from Thornaby, North Yorkshire, causing the bombs to explode. The crew all rest locally in Thornaby-on-Tees Cemetery.

269 Sqn	**Hudson I**	N7361	UA-G	**Op:**	Trondheim
	Sgt E B Lascelles	580224	PoW	Base:	Sumburgh
	Sgt A M S Brodie	565699	PoW	T/o time:	11:30
	Sgt E T D Machell MiD	524148	DoW		
	Sgt J G Hepburn	551354	PoW		

On operation with 11 other 269 Squadron Hudsons to Trondheim when shot down by Me109s into Gulosen Fjord. Sgt Machell died of his wounds and rests in Stavne Cemetery, Trondheim.

269 Sqn	**Hudson I**	P5131	UA-P	**Op:**	Trondheim, Norway
	Sgt G W Robson	580228	+	Base:	Sumburgh
	Sgt A Sherwood	. . . . . .	Evaded	T/o time:	11:30
	Sgt J Craig	759047	+		
	Sgt A Napier	614218	PoW		

Shot down by flak over Trondheim after pattern bombing the *Gneisenau*, *Admiral Hipper* and *Scharnhorst* and crashed into Buvik Harbour. Sgt Sharwood escaped by parachute, alighting at the edge of a fjord some way from the hostilities. Hiding until nightfall, he made contact with a Norwegian group. With food, maps and clothes supplied by them, he walked 150 miles over the mountains to the Swedish frontier arriving there nine days later. He was interned, eventually reaching this country when the Swedish Government released certain groups of German and British internees. Both Sgt Robson and Sgt Craig are commemorated on the Runnymede Memorial.

12th June 1940

254 Sqn	**Blenheim IV**	N3627	QY-R	**Op:**	Reconnaissance
	Sgt R H Brown	561051	+	Base:	Sumburgh
	Sgt H G J Gannaway	627060	+	T/o time:	?
	Sgt W Dixon	751307	+		

Took off tasked with an operation to Trondheim. Shot down at 22:30 hrs by Oblt Walter of I/ZG76 and crashed west of Romsdalsfjord. The crew are commemorated on the Runnymede Memorial.

13th June 1940

42 Sqn	**Beaufort I**	L4489	AW-A	**Op:**	Vaernes
	Sgt F D Flinn	44120	Safe	Base:	Sumburgh
	Sgt S W Shirley	516023	Safe	T/o time:	23:15
	LAC Thomas	. . . . . .	Safe		
	AC F A O'Malley	544944	Safe		

Carried out a dive bombing attack on Vaernes from 6000 ft. Released two 250 lb GP bombs at 2100 ft and reported that both bombs hit a barrack block. Hit by machine-gun nest at Trondheim Station in position 10 30 E, 63 13N and the starboard aileron wire was shot away. The Beaufort returned to base but crashed at 04:50 hrs into the sea when attempting to land. Crew were reported as safe apart from minor cuts and shock.

500 Sqn	**Anson I**	N5225	MK-M	**Op:**	Patrol S.A.6
	Sgt N J Sparks	754915	+	Base:	Detling
	F/O R K Curzon	70156	+	T/o time:	21:48
	AC1 L V Pepper	627043	+		
	Sgt G A Mitchell	812090	+		

Missing from a convoy escort. The crew are commemorated on the Runnymede Memorial.

14th June 1940

224 Sqn	Hudson I	N7359	QX-Q	Op:	Special Coastal Recce
	P/O T N C Rothwell	41475	PoW	Base:	Leuchars
	P/O R C Wood	41514	PoW	T/o time:	09:35
	Sgt W E Harding	627362	+		
	Sgt C L Hand	544342	+		

Shot down by flak-ships of 3./Raumbootflottille NW of Stavanger. Both Sgt Harding and Sgt Hand are commemorated on the Runnymede Memorial.

15th June 1940

224 Sqn	Hudson I	N7217	QX-W	Op:	Soma, Norway
	Sgt T H Nicholls	561837	+	Base:	Leuchars
	P/O R B Askquith-Ellis	42477	+	T/o time:	06:25
	AC1 S J W Baines	630891	+		
	Sgt J Long	621505	+		

Tasked to bomb an ammunition dump but was shot down at 09:00 hrs by either Ofw A Hackl or Fw Petermann of 5./JG77 off Sola, Norway. All are commemorated on the Runnymede Memorial.

224 Sqn	Hudson I	N7270	QX-V	Op:	Soma
	P/O C S Greenaway	43638	+	Base:	Leuchars
	Sgt S G H Stephens	566150	+	T/o time:	06:25
	LAC A F King	546844	+		
	Cpl A J Hull	358791	+		

Tasked to bomb an ammunition dump and shot down by flak at about 09:00 hrs off Stavanger, Norway. Both P/O Greenaway and Cpl Hull rest in Sola Churchyard while the other crew members are commemorated on the Runnymede Memorial.

224 Sqn	Hudson I	N7279	QX-U	Op:	Soma
	P/O N Ewart	41838	+	Base:	Leuchars
	P/O F S Crawford	41558	+	T/o time:	06:25
	Sgt E Pearce	624941	+		
	AC1 T Morton	615295	+		

Tasked to bomb an ammunition dump but shot down at 09:00 hrs by either Ofw A Hackl or Fw Petermann of 5./JG77 off Sola, Norway. P/O Ewart, a New Zealander from Wellington, P/O Crawford, from Auckland, New Zealand, Sgt Pearce and AC1 Morton are all commemorated on the Runnymede Memorial.

254 Sqn	Blenheim IV	L9480	QY-F	Op:	Trondheim
	P/O P C Gaylard	41995	+	Base:	Sumburgh
	Sgt J D Wicks	751253	+	T/o time:	09:45
	Sgt C A C Burran	552645	+		

Last seen flying into cloud on the NE side of Trondheim Harbour. Shot down at 12:45 hrs by Ltn Bender, W of Smola Island. All rest locally in Stavne Cemetery, Trondheim.

16th June 1940

608 Sqn	Anson I	N5067	UL-L	Op:	?
	P/O Duncan	. . . . .	Injured	Base:	Thornaby
	Sgt L B Walpole	745085	DoI	T/o time:	

Hit high-tension cables on high ground in bad visibility and overturned near Saltburn, 4 miles from Guisborough, North Yorkshire. P/O Duncan and Sgt Walpole were seriously injured and taken to North Ormesby Hospital. Sgt Walpole died of his injuries on 19th June and is buried in SS Mary and Margaret Churchyard, Castle Bromwich, Warwickshire.

19th June 1940

PDU	Spitfire I (PR) type B	P9392		Op:	Emden/Bremen
	P/O J H Nicholson	41052	+	Base:	Heston
				T/o time:	1745

Failed to return from a photo-reconnaissance sortie.
P/O Nicholson rests in Hannover War Cemetery, Germany.

206 Sqn	Hudson I		P5120	VX-C	Op:	Patrol S.A.2
	F/O	Marvin	. . . . .	Safe	Base:	Bircham Newton
	P/O	J A Gilbert	41399	Safe	T/o time: 23:50	
	AC	Garrety	. . . . . .	Safe		
	LAC	Thompson	. . . . . .	Safe		

Took off in company with two other aircraft of the squadron. Hit a ridge on the approach, bounced, stalled and the u/c collapsed at 03:15 hrs.

20th June 1940

235 Sqn	Blenheim IV		N3534	LA-X	Duty:	?
					Base:	Thorney Island
	Crashed. No further details.				T/o time: ?	

236 Sqn	Blenheim I		L1334	FA-	Duty:	Training
	F/O	W S Moore	40007	Safe	Base:	Middle Wallop
					T/o time: 00:05	

U/c jammed halfway and the aircraft was belly-landed in a field adjacent to the aerodrome.

21st June 1940

42 Sqn	Beaufort I		L4486	AW-C	Op:	Scharnhorst
	F/O	H J Seagrim	39176	+	Base:	Wick
	Sgt	F J Willoughby	565351	+	T/o time: 14:20	
	LAC	C A Malcolm	523441	+		
	LAC	J White	627575	+		

Took off along with other squadron aircraft and last seen over the target flying North. Shot down by Me109s of II/JG77 into the North Sea off Bergen, Norway. Sgt Willoughby rests in Mollendal Church Cemetery, Bergen, while the others are commemorated on the Runnymede Memorial.

42 Sqn	Beaufort I		L4501	AW-A	Op:	Scharnhorst
	P/O	A G Rigg	.41067	+	Base:	Wick
	P/O	M A Phillips	44259	+	T/o time: 14:20	
	AC1	G E Tanner	625471	+		
	LAC	D Gow	532923	+		

Took off as part of a maximum effort strike. Bombed the target then was last seen doing a climbing right hand turn off the water. Claimed as shot down by II/JG77 into the North Sea off Bergen. P/O Rigg and his crew are commemorated on the Runnymede Memorial.

42 Sqn	Beaufort I		L9810	AW-M	Op:	Scharnhorst
	F/O	W Barrie-Smith	39178	+	Base:	Wick
	P/O	M A Butler	42103	+	T/o time: 14:25	
	Cpl	W J Bates	567448	+		
	Cpl	F Dale	508348	+		

Tasked with a strike along with other squadron aircraft. Caught up with the formation after being attacked by two Me109s of II/JG77. The starboard u/c suddenly dropped, engine burst into flames and crashed into the North Sea. F/O Barrie-Smith and Cpl Dale are commemorated on the Runnymede Memorial, Cpl Bates rests in Rossebo Var Frelsers Cemetery, Haugesund, Norway, and P/O Butler, from Ontario, is buried in Hjaardemaal Klit Churchyard, Denmark.

224 Sqn	Hudson I		N7287	ZS-P	Op:	Convoy Escort
	F/Lt	A E Williamson	37370	+	Base:	Leuchars
	P/O	A S T Cargill DFM	43197	+	T/o time: 17:05	
	Sgt	C F Fennell	531039	+		
	Sgt	P W Weightman	533027	+		

The Hudson was borrowed from 233 Squadron. Failed to return from escorting Convoy 18CS. F/Lt Williamson and his crew are all commemorated on the Runnymede Memorial.

233 Sqn	Hudson I		N7246	ZS-X	Op:	Scharnhorst
	S/Ldr	D Y Feeny	32076	+	Base:	Leuchars
	F/O	C A Wallis	39180	+	T/o time: 12:45	
	Sgt	C G McN Wilson	519827	+		
	Sgt	G W E Walton	568459	+		

Set course from Leuchars in formation with N7340 and two aircraft of 224 Squadron to attack the *Scharnhorst* and eight German destroyers. The flight located their objective in position LXOX 2543 on course 065° True, speed 25 kts. An attack was carried out with 2x500lb S.A.P. bombs on bearing of 310° True, but the bombs overshot by 200 yards. Intense flak was encountered and the flight was engaged by between 40 and 50 Me110 and Me109 fighters. S/Ldr Feeny's aircraft was shot down in flames off Utsire and other a/c in the formation were badly damaged. S/Ldr Feeny's Hudson was claimed by Oblt Jung of 5./JG77; the second pilot F/O Wallis is buried in Rossebo Var Frelsers Cemetery, Haugesund, while the rest of the crew are commemorated on the Runnymede Memorial.

24th June 1940

254 Sqn	Blenheim IV	L9409	QY-J	Op:	Trondheim
	F/Lt P S Jolliffe	33263	+	Base:	Sumburgh
	Sgt A B Norfolk	751127	+	T/o time:	03:35
	Sgt J Price	626267	+		

Took off in formation with other squadron aircraft. Attacked escort ship Schiff 47 with bombs and machine-guns at 06:35 hrs. H/254 reported wingman missing and the ship claimed one Blenheim shot down. The crew of L9409 are commemorated on the Runnymede Memorial.

254 Sqn	Blenheim IV	R3826	QY-Q	Op:	Stavanger
	Sgt H G Hughes	580302	+	Base:	Sumburgh
	Sgt J F Borrows	624811	+	T/o time:	?
	Sgt S Longstaff	755125	+		

Shot down west of Stavanger by Ofw Jakob Arnoldy of 4./JG77 at 13:30 hrs. Sgt Hughes had possibly attacked Sola airfield with bombs. The crew are commemorated on the Runnymede Memorial.

25th June 1940

254 Sqn	Blenheim IV	N3604	QY-	Op:	Stab
	F/Sgt P G Cory	564105	+	Base:	Sumburgh
	Sgt D F S Campbell	743031	+	T/o time:	12:48
	Sgt F G Kinghan	535306	+		

Shot down by Ofw Arnoldy of 4./JG77 at approximately 14:25 hrs, while attacking a ship off Stavanger. F/Sgt Cory and his crew rest in Rossebo Var Frelsers Cemetery, Haugesund, Norway.

254 Sqn	Blenheim IV	R3622	QY-K	Op:	Stab
	P/O A J Hill	42004	PoW	Base:	Sumburgh
	Sgt G W H Kendall	563559	+	T/o time:	12:48
	Sgt R C Trowbridge	550858	+		

Shot down by Ofw Arnoldy of 4./JG77 at approx 14:25 hrs on a sweep to Stavanger/Bergen. Both Sgt Kendall and Sgt Trowbridge are commemorated on the Runnymede Memorial.

27th June 1940

235 Sqn	Blenheim IV	L9447	LA-Y	Op:	Patrol
	P/O J R Cronan	42109	+	Base:	Bircham Newton
	Sgt A O Lancaster	755199	PoW	T/o time:	12:55
	Sgt P L Lloyd	551596	DoW		

Tasked with a patrol of the IJsselmeer. The flight made landfall near Noordwijk and turned towards Amsterdam. Just south of Schipol they were attacked at 15:00 hrs by a large number of Me109s which had just taken off from Soesterberg on an interception. The Blenheim was hit by either Uffz W Schilling of 3./JG21 or Oblt R von Aspern, Staffelkapitan of 2./JG76, the burst of machine-gun fire mortally wounding Sgt Lloyd and hitting P/O Cronan in the shoulder. Sgt Lancaster was wounded in the left leg and saw the pilot slump over the controls unconscious and reached over to remove him from the seat. As he was being moved P/O Cronan recovered and tried to take control of the aircraft again but found that the controls had been shot away. P/O Cronan ordered Sgt Lancaster to abandon through the lower escape hatch but this was jammed and the Sgt then tried to exit through the main hatch but this was also damaged. P/O Cronan released the canopy hatch and jumped to clear the way for Sgt Lancaster. As Sgt Lancaster stood on the seat preparing to exit there was a sudden jerk and bang and he was knocked unconscious. When he recovered he was tumbling in the air and managed to pull the ripcord just before he hit the ground. After walking to a farm he was tended by a doctor and nurse before being taken PoW. P/O Cronan had hit the tail of the aircraft with the side of his face and failed to open his parachute. Sgt Lloyd was found with severe burns and died shortly afterwards. The Blenheim crashed at the Hoogen Dijk, Waverveen near Vinkeveen. Both P/O Cronan, from Auckland in New Zealand, and Sgt Lloyd now rest in Bergen-op-Zoom Canadian War Cemetery, Noord-Brabant.

235 Sqn	Blenheim IV	N3543	LA-U	Op:	Patrol
	P/O A R Wales	41968	+	Base:	Bircham Newton
	Sgt J W Needham	742691	+	T/o time:	12:55
	Sgt T C Jordan	629644	+		

Tasked with a patrol of the IJsselmeer. The flight made landfall near Noordwijk and turned towards Amsterdam. Just south of Schipol they were attacked at 15:00 hrs by a large number of Me109s which had just taken off from Soesterberg on an interception. The Blenheim was shot down at 15:30 hrs by Lt J Schypek of 2./JG76 and tried to make a forced landing but ploughed through a meadow and came to rest against the embankment of a ditch in a field along the Valkenburgerweg at Oegstgeest close to the community border of Rijnsburg. The aircraft broke up due to the impact, throwing some parts 150 metres beyond, the starboard engine and fuel tank ending up some distance from the main wreckage. Sgt Jordan was found by local farm workers lying in the meadow but died shortly afterwards. Sgt Needham was found on the other side of the meadow and P/O Wales only when the Germans salvaged the aircraft. P/O Wales and his crew were later reportedly shot down again in a French aircraft while trying to escape on 29th June, but this originated from a rumour caused by confusion of the RAF fin flash colours and the Dutch/French national flags. The crew died in the crash of N3543 and are buried in Oegstgeest Protestant Churchyard, Zuid-Holland.

235 Sqn	Blenheim IV	P6957	LA-R	Op:	Patrol
	P/O P Weil	41971	+	Base:	Bircham Newton
	Sgt S K Bartlett	755198	+	T/o time:	12:55
	Sgt A Kempster	627208	+		

Tasked with a patrol of the IJsselmeer. Attacked by a large number of Me109s and shot down at 15:30 hrs by either Uffz W Schilling of 3./JG21 or Oblt R von Aspern, Staffelkapitan of 2./JG76 into the North Sea SSW of Noordwijk, Holland. The crew rest in various cemeteries: P/O Weil in Becklingen War Cemetery; Sgt Bartlett's body was recovered near Scheveningen on the 8th July and was buried in Westduin General Cemetery, The Hague; and Sgt Kempster, who was washed ashore on the 20th July and initially buried in Egmond aan Zee, now rests in Jonkerbos War Cemetery.

235 Sqn	Blenheim IV	P6958	LA-D	Op:	Patrol
	P/O H S Pardoe-Williams	41974	+	Base:	Bircham Newton
	Sgt C W Thorley	751531	+	T/o time:	13:00
	P/O E A Saunders	77342	+		

Tasked with a patrol of the IJsselmeer. Attacked by a large number of Me109s and shot down at Ouderkerk aan de Amstel at 15:00 hrs by either Uffz W Schilling of 3./JG21, Ofw M Stotz of 1./JG76 or Oblt F Eckerle of 3./JG76. P/O Pardoe-Williams and his crew are buried in Amsterdam New Eastern Cemetery.

269 Sqn	Hudson I	N7330	UA-C	Op:	Reconnaissance
	P/O P N Trolove	36183	+	Base:	Wick
	Sgt R H Radford	564970	+	T/o time:	06:15
	Sgt W H Gray	548063	+		
	P/O B C Lea	77273	+		

Missing off Lister, Norway. Possibly shot down by Ofw A Hackl of 5./JG77 at 09:40 hrs. P/O Trolove, from Canterbury, New Zealand, and his crew are commemorated on the Runnymede Memorial.

28th June 1940

206 Sqn	Hudson I	N7299	VX-	Op:	Reconnaissance
	Sgt Cullen	. . . . . .	Safe	Base:	Bircham Newton
	Sgt McMahon	. . . . . .	Safe	T/o time:	21:20
	AC Field	. . . . . .	Safe		
	AC W L Johnston	759044	Safe		

Flew into the runway when the flare-path was extinguished without warning at 00:15 hrs due to an invasion scare.

500 Sqn	Anson I	N5226	MK-E	Op:	Boulds
	P/O I F Lothian	42717	+	Base:	Detling
	P/O A Swainston	90610	+	T/o time: 14:00	
	Sgt J P Morgan	626428	+		
	Sgt J W T Alderslade	903455	+		

Missing from a convoy escort. The entire crew are commemorated on the Runnymede Memorial.

29th June 1940

209 Sqn	Lerwick I	L7261	WQ-L	Op:	Escort
	F/O E M Pain	40640	Safe	Base:	Oban
	F/O W H Flint	40101	Safe	T/o time: 03:35	
	P/O W E Ogle-Skan	41609	Safe		
	+ 6 other crew members		Safe		

Took off for an escort operation but ran into bad weather west of Coll and returned to base. Waterborne at 04:30 hrs. When taxying across wind to take up moorings the starboard float apparently broke adrift and the aircraft subsequently capsized and sank in Ardantrive Bay at about 05:00 hrs. The aircraft was later recovered.

210 Sqn	Sunderland I	N9026	DA-D	Op:	Convoy Patrol
	F/Lt A S Ainslie DFC	37310	+	Base:	Pembroke Dock
	F/O C F Elder	70787	+	T/o time: 04:30	
	P/O G N Gaylard	41398	+		
	Sgt F E G Balley	755360	+		
	Sgt G L Walters	533619	+		
	Sgt A G N Hayes	522076	+		
	Sgt D T Crockett	570634	+		
	LAC E R Morris	536055	+		
	LAC E Peacock	620950	+		

Missing off the SW coast of Ireland and believed to have been shot down. A Milford Haven trawler later recovered Sgt Hayes' gas mask bag and pieces of wreckage identified as coming from the nose of a Sunderland. F/Lt Ainslie, from South Africa and his crew are all commemorated on the Runnymede Memorial.

1st July 1940

236 Sqn	Blenheim I	L1278	FA-	Duty:	Air Test
	P/O A R de L Inniss	. . . . .	Safe	Base:	Middle Wallop
				Time:	20:40

While taxying for take-off for R/T and night-flying test, the u/c collapsed. The aircraft u/c had been worked on four hours previously and been raised and lowered several times. It was found that the u/c lever had been wrongly repositioned after the work was finished leaving the u/c unlocked. Although initially classed as repairable the aircraft was later struck off charge.

4th July 1940

206 Sqn	Hudson I	N7368	VX-	Duty:	Air Sea Rescue Search
	P/O S R Henderson DFC	40826	+	Base:	Bircham Newton
	Sgt G H Goldsmith	526218	+	T/o time: 05:50	
	LAC J L Williamson	534498	+		
	Sgt G C Sumner	568173	+		

Took off on a search for missing Handley Page Hampden P4352 ('J' of 44 Squadron). P/O Henderson and his crew were presumed lost near Texel and are commemorated on the Runnymede Memorial.

206 Sqn	Hudson I	P5162	VX-V	Duty:	Air Sea Rescue Search
	P/O J E MacKinnon	41439	+	Base:	Bircham Newton
	P/O S J Lester	41434	+	T/o time: 05:50	
	Sgt K S Bushell	546956	+		
	Sgt K E Lewis	746918	+		

Failed to return from off Texel, on a search for missing Hampden P4352 ('J' of 44 Squadron). P/O Lester, a New Zealander from Nelson, P/O MacKinnon, a Canadian from Moncton, New Brunswick, Sgt Bushell and Sgt Lewis are all commemorated on the Runnymede Memorial.

6th July 1940

254 Sqn	Blenheim IV	L8842	QY-R	Op:	Escort
	Sgt A W Tubbs	564445	Safe	Base:	Sumburgh
	Sgt R A McVeigh	745470	DoW	T/o time:	08:30
	Sgt A C Johnston	969948	Safe		

Shot down by Uffzr Zickler of 3./ZG76 approximately 50 miles off the coast of Norway. The Blenheim was hit in both the starboard oil tank and port petrol tank. Sgt Tubbs landed his a/c near the destroyer HMS *Cossack* and all three crew were rescued by the destroyer's sea boat. Sgt McVeigh died on board of his wounds and was buried at sea that day.

254 Sqn	Blenheim IV	P6950	QY-	Op:	Escort
	P/O V J Pattison	33442	+	Base:	Sumburgh
	Sgt R D McLaren	......	Wounded	T/o time:	08:30
	Sgt A P Savage	......	Safe		

Shot down at 10:50 hrs by Lt Rott of 6./JG77. P/O Pattison, who is commemorated on the Runnymede memorial, crashed vertically into the sea in flames SW of Stavanger. His two crewmen were later rescued by HMS *Fortune*.

9th July 1940

21 Sqn	Blenheim IV	L8872	YH-M	Op:	Stavanger
	F/Lt J D W Murray	39559	+	Base:	Lossiemouth
	Sgt W Hartley	581153	+	T/o time:	08:00
	Sgt G E Duck	551700	+		

Lost without trace. Claimed by JG77 at about 10:10 hrs. F/Lt Murray, of Otago, New Zealand, and his crew are commemorated on the Runnymede Memorial.

21 Sqn	Blenheim IV	N3619	YH-K	Op:	Stavanger
	P/O W D Macley	42415	+	Base:	Lossiemouth
	Sgt W L Rawson	580595	+	T/o time:	08:00
	Sgt J B Dorrington	900499	+		

Lost without trace: all commemorated on Runnymede Memorial. Claimed by JG77 at c.10:10 hrs.

21 Sqn	Blenheim IV	R3732	YH-L	Op:	Stavanger
	W/C L C Bennett	16216	+	Base:	Lossiemouth
	Sgt A T Summers	563808	+	T/o time:	08:00
	Sgt C J Burt	629928	+		

Crashed into the sea after sending a message that they had sustained battle damage at 11:45 hrs. Claimed by JG77. W/C Bennett rests in Lonstrup Churchyard, Denmark while the others are commemorated on the Runnymede Memorial.

21 Sqn	Blenheim IV	R3822	YH-O	Op:	Stavanger
	P/O J A Heath-Brown	42344	+	Base:	Lossiemouth
	Sgt W A Hamlyn	581386	+	T/o time:	08:00
	Sgt E Williams	638749	+		

Lost without trace: all commemorated on Runnymede Memorial. Claimed by JG77 at c.10:10 hrs.

21 Sqn	Blenheim IV	R3876	YH-Q	Op:	Stavanger
	Sgt J B M Brown	741269	+	Base:	Lossiemouth
	Sgt C D Stevens	581538	+	T/o time:	08:00
	Sgt J Morton	642718	+		

Crashed into the sea. Claimed by JG77 at about 10:10 hrs. Sgt Brown rests in Stavne Cemetery, Trondheim, Norway, while his crew are commemorated on the Runnymede Memorial.

57 Sqn	Blenheim IV	R3750	DX-	Op:	Stavanger
	P/O R A Hopkinson	70324	+	Base:	Lossiemouth
	Sgt J G Andrew	746706	+	T/o time:	?
	Sgt G A Miles	751326	+		

Lost without trace. Claimed by JG77.

57 Sqn	Blenheim IV	R3847	DX-	Op:	Stavanger
	Sgt F G Mills	740119	+	Base:	Lossiemouth
	Sgt S J Newcombe	746922	+	T/o time:	?
	Sgt T J Jervis	551360	+		

Lost without trace. Claimed by JG77.

59 Sqn	**Blenheim IV**	**R3637**	**TR-C**	**Op:**	**Hach Patrol**
	P/O A D Hopkin	36220	+	Base:	Thorney Island
	Sgt T J Rowles	581474	+	T/o time:	22:20
	Sgt J Falconer	551873	+		

Blew up at night near Cardiff, at 03:00 hrs. All are commemorated on the Runnymede Memorial.

201 Sqn	**Sunderland I**	**N6133**	**ZM-Y**	**Op:**	**Patrol S.A.1.B**
	F/Lt J D Middleton	33326	+	Base:	Sullom Voe
	P/O D M Harry	40823	+	T/o time:	13:00
	P/O J Seeds	33445	+		
	Sgt L E Worthington	745453	+		
	LAC M J E Jarvis	530166	+		
	LAC J H Lane	517249	+		
	LAC R H F Hammond	536608	+		
	LAC J F Hindle	546994	+		
	AC1 J B Belderson	570289	+		
	AC1 P Clark	623619	+		

Shot down by Oblt Gollob of 3./ZG76 at 14:47 hrs some 90 miles SW of Sumburgh Head, Shetland. F/Lt Middleton and his crew are commemorated on the Runnymede Memorial. On 14th November 1939, F/Lt Middleton had survived ditching into the North Sea when London K5912 was lost.

233 Sqn	**Hudson I**	**N7377**	**ZS-J**	**Op:**	**Patrol S.A.2**
	P/O L J E Ewing MiD	41274	+	Base:	Leuchars
	P/O R M Buchanan	42556	+	T/o time:	15:34
	Sgt D C Sinclair	615825	+		
	Sgt R G Ireland	529709	+		

P/O Ewing from Wellington, New Zealand, and P/O Buchanan from Toronto, Ontario, failed to return from a routine patrol. It is believed that the Hudson was shot down by Oblt Gollob of 3./ZG76 off Shetland at 17:20 hrs. The crew are commemorated on the Runnymede Memorial.

10th July 1940

59 Sqn	**Blenheim IV**	**R3881**	**TR-A**	**Op:**	**Hach Patrol**
	P/O J Rex	78982	+	Base:	Thorney Island
	Sgt J S Jeffery	581226	+	T/o time:	00:05
	Sgt J W Liddle	638666	+		

Detailed for Reconnaissance of Le Havre, France. When flying in low clouds and mist at 03:15 hrs the Blenheim struck an electric power pole on high ground, swung into Titterstone Quarry spoil dump on Clee Hill, Shropshire, and caught fire. From examination of the crash it was noted that P/O Rex was in level flight at normal cruising speed when the aircraft struck the ground but that the W/Op was unable to achieve R/T or W/T contact. P/O Rex rests in St Mary Churchyard, Shawbury, Shropshire, Sgt Jeffery in Greenwich Cemetery, London and Sgt Liddle in Bishopwearmouth Cemetery, Sunderland, County Durham.

11th July 1940

500 Sqn	**Anson I**	**N5228**	**MK-F**	**Op:**	**Dundee**
	Sgt J Wilson	748404	+	Base:	Detling
	Sgt W G Shier	580983	+	T/o time:	02:05
	Sgt L F J O'Kelly	550918	+		
	Sgt H G Worton	903377	+		

Control was lost after a night take-off in bad visibility half a mile SE of Detling. Sgt Wilson rests in Kilmaurs Cemetery, Ayrshire; both Sgt Shier and Sgt O'Kelly locally in St Martin Churchyard Extension, Detling. Sgt Worton is buried in Hertford Road Cemetery, Enfield, Middlesex.

500 Sqn	**Anson I**	**N5220**	**MK-D**	**Op:**	**Hookos Patrol**
	F/O A W A Whithead	70731	+	Base:	Detling
	P/O A R Mathias	41603	+	T/o time:	21:15
	AC1 W C Hubbard	625793	+		
	Sgt H W J Smith	812199	PoW		

Took off for a North Sea patrol but crashed at 23:30 hrs south west of Den Brielle after an attack by He111s. The Anson was shot down by flak and crashed along the Vondelingenweg at Pernis, south of Schiedam. Those who died rest in Crooswijk General Cemetery, Rotterdam, Holland.

12th July 1940

53 Sqn	Blenheim IV	L9474	PZ-L	Op:	Leiden
	W/C E C T Edwards	05146	Safe	Base:	Detling
	Sgt Morriss	. . . . . .	Safe	T/o time: 21:03	
	Sgt W E Williams	645116	Safe		

The crew released their bombs over the target and saw poor AA fire. Bearings were obtained from Detling and Manston but were unreadable due to bad reception. W/C Edwards ordered the crew to abandon the aircraft when the fuel ran low and all landed safely by parachute. The Blenheim crashed near Bulphan, Essex, at approximately 02:45 hrs.

13th July 1940

59 Sqn	Blenheim IV	R3665	TR-P	Op:	Bruges
	P/O H A Clark	72590	+	Base:	Thorney Island
	Sgt D D Morton	581239	+	T/o time: 22:50	
	Sgt F Clayton	643566	+		

At about 02:22 hrs on the 14th of July the Brighton coast-watching Sea Scout reported that an aeroplane was down in the sea 2 miles S of Saltdean. The sea was smooth with light north-easterly airs. The motor lifeboat *Rosa Woodd and Phyllis Lunn* was launched at 03:08 hrs, and at about 04:00 hrs found the wreckage of an RAF machine. She picked up three bodies and brought them in, returning to her station at 07:00 am. It is believed that the Blenheim had been shot down by enemy fighters. P/O Clark rests in St Peter Churchyard, Boughton Monchelsea, Kent; Sgt Morton locally in St Nicholas Churchyard, West Thorney and Sgt Clayton in Thorne Cemetery, Yorkshire.

220 Sqn	Hudson I	N7231	NR-S	Op:	Patrol S.A.3
	P/O G W F Carey DFC	36169	+	Base:	Thornaby
	P/O P K Vartan	41632	+	T/o time: 18:46	
	Sgt V G Gent	624628	+		
	Sgt G A Matthews	538451	+		

On the return from the operation the Hudson hit a balloon cable and crashed at Boldon Colliery, County Durham. After the crash the aircraft caught fire and the bomb-load exploded. Both P/O Carey, a New Zealander from Canterbury, and P/O Vartan, a New Zealander from Hawke's Bay, rest in Castletown Cemetery, Hylton, Durham, Sgt Gent in Linthorpe Cemetery, Middlesborough, and Sgt Matthews in St Patrick Churchyard and Hookergate Cemetery, Winlaton, Durham.

14th July 1940

53 Sqn	Blenheim IV	N3551	PZ-E	Op:	Ghent
	F/O A D Panton DFC	33331	PoW	Base:	Detling
	Sgt A E Farrow	511965	PoW	T/o time: 21:35	
	Sgt L H Stride MiD	546871	+		

Missing from a raid on an oil depot. Sgt Stride is buried in Eeklo Communal Cemetery, Belgium.

17th July 1940

59 Sqn	Blenheim IV	R3694	TR-E	Op:	Cherbourg
	P/O A K Jackson	42840	+	Base:	Thorney Island
	Sgt R V Kingshott	751190	+	T/o time: 08:42	
	Sgt J A Hunter	628333	+		

Missing. Sgt Hunter rests in Cayeux-sur-Mer Communal Cemetery, Somme, and the other crewmen are commemorated on the Runnymede Memorial.

18th July 1940

53 Sqn	Blenheim IV	R3661	PZ-A	Op:	Vlissingen
	F/O J E Mahony	39237	+	Base:	Detling
	Sgt D A Keetley	747771	+	T/o time: 12:02	
	Sgt G E Exton	640689	+		

Shot down at 14:00 hrs by an Me109 of 6./JG54 operating from Haamstede and crashed into the mouth of the Scheldt. F/O Mahony and Sgt Keetley are commemorated on the Runnymede Memorial while Sgt Exton was initially buried Klemskerke but now is buried in Adegem Canadian War Cemetery in Belgium.

235 Sqn	**Blenheim IV**	**N3541**	**LA-**	**Op:**	**Convoy Patrol**
	P/O R L Patterson	77529	+	Base:	Bircham Newton
	Sgt L H M Reece	747825	+	T/o time: 10:00	
	Sgt R Y Tucker	552711	+		

Failed to return from the North Sea after being separated from a formation in very low cloud and low visibility. Having no known graves, the crew are commemorated on the Runnymede Memorial.

236 Sqn	**Blenheim I**	**L6639**	**FA-**	**Op:**	**Escort**
	P/O R H Rigby	42149	+	Base:	Thorney Island
	Sgt D D MacKinnon	745928	+	T/o time: 11:20	

Missing on an operation to Le Havre, France, in bad weather. Presumed shot down by Uffz W Melchert of II/JG2 near Cap-de-la-Hague at about 12.15 hrs. P/O Rigby rests in Ste Marie Cemetery, Le Havre; Sgt MacKinnon is buried in Villerville Communal Cemetery, Calvados.

236 Sqn	**Blenheim I**	**L6779**	**FA-**	**Op:**	**Escort**
	P/O C R D Thomas	40031	+	Base:	Thorney Island
	Sgt H D B Elsdon	743044	+	T/o time: 11:20	

Missing on a photo operation to Le Havre, France, in bad weather. Possibly shot down by Hptm W Schellmann of II/JG2 near Cap-de-la-Hague at about 12:15 hrs. P/O Thomas is buried in Quiberville Churchyard while Sgt Elsdon is commemorated on the Runnymede Memorial.

20th July 1940

236 Sqn	**Blenheim I**	**L1300**	**FA-A**	**Op:**	**Escort**
	Sgt E E Lockton	740005	+	Base:	Thorney Island
	Sgt H Corcoran	519958	+	T/o time: 17:45	

Shot down by Me109s and seen to spin into the sea at 18:20 hrs, off Cherbourg. Claimed by Hptm Neumann of JG27. Both Sgt Corcoran (who had joined 236 Sqn the previous day) and Sgt Lockton are commemorated on the Runnymede Memorial.

21st July 1940

204 Sqn	**Sunderland I**	**N9028**	**KG-A**	**Op:**	**Reconnaissance**
	W/C E S C Davis OBE AFC	16107	+	Base:	Sullom Voe
	F/Lt F Phillips DFC	37827	+	T/o time: ?	
	P/O G E MacDonald	42067	+		
	P/O R T Pareezer	42076	+		
	Sgt D P Dixon	610629	+		
	Sgt W G Lillie DFM	538981	+		
	Sgt E W Ovens	550833	+		
	LAC D J Frame	535408	+		
	LAC T P J Trickey	635359	+		
	AC1 J A McL G White	967530	+		
	AC1 L C Bennett	570382	+		
	AC2 E Sneyd	935024	+		

Took off tasked for an operation to the Trondheim area. Missing, presumed shot down by Me110s near Linaero possibly at 05:15 by Oblt Weber of 8./JG77. All, including P/O MacDonald from Seattle Heights, Washington, USA, are commemorated on the Runnymede Memorial.

224 Sqn	**Hudson I**	**N7305**	**QX-X**	**Op:**	**Strike**
	P/O V C R Morrison	43204	+	Base:	Leuchars
	Sgt E A Cotton	742495	+	T/o time: 10:27	
	Sgt D Middleton	551824	+		
	Sgt S W Curry	551339	+		

Detailed to bomb four minesweepers from 1.Minensuchflottille and the 12000 ton tanker *Nordmark* in position JZUB 4545. Listed as missing at 13:43 hrs after an attack in position JGYG 2628, W of Hestholmen, Norway. Shot down at 14:45 hrs by either Lt Eckhardt or Uffz Ladwein of II/ZG76. All are commemorated on the Runnymede Memorial.

233 Sqn	**Hudson I**	**N7242**	**ZS-Z**	**Op:**	**Strike**
	P/O W L Ather	44226	+	Base:	Leuchars
	Sgt J J Crabtree	523092	+	T/o time: 10:29	
	Sgt B J Mahon	635470	+		
	Sgt A W Lamont	523170	+		

Detailed to bomb four minesweepers of 1.Minensuchflottile and the 12,000 ton tanker *Nordmark* in position JZUB4545. The Hudson was shot down at 14:45 hrs by either Ltn Eckhardt or Uffz Ladwein of II/ZG76. P/O Ather and his crew are commemorated on the Runnymede Memorial.

22nd July 1940

59 Sqn	Blenheim IV	R3639	TR-Z	Op:	Amsterdam
	P/O A P Hovenier	41927	Safe	Base:	Thorney Island
	Sgt L E Magee	581233	Safe	T/o time:	23:40
	Sgt J B Scotchmere	552935	Safe		

Destroyed on landing at Thorney Island when the port u/c collapsed and the bomb-load exploded.

254 Sqn	Blenheim IV	R3887	QY-	Duty:	Training
	F/Sgt W G Tyler	516399	+	Base:	Sumburgh
				T/o time:	?

F/Sgt Tyler took off on his second day at the squadron to carry out a local solo flight. He was offered some dual training on the Blenheim but this was refused as he felt confident of his ability. He made two normal landings but on his third landing he turned sharply off the approach to avoid a collision with two lorries, stalled and burst into flames on the ground. F/Sgt Tyler rests in Uplands Cemetery, Smethwick, Staffordshire.

23rd July 1940

21 Sqn	Blenheim IV	R3872	YH-P	Duty:	Training
	P/O A F C Carson	42693	Safe	Base:	Lossiemouth
				T/o time:	?

Overshot on landing and ran into the watch office.

21 Sqn	Blenheim IV	R3820	YH-J	Duty:	Training
	P/O T J Powell	42643	+	Base:	Lossiemouth
	Sgt C J Smewin	580591	+	T/o time:	?
	Sgt D V Mobberley	641364	+		

Spun into the North Sea at 10:08 hrs, 1 mile N of Lossiemouth airfield, Morayshire. Sgt Smewin rests in All Saints Churchyard, Publow, Somerset, Sgt Mobberley in Glanadda Cemetery, Bangor, while P/O Powell is commemorated on the Runnymede Memorial.

269 Sqn	Hudson I	P5152	UA-J	Op:	Escort O.A.188
	F/Lt C D W Price	37985	+	Base:	Wick
	P/O J T T Fleming	41277	+	Time:	04:15
	P/O W Appleby	42975	+		
	Sgt L Land	623762	+		

Collided with Hurricane P2862 whilst taking off and crashed. F/Lt Price rests in St Cattwg Churchyard, Llanspyddid, Brecknockshire; P/O Appleby in SS Mary and James Churchyard, Morpeth, Northumberland; while both P/O Fleming, from Wellington, New Zealand, and Sgt Land are buried locally in Wick Cemetery.

25th July 1940

53 Sqn	Blenheim IV	R3836	PZ-X	Op:	Patrol S.A.9
	P/O D B Starky	41752	+	Base:	Detling
	Sgt H W Hunt	580545	+	T/o time:	06:02
	Sgt B Moriarty	615346	+		

Shot down by ship's flak off Ballum, Ameland, during a raid on invasion barges and crashed on the Koffieboon Plaat sand bank. Sgt Hunt, a Canadian from Vancouver, is buried in Jonkerbos War Cemetery, Gelderland, Holland. Both P/O Starky, a New Zealander from Opotiki, and Sgt Moriarty, from Eire, are commemorated on the Runnymede Memorial.

59 Sqn	Blenheim IV	L9473	TR-K	Duty:	Air Sea Rescue
	F/O H Haswell	72482	+	Base:	Thorney Island
	Sgt R B Martin	751104	+	T/o time:	12:00
	Sgt D B Simpson	755136	+		

Failed to return when tasked to identify an area to destroyers where rafts had been seen that morning. F/O Haswell, a South African from Johannesburg, and his crew are commemorated on Runnymede Memorial.

26th July 1940

59 Sqn	Blenheim IV	T1801	TR-T	Op:	Cherbourg
	P/O M R Turnbull	42915	+	Base:	Thorney Island
	Sgt G P Rowe	751202	+	T/o time:	03:15
	Sgt D Wallace	628797	+		

Missing. Both P/O Turnbull and Sgt Rowe are commemorated on the Runnymede Memorial while Sgt Wallace rests in Criel-sur-Mer Communal Cemetery, France.

320 Sqn	Fokker T-VIIIW	AV964	TD-R	Op:	Convoy Escort
	Off VI 1e Klas E Martare RNNAS	. . . . .	+	Base:	Pembroke Dock
	Off VI 3e Klas J C Den Hollander RNNAS		+	T/o time:	10:31
	Kpl Telegrafist KMR J G Ras RNNAS	12062	+		
	Sergt-Maj. VI A de Knegt RNNAS	. . . . .	+		

Hit the water near a convoy in the Irish Sea at 12:15 hrs. A message was received that the aircraft had left the convoy at 12.10 hrs at position 5135N 0531W, its PLE (prudent limit of endurance). Coastguard watch reported an unknown object drifting at sea, about 7 miles SSE of St Govens Head and some ships nearby. A Saro Lerwick took off at 15:15 hrs, headed for St Govens Head and from there set course in a SE direction. At about 13 nautical miles ESE of St Govens Head the fishing boat *King Edward* was sighted, towing the wreckage of AV964. The Dutch vessel SS *Prima* delivered two bodies to Cardiff. Both Off Martare and Kpl Ras rest in Llanion Cemetery, Pembroke Dock, Pembrokeshire.

Several of these modern Fokker T-VIIIW twin-engined patrol seaplanes were evacuated to Britain when the Germans invaded the Netherlands. They were impressed into RAF service to continue the fight, manned by Dutch crews, initially patrolling the Western approaches from their base at Pembroke Dock. This particular machine had been serialled 'R-10' during its previous service with the Royal Netherlands Naval Air Service.

30th July 1940

236 Sqn	Blenheim IV	R2777	FA-	Duty:	?
	F/Lt R M Power	39471	Safe	Base:	Carew Cheriton
				Time:	13:20

Construction work on the aerodrome had resulted in restricted take-off runs. F/Lt Power thought that his run would take him clear of the runway under construction but he hit bags of cement and the u/c collapsed.

31st July 1940

233 Sqn	Hudson I	N7224	ZS-O	Op:	Patrol S.A.2
	P/O J M Horan	41417	+	Base:	Leuchars
	P/O B C Paton	42021	+	T/o time:	08:52
	Sgt W G Cameron	548486	+		
	Sgt S Morgan	539583	+		

P/O Horan, an Australian, took off to undertake a patrol on Tracks R and Q but failed to return. It is believed that they were shot down by Ofw Arnoldy of II/JG77 off the coast of Norway where P/O Paton rests in Kristiansand Civil Cemetery. The bodies of the rest of the crew were not recovered and they are commemorated on the Runnymede Memorial.

48 Sqn	Anson I	K8829	OY-	Duty:	Training
	Sgt A J Daniels RNNAS	. . . . . .	Injured	Base:	Carew Cheriton
	Lt/Cmdr Kolff	. . . . .	Injured	T/o time:	04:31
	Cpl J Van de Schaaf RNNAS	. . . . . .	Injured		
	F/Sgt S P Tomley	565434	+		
	Sgt A G Willis	568341	+		

Assigned to the RNNAS. On taking off while carrying a mixed crew of three Dutch and two RAF, the Anson crashed into a dispersed Battle (N2050) and burst into flames. F/Sgt Tomley rests in Seaford Cemetery, Sussex, while Sgt Willis is buried locally in St Mary New Churchyard, Carew.

Chapter 6

1st August 1940 to 25th September 1940

In August Hitler turned his attention to the invasion of Britain and Coastal Command now found its Channel Convoy protection task hampered by the presence of the *Luftwaffe* only a few minutes flying away. Invasion barges were collecting in Dutch ports requiring strike operations to be added to the growing demands on the scarce resources of Coastal Command along the south coast.

U-boats operating from Biscay ports now ranged deep into the Atlantic stretching the patrol areas of the anti-submarine aircraft and highlighting the lack of suitable airfields in the South West. A change in U-boat tactics in August to night attacks further reduced the interceptions by the anti-submarine crews, since only one in five of their aircraft were fitted with ASV radar – delivery of the improved Mk.II version having been delayed to satisfy the production needs of fighter AI (Airborne Interception) sets. Coastal Command land bases were now in the front line with aircraft losses during air raids on Detling, Thorney Island, Manston, St Eval and Filton.

The first examples of the Martin 167 Maryland twin-engined three-seat reconnaissance bomber began to arrive in the UK in July, having been diverted from an original French order. Some early deliveries went to 'C' Flight of 22 Squadron, for crew-training, the crews moving on to Malta to join 431 Flight. Most Marylands went to Middle East units; their sojourn with Coastal Command being quite brief, although a few were retained by the Photographic Reconnaissance Unit. In August another new aircraft type, the Blackburn Botha, began to re-equip 608 and 502 Squadrons but proved inadequate to the role and was withdrawn after only a few months. Problems were also encountered with the high dropping speeds of the modern torpedo-bombers leading to failures of the standard naval air to surface torpedo. Modified weapons were not available until the beginning of September when the Beaufort units began operations against the invasion barge concentrations.

On the 17th August a total blockade of Britain was declared and all neutral ships running the blockade liable to be sunk. Focke-Wulf Fw 200 Condor long-range aircraft started to operate from Bordeaux in September, attacking single vessels and shadowing convoys just out of range from the anti-submarine patrols or the convoy defences. The sighting reports allowed the U-boats to converge on the convoy and follow it by day and attack at night as a 'Pack'.

1st August 1940

PRU	Spitfire I (PR ?)	K9879	LY-	Duty:	Training
	Lt Cdr G D Kingdon	–	+	Base:	Heston
				T/o time:	?

Pilot believed collapsed from oxygen starvation while flying at 30,000ft on a cross-country training exercise. The aircraft dived into the ground 3½ miles NW of Crewkerne, Somerset. Lt Cdr Kingdon was assigned to HMS *President* and rests in Weston Mill Cemetery, Plymouth, Devon.

59 Sqn	Blenheim IV	L8792	TR-A	Op:	Cherbourg
	W/C R G S Morgan-Weld-Smith 05224		+	Base:	Thorney Island
	P/O D H Davis AFM	44271	+	T/o time:	15:00
	Sgt P Pryde	551852	+		

Failed to return. W/C Morgan-Weld-Smith MiD, is buried in St Pierre-en-Port Communal Cemetery. Sgt Pryde is buried in Veules-les-Roses Communal Cemetery and P/O Davis twice MiD rests in St Valery-en-Caux Franco-British Cemetery.

220 Sqn	Hudson I	N7314	NR-B	Op:	Patrol S.A.3
	F/Lt H W A Sheahan DFC	37266	+	Base:	Thornaby
	P/O C J Allsup	41539	+	T/o time:	18:02
	Sgt S Smith	623798	+		
	Sgt Butler	Injured			

Hit a high-tension (HT) cable at Maltby, Yorkshire, and crash-landed at 23:48 hrs. The bomb-load exploded on impact. F/Lt Sheahan, a South African, and Sgt Smith both rest locally in Thornaby-on-Tees Cemetery while P/O Allsup, a Canadian from Vancouver, was taken to All Saints Churchyard, Sanderstead, Surrey, for burial.

236 Sqn	Blenheim IV	N3601	FA-K	Op:	Cherbourg
	S/L P E Drew	26199	+	Base:	Thorney Island
	F/O B Nokes-Cooper	77362	+	T/o time:	15:05

Last seen diving to attack over the airfield and was possibly shot down by either flak or Oblt Adolph of III/JG27. F/O Nokes-Cooper, who was the Squadron Signals Officer, is buried in Bayeux War Cemetery while his pilot rests in Biville Churchyard.

236 Sqn	Blenheim IV	R2774	FA-N	Op:	Cherbourg
	P/O B M McDonough	42137	+	Base:	Thorney Island
	Sgt F A P Head	902546	+	T/o time:	15:05

Last seen diving to attack over the airfield and was shot down either by flak or by Oblt Dullberg of III/JG27. Both P/O McDonough, an Australian, and Sgt Head are commemorated on the Runnymede Memorial.

254 Sqn	Blenheim IV	L9299	QY-		
	Struck off charge. No further details.			Base:	Sumburgh

2nd August 1940

59 Sqn	Blenheim IV	N3587	TR-K	Op:	Cherbourg
	P/O D A Drew	79539	+	Base:	Thorney Island
	Sgt A G Herbert	749485	+	T/o time:	09:05
	Sgt J R Close	653790	+		

Took off to search for A/59 which was lost the previous day, then to carry out a reconnaissance of Le Havre. Shot down N of Le Havre by Oblt P Temme at 11:05 hrs. P/O Drew and his crew rest in Ste Marie Cemetery, Le Havre, France.

3rd August 1940

53 Sqn	Blenheim IV	L8794	PZ-T	Op:	'49'
	S/Ldr D C Oliver	34109	Safe	Base:	Detling
	Sgt Dunjey	. . . . . .	Safe	T/o time:	19:48
	Sgt Thirlby	. . . . . .	Safe		

Abandoned in bad visibility and crashed at 01:10 hrs, Broxhead Common, near Bordon, Hampshire, on the return from the target due to problems with wireless communications. S/Ldr Oliver landed by parachute between Farnham and Petersfield and Sgt Dunjey near Farnham.

53 Sqn	Blenheim IV	L9475	PZ-V	Op:	Emden Harbour
	P/O H C Corbett	72466	+	Base:	Detling
	Sgt S E Riddington	751028	+	T/o time:	19:48
	Sgt K W Crane	526095	+		

Failed to return. At 00:45 hrs bearings indicated the aircraft flying out to sea north of Bircham Newton. Wireless transmission from the Blenheim broke off abruptly at 01:05 hrs. P/O Corbett was washed ashore on the 29th of August and is buried locally in Schoorl General Cemetery, Holland, Sgt Riddington in Thurmaston Cemetery, Leicestershire and Sgt Crane is commemorated on the Runnymede Memorial.

206 Sqn	Hudson I	T9282	VX-E	Op:	Patrol S.A.4
	P/O J A Gilbert	41399	+	Base:	Bircham Newton
	Sgt B P Gannon	741151	+	T/o time:	20:40
	Sgt W L Johnston	759044	+		
	Sgt P W Swinson	620418	+		

Failed to return. P/O Gilbert and his crew are commemorated on the Runnymede Memorial.

5th August 1940

206 Sqn	Hudson I	P5133	VX-D	Duty:	Search
	P/O R T Kean DFC	41295	+	Base:	Bircham Newton
	P/O R Rustom	42079	+	T/o time:	15:05
	Sgt F H Hull	755799	+		
	Sgt D Mannion	627225	+		

Stalled after a steep turn, hit the ground at 18:05 hrs and blew up at Syderstone, Norfolk. P/O Kean, a New Zealander from Otago , rests in New Hunstanton Cemetery, Norfolk, P/O Rustom locally in St Mary's Churchyard, Great Bircham, Norfolk, Sgt Hull in Solihull Cemetery, Warwickshire and Sgt Mannion in Nottingham Road Cemetery, Derby.

206 Sqn	Hudson I	T9272	VX-	Duty:	Transit Flight
	P/O A P Davis	41261	Safe	Base:	?
				T/o time:	?

Took off to transport heavy stores. Damaged beyond repair in a heavy landing at Aldergrove, 17:50 hrs. See also 5th January 1940.

6th August 1940

206 Sqn	Hudson I	P5153	VX-O	Op:	Patrol SA 4/1
	F/O Feeneley	. . . . .	Safe	Base:	Bircham Newton
	Sgt Bracken	. . . . .	Safe	T/o time:	20:40
	Sgt J Wallace	638965	Safe		
	Sgt G R Ellerington	627175	Safe		

Crashed on landing at Docking and the bomb-load exploded at 22:30 hrs. All crew escaped safely.

7th August 1940

206 Sqn	Hudson I	N7395	VX-N	Op:	Patrol S.A.4.1
	P/O Burn	. . . . .	Safe	Base:	Bircham Newton
	P/O Huert	. . . . .	Safe	T/o time:	20:45
	Sgt Willet	. . . . . .	Safe		
	Sgt McGlyn	. . . . . .	Safe		

Overshot during landing at 00:15 hrs, swung and the u/c collapsed slewing the Hudson into another aircraft at Docking before the bombs exploded.

224 Sqn	Hudson I	N7282	QX-F	Op:	Special Reconnaissance
	P/O R B Forbes	41391	+	Base:	Leuchars
	Sgt J M Oliver	700059	+	T/o time:	10:49
	Sgt G D Tennant	550847	+		
	Sgt S Grant	539039	+		

Attacked escort ship NB02 in Fedjefjorden and was shot down at 14:10 hrs by Fw Ladwein of II/ZG76 off Bergen, Norway. P/O Forbes, a Canadian from Winnipeg, Sgt Oliver and Sgt Tennant are commemorated on the Runnymede Memorial while Sgt Grant rests in Stavne Cemetery, Trondheim.

248 Sqn	Blenheim IV	L9456	WR-R	Op:	Trondheim
	P/O R H Haviland	76571	Safe	Base:	Sumburgh
	P/O M L Wells	78260	Safe	T/o time:	?
	Sgt A Kay	647610	Injured		

Owing to bad visibility it was impossible to see Trondheim. P/O Haviland continued south along the Norwegian coast to fix position before setting course for base. After 8.25 hours flight, owing to lack of fuel, they ditched into sea near Farne Island off St Abbs Head. The crew took to their rubber boat before being picked up by trawler, and landed at South Shields. The aircraft was salvaged and the crew were none the worse for their experience apart from minor injuries to the Observer's leg. Also see entry for 28th August 1940 for P/O Haviland.

8th August 1940

59 Sqn	Blenheim IV	N3590	TR-F	Op:	Cherbourg
	P/O H L N Davis	72988	+	Base:	Thorney Island
	Sgt G H Coulton	619184	+	T/o time:	15:50
	Sgt B W Beaumont	744953	+		

Missing on Reconnaissance Both P/O Davis and Sgt Coulton are commemorated on the Runnymede Memorial while Sgt Beaumont rests in Dieppe Canadian War Cemetery, Hautot-sur-Mer, France.

9th August 1940

321 Sqn	Anson I		K6285	F	Duty:	Training
	Sgt	J P J Bielfeldt RNNAS	12682	Safe	Base:	Carew Cheriton
					T/o time:	00:30

Became lost while carrying out local flying practice and force-landed at the east end of Pendine Sands, Dyfed. As Sgt Bielfeldt was landing he hit one of the anti-invasion beach obstructions and crashed into the sea. He reached shore safely, the Anson was later recovered to become 2398M

500 Sqn	Anson I		N5356	MK-B	Op:	Hookos Patrol
	P/O	H G R Pirie	42077	+	Base:	Detling
	P/O	J B S Brockway	78530	PoW	T/o time:	02:35
	Sgt	S R Croft	632266	PoW		
	Sgt	M A Prentice	812244	+		

Crashed into the North Sea off Katwijk. P/O Pirie rests in Noordwijk General Cemetery, Holland, and Sgt Prentice is buried in Bergen-op-Zoom Canadian War Cemetery, Holland.

11th August 1940

53 Sqn	Blenheim IV		T1816	PZ-K	Op:	Dundee 2
	P/O	P J Coleman	42695	Evaded	Base:	Detling
	Sgt	I Inskip	581339	+	T/o time:	10:24
	P/O	G M Bardolph	78695	DoW		

Missing off the coast of France. Sgt Inskip has no known grave and is commemorated on the Runnymede Memorial. P/O Bardolph, a Canadian from Vernon, was severely wounded and died from his wounds in the German Military Hospital at Château-des-Domaines, Hardinghen on the 17th August. He is buried in Hardinghen Churchyard, Pas-de-Calais.

217 Sqn	Anson I		K8813	MW-V	Op:	Patrol S.A.12
	P/O	A Gordon-Peiniger	40904	+	Base:	St Eval
	P/O	R M Coulman	41557	+	T/o time:	12:15
	Sgt	E K Mellody	969831	+		
	Sgt	E Hopperton	625352	+		

At 16:57 hrs a message requesting help was received. Blenheims of 236 Squadron took off to search position 4040N 0735W but could not find any trace of the Anson. P/O Gordon-Peiniger and his crew were presumed lost at sea after an enemy attack and are commemorated on the Runnymede Memorial.

12th August 1940

53 Sqn	Blenheim IV		T1937	PZ-E	Op:	'54'
	F/O	Jameson	. . . . .	Safe	Base:	Detling
	Sgt	Butler	. . . . . .	Safe	T/o time:	21:15
	Sgt	Andrews	. . . . . .	Safe		

Made landfall on the return over the east coast of Kent. From Manston F/O Jameson set course for Detling but failed to locate the aerodrome. The crew received no bearings from Detling but they did receive another QDM from Manston from which the Blenheim again set course for Detling, but again failed to locate the airfield. The crew baled out at 01:45 hrs at 7,000 ft, F/O Jameson then baled out at 9,000 ft leaving the aircraft to crash and burn at Conghurst, Hawkhurst, Kent.

13th August 1940

53 Sqn	Blenheim IV	R3677	PZ-	Ground Loss	
	Blenheim IV	R3819	PZ-	Ground Loss	
	Blenheim IV	R3849	PZ-	Ground Loss	
	Blenheim IV	T1938	PZ-	Ground Loss	
				Base:	Detling
				Time:	16:05

All four aircraft destroyed in an air raid.

14th August 1940

206 Sqn	Hudson I		N7401	VX-	Op:	Reconnaissance
	P/O	H G Ballantyne	36265	+	Base:	Docking

P/O J O L Stephenson	41623	+	T/o time: 03:15
Sgt J Steel	644325	Safe	
Sgt E Fitzgerald	545600	+	

Control lost in the circuit after take-off. The Hudson dived into the ground at Sunderland Farm, Docking, Norfolk. Both P/O Ballantyne, a New Zealander from Hawke's Bay, and P/O Stephenson, a New Zealander from Taranaki, rest locally in St Mary's Churchyard, Great Bircham, Norfolk and Sgt Fitzgerald in The Rosary Cemetery, Norwich, Norfolk.

16th August 1940

PRU	Spitfire I (PR) type ?	?	LY-	Op:	Ruhr
	P/O A B Corbett	41666	PoW	Base:	Heston
				T/o time: ?	

Pilot reported as a PoW on 19th August. P/O Corbett's aircraft identity remains in doubt. The Unit ORB records a Spitfire failing to return on 16th, but does not mention the aircraft serial. Another source quotes N3116, a Spitfire Mk.I (PR) type B, as failing to return on 15th August, and it being struck off their charge on the 26th. Clarification still required.

59 Sqn	Blenheim IV	R3835	TR-		Ground Loss
				Base:	Manston
	Destroyed in an air raid.			Time:	?

59 Sqn	Blenheim IV	T1815	TR-		Ground Loss
				Base:	Thorney Island
	Damaged beyond repair in an air raid.			Time:	18:14

220 Sqn	Hudson I	N7316	NR-Y	Duty:	Training
	S/Ldr D W Lydall	. . . . .	Injured	Base:	Thornaby
	P/O J T Wardlaw	42920	DoI	T/o time: 17:30	

S/Ldr Lydall was converting P/O Wardlaw onto the Hudson type when an engine failed shortly after take-off. Both crew were transferred to Stockton Hospital where P/O Wardlaw died of his injuries on 22nd August and was buried in Sunnyside Cemetery, Alloa, Clackmannanshire.

17th August 1940

PRU	Spitfire I (PR) type B (?)	K9791	LY-	Op:	Ruhr
	F/Sgt J D T Taylor-Gill	590406	PoW	Base:	Heston
				T/o time: ?	

Failed to return from PR sortie over the Ruhr.
Aircraft K9791 had flown 126 hours when lost.

235 Sqn	Blenheim IV	L4833	LA-	Op:	Escort
	?	. . . . .		Base:	Thorney Island
	?	. . . . .		T/o time: ?	

Upon return from Boulogne crashed into the sea on a night approach at Thorney Island, Hampshire.

235 Sqn	Blenheim IV	N3540	LA-X	Op:	Escort
	Sgt S J Hobbs	. . . . . .	Safe	Base:	Thorney Island
	Sgt H W Ricketts	. . . . . .	Safe	T/o time: 19:15	
	Sgt T A Maslen	615059	Safe		

Tasked with escort of Battles to Boulogne. Overshot on landing and the u/c collapsed but the crew escaped without injury.

18th August 1940

235 Sqn	Blenheim IV	T1805	LA-M	Op:	Defensive Patrol
	?			Base:	Thorney Island
	Damaged by return fire from an enemy aircraft.			T/o time: 14:20	

19th August 1940

59 Sqn	Blenheim IV	R2795	TR-D		Op:	Caen
	P/O B Reynolds	42528	DoW		Base:	Thorney Island
	Sgt W G F Whiting	581252	+		T/o time:	22:00
	Sgt W G J Wilkinson	546143	+			

Failed to return. P/O Reynolds died of his wounds on the 20th of August and lies along with his crew in Bayeux War Cemetery, Calvados, France.

248 Sqn	Blenheim IV	L9457	WR-S		Op:	Reconnaissance
	Sgt J H Round	740667	+		Base:	Sumburgh
	Sgt W H Want	745927	+		T/o time:	?
	Sgt M P Digby-Worsley	649007	+			

Failed to return from the coast, south of Norway. Engaged by flak from Kvingsoy Island at 15:00 hrs then shot down by four Me109s. All are commemorated on the Runnymede Memorial.

21st August 1940

236 Sqn	Blenheim IV	R2776	FA-			Ground Loss
	Blenheim IV	T1944	FA-			Ground Loss
					Base:	St Eval
					Time:	13:52

The airfield was attacked by three Ju88s which bombed a hangar and machine-gunned aircraft at dispersal, destroying the above aircraft.

240 Sqn	Stranraer I	K7301	BN-			Ground Loss
					Base:	Stranraer
					Time:	?

Sank at its mooring during a gale. The Stranraer was later salvaged but deemed beyond repair.

23rd August 1940

224 Sqn	Hudson I	N7244	QX-		Duty:	?
	P/O A T Harrison	42604	+		Base:	Leuchars
	P/O B D Clarkson	42674	DoI		T/o time:	12:15

Crashed into a river near Leuchars due to unknown causes. P/O Harrison died in the crash and was taken to South Ealing Cemetery, Middlesex for burial. P/O Clarkson died later in St Andrews Cottage Hospital and is buried in Piershill Cemetery, Edinburgh.

269 Sqn	Hudson I	T9299	UA-Y		Duty:	Training
	P/O S J Herring	42605	+		Base:	Wick
	S/Ldr R H S McConnell DFC	34023	+		T/o time:	?

Took off for first flight on type. Engine cut on overshoot and the Hudson, stalled, spun in and caught fire. Both S/L McConnell and P/O Herring are buried locally in Wick Cemetery.

24th August 1940

53 Sqn	Blenheim IV	T2035	PZ-F		Op:	Hookos Patrol
	F/O S C Rochford	70584	+		Base:	Detling
	Sgt W Briggs	751402	+		T/o time:	20:59
	Sgt D Brook	648603	+			

Crashed at Dover hitting two houses and bursting into flames while returning from an attack on the Channel Ports. F/O Rochford rests in Hertford Corporation Cemetery, Sgt Briggs in St John the Baptist Churchyard, Westwood, Warwickshire while Sgt Brook was taken to Anlaby Tranby Lane Cemetery, Haltemprice, Yorkshire.

235 Sqn	Blenheim IV	T1804	LA-E		Op:	Patrol
	P/O D N Woodger	42666	+		Base:	Thorney Island
	Sgt D L Wright	552618	+		T/o time:	16:30

Took off to provide aerodrome fighter protection during an air raid. Shot down 5 miles S of Thorney Island at 16:45 hrs by a Hurricane of 1 (RCAF) Squadron and crashed into Bracklesham Bay. A search of the crash area by the Shoreham Harbour lifeboat was unsuccessful. Sgt Wright's body was later recovered from the sea and he rests in St Ann Churchyard, Chasetown, Staffordshire. P/O Woodger is commemorated on the Runnymede Memorial.

608 Sqn	Botha I	L6209	UL-O	Op:	Convoy Escort
	P/O D H F Horner	. . . . .	Injured	Base:	Thornaby
	P/O Reid	. . . . .	Safe	T/o time:	?

Engine cut after take-off for a convoy escort. The Botha was belly-landed but hit a hedge then ran into a ditch at Ormesby, County Durham.

25th August 1940

254 Sqn	Blenheim IV	L9407	QY-	Duty:	Training
	F/O G D Sise RNZAF	. . . . .	Injured	Base:	Dyce
	F/Lt W P Bain	. . . . .	Injured	T/o time:	15:10

Carrying out circuit and landing flying practice when the Blenheim approached too slow, undershot, struck a boundary wall, stalled and then fell to the ground heavily.

26th August 1940

500 Sqn	Anson I	N5229	MK-	Op:	Anti-Submarine Patrol
	?			Base:	Detling
				T/o time:	?

Crashed on t/o for an anti-submarine sweep; caught fire.

500 Sqn	Anson I	N9898	MK-Y	Op:	Sweep
	P/O P W Peters	. . . . .	Safe	Base:	Detling
	Sgt Stanley	. . . . . .	Safe	T/o time:	01:15
	Sgt Collorrossi	. . . .	Safe		
	Sgt C H Newton	812249	Safe		

Crashed and caught fire on take-off. P/O Peters (and his crew?) then immediately ran to the spare aircraft, N5317, and took off in that, only to crash a few minutes later.

500 Sqn	Anson I	N5317	MK-	Op:	Patrol
	P/O P W Peters	. . . . .	Injured	Base:	Detling
	Crew ?			T/o time:	01:20

Swung on take-off and stalled in bad visibility. It has not been possible todate to ascertain whether the exact same crew of N9898 joined P/O Peters in N5317.

27th August 1940

PRU	Hudson I	N7321		Op:	Cuxhaven
	F/O Bamber	. . . . .	Safe	Base:	Coltishall
	Sgt Rowland	. . . . . .	Safe	T/o time:	11:05
	Sgt Walker	. . . . . .	Safe		
	LAC Hatfield	. . . .	Safe		
	Sgt F C Sawyer	638724	+		

Crossed the enemy coast near Husum. When over Cuxhaven the Hudson was hit by flak which damaged a fuel tank and the tailplane. The aircraft ran short of fuel and was ditched 15 miles off Sheringham, Norfolk. All the crew got clear safely but the aircraft sank in just over a minute. F/O Bamber spent an hour swimming in the sea before being picked up by a trawler. 236 Sqn a/c reported 3 crew picked up by drifter but only found oil on the water. At about 16:30 hrs, RAF Chatham reported that an aircraft was down in the sea 17 miles N of Sheringham. A moderate NNE wind was blowing, with a moderate sea. The No 1 motor lifeboat H.F. Bailey was launched at 16:40 hrs and found some articles and gear belonging to the Hudson, also a large patch of oil. When a RAF HSL arrived with the news that the crew were safe on a patrol boat, the lifeboat returned, arriving at 21:00 hrs. Sgt Sawyer is commemorated on the Runnymede Memorial.

248 Sqn	Blenheim IV	L9449	WR-U	Op:	Reconnaissance
	P/O C J Arthur	42090	+	Base:	Sumburgh
	Sgt R C R Cox	747819	+	T/o time:	10:50
	Sgt E A Ringwood	629710	+		

Lost off the coast of Norway at mid-day. Claimed by Ltn Setz of 6./JG77. Sgt Cox's body was washed ashore near Stromstad and initially buried at Tjärnö north of Gothenburg but is now buried in Kviberg Cemetery, Sweden. Both P/O Arthur and Sgt Ringwood are commemorated on the Runnymede Memorial.

28th August 1940

53 Sqn	Blenheim IV	T2046	PZ-J	Op:	Hookos Patrol
	P/O W E Fitzpatrick	79540	+	Base:	Detling
	Sgt J Bann	581165	+	T/o time:	20:54
	Sgt H Dunnington	612371	+		

Took off tasked for a patrol from the Hook of Holland to Oostende including the seaplane base at Schellingwoude but failed to return. P/O Fitzpatrick and his crew are commemorated on the Runnymede Memorial.

59 Sqn	Blenheim IV	R2794	TR-F	Op:	Caen
	P/O J Dellow	42812	+	Base:	Thorney Island
	Sgt K A Edwards	745956	+	T/o time:	20:15
	Sgt L E Bettis	900253	+		

Flew into the ground at night in bad visibility 1½ miles NW of Littlehampton, Sussex, on the return from the target. P/O Dellow is buried locally in St Nicholas Churchyard, West Thorney, while his crew rest in various cemeteries in England.

248 Sqn	Magister I	R1832	WR-	Duty:	Training
	P/O R H Haviland	76571	+	Base:	Sumburgh
	AC2 R Moon	909698	+	T/o time:	?

Hit the ground during low aerobatics and crashed into hills some 4 to 5 miles from the aerodrome. P/O Haviland rests in Aberdeen Crematorium and AC2 Moon in Lerwick New Cemetery, Shetland. Also see 7th August 1940 for P/O Haviland.

Miles Magister two-seat single-engine monoplane elementary trainers were widely used by RAF squadrons for 'hack' and communication duties.

29th August 1940

22 Sqn	Maryland I	AR704	OA-	Duty:	Training
	Sgt I F Meathrel	580298	+	Base:	North Coates
	Sgt W J Davies	624095	+	T/o time:	?
	Sgt D F G Sanders	759256	+		

Hit trees on the approach to Aldergrove, County Antrim, during night flying trials. Sgt Meathrel rests in Bromley Hill Cemetery, Surrey; Sgt Davies is buried in Chester General Cemetery and Sgt Sanders is buried locally in Glenavy Roman Catholic Churchyard, County Antrim. The Martin Marylands were in use with 'C' Flight of this Squadron, and this was their first loss of this type.

30th August 1940

235 Sqn	Blenheim IV	L9262	LA-	Duty:	Training
	P/O J S Priestley RNZAF	39934	+	Base:	Bircham Newton
	Sgt E A Graves	632826	+	T/o time:	?

Spun into the ground during practice circuits and crashed at Barwick Farm at 11:15 hrs. P/O Priestley, from Wellington in New Zealand, rests locally in St Mary's Churchyard, Great Bircham while Sgt Graves was taken to Langney Cemetery, Eastbourne.

31st August 1940

53 Sqn	Blenheim IV	T1940	PZ-D	Op:	Pernis
	W/C E C T Edwards	05146	+	Base:	Detling
	Sgt L L Benjamin	751790	+	T/o time:	19:40
	Sgt J T Beesley	552175	+		

Shot down at 21:10 hrs local time by Flakgruppe 261 while attacking the Pernis oil refinery and crashed in flames near the Welplaat. W/C Edwards and his crew rest in Crooswijk General Cemetery, Rotterdam, after being initially buried near the crash.

59 Sqn	Blenheim IV	R3880	TR-S	Op:	Cherbourg
	P/O J J Finlay	42826	+	Base:	Thorney Island
	Sgt F J Leonhardt	751200	+	T/o time:	04:15
	Sgt A L Peddie	747834	+		

Missing. Both P/O Finlay and Sgt Leonhardt are commemorated on the Runnymede Memorial and Sgt Peddie rests in Quiberville Churchyard, France.

254 Sqn	Blenheim IV	L8786	QY-	Duty:	Training
	P/O H R Rose	. . . . .	Safe	Base:	Dyce
				T/o time:	15:20

P/O Rose took off to carry out local flying practice. When landing he overshot, opened up, climbed with the flaps down and failed to gain sufficient height to clear a hill half a mile north of the aerodrome before hitting a tree with a wing.

608 Sqn	Botha I	L6165	UL-	Duty:	Training
	P/O T H Creed	42697	+	Base:	Thornaby
	P/O Barrett	. . . . .	Wounded	T/o time:	
	AC1 T E Corrigan	808373	+		
	AC2 G Beadnall	808387	+		

Took off for a training flight but was unable to land due to the presence of intruders. The Botha was presumed to have ditched into the North Sea. Those who died are commemorated on the Runnymede Memorial.

1st September 1940

59 Sqn	Blenheim IV	T1880	TR-P	Op:	Lorient
	P/O Short	. . . . .	Safe	Base:	Thorney Island
	Sgt Hewitt	. . . . . .	Safe	T/o time:	20:20
	Sgt Burney	. . . . . .	Safe		

P/O Short reported that they had dropped a stick of bombs on the docks from 8,000 ft and had seen fires start. The Blenheim was hit by accurate heavy flak and subsequently crashed into a creek on approaching the aerodrome to land.

206 Sqn	Hudson I	N7367	VX-E	Op:	Convoy
	P/O Blackett	. . . . .	Safe	Base:	Bircham Newton
	P/O J F Bendix	. . . . .	Safe	Time:	17:35
	Sgt Elford	. . . . . .	Safe		
	Sgt Hayward	. . . . . .	Safe		

Swung on take-off, the u/c collapsed causing the Hudson to catch fire and the bombs to explode

235 Sqn	Blenheim IV	Z5724	LA-	Duty:	Training
	P/O J C Kirkpatrick	. . . . .	Safe	Base:	Bircham Newton

Took off at 15:00hrs for a cross country flight to Hooton Park for training in navigation and D/F homing. An engine failed in flight due to mishandling and the Blenheim was belly-landed 4 miles SE of Lincoln, crashing through a hedge. The Court of Inquiry found that the pilot had been fatigued due to being duty officer right up to take-off time and was poorly trained in fault finding to correct the engine failure in flight.

500 Sqn	Anson I	N9538	MK-		Ground Loss
				Base:	Detling
	Destroyed in an air raid.			Time:	16:37

2nd September 1940

10 (RAAF) Sqn	Sunderland I	P9602	RB-G	Op:	Convoy patrol
	F/Lt J A Cohen RAAF	. . . . .	Safe	Base:	Oban
	P/O Butcher	. . . . . .	Safe	T/o time:	10:25
	LAC F L Gardner RCAF	C/3215	Injured		

Arrived back from patrol at 23:15 hrs but overshot the flare-path. The Sunderland's landing lights were switched on to reveal Lismore Island, Argyll, and avoiding action was taken but the port wingtip and float hit causing the loss of aircraft as it ran aground. Subsequent recovery attempts were hindered by the lack of suitable marine salvage experts to assist.

22 Sqn	Beaufort I	L9879	OA-C	Op:	Flushing
	W/C F J St C Braithwaite	. . . . .	Safe	Base:	Bircham Newton
	P/O Hatton	. . . . .	Safe	T/o time:	16:30
	Sgt Coulson	. . . . . .	Safe		
	P/O E Pennington	77122	Safe		

Undershot and crash-landed at 23:20 hrs into a field 50 yards short of North Coates on the return from the operation.

210 Sqn	Sunderland I	T9043	DA-F	Op:	Convoy Patrol
	F/Lt P D Parry-Jones	40012	+	Base:	Oban
	F/O B L A Pusey	77124	+	T/o time:	10:30
	P/O I W Phillips	33474	+		
	P/O M H Dalzell-McKean	33538	+		
	Sgt R G Fitzgerald	968419	+		
	Sgt M A F Drewitt	570399	+		
	LAC W T James	570180	+		
	AC1 L E Stokes	541918	+		
	AC1 L J Caunter	935081	+		
	AC1 W H Blackmore	572892	+		
	AC1 D H Jones	967075	+		

Missing from patrol. All, including Sgt Fitzgerald from Eire, are commemorated on the Runnymede Memorial.

3rd September 1940

206 Sqn	Hudson I	N7351	VX-	Op:	Patrol S.A.51
	P/O Curtiss	. . . . .	Safe	Base:	Bircham Newton
	Sgt Pendy	. . . . . .	Safe	T/o time:	00:15
	Sgt Kilburn	. . . . . .	Safe		
	Sgt Humphries	. . . . .	Safe		

Hit some trees on take-off and belly-landed.

254 Sqn	Blenheim IV	N3529	QY-	Duty:	Transit Flight
	Sgt R C Hanna	816023	+	Base:	Dyce
	AC2 J E Mangion	948167	+	T/o time:	?

Crashed while engaged in aerial tactics 9 miles N of Dyce and burned out . Sgt Hanna is buried in Knockbreda Church of Ireland Churchyard, County Down, while AC2 Mangion, from Malta, rests in Dyce Old Churchyard, Aberdeenshire.

254 Sqn	Blenheim IV	N3608	QY-	Duty:	Transit Flight
	P/O J R J Laidlay	79740	+	Base:	Dyce
	AC1 D Campbell	638834	+	T/o time:	?
	Sgt R J Whiffen	747997	+		

Crashed while engaged on aerial tactics, 8 miles N of Dyce, and caught fire. P/O Laidlay is buried in Abdie Old Churchyard, Fife; AC1 Campbell locally in Dyce Old Churchyard, Aberdeenshire and Sgt Whiffen in Bournemouth East Cemetery, Hampshire.

4th September 1940

22 Sqn	Beaufort I	. . . . .	OA-	Op:	?
	?			Base:	?
	?			T/o time:	?

Aircraft destroyed on landing after operations. No further details.

53 Sqn	Blenheim IV	L9460	PZ-	Ground Loss	
				Base:	Detling
				Time:	?

Struck off charge. Possibly damaged on 2nd September when enemy aircraft attacked and damaged 'C' Flight hangar.

5th September 1940

21 Sqn	Blenheim IV	R3755	YH-	Op:	Anti-Shipping
	Sgt J E Moss	745478	+	Base:	Lossiemouth
	Sgt K L Daly	581504	+	T/o time:	08:15
	Sgt C Mein	638466	+		

Lost without trace. Sgt Moss and his crew are all commemorated on the Runnymede Memorial.

6th September 1940

612 Sqn	Anson I	R3333	WL-M	Op:	Convoy WN13
	P/O W J R Redman	. . . . .	Safe	Base:	Stornoway
	Sgt Strain	. . . . . .	Safe	T/o time: 08:25	
	Sgt Abercrombie	. . . . . .	Safe		
	LAC Fraser	. . . . . .	Safe		

Ran out of fuel at 13:30 hrs and ditched 25 miles NE of Tiumpan Head, Lewis.
The crew were rescued by the trawler *Sophy*.

7th September 1940

206 Sqn	Hudson I	T9276	VX-	Duty:	?
	F/O J W B Davis	. . . . .	Safe	Base:	Bircham Newton
				T/o time: 12:20	

The Hudson was landing into wind when a Hurricane cut across the flight path.
F/O Davis pulled up to avoid the collision, stalled, crashed and burst into flames.

8th September 1940

53 Sqn	Blenheim IV	R3779	PZ-Z	Op:	Cal 2
	F/Lt I H Bartlett	25095	+	Base:	Detling
	Sgt R E Aldridge	517434	+	T/o time: 11:42	
	Sgt E D Sheldrick MiD	551845	+		

Shot down by Me109s during a convoy attack off Calais.
F/Lt Bartlett and his crew are commemorated on the Runnymede Memorial.

53 Sqn	Blenheim IV	T2042	PZ-H	Op:	Cal 2
	P/O R G Hall	42749	+	Base:	Detling
	Sgt J D Randall	581064	+	T/o time: 11:49	
	Sgt M B Conacher	552142	+		

Shot down by an Me109 while on a shipping strike off Calais. P/O Hall, a New Zealander from
Wellington, and his crew are commemorated on the Runnymede Memorial.

224 Sqn	Hudson I	N7268	QX-D	Op:	Patrol S.A.2
	F/O R G Cuthbert	41260	+	Base:	Leuchars
	F/O I H Dolman	41264	+	T/o time: 07:47	
	Sgt E Duffield	546967	+		
	Sgt M Rees	637154	+		

Failed to return from a North Sea Patrol.
Possibly shot down off Mandal, Norway, by Ofw E Sawallisch of 4./JG77.
All the crew are commemorated on the Runnymede Memorial.

9th September 1940

42 Sqn	Beaufort I	L4506	AW-	Duty:	Air Test
	Sgt J E Woodward	515054	Safe	Base:	Wick
	F/O Wickenden	. . . . . .	Wounded	T/o time: 15:45	

Crashed through a hedge after the port engine failed on the approach to Wick. Sgt Woodward
was admitted to hospital with concussion and F/O Wickenden to the SSQ with a severe wound
to his right foot.

10th September 1940

22 Sqn	Beaufort I	N1146	OA-R	Op:	Boulogne
	Sgt R D Gunn	580002	+	Base:	Bircham Newton
	Sgt S G Twitchin	590984	+	T/o time: 01:30	
	Sgt J Murray	625327	+		
	Sgt C S F Beer	751495	+		

Took off and was last heard on W/T at 02:40 hrs. Sgt Gunn is buried in St Margaret Churchyard,
Old Catton, Norfolk, while Sgt Beer's body was recovered from the other side of the North Sea
on 28th September near beach pole 13 on Texel and is buried locally in Den Burg Cemetery.
Sgt Twitchin and Sgt Murray are both commemorated on the Runnymede Memorial.

42 Sqn	Anson I	N5198	AW-	Duty:	Ferry Flight
	P/O O O'N Briginshaw	72051	+	Base:	Wick
	AC2 L T Flavell	623489	+	T/o time:	?

Collided with Anson N5053 and crashed into the sea off Wick Harbour. Both P/O Briginshaw and AC2 Flavell are commemorated on the Runnymede Memorial.

11th September 1940

235 Sqn	Blenheim IV	L9396	LA-E	Op:	Escort
	P/O P C Wickings-Smith	42929	+	Base:	Thorney Island
	P/O A W V Green	78082	+	T/o time:	15:55
	Sgt R D H Watts	746868	+		

Shot down at 17:30 hrs possibly by III/JG26 while escorting FAA Fairey Albacores raiding Calais, France. Sgt Watts was seen to continue firing until the Blenheim fell into the sea. All are commemorated on the Runnymede Memorial.

235 Sqn	Blenheim IV	Z5725	LA-G	Op:	Escort
	F/Lt F W Flood	37582	+	Base:	Thorney Island
	P/O N B Shorrocks	78265	+	T/o time:	15:55
	Sgt B R Sharp	628218	+		

Shot down at 17:30 hrs possibly by III/JG26 while escorting FAA Fairey Albacores raiding Calais, France. F/Lt Flood and his crew are commemorated on the Runnymede Memorial.

13th September 1940

98 Sqn	Battle I	L5343		Duty:	Ferry Flight
	F/Lt H C G Wilcox RCAF	. . . . .	Safe	Base:	Kaldadarnes (Iceland)
	Lt Col H L Davies DSO MC	. . . . .	Safe	T/o time:	?

F/Lt Wilcox had taken off from Kaldadarnes for Melgerdi Field (near Akureyri). Lt Col Davies was a passenger, going to visit and inspect the army garrison at Akureyri. A low ceiling and bad visibility prevented the pilot from finding the airfield and the Fairey Battle set course back to Kaldadarnes. When the a/c was a short distance from the glacier Hofsjökull, the engine suddenly stopped. F/Lt Wilcox made a forced landing in hostile and boulder-strewn terrain and the a/c came to a standstill within 25 yards. F/Lt Wilcox sustained only minor injuries and Lt Col Davies escaped unhurt. The aircraft received extensive damage to its u/c (which was extended) and airframe. Both travelled by foot for almost two days before being met by a rescue party (Royal Regiment of Canada) that was proceeding to the crash site following its discovery from the air. Shortly after the crash a salvage team went to the site and removed the a/c guns, radio and instruments before setting fire to the broken airframe. The fuselage of this aircraft was salvaged from Iceland in the early 1970s and after restoration at RAF St Athan is now on display at the RAF Museum, Hendon.

235 Sqn	Blenheim IV	L9393	LA-	Duty:	Training
	Sgt Le Jeune	1299997	Safe	Base:	Bircham Newton
				T/o time:	12:11

Engaged in local formation flying practice. Suffered an engine failure due to mishandling and force-landed with the u/c retracted near Grimston, Norfolk. Sgt Le Jeune was from Belgium.

248 Sqn	Blenheim IV	L9451	WR-V	Op:	Reconnaissance
	Sgt W J Garfield	740997	+	Base:	Sumburgh
	Sgt B W Mesner	745987	+	T/o time:	05:35
	Sgt A Kay	647610	+		

Crashed into the North Sea at 07:00 hrs while on an operation to the Norwegian coast from Feje to Stadlandet. Claimed by Fw Dyck of 4./JG77. Sgt Garfield rests in Mollendal Church Cemetery, Bergen, Norway while the other crewmen are commemorated on the Runnymede Memorial.

4th September 1940

PRU	Spitfire I (PR) type E (?)	P9453		Op:	French Coast
	F/O A E Hyde Parker	37971	+	Base:	?
				T/o time:	07:55

Missing on low altitude PR sortie from Boulogne to Cherbourg in Green Spitfire. F/O Hyde Parker is commemorated on the Runnymede Memorial.

PRU	Spitfire I (PR) type E	R6879	LY-		Op:	Belgian Coast
	F/O P L Dakeyne	39068	PoW		Base:	Heston
					T/o time:	?

Failed to return from low altitude PR sortie over the Belgian coast. In a letter to his CO from Dulag Luft, F/O Dakeyne reported that he suffered a direct hit which stopped the propeller. He abandoned by parachute, landing among an enemy troop concentration. Aircraft R6879 (fitted with Merlin III engine 23213) was delivered to the unit by air from Tern Hill on 13th August 1940.

98 Sqn	Battle I	P6570			Duty:	Transit Flight
	Sgt. F W Townsend	.....	Safe		Base:	Wick
	?	......	Safe		T/o time:	?
			(Observer)			
	P/O C E Blair	.....	Injured			

Force-landed on the edge of Kaldadarnes, Iceland, at 17:15 hrs. The propeller from P6570 survives and is fitted to Battle L5343 on display at the RAF Museum, Hendon. (See 13th September 1940).

15th September 1940

220 Sqn	Hudson I	N7233	NR-		Duty:	Air Test
	P/O J I Humphreys	43202	+		Base:	Thornaby
	P/O Billings	.....	Injured		T/o time:	?
	AC Hildreth	......	Injured			
	AC Bellas	......	Injured			

Lost height after take-off and flew into ground. The injured were transferred to hospital with burns and P/O Humphreys rests in Darlington Crematorium, Durham.

16th September 1940

21 Sqn	Blenheim IV	N3564	YH-		Duty:	Training
	P/O A F C Carson	42693	+		Base:	Lossiemouth
	Sgt N C Manser	581517	+		T/o time:	?
	Sgt Burton	.....	Injured			
	AC2 T G Adams	936634	+			

Crashed on take-off for a practice bombing sortie. P/O Carson rests locally in Lossiemouth Burial Ground, Morayshire, while Sgt Manser was taken to Crystal Palace District Cemetery, Kent. AC2 Adams was from 57 Sqn.

42 Sqn	Beaufort I	L9882	AW-		Duty:	?
	P/O M F Llewelyn Thomas	.....	Injured		Base:	Wick
	Sgt Thomas	......	Injured		Time:	10:20

Swung on opening the throttles for take-off, bounced over a road and crashed into the bomb dump. P/O Llewelyn Thomas was placed on the dangerously ill list and admitted to Bagnoll hospital with multiple skull fractures. Sgt Thomas fractured a shoulder, injured his 'stern' and lost his little finger on the right hand.

17th September 1940

22 Sqn	Beaufort I	L4508	OA-K		Op:	Cherbourg
	P/O T Atherton	43763	+		Base:	Thorney Island
	P/O R A MacFarlane	33546	+		T/o time:	13:30
	Sgt J L Feather	641705	+			
	Sgt C J Harvey	751693	+			

Crashed at Tourlaville, north of Cherbourg while participating in a set-piece night torpedo strike against shipping in Cherbourg's outer harbour, in company with five other 22 Squadron Beauforts plus a total of 12 Blenheims drawn from 53 and 59 Squadrons. All the crew of K/22 are buried in the Bayeux War Cemetery, Calvados, France.

19th September 1940

53 Sqn	Blenheim IV	T2045	PZ-F		Op:	Dundee 2
	P/O C F Tibbitts	43050	+		Base:	Detling
	Sgt R W Grace	751623	+		T/o time:	14:55
	Sgt E Harrold	805497	+			

Missing off Berck-sur-Mer. P/O Tibbitts, from Tauranga, New Zealand, and his crew are commemorated on the Runnymede Memorial.

20th September 1940

59 Sqn	**Blenheim IV**	**R3635**	**TR-V**	**Op:**	**Cherbourg**
	P/O K V Palmer	42874	+	Base:	Thorney Island
	Sgt E E Wright	580992	+	T/o time: 21:25	
	Sgt D A Walters	642945	+		

Missing. P/O Palmer and his crew are buried in Le Vast Churchyard, Manche, France.

23rd September 1940

22 Sqn	**Beaufort I**	**L9852**	**OA-L**	**Duty:**	**Training**
	P/O J R Barry	. . . . .	Safe	Base:	North Coates
				T/o time: ?	

Took off for night landing practice at Docking, Norfolk, with three pilots onboard. P/O Barry failed to see the ground by the light of the aircraft landing lights and glim lamps, held off too high and stalled into the ground at 22:00 hrs. All three pilots escaped with only slight injuries.

25th September 1940

22 Sqn	**Beaufort I**	**L9827**	**OA-**		**Ground Loss**
	Beaufort I	**L9880**	**OA-**		**Ground Loss**
				Time: ?	

Damaged beyond repair during an air raid while at Filton for modifications.

42 Sqn	**Beaufort I**	**L4507**	**AW-**		**Ground Loss**
				Time: ?	

Damaged beyond repair during an air raid while at Filton for modifications.

59 Sqn	**Blenheim IV**	**L8793**	**TR-J**	**Op:**	**Moon 2**
	P/O R F W Johnson	82699	+	Base:	Thorney Island
	Sgt Abell	. . . . .	Safe	T/o time: 01:15	
	Sgt Andrews	. . . . .	Safe		

Stalled on the approach and crashed into the sea at Thorney Island. The Selsey lifeboat carried out a search and as she approached Chichester harbour, she saw oil on the water, and learnt later that two airmen had been picked up by another boat. The Blenheim had crashed just inside the harbour entrance. P/O Johnson, the only casualty, was buried locally in St Nicholas Churchyard, West Thorney.

Chapter 7

26th September to 31st December 1940

On 26th September a 42 Squadron detachment resumed operations with 'Gardening' (mining) sorties off the Channel ports before returning to Wick. *Luftwaffe* air raids on Carew Cheriton, St Eval, Wick and Mount Batten continued to destroy much needed Coastal Command aircraft. With the threat of invasion receding, Coastal Command strike units gradually moved onto the offensive with 'Gardening' operations off the Biscay ports and the introduction of the first 'Intruder' sorties over *Luftwaffe* airfields in occupied France. Further north offensive operations were commenced against shipping in Norwegian waters and strikes against rail and communication targets in the north of Norway.

Changes in U-boat tactics had increased their effectiveness over the Autumn and early Winter with over 350,000 tonnes of shipping being lost in October and a similar amount in November. These losses were beyond the replacement ability of the shipyards and changed the priority of supply from fighter AI sets to Mk.II ASV radar.

New squadrons were formed with Whitley and Wellington aircraft, albeit with aircraft released as obsolescent by Bomber Command. No 502 Squadron at Aldergrove began to replace their Ansons with Whitley Vs in October, and the following month 612 Squadron at Dyce did likewise. Also, towards the end of November, 221 Squadron reformed with Wellington ICs at Bircham Newton, although this unit did not become operational until February. These new types started to work up with the new radar sets which gave better definition, longer ranges and sideways looking instead of forward. Also approved at this time were orders for long-range Catalina and Liberator aircraft to increase the effective patrol range into the mid-Atlantic gap. Until these new aircraft reached squadron service the Blenheims of 235, 236 and 254 Squadrons all operated from Aldergrove on interception patrols for the Focke-Wulf Fw 200 Condors that shuttled between Bordeaux and Norway.

As the recce role expanded, the PRU underwent a further re-designation, to become 1 PRU, on 16th November – coincidental with the formation of 3 PRU in Bomber Command. The first operational sortie by a 'bowser-wing' Spitfire Mk.I (PR) type D conversion, was a 5 hour 25 min flight to Stettin on 29th October, although it was 5th April 1941 before the production version of the 'bowser' – known as the PR Mk.IV – would be operational.

1940 closed with the strike squadrons learning new skills and the anti-submarine squadrons struggling with their obsolete equipment.

26th September 1940

217 Sqn	**Anson I**		**N9890**	**MW-J**	**Op:**	**Shipping Strike**
	F/Lt	Arnold	. . . . .	Safe	Base:	St Eval
	P/O	Kerr	. . . . .	Safe	T/o time:	00:05
	Sgt	Grenivier	. . . . . .	Safe		
	Sgt	W B Miflin	550750	Safe		

Short of fuel on return from Cherbourg, belly-landed on the beach at Rhossili, Glamorganshire. The Anson had sustained slight flak damage to the fuselage and port mainplane.

320 Sqn	**Fokker T-VIIIW**	**AV963**	**TD-**	**Op:**	**Patrol**
	Off VI 3-KM J A L Schevenhoven RNNAS	+		Base:	Carew Cheriton
	Sgt VI-KM H G A Akkers RNNAS	+		T/o time:	?
	Seinersmaat KM L J Scholman RNNAS	+			

Took off for a convoy patrol. Missing over St George's Channel. Aircraft was ex-RNNAS 'R-9'.

27th September 1940

22 Sqn	**Beaufort I**	**N1117**	**OA-A**	**Duty:**	**Training**
	P/O J R Hyde	. . . . .	Safe	Base:	North Coates
				T/o time:	01:30

Crashed on the approach to Docking, Norfolk. P/O Hyde failed to see the ground due to the limited range of the aircraft landing lights.

---

53 Sqn	Blenheim IV	T2221	PZ-J	Op:	Helder
	P/O P J E Ritchie	. . . . .	Safe	Base:	Detling
	Sgt R H Trafford	552655	Safe	T/o time:	01:29
	Sgt Gotham	. . . . . .	Injured		

Hit a tree on take-off and crashed. Sgt Trafford, a Canadian from British Columbia, suffered abrasions to his face and injuries to a leg.

28th September 1940

42 Sqn	Beaufort I	N1149	AW-V	Op:	Gardening
	F/Lt J R Bendell	39409	+	Base:	Thorney Island
	Sgt C K Woolnough	565451	+	T/o time:	19:40
	Sgt C F Masson	622651	+		
	Sgt J A MacNaughton	522280	+		

Shot down by a flak-ship and crashed into the sea off Finistère while on a mining operation. F/Lt Bendell rests in Lanriec Communal Cemetery; Sgt Woolnough and Sgt MacNaughton are buried in Tregunc Communal Cemetery, and Sgt Masson in Fouesnant Communal Cemetery, all in Finistère district, France.

269 Sqn	Hudson I	P5129	UA-E	Op:	Patrol S.A.1
	P/O L B Emeno	41160	+	Base:	Wick
	Sgt J W C Heath	519449	+	T/o time:	16:20
	Sgt J N MacDonald	524731	+		
	Sgt P S Brown	755766	+		

FTR from patrol after sending a brief report near the Norwegian coast that enemy aircraft had been sighted. P/O Emeno overflew Herdla airfield at low level just before two Me109s took off for patrol. The Hudson was chased out to sea and shot down at 19:43 hrs by Uffz Neimayer of 4./JG77. P/O Emeno, from Winnipeg, and his crew are commemorated on the Runnymede Memorial.

30th September 1940

42 Sqn	Beaufort I	L9942	AW-Q	Duty:	Training
	P/O E G Pett	. . . . .	Safe	Base:	Wick
	Sgt Bower	. . . . . .	Safe	T/o time:	11:10
	Sgt Riccard	. . . . . .	Safe		

While taking part in a practice light attack at 70 feet in calm sea conditions, P/O Pett misjudged the height and allowed the propellers to strike the sea causing severe vibration and loss of power. The aircraft was ditched into Sinclair Bay off Wick, the crew taking to their dinghy.

53 Sqn	Blenheim IV	T2044	PZ-G	Op:	Rotterdam
	P/O S R Bevan-John	81933	+	Base:	Detling
	Sgt S Macquire	747938	+	T/o time:	18:23
	Sgt H A Shaw	630002	+		

Crashed into the North Sea *en route*. P/O Bevan-John rests in St Illtyd Churchyard, Pembrey, Carmarthenshire and Sgt Macquire is buried in Kingsthorpe Cemetery, Northampton. Sgt Shaw has no known grave and is commemorated on the Runnymede Memorial.

224 Sqn	Hudson I	T9326	QX-V	Op:	Convoy Escort
	Sgt K Posgate	565653	+	Base:	Aldergrove
	Sgt A J Gibbs	748374	+	T/o time:	04:45
	Sgt R C Cox	740172	+		
	Sgt S Swann	551592	+		
	Sgt J P O'Connor	627424	+		

Took off to escort convoy HX74. Crashed just after take-off, 2 miles from the western edge of the aerodrome after a normal left turn, reached a height of 200 feet and stalled. Engine trouble was suspected as the cause of the crash but the Court of Inquiry stated that both engines had been running normally when the aircraft hit the ground. Both Sgt Gibbs and Sgt Swann rest in St Catherine Church of Ireland Churchyard, Killead, County Antrim; Sgt Posgate in Killead Presbyterian Churchyard; Sgt Cox in Hull Northern Cemetery and Sgt O'Connor in St Joseph's Roman Catholic Cemetery, North Ormesby, Yorkshire.

1st October 1940

248 Sqn	Blenheim IV	R3626	WR-J	Op:	Reconnaissance
	P/O C C Bennett	42097	+	Base:	Sumburgh
	Sgt G S Clarke	747818	+	T/o time:	13:20
	Sgt G B Brash	639109	+		

Failed to return from a PR sortie to the coast of Norway from Lister to Stadlandet. P/O Bennett, an Australian from Adelaide, and his crew are commemorated on the Runnymede Memorial.

320 Sqn	Anson I	K6175	NO-		Ground Loss
321 Sqn	Anson I	K8823			Ground Loss
				Base:	Carew Cheriton
				Time:	07:00

Both aircraft destroyed in an air raid.
K6175 was assigned to station flight.

3rd October 1940

217 Sqn	Anson I	K8783	MW-A		Ground Loss
				Base:	St Eval
				Time:	07:10

Caught fire and burned out in No 3 hangar during a daylight air raid.

4th October 1940

42 Sqn	Beaufort I	L4488	AW-F	Op:	Coastal Patrol
	P/O F D Flinn	44120	PoW	Base:	Thorney Island
	Sgt S W Shirley	516023	PoW	T/o time:	12:35
	Sgt F A O'Malley	544944	PoW		
	Sgt A M B Robertson	523060	PoW		

Took off tasked with patrolling between Oostende and IJmuiden.
Shot down into the North Sea by Me109s off the coast of Belgium.

5th October 1940

53 Sqn	Blenheim IV	R2771	PZ-A	Op:	Hookos Patrol
	P/O K A Faulkner	. . . . .	Injured	Base:	Detling
	Sgt A R S Hall	755403	+	T/o time:	19:16
	Sgt G B Fielder	755751	Injured		

Lost height in the circuit in bad visibility on the return from a sweep. The Blenheim flew into the ground at Manston, Kent, at 23:30 hrs and burst into flames. Sgt Hall is buried in London Road Cemetery, Brentwood, Essex.

233 Sqn	Hudson I	P5117	ZS-S	Op:	Patrol S.A.2
	F/O G K Brackenridge	70074	+	Base:	Leuchars
	P/O J McIntosh	43289	+	T/o time:	14:09
	Sgt D Bruce	536872	+		
	Sgt A Russell	533654	+		

The patrol track of the Hudson was extended and the aircraft did not reach coast again until after dark. Weather was appalling and F/O Brackenridge and crew failed to locate their base. The cause of the loss was attributed to the inability to ascertain whereabouts due to failure of W/Op to receive signals. Various messages were received and bearings passed. The last bearing at 19:56 hrs was not acknowledged by the aircraft. Landing was deemed impracticable due to bad weather and growing darkness. Finally the aircraft was abandoned by the crew over the North Sea and thought to have been left on automatic pilot. P5117 eventually crashed near the hamlet of Oxford, 1 mile SW of Scremerston, Northumberland. The bodies of the crew were not recovered and they are commemorated on the Runnymede Memorial.

6th October 1940

220 Sqn	Hudson I	T9323	NR-W	Op:	Offensive Patrol
	Sgt P H Fletcher	566110	+	Base:	Thornaby
	Sgt L Dudley	741157	+	T/o time:	09:05
	Sgt J C Murray	552235	+		
	P/O H Parkinson	42954	+		

Shot down by ship's flak off the coast of Denmark. The Hudson was seen to climb to nearly 2,000 feet and fire to spread rapidly across the aircraft which at this point turned vertically over to port and then dived head first into the sea. A second later a red explosion was followed by a dense cloud of black smoke from where it had disappeared. The crew are commemorated on the Runnymede Memorial.

8th October 1940

PRU	**Spitfire I (PR) type ?**	P9382	**LY-**	**Op:**	**Kiel**
	F/Lt J R T Smalley DFC	39345	PoW	**Base:**	Heston
				T/o time:	09:18

Took off for a PR sortie to Kiel. Experienced problems when switching fuel tanks over the Friesian Islands and turned back towards England in preparation for abandoning the aircraft.
Just E of Groningen at 33,000 feet the pilot heard a loud bang and the cockpit filled with smoke. Eyewitnesses on the ground saw the Spitfire attacked by another aircraft and observed white smoke from the radiator under the starboard wing. F/Lt Smalley was wounded in the right leg and lost consciousness. At 2,000 feet he recovered while the aircraft was in a flat spin, so he abandoned. A local doctor tended the pilot's wounds received both in the air and on the ground, the latter caused by being pulled through two ditches while entangled in his parachute. The Germans found F/Lt Smalley at the doctor's house and took him prisoner. The Spitfire crashed into a front garden in Hoofdweg at Noordbroek, 15 km (c 9½ miles) E of Groningen, Netherlands.

PRU	**Spitfire I (PR) type ?**	R6894	**LY-**	**Op:**	**Enemy Coast**
	F/O W B Parker RNZAF	. . . . .	Injured	**Base:**	Heston
				T/o time:	10:25

Took off tasked for a sortie from Flushing to Le Havre. Shot down in flames by an Me109 at Adisham Court Farm, 6 miles SE of Canterbury, Kent, on the return. F/O Parker baled out and was taken to Canterbury Hospital suffering from severe burns.

42 Sqn	**Beaufort I**	L4484	**AW-E**	**Op:**	**Coastal Patrol**
	F/Lt J Kerby	. . . . .	Safe	**Base:**	Thorney Island
	Sgt Baker	. . . . . .	Safe	**T/o time:**	18:45
	Sgt W H Bolton	535103	Safe		
	Sgt Mills	. . . . . .	Safe		

Commenced patrol from Selsey. Chased a He111 but lost it in a rainstorm. At Cherbourg F/Lt Kerby encountered an enemy ship, seen only by wake, and made an attack. The ship stopped and was lost from sight. Nothing more was seen of the enemy ship so the Beaufort returned to base where, due to engine failure, it crashed and burned near Chidham, Sussex, at 20:40 hrs.

53 Sqn	**Blenheim IV**	T2036	**PZ-K**	**Op:**	**Gravelines**
	P/O J C Mallon	42719	DoW	**Base:**	Detling
	Sgt W P Whetton DFM	562350	+	**T/o time:**	18:45
	Sgt A T Shackleford	613282	+		

Shot down by flak and crashed at Frethun, 5 km (c 3miles) SW of Calais, at 22:45 hrs.
P/O Mallon, a New Zealander from Taranaki, died of his wounds and is buried along with his crew in Guines Communal Cemetery, Pas de Calais.

9th October 1940

201 Sqn	**Sunderland I**	P9621	**ZM-**	**Op:**	**Anti-Submarine Patrol**
	F/Lt E J Brooks	. . . . .	Safe	**Base:**	Sullom Voe
				T/o time:	?

Force-landed in bad weather and ran aground at Scalasaig Bay, Colonsay. SoC 4th December 1940.

206 Sqn	**Hudson I**	T9357	**VX-**	**Op:**	**Reconnaissance**
	F/Lt B O Dias	. . . . .	Safe	**Base:**	Bircham Newton
	P/O Patrick	. . . . .	Safe	**T/o time:**	18:05
	P/O J R H Lascelles	41030	Safe		
	Sgt Saraton	. . . . . .	Safe		
	Sgt J T Farlowe	755909	Safe		

Pilot mistook the boundary hedge for a dummy hedge, landing at 22:40 hrs at Docking, Norfolk.

235 Sqn	**Blenheim IV**	N3530	**LA-S**	**Op:**	**Hach Patrol**
	P/O J C Kirkpatrick	81630	+	**Base:**	Thorney Island
	P/O R C Thomas	82731	+	**T/o time:**	16:30

Sgt	G E Keel	751079	+		

Shot down at 17:30 hrs over the Channel. P/O Kirkpatrick is commemorated on the Runnymede Memorial, P/O Thomas rests in Cathays Cemetery, Cardiff, and Sgt Keel in Eastney Cemetery, Portsmouth.

10th October 1940

42 Sqn	Beaufort I	L4491	AW-R	Op:	Rover
	F/O G S P Rooney DFC	39245	Wounded	Base:	Thorney Island
	F/O Simmonds	. . . . .	Wounded	T/o time: 17:00	
	Sgt R F Henry	627041	Safe		
	Sgt W R J Little	539889	Safe		

Attacked by four Me109s off Boulogne, France, after releasing the torpedo into the inner harbour. The first burst from the enemy aircraft put the hydraulics and turret out of action. F/O Rooney, although wounded, dropped down to sea level, took avoiding action and after shaking off the attack handed control over to F/O Simmonds, who carried out a wheels-up landing at base.

12th October 1940

217 Sqn	Anson I	K8769	MW-Q	Op:	Strike
	F/O Bursey	. . . . .	Safe	Base:	St Eval
	Sgt Wood	. . . . .	Safe	T/o time: 01:47	
	Sgt Bruce	. . . . .	Safe		
	Sgt Alexander	. . . . . .	Safe		

Suffered an engine failure, lost height and belly-landed on sand dunes 1 mile SE of Trevose Head, Cornwall, at 01:55 hrs.

14th October 1940

206 Sqn	Hudson I	N7362	VX-F	Op:	Patrol S.A.4A/2
	F/O J R H Lascelles	41030	+	Base:	Bircham Newton
	F/O J G I Acheson	74322	+	T/o time: 05:05	
	Sgt R E Garstin	616246	+		
	Sgt J T Farlowe	755909	+		

Failed to return. F/O Lascelles and his crew are commemorated on the Runnymede Memorial.

233 Sqn	Hudson I	T9343	ZS-Z	Op:	Reconnaissance
	F/Lt L P Rowley	27146	+	Base:	Leuchars
	P/O R A Hanks	42706	+	T/o time: 11:30	
	Sgt J W Purt	553164	+		
	Sgt J J Wilks	524023	+		

Failed to return from off coast of Norway. Oberleutnant Horst Carciganico of Stab/JG.77 claimed one Hudson in aerial combat on this day. F/Lt Rowley and his crew are commemorated on the Runnymede Memorial.

235 Sqn	Blenheim IV	Z5741	LA-X	Op:	Hach Patrol
	Sgt R F Tatnell	748556		Base:	Thorney Island
				T/o time: 16:04	

At ZJVD 0043 sighted a concentration of enemy fighters at 10,000 feet. Returned to base, stalled on landing and the u/c collapsed at Thorney Island at 16:55 hrs.

254 Sqn	Blenheim IV	T1952	QY-	Duty:	?
	F/O D Shawe	. . . . .	Injured	Base:	Dyce
				T/o time: 11:00	

Force-landed at 15:45 hrs due to the weather, struck anti-invasion pole on Aberdeen Beach, swung out to sea and overturned. One crewman was injured. The Blenheim was salvaged to become ground instruction airframe 2363M.

15th October 1940

21 Sqn	Blenheim IV	N3588	YH-	Duty:	Training
	P/O J K Rodger	. . . . .	Safe	Base:	Lossiemouth ?
				T/o time: ?	

Overshot and crashed at 12:20 hrs just beyond the perimeter of Exeter aerodrome, while attempting to land in heavy rain.

206 Sqn	Hudson I	T9303	VX-V	Op:	Patrol S.A.5
	P/O D E Teden	90486	+	Base:	Bircham Newton
	P/O J L De Keyser	79166	+	T/o time: 22:30	
	Sgt W Kent	518350	+		
	Sgt J Steel	644325	+		

Failed to return. All the crew including P/O De Keyser, a South African from Johannesburg, are commemorated on the Runnymede Memorial.

16th October 1940

224 Sqn	Hudson I	T9328	QX-F	Op:	Anti-Submarine Patrol
	F/Lt F C Scott	34055	+	Base:	Aldergrove
	P/O R J Davies	42593	+	T/o time: 07:55	
	P/O A B Tisdall	74693	+		
	Sgt A B Nayler	553802	+		
	Sgt A F Thomas	521431	+		

Flew into Slievenanee Mountain, Northern Ireland at 08:10 hrs in cloud and off course. F/Lt Scott, P/O Davies and P/O Tisdall rest in St Catherine Church of Ireland Churchyard, Killead, County Antrim; Sgt Nayler in Woodlands Cemetery, Gillingham, Kent, and Sgt Thomas in Nottingham Road Cemetery, Derby.

17th October 1940

PRU	Spitfire I (PR) type ?	P9384	LY-	Duty:	Ferry flight
	P/O M N Hesketh	41021	+	Base:	Heston
				T/o time: ?	

Pilot failed to arrive at Wick. Possibly flew into Loch Ness due to bad visibility but unconfirmed. P/O Hesketh is commemorated on the Runnymede Memorial. An entry in the Unit ORB indicates that P9384 was written-off the unit inventory on 29th October.

PRU	Spitfire I (PR) type ?	X4332	LY-	Duty:	?
	?			Base:	?
				T/o time: ?	

Reported as lost on this date, but no further details. The PRU ORB declares it written-off on 29th October 'after enemy action', also that its Merlin III engine, 30351, went to 71MU on that date.

22 Sqn	Beaufort I	L9856	OA-K	Op:	Rover Patrol
	F/Lt R P M Gibbs	. . . . .	Safe	Base:	North Coates
	Sgt R E Cree	746709	Wounded	T/o time: 11:35	
	Sgt J Coulson	. . . . . .	Safe		
	P/O McFadden	. . . . .	Wounded		

Took off and set course for IJmuiden then flew north up the coast of Holland. During an abortive attack on a tanker and three escort flak-ships, Sgt Cree and P/O McFadden were wounded and F/Lt Gibbs nursed the flak-damaged Beaufort to Sutton Bridge where it crashed on landing at 15:20 hrs. This action is described in the pilot's autobiography *Not Peace But a Sword*, published by Grub Street, 1993. See Beaufort N1147 loss on 6th April 1941 for a later reference to Sgt Cree.

59 Sqn	Blenheim IV	T2319	TR-D	Op:	Bombing of Destroyers
	P/O E E Hives	81354	+	Base:	St Eval
	Sgt B D Jones	755459	+	T/o time: 17:15	
	Sgt E Jones	546188	+		

Last seen in formation before an attack on destroyers off Brest. P/O Hives is commemorated on the Runnymede Memorial, Sgt B Jones rests in Danygraig Cemetery, Risca, Monmouthshire, while Sgt E Jones is buried in Lawns Wood Cemetery, Leeds, Yorkshire.

18th October 1940

PRU	Magister I	P6347		Duty:	Training
	W/C J H Hutchinson	16112	+	Base:	Pembrey
	?	. . . . .	+	T/o time: ?	

Took off for a cross-country flight to Northolt but hit a balloon cable at 700 feet and crashed at Langley, Buckinghamshire, at 11:57 hrs. The aircraft was probably slightly off course when approaching Northolt, due to the weather conditions and the balloon was flying in cloud at 4,500 feet. The Magister came out of the cloud at 1,000 feet and was first seen some 300 yards from the cable. W/C Hutchinson rests in St Illtyd Churchyard, Pembrey, Carmarthenshire.

20th October 1940

248 Sqn	Blenheim IV	L9453	WR-Z	Op:	Reconnaissance
	P/O S R Gane MiD	42117	+	Base:	Sumburgh
	P/O M D Green	78363	+	T/o time:	07:16
	Sgt N J Stocks	552636	+		

Lost on a sortie to the coast of Norway from Stadlandet to Trondheim. Possibly shot down by Unteroffizier Ludvig Fröba of 4./JG77 at 10:57 hrs. P/O Gane rests in Stavne Cemetery, Trondheim while the other crew members are commemorated on the Runnymede Memorial.

248 Sqn	Blenheim IV	P6952	WR-X	Op:	Patrol S.A.1.E
	P/O G M Baird	42094	PoW	Base:	Sumburgh
	Sgt R Copcutt	581146	+	T/o time:	07:25
	Sgt D L Burton RNZAF	40187	PoW		
	Sgt S V Wood	649800	PoW		

Engaged and shot down a Do215 and was then attacked by three Me109s. One engine was put out of action, possibly by Lt Heinrich Setz of 6./JG77 at 10:23 hrs, and the cockpit filled with smoke. P/O Baird descended to sea level and struck the water surface in position 5910N 0210E. P/O Baird rescued Sgt Burton who was unconscious but was unable to reach Sgt Copcutt who had also been knocked out by the crash. Sgt Wood escaped and launched the dinghy.
The crew was seen by Blenheim 'C' of 248 Squadron on the 21st, rowing for the coast in a dinghy. Sgt Wood was treated in Oslo Hospital and Sgt Burton was admitted to Stavanger Hospital. Sgt Copcutt is commemorated on the Runnymede Memorial.

21st October 1940

53 Sqn	Blenheim IV	R3699	PZ-U	Op:	Patrol S.A.9
	P/O H J W Meakin	. . . . .	Wounded	Base:	Detling
	Sgt G Hutson	751510	Safe	T/o time:	07:58
	Sgt G T Hadnam	755274	Safe		

The aircraft was hit while on patrol between 10:00 and 10:30 hrs and became uncontrollable. After passing the aerodrome in low cloud the Blenheim was abandoned by the crew near Tonbridge, Kent. At approximately 10:30 hrs the Blenheim crashed into Dernier Road, Tonbridge, killing one person and seriously injuring 16.

22nd October 1940

217 Sqn	Beaufort I	L9822	MW-	Duty:	?
				Base:	St Eval
				Time:	?
	Swung on take-off and hit a truck				

24th October 1940

269 Sqn	Hudson I	P5132	UA-F	Op:	Patrol S.A.1
_	F/Lt N B Mole	37779	+	Base:	Wick
	Sgt D A J Smith	742822	+	T/o time:	07:11
	Sgt J E R Sharvin	550430	+		
	Sgt A W Campbell	545658	+		

Failed to return. Believed to have been shot down by Ltn Deutschle of 6./JG77. F/Lt Mole, from the Republic of Ireland, and his crew, are commemorated on the Runnymede Memorial.

25th October 1940

224 Sqn	Hudson I	N7240	QX-Q	Op:	Convoy Escort
	P/O J H H Gladdis	42404	+	Base:	Aldergrove
	P/O A R Carrick	78273	+	T/o time: 07:55	
	Sgt T A Hughes	748737	+		
	Sgt J D Dowson	526769	+		
	Sgt J McGhie	541465	+		

Took off to escort Convoy CAB 233 but failed to return from the Atlantic Ocean.
P/O Gladdis and his crew are all commemorated on the Runnymede Memorial.

254 Sqn	Blenheim IV	R3629	QY-P		Ground Loss
				Base:	Montrose

Destroyed during an air raid at 18:25 hrs. The Blenheim had been damaged by a Hurricane while
on convoy escort on the 2nd of October and the u/c had collapsed on landing at Montrose.

26th October 1940

PRU	Hudson I	N7301	LY-	Op:	Recce
	F/Lt A A Rumsey	22246	PoW	Base:	Heston ?
	P/O C G Broome	84688	+	T/o time: ?	
	Sgt Williams	. . . . . .	PoW		
	Sgt Phillips	. . . . . .	PoW		
	LAC A J Dixon	820009	PoW		

Failing to return from a PR sortie to the Scheldt Estuary. F/Lt Rumsey confirmed that all five men
abandoned the burning aircraft by parachute at between 200 and 600 feet. P/O Broome rests in
Vlissingen Cemetery, Flushing, Zeeland, Netherlands.

21 Sqn	Blenheim IV	R3760	YH-		Ground Loss
	Blenheim IV	T2233	YH-		Ground Loss
	P/O Slater	. . . . .	+	Base:	Lossiemouth
	Sgt Jones	. . . . . .	+	Time:	18:30
	Cpl Holland	. . . . . .	+		
	Sgt Green	. . . . . .	Injured		
	AC1 Windeler	. . . . . .	Injured		
	AC1 Bristow	. . . . . .	Injured		

Both aircraft were destroyed in an air raid at 18:30 hrs when Heinkels attacked the airfield during
preparations for night flying. Three aircrew were killed and three injured during the raid, though
it is not certain which individuals were assigned to which aircraft.

42 Sqn	Beaufort I	L9813	AW-	Op:	Shipping Strike
	S/Ldr F G L Smith DFC	29181	PoW	Base:	Wick
	P/O H F Burns	41551	PoW	T/o time: 13:08	
	Sgt E A Brown	751798	PoW		
	Sgt W R Perrin	747777	+		

Shot down by Me109s of 4./JG77 into Sogne Fjord while leading two other 42 Squadron Beauforts
(inc N1159) against shipping in the Fjord. Sgt Perrin is buried in Stavne Cemetery, Trondheim.

42 Sqn	Beaufort I	N1159	AW-	Op:	Shipping Strike
	Sgt G R Brocklehurst	580180	+	Base:	Wick
	Sgt V W Gadson	523417	+	T/o time: 13:08	
	Sgt W H Bolton	535103	+		
	F/O A MacRury	41125	+		

Released the torpedo at Norwegian vessel *H J Kyvik* in Aspo Fjord. The Beaufort was then
shot down by Me109s of 4./JG77 into Sogne Fjord. All are commemorated on the Runnymede
Memorial.

269 Sqn	Hudson I	P5130	UA-		Ground Loss
				Base:	Wick
				T/o time: 18:25	

At 18:25 hours on the 26th October, 1940, three Heinkel medium bombers approached Wick
aerodrome from a Southerly direction. Flying low they machine-gunned the streets of Wick town
and proceeded to attack the aerodrome. Twenty-four x 250 kg. HE bombs were dropped on the
aerodrome and the aerodrome boundary. One hangar was damaged superficially and this
Hudson aircraft was set on fire and destroyed as a result of the machine-gun attack.

27th October 1940

53 Sqn	Blenheim IV	L8789	PZ-E	Op:	Emvee
P/O	R L Buckley	84916	+	Base:	Detling
Sgt	C Henderson	755515	+	T/o time:	11:40
Sgt	P E J Neale	749451	+		

Shot down by Me109s into the Channel during a shipping strike off Folkestone. RAF HSLs recovered a parachute and flying jacket which were later identified as coming from the Blenheim. All are commemorated on the Runnymede Memorial.

224 Sqn	Hudson I	N7266	QX-G	Op:	Convoy Escort
Sgt	K B Files	523740	Safe	Base:	Aldergrove
Sgt	W M Bryon	......	Safe	T/o time:	07:52
Sgt	R Stevens	......	Safe		
Sgt	R W Willis	552094	Safe		

Took off to escort Convoy CAB 234 and was damaged during an attack by a Fw200 in position 5604N 0140W at 09:50 hrs. Landed safely at 14:20 hrs but was SoC on 1st January 1941.

28th October 1940

204 Sqn	Sunderland I	P9620	KG-K	Op:	Patrol
F/Lt	S R Gibbs	.....	Safe	Base:	Oban
P/O	Neugebauer	.....	Safe	T/o time:	16:40
P/O	J M Ennis	.....	Safe		
Sgt	Gough	......	Safe		
Sgt	H W Taylor	755791	Safe		
Sgt	Cushworthy	......	Safe		
LAC	Gay	.....	Safe		
AC	Hicks	.....	Safe		
AC	Bond	.....	Safe		
LAC	M E Towe	744561	+		
Sgt	S H MacDonald RNZAF	39866	+		
AC1	K W Beavis	642035	+		
Sgt	M S Ross	755445	+		

Encountered a severe electrical storm which affected the compass. Ran short of fuel and then force-landed into the sea some 200 miles NW of Cape Wrath at 06:15 hrs on the 29th. The aircraft stayed afloat for almost nine hours in a full gale, only to break up and sink shortly after the rescue ship was sighted. Nine survivors were rescued by HMS *Australia*. All those killed, including Sgt MacDonald, from Wellington, New Zealand, are commemorated on the Runnymede Memorial.

29th October 1940

22 Sqn	Beaufort I	L9800	OA-D	Op:	Rover Patrol
Sgt	J P Rylands	741175	+	Base:	North Coates
Sgt	D D Palmer	580975	+	T/o time:	05:30
Sgt	P W Ripley	751060	+		
Sgt	N H Jackson	749426	+		

Suffered problems shortly after take-off and crashed into sea half a mile offshore. Sgt Ryland's body was not recovered and he is commemorated on the Runnymede Memorial. Sgt Palmer, Sgt Ripley and Sgt Jackson rest in Ryde Borough Cemetery, Bognor Regis Cemetery and Manchester Southern Cemeteries respectively.

201 Sqn	Sunderland I	P9622	ZM-W	Duty:	Air Sea Rescue Search
P/O	Field	.....	Injured	Base:	Sullom Voe
P/O	Rabou	.....	Injured	T/o time:	09:18
P/O	Cooper	.....	Injured		
Sgt	R Lauder	507615	+		
Sgt	Corbin	......	Injured		
Sgt	J L Carson	543418	+		
Sgt	R W J Phelps	644168	+		
Sgt	Ault	......	Safe		
Cpl	Wells	......	Injured		
Sgt	Anderson	......	Safe		
AC1	G A Nangle	973249	+		

While lost at Dunnet Head, Caithness, flew into a hill about 28 miles SW of Wick and caught fire. Sgt Lauder rests in Wick Cemetery; Sgt Carson in Holy Evangelists Church of Ireland Churchyard Extension, Carnmoney, County Antrim; Sgt Phelps in Stony Stratford Cemetery, Wolverton, Buckinghamshire and AC1 Nangle in Airbles Cemetery, Dalziel, Lanarkshire.

204 Sqn	Sunderland I	T9045	KG-	Duty:	Air Sea Rescue Search
	S/Ldr Cumming	. . . . .	Safe	Base:	Sullom Voe
	F/O Tremear	. . . . .	Safe	T/o time:	09:10
	P/O Douglas	. . . . .	Safe		
	P/O Smith-Bingham	. . . . .	Safe		
	P/O Fitzearle	. . . . .	Safe		
	and a further 9 airmen crew		Safe		

Took off to search for Sunderland P9620 but was forced to land in the sea at 21:45 hrs due to darkness and veering wind. The starboard float was smashed on landing and a trawler in the vicinity came alongside and lines were passed. Attempts to tow the aircraft were foiled owing to the roughness of sea, and after the port float had been stoved in by the trawler, it was decided to abandon the aircraft. All personnel were safely transferred to trawler *A76* and the aircraft eventually sank about 5 miles E by S from Strathie Point, Caithness.

31st October 1940

233 Sqn	Hudson II	T9377	ZS-R	Op:	Offensive Patrol
	P/O W O Weaber	83709	+	Base:	Leuchars
	P/O B P Erskine	44190	+	T/o time:	10:20
	Sgt H Dean	642917	+		
	Sgt J A Wallace	568661	+		

Three aircraft reached the Norwegian coast in formation at 12:44 hrs 6 miles N of Lister and observed one vessel of 3000 tons heavily laden with timber, one of 500 tons and (1 mile ahead of them) a flak-ship of 1000 tons, all steaming on a course of 350°. All three a/c attacked the 3000 ton vessel. P/O Weaber was seen to make an attack, but his bombs missed and he was later seen flying over the flak-ship. He was not seen again but at 12:55 hrs a sheet of flame was seen on the beach 10 miles N of Lister. Sgt Dean has no known grave and is commemorated on the Runnymede Memorial while the rest of the crew lie in Sola Churchyard.

Ten miles W of Ogne the 1600 ton German merchant vessel *Ilse L M Russ* and minesweeper M.1103 were unsuccessfully attacked by 15 bombs from three Hudsons. M.1103 claimed a Hudson shot down and fighters from II/JG77 also claimed a Hudson shot down. T9377 was probably shot down by a combination of fire from M.1103 and from Me109s attacking at the end.

2nd November 1940

59 Sqn	Blenheim IV	T2137	TR-P	Op:	Cap Gris Nez
	P/O W F Lewis	84310	+	Base:	Thorney Island
	Sgt I C Greening	742294	+	T/o time:	04:05
	Sgt J S Peckham	755635	+		

Crashed at Halinghen after an attack on the Cap Gris Nez guns. All rest in Halinghen Communal Cemetery, Pas de Calais, France.

3rd November 1940

22 Sqn	Beaufort I	L9892	OA-I	Duty:	?
				Base:	?
				Time:	?

Damaged beyond repair and became ground instructional airframe 2387M. No further details.

233 Sqn	Hudson I	N7374	ZS-N	Op:	Offensive Patrol
	P/O L G Williams	42550	+	Base:	Leuchars
	P/O H G Gilbert	44192	+	T/o time:	08:40
	Sgt J Greig	619903	+		
	Sgt H F Thorndyke	747794	+		

Reached the Norwegian coast in position XZUB 0010 at 10:57 hrs, flying at 3000 ft. The formation turned south, and saw two 1000 ton coastal vessels, both on a northerly course, one just north and one 3 miles south of Egersund. At 11:10 hrs the three aircraft reached Lister and prepared to bomb the aerodrome. They were running up from the SW at 3000 feet when they were attacked by six Me110s and climbed to cover at 5000 feet. P/O Williams' Hudson on the port side of the vic formation was concentrated on by the enemy aircraft and lost formation, with flames coming from the starboard bow. At the debriefing the Captains of the other aircraft said that they thought the crew had reasonable chance of baling out or force-landing, but the crew were lost without trace and are commemorated on the Runnymede Memorial.

236 Sqn	Blenheim IV	R3886	FA-	Duty:	Training
	P/O J M Derbyshire	42110	Injured	Base:	St Eval
				T/o time:	

Engine cut due to mishandling on night flying training causing the Blenheim to crash during a forced landing after hitting high tension cables at Carnanton, Cornwall at 19:07 hrs. P/O Derbyshire was taken to Truro Hospital with a broken ankle and fractured skull.

248 Sqn	Blenheim IV	L9392	WR-G	Op:	Interception
	P/O A H H Garrad	42119	+	Base:	Sumburgh
	Sgt E J Bayliss	581431	+	T/o time:	10:11
	Sgt H F J Moynham	634201	+		

Last seen making a second attack on a He111K near sea level. Claimed by Uffz Richard Woick of 7./JG54 operating from Katwijk. Crashed into North Sea. The lifeboat *Arthur* left Scheveningen harbour at 21:00 hrs but returned on the 4th at 05:30 hrs without finding any sign of the aircraft. P/O Garrad and his crew are commemorated on the Runnymede Memorial.

5th November 1940

22 Sqn	Beaufort I	L4511	OA-H	Duty:	Transit Flight
	P/O I N W MacKie	70432	Safe	Base:	North Coates
				T/o time:	11:30

Took off for advanced operations and overshot in bad visibility while landing at St Eval, Cornwall, 13:05 hrs. The accident was attributed to a waterlogged downhill surface which caused the Beaufort to skid and hit an obstruction. All the crew escaped safely.

22 Sqn	Beaufort I	L9871	OA-U	Duty:	Transit Flight
	Sgt D G How	742696	Safe	Base:	North Coates
	Sgt P V Renai	580978	Safe	T/o time:	11:30

Took off for St Eval for advanced operations. Suffered an engine failure in flight and height was lost. During the subsequent forced landing at Whimple, Devon, the Beaufort's tail hit a tree and crashed at 12:30 hrs. One of the crew was injured. The aircraft was returned to Bristol's for repair and was eventually struck off charge in March of 1942.

502 Sqn	Whitley V	P5064	YG-	Duty:	Training
	S/Ldr A M Scott AFC	90369	+	Base:	Kinloss
	F/O A R Nivison-Smith	41454	+	T/o time:	21:10
	Sgt S Nicholls	973969	+		

Crashed after take-off 2 miles E of Kinloss, Morayshire. F/O Nivison-Smith, of 612 Sqn, rests in Dyce Old Churchyard, Aberdeenshire; Sgt Nicholls in New Hall Lane Cemetery, Preston and S/Ldr Scott, of 612 Sqn, in Springbank Cemetery, Aberdeen. This was the unit's first loss of a Whitley V since it had begun to convert to the type the previous month.

7th November 1940

220 Sqn	Hudson I	N7295	NR-F	Op:	Anti-Submarine Patrol
	P/O Mallinson	. . . . .	Safe	Base:	St Eval
	P/O Wickman	. . . . .	Safe	T/o time:	14:15
	Sgt Shadwell	. . . . . .	Safe		
	Sgt Sutton	. . . . . .	Safe		

Returned low on fuel at 19:40 hrs and overshot during landing, ran through a hedge and ended up in a ditch. The crew were uninjured but were treated for shock.

220 Sqn	Hudson I	N7291	NR-K	Op:	Anti-Submarine Patrol
	F/Lt Barron	. . . . .	Safe	Base:	St Eval
	P/O Ainsworth	. . . . .	Safe	T/o time:	14:30
	Sgt Hugill	. . . . . .	Safe		
	Sgt E Cook	. . . . . .	Safe		

It was dark, fuel had been exhausted, the aircraft was unable to reach base at St Eval, and the crew jumped by parachute. Their aircraft crashed near Sancreed, Cornwall at 20:50 hrs.

220 Sqn	Hudson I		P5124	NR-R	Op:	Anti-Submarine Patrol
	F/Sgt	Knowles	. . . . . .	Safe	Base:	St Eval
	Sgt	Travell	. . . . . .	Safe	T/o time:	14:30
	Sgt	Chester	. . . . . .	Safe		
	Sgt	Butler	. . . . . .	Safe		

Short of fuel the Hudson was crash-landed on Gwithian Beach 1 mile N of Hayle, Cornwall, at 22:15 hrs with little damage and no crew injuries. The aircraft became 2429M.

8th November 1940

248 Sqn	Blenheim IV		T2130	WR-G	Duty:	Taxying Test
	F/O	A E Hill	42125	Safe	Base:	Sumburgh
					T/o time:	09:10

Failed to gain height and crashed on take-off with the u/c retracted. Frozen snow on mainplanes and control surfaces and slippery state of ground were blamed for the crash. The Court of Inquiry found that the Blenheim was practically stalled from the time it became airborne. The ground crew had only partially cleared wings of ice as they were under the impression that the aircraft was only required for taxi test. The pilot should have reported the state of the runways before attempting to do circuit and test them under flying conditions.

9th November 1940

PRU	Spitfire I (PR) type ?		P9313	LY-	Op:	French Coast
	F/Lt	J W S Fowler	37765	+	Base:	Heston

Took off at 09:30 hrs tasked with a Group A sortie but failed to return.
F/Lt Fowler is commemorated on the Runnymede Memorial.

240 Sqn	Stranraer I	K7291	BN-		Ground Loss
				Base:	Stranraer

Sank at its mooring after being struck by a Walton Boat at approximately 06:30 hrs.
The aircraft was recovered but had been damaged beyond repair.

15th November 1940

224 Sqn	Hudson I		T9338	QX-D	Op:	Escort
	Sgt	A Norman	. . . . . .	Safe	Base:	Aldergrove
	Sgt	F L Ingersent	553881	+	T/o time:	07:50
	Sgt	E Mill	740701	+		
	Sgt	L G Castle	502661	Safe		
	Sgt	E E Owen	551167	+		

Crashed on take-off due to a combination of icing, attempting to pull off before reaching flying speed and an uphill runway. Hit a barrack hut killing both occupants. Sgt Mill rests in Vicarsford Cemetery, Forgan, Fife; Sgt Ingersent in St Peter Churchyard, Bishopsworth, Somerset and Sgt Owen in Glyntaff Cemetery, Pontypridd, Glamorganshire.

16th November 1940

206 Sqn	Hudson II		T9382	VX-V	Op:	Abbeville
	F/Lt	B O Dias	. . . . .	Safe	Base:	Bircham Newton
	P/O	M K Warren	79560	Safe	T/o time:	17:25
	Sgt	Chufield	. . . . .	Safe		
	Sgt	V C D Hayward	906000	Injured		

When over the target a shell hit one engine. F/Lt Dias jettisoned the bombs and turned for home. The crew tried to make for Manston but the other engine failed and at 20:15 hrs the Hudson was force- landed in the sea, at Birchington, Kent. The airmen waded ashore with only Sgt Hayward sustaining a sprained ankle and catching a chill.

217 Sqn	Anson I		N9889	MW-S	Op:	Patrol S.A.12
	P/O	R E Troward	42914	PoW	Base:	St Eval
	Sgt	A R Weston	940106	PoW	T/o time:	08:00
	Sgt	Wilson	. . . . .	PoW		
	Sgt	J B Steedman	973774	PoW		

At 13:50 hrs an SOS was picked up by St Eval D/F on a bearing of 139° True. The aircraft ditched into the Channel and the crew landed in Guernsey by dinghy.

18th November 1940

235 Sqn	**Blenheim IV**		**Z5732**	**LA-Y**	**Op:**	**Escort**
	F/Lt	Goddard	.....	Wounded	Base:	Bircham Newton
	Sgt	Wedlock	......	Safe	T/o time:	07:30
	Sgt	Dawson	......	Safe		

Damaged by return fire from He115s and belly-landed at North Coates, Lincolnshire. The Blenheim was deemed DBR (damaged beyond repair).

502 Sqn	**Whitley V**		**P5054**	**YG-C**	**Op:**	**Anti-Sub Sweep (2) North**
	Sgt	A W Wood	740518	Safe	Base:	Aldergrove
	S/Lt	L E H Scholefield RN	–	+	T/o time:	23:35
	Sgt	Holland	......	Safe		
	Sgt	G Brown	550231	Safe		
	Sgt	F Brown	943001	Safe		
	F/O	de Vere Hunt	.....	Safe		

Ditched on an anti-submarine sweep in position 5513N 0650W at 03:00 hrs off Downhill, Londonderry. S/Lt Scholefield was assigned to HMS *Daedalus*.

19th November 1940

206 Sqn	**Hudson I**		**N7300**	**VX-B**	**Op:**	**Convoy**
	F/O	H A Skeats	72003	+	Base:	Bircham Newton
	Sgt	P L Brace	745496	+	T/o time:	13:25
	Sgt	J H Moss	905501	+		
	Sgt	S Bradley	749429	+		

Homed on D/F to Bircham Newton at 16:30 hrs, and then told on R/T to go to Langham. F/O Skeats replied that visibility was bad and was then told to go to Coltishall. The Hudson then crashed two minutes later on fire into a wood near West Raynham Hall, Norfolk, on the main Fakenham to Swaffam Road. The O/C noted that the crash was a clear case of the pilot losing his head. F/O Skeats rests in Cambridge Crematorium; Sgt Brace in Islington Cemetery, Middlesex; Sgt Moss in St Mary's Churchyard, Great Bircham, Norfolk and Sgt Bradley in All Saints Churchyard, Mickleover, Derbyshire.

500 Sqn	**Anson I**		**R3435**	**MK-**	**Op:**	**Anti-Submarine Patrol**
	Sgt	R B Barr MiD	741009	+	Base:	
	F/O	L E Sanderson	90014	+	T/o time:	
	AC1	G E Crocker	812067	+		
	Sgt	Gilham	......	Safe		

Stalled at low altitude at 15:40 hrs when pulling out near the ground while locating their position in thick fog and crashed at Walcot, near Diss, Norfolk. One crew member was injured. Sgt Barr is buried in Hove New Cemetery, Sussex; F/O Sanderson rests in Cambridge Crematorium and AC1 Crocker in Maidstone Cemetery, Kent.

20th November 1940

224 Sqn	**Hudson I**		**N7272**	**QX-L**	**Op:**	**Escort**
	P/O	J Atkinson	......	Safe	Base:	Aldergrove
	P/O	Fowler	......	Safe	T/o time:	11:15
	Sgt	Wright	.....	Safe		
	Sgt	Wall	.....	Safe		

Took off tasked for an escort to convoy OB245. The W/T failed and the Hudson was abandoned out of fuel 3 miles NW of Luss, Dumbartonshire and left to crash into Loch Lomond.

21st November 1940

1 PRU	**Spitfire I (PR) type ?**	**P9426**	**LY-**	**Op:**	**?**
	P/O R B Dyrgalla	.....	Injured	Base:	Heston
				T/o time:	?

Took off with AC1 H Rhodes, a mechanic, on the tail. On two occasions the pilot snatched the aircraft back from spinning before it became so unstable that it was impossible to retain sufficient control to land, and the Spitfire stalled and crashed at 14:30 hrs from 100ft. AC1 Rhodes sustained two broken ribs. The pilot was knocked out and when he came to complained that the aircraft was tail heavy. It was suggested that the Polish pilot misunderstood the procedure whereby a mechanic remained on the tail to keep the tail down when taxying in mud, and then would clean the camera lens prior to take-off.

209 Sqn	Lerwick I	L7251	WQ-			Ground Loss
					Base:	Stranraer
	Sank at its mooring.				Time:	?

210 Sqn	Sunderland I	T9044	DA-			Ground Loss
					Base:	Pembroke Dock
	Sank in a gale.				Time:	?

217 Sqn	Anson I	R9701	MW-L		Duty:	Air Sea Rescue Search
	F/O	Holgate	. . . . .	Safe	Base:	St Eval
	Sgt	Hickson	. . . . .	Safe	T/o time:	08:05
	Sgt	Taylor	. . . . .	Safe		
	Sgt	Cowley	. . . . .	Safe		

Took off tasked with a search for Gladiator N5644 of 247 Squadron that was thought to have been lost off Kelland Head. Suffered a failure of the starboard engine, lost height and ditched 5 miles NE of Trevose Head, Cornwall. All the crew were picked up by trawlers of the River Camel Patrol. The Anson was salvaged but later sank off Port Isaac while being towed.

240 Sqn	Stranraer I	K7290	BN-X			Ground Loss
					Base:	Stranraer
	Sank in a gale.				Time:	?

23rd November 1940

22 Sqn	Beaufort I	L9946	OA-V		Op:	Den Helder
	P/O	Moore	. . . . .	Safe	Base:	North Coates
	Sgt	S Goldberg	746710	+	T/o time:	15:50
	Sgt	I T C Edwards	639611	Safe		
	Sgt	Kemp	. . . . . .	Safe		

Tasked with a bombing operation to Den Helder, the crew released their Time Impact Mine and reported an explosion in the centre of the target. On the return flight an engine cut and the Beaufort lost height before force-landing at 18:50 hrs near Fleming Hall, Southolt, Sussex. Sgt Goldberg baled out prior to the forced landing but died in the descent and is buried in Brighton and Hove Jewish Cemetery, Sussex.

59 Sqn	Blenheim IV	R2783	TR-V		Op:	Lorient
	P/O	J C E Beelaerts van Blokland	78859	+	Base:	Thorney Island
	Sgt	J C Woodcock	580991	+	T/o time:	15:35
	Sgt	L S Carvil	549762	+		

Shot down by an Me109 into the Channel. P/O Beelaerts van Blokland, from The Netherlands, and his crew are commemorated on the Runnymede Memorial.

235 Sqn	Blenheim IV	T1999	LA-S		Op:	Danish Sweep
	P/O	Davidson	. . . . .	Injured	Base:	Bircham Newton
	Sgt	Brazier	. . . . . .	Safe	T/o time:	11:00
	Sgt	Aslett	. . . . . .	Injured		

Damaged by flak off the coast of Denmark. Crashed on landing due to u/c damage, caught fire, causing the hung up bombs to explode, further injuring Sgt Aslett. P/O Davidson and Sgt Brazier rescued Sgt Aslett from the flames.

502 Sqn	Whitley V	P5090	YG-L		Op:	Convoy Escort
	Sgt	W J Barnfather	754627	+	Base:	Limavady
	Sgt	J J Westoby	741729	+	T/o time:	20:00
	P/O	J Whitsed	758109	+		
	Sgt	J G Curtis	943020	+		
	Sgt	J Perfect	942632	+		
	Sgt	W S Hamilton	816222	Injured		

Crashed into Fathan Glinne 1 mile W of Balquhidder, Perthshire, on the return from convoy escort to SC11. Sgt Hamilton was injured and taken to Stirling Infirmary while the others rest in Grandsable Cemetery, Grangemouth, Stirlingshire.

24th November 1940

272 Sqn	Blenheim IV	Z5734	XK-D	Op:	Convoy Escort
	P/O B H Herrick	42003	+	Base:	Aldergrove
	Sgt P R Smith	581477	+	T/o time:	16:20
	Sgt J G Hair	970690	+		

Found the wrong convoy and was involved in a dogfight with a Fairey Fulmar. Eye witnesses on HMS *Vesper* reported that the Blenheim stalled off a turn and dived into the North Channel. P/O Herrick, a New Zealander from Hawke's Bay, and his crew are commemorated on the Runnymede memorial.

26th November 1940

22 Sqn	Beaufort I	L9889	OA-T	Op:	Rover Patrol
	S/Ldr F H Roberts	34177	+	Base:	North Coates
	Sgt S F Martin	755974	+	T/o time:	12:30
	Sgt S N Douglas	623918	+		
	Sgt T Pickering	937061	PoW		

Set course for Holland, leading one other Beaufort, on his first operation for the Squadron. The flight made landfall at Den Helder at 13:35 hrs and S/Ldr Roberts sighted two merchant vessels, each between 3,000 and 4,000 tons, some 8 km (c 5 miles) NW of Den Helder. After circling the ships for about ten minutes in medium and heavy flak the Beaufort was seen to drop its torpedo and continue the attack run, turning slightly to port, before crashing into the North Sea 400 yards beyond the ship at approx 14:25 hrs. The Beaufort was claimed by Vorpostenboot 1101. S/Ldr Roberts and Sgt Douglas both rest in Sage War Cemetery while Sgt Martin was washed ashore on 8th January 1941 and buried locally in Vredenhof Cemetery on Schiermonnikog, Holland.

53 Sqn	Blenheim IV	N3630	PZ-N	Op:	Ghent
	P/O M M Barbour	83284	+	Base:	Thorney Island
	Sgt A Cowling MiD	628158	+	T/o time:	16:35
	Sgt G A Hinton	749321	+		

Missing from an attack on the oil depot. P/O Barbour, Sgt Hinton and Sgt Cowling are all commemorated on the Runnymede Memorial.

53 Sqn	Blenheim IV	V5371	PZ-T	Op:	Ghent
	P/O R E Maurer	42569	+	Base:	Thorney Island
	Sgt I S MacAulay	747942	+	T/o time:	16:35
	Sgt B L Bembridge	900946	+		

Missing from an attack on the oil depot. The Blenheim is presumed to have crashed into the sea because P/O Maurer is commemorated on the Runnymede Memorial and his crewmen are buried on either side of the Channel.

59 Sqn	Blenheim IV	R3889	TR-G	Op:	Lorient
	P/O K W Jerwood	84915	+	Base:	Thorney Island
	Sgt F J Newman RNZAF	40626	+	T/o time:	15:50
	Sgt E F Battle	637571	+		

Missing, failed to return. Sgt Newman, from Auckland, and the rest of the crew are commemorated on the Runnymede Memorial.

27th November 1940

10 (RAAF) Sqn	Sunderland I	N9048	RB-B		Ground Loss
				Base:	Mount Batten
				Time:	18:40

The Sunderland had been beached and drawn into a hangar for maintenance earlier in the day. The hangar was hit by a bomb during an air raid at 18:40 hrs setting it and the aircraft alight. During the blaze the hangar roof collapsed onto the aircraft fuselage, leaving only the tail in a recognisable shape.

10 (RAAF) Sqn	Sunderland I	P9601	RB-		**Ground Loss**
				Base:	Mount Batten
				Time:	18:40

During an air raid, a stick of high explosive bombs, four of which fell into the Cattewater, caused a fire on the aircraft which was at moorings. The port wingtip caught fire first before the fire spread to the front of the fuselage and along the starboard wing. The flames and reflection from the aircraft illuminated the whole station and surrounding areas. The Sunderland finally sank at its moorings where it was later salvaged. During this air raid two other 10 Squadron Sunderlands moored in the Cattewater (P9605 and T9047) were slightly damaged by shrapnel.

28th November 1940

320 Sqn	Fokker T-VIIIW	AV958	TD-	**Duty:**	?
		. . . . .		Base:	?
		. . . . . .		T/o time:	?

Ran out of fuel and crashed at Middleton, Suffolk. No further details.
This aircraft was formerly 'R-1' when operated by the Royal Netherlands Naval Air Service.

29th November 1940

22 Sqn	Beaufort I	L9792	OA-S	**Op:**	**Rover Patrol**
	F/Lt R P M Gibbs	. . . . .	Injured	Base:	North Coates
	Sgt Barton	. . . . .	Injured	T/o time:	16:42
	Sgt J Coulson	. . . . . .	Safe		
	Sgt Traynor	. . . . . .	Injured		

On a patrol earlier in the day this crew successfully attacked an enemy convoy. They returned to North Coates to refuel and re-arm before leading other squadron aircraft to the location for a second attack. Upon arrival, gathering darkness prevented the strike taking place and the flight returned to North Coates at 18:35 hrs. On the approach F/Lt Gibbs undershot, hit a ditch and the Beaufort cartwheeled and came to rest on its back.
    The pilot's autobiography *Not Peace But a Sword* suggests that the aircraft involved in this incident was his personal a/c, coded 'K' for Kitty, L9856.

59 Sqn	Blenheim IV	N3614	TR-E	**Op:**	**Moon Patrol**
	F/O A P Hovenier	41927	+	Base:	Thorney Island
	Sgt L E Magee	581233	+	T/o time:	14:30
	Sgt J B Scotchmere	552935	+		

Missing, failed to return. Sgt Magee, from Eire, and the rest of the crew are commemorated on the Runnymede Memorial.

321 Sqn	Anson I	N9742	Y	**Op:**	**Convoy Patrol**
	Sgt C L Van Kooy	12734	Injured	Base:	Carew Cheriton
	?	. . . . .	Injured	T/o time:	?
	?	. . . . .	Injured		

The Anson suffered an engine failure and ditched off Holyhead, Anglesey, at 15:30 hrs. The aircraft sank and three crew were injured.

30th November 1940

59 Sqn	Blenheim IV	L9463	TR-O	**Op:**	**Lorient**
	P/O Christie	. . . . .	Injured	Base:	Thorney Island
	Sgt Taverner	. . . . . .	Injured	T/o time:	05:45
	Sgt G E Crout	755728	+		

Stalled after take-off and hit the ground. Sgt Crout is buried in Earlsfield Cemetery, Wandsworth, London.

502 Sqn	Whitley V	T4219	YG-P	**Op:**	**Anti-Submarine Patrol**
	P/O L R de M Thompson	74342	+	Base:	Aldergrove
	Sgt G D Hutchings	742519	+	T/o time:	02:53
	Sgt R N Wain	758044	+		
	F/Sgt A F Scragg	511845	+		
	Sgt J A Kerr	816249	+		

Missing on patrol. All are commemorated on the Runnymede Memorial.

1st December 1940

59 Sqn	**Blenheim IV**	**N3537**	**TR-J**	**Op:**	**Reconnaissance**
	P/O L B Hinman	85235	+	Base:	Thorney Island
	Sgt D A Walden	751116	+	T/o time: ?	
	?	. . . . . .	Injured		

Took off tasked for a Reconnaissance and returned at 11:00 hrs. P/O Hinman landed downwind and saw another a/c landing into wind so he opened up to go round again. The Blenheim turned to the left but had insufficient height to avoid hitting trees and house before crashing onto the road. After the crash it was found that one propeller was in fine pitch and one in coarse pitch and that this may have caused the yaw. P/O Hinman is buried locally in St Nicholas Churchyard, West Thorney, while Sgt Walden rests in St Andrew Churchyard, Kinson, Hampshire.
The WOp/AG injured in this incident has yet to be identified .

2nd December 1940

48 Sqn	**Anson I**	**K6242**	**OY-**	**Duty:**	**Transit Flight**
	P/O C D Maxwell	. . . . .	Safe	Base:	Sydenham
	P/O Duclos	. . . . .	Safe	T/o time: 09:50	
	Sgt O'Reilly	. . . . . .	Safe		
	Sgt Harris	. . . . . .	Safe		

Stalled on the approach to Stornoway due to the reflection of the sun and the u/c collapsed in the resultant heavy landing at 13:00 hrs. The Anson was deemed to be beyond economic repair.

4th December 1940

220 Sqn	**Hudson I**	**P5135**	**NR-O**	**Op:**	**Hornli Patrol**
	F/O D Lingwood	41305	+	Base:	Thornaby
	F/O R D Masters	72528	+	T/o time: 10:50	
	Sgt D V Taylor	623170	+		
	Sgt E J Pritchard	568713	+		

Crashed into the North Sea off Hartlepool, County Durham. Several ETA's by the crew were transmitted then finally a D/F at 17:35 hrs. All are commemorated on the Runnymede Memorial.

233 Sqn	**Hudson I**	**T9365**	**ZS-K**	**Op:**	**Stand Patrol**
	P/O J G Forbes	72990	+	Base:	Leuchars
	P/O H B Allan	42782	+	T/o time: 06:15	
	Sgt T Rutter	974038	+		
	Sgt A G Davidson	537408	+		

Lost height after take-off and flew into the ground at Guardbridge, Fife, killing all four crew. Both P/O Forbes and P/O Allan are buried locally in Leuchars Cemetery while Sgt Rutter and Sgt Davidson were taken to St Mary Churchyard, Whalley, Lancashire and Banchory Ternan Parish Churchyard, Kincardineshire respectively.

5th December 1940

22 Sqn	**Beaufort I**	**L9936**	**OA-B**	**Op:**	**Rover Patrol**
	F/Lt A R H Beauman DFC	39207	+	Base:	North Coates
	P/O P H Telford	83292	+	T/o time: 06:45	
	Sgt T J James	635439	+		
	P/O F W Hicks	78544	+		

Last seen at 09:00 hrs over the North Sea off Wilhelmshaven, Germany. German Radio later reported the Beaufort as shot down. F/Lt 'Dick' Beauman and his crew are commemorated on the Runnymede Memorial.

53 Sqn	**Blenheim IV**	**T2218**	**PZ-W**	**Op:**	**Guns**
	P/O P E Gibbs	. . . . .	Safe	Base:	Thorney Island
	Sgt Wood	. . . . . .	Safe	T/o time: 19:00	
	Sgt Oram	. . . . . .	Safe		

Wireless became u/s on the return and no D/F bearings could be obtained. Abandoned when lost in bad weather on the return from Cap Griz Nes, France, and left to crash at Occuld, Suffolk.

6th December 1940

53 Sqn	Blenheim IV	V5420	PZ-H	Duty:	Air Test
	P/O S R E Weatherle	84003	+	Base:	Thorney Island
	Sgt H S Parrott	759225	+	T/o time:	
	Sgt S McAndrew	543725	Injured		

Overshot while landing in heavy rain and hit some trees at 15:30 hrs. P/O Weatherle is buried in Hendon Cemetery; Sgt Parrott was taken to St James Churchyard, Rowledge, Surrey for burial.

209 Sqn	Lerwick I	L7255	WQ-A		Ground Loss
				Base:	Stranraer
				Time:	?

Lost a float in gale while at a mooring and sank.

254 Sqn	Blenheim IV	Z5726	QY-N	Op:	Protective Patrol
	Sgt D K Leaver	748367	+	Base:	Dyce
	Sgt A F Bean	581432	+	T/o time:	09:45
	Sgt A C Johnston	969948	+		

Missing from a patrol to Flamborough Head. The Blenheim was believed to have ditched off Montrose, Angus, after flying into snow. The crew is commemorated on the Runnymede Memorial.

7th December 1940

53 Sqn	Blenheim IV	T2395	PZ-N	Op:	Hookos
	P/O A K Steel	43083	+	Base:	Thorney Island
	Sgt W R Hemsley	745314	+	T/o time:	17:27
	Sgt D Robson	755168	Wounded		

Crashed at Shingle Point, Pegwell Bay, Deal, Kent, returning from shipping reconnaissance at approximately 19:50 hrs after hitting a balloon cable. P/O Steel rests in Bishopwearmouth Cemetery, Sunderland and Sgt Hemsley in Nottingham Road Cemetery, Derby.

217 Sqn	Beaufort I	N1154	MW-B	Op:	Brest
	F/O H E Mussenden	41198	+	Base:	St Eval
	P/O G H Brooks	78459	+	T/o time:	20:25
	Sgt J W Pratt	627713	+		
	Sgt T J G Eede	527729	+		

Failed to return. Some remains of this aircraft are reported to be on display in Hopital-Camfrout Town Hall. All the crew are buried in Hôpital-Camfrout Communal Cemetery, Finistère, France.

502 Sqn	Whitley V	T4277	YG-J	Duty:	Anti-Sub Search (2) North
	F/Lt C W Rees	90050	+	Base:	Limavady
	P/O M L Worthington	76024	+	T/o time:	18:35
	Sgt W A Adams	564507	+		
	Sgt P J Miller	625296	+		
	Sgt V S Brown	816242	Injured		

Dived into the ground near Ballykelly at approximately 18:50 hrs after a night take-off. F/Lt Rees rests in St Catherine Church of Ireland Churchyard, Killead, County Antrim; P/O Worthington in St Peter Churchyard, Prestbury, Cheshire; Sgt Adams in Weston Mill Cemetery, Plymouth, and Sgt Miller in Londonderry City Cemetery.

9th December 1940

224 Sqn	Hudson I	N7265	QX-J	Op:	Stand Patrol
	F/O G J M Dewar	41385	+	Base:	Leuchars
	P/O A Bilderbeck	33535	+	T/o time:	10:35
	Sgt G Bell	551726	+		
	Sgt W E Woolley	755114	+		

Failed to return. Possibly shot down by III/ZG76. F/O Dewar and his crew are commemorated on the Runnymede Memorial.

224 Sqn	Hudson I	T9277	QX-W	Op:	Stand Patrol
	F/O L D P Murphy	41196	+	Base:	Leuchars
	P/O F A Roach	85228	+	T/o time:	10:40
	Sgt W Steele	523780	+		
	Sgt T J Crawley	901761	+		

Failed to return from off Norway. Possibly shot down by III/ZG76. All are commemorated on the Runnymede Memorial.

11th December 1940

204 Sqn	Sunderland I	N9046	KG-F		**Ground Loss**
				Base:	Sullom Voe
	Destroyed by fire and sank at its moorings.			Time:	13:30

13th December 1940

248 Sqn	Blenheim IV	L9455	WR-B	**Duty:**	**Transit Flight**
	P/O J D Dodd	84322	+	Base:	Sumburgh
	P/O A F Pettet	85011	+	T/o time:	13:12
	Sgt A Hook	647887	+		
	LAC L S J Bright	653093	+		
	AC1 A E H Moore	634717	+		

Soon after take-off collided with Blenheim 'S 'of 248 Squadron and dived into the sea off Wick, Caithness. All are commemorated on the Runnymede Memorial.

248 Sqn	Blenheim IV	R3625	WR-S	**Duty:**	**Transit Flight**
	Sgt J S Hamilton	754020	+	Base:	Sumburgh
	Sgt H W Walmesley	755997	+	T/o time:	13:14
	Sgt J H May	759336	+		
	AC1 S Julian	636478	+		
	AC1 G W Monks	907460	+		

Collided with Blenheim 'B' of 248 squadron and dived into the sea off Wick, Caithness. Sgt Hamilton, crew and passengers are all commemorated on the Runnymede Memorial.

15th December 1940

201 Sqn	Sunderland I	N9021	ZM-P	**Op:**	**Convoy Escort**
	F/O D J Fletcher	41166	Safe	Base:	Sullom Voe
	P/O George	.....	Safe	T/o time:	08:15
	P/O Parsons	.....	Safe		
	Sgt Walker	......	Safe		
	LAC Hamilton	......	Safe		
	AC1 W M Kinnish	966738	Safe		
	AC Todd	......	Safe		
	LAC Thompson	......	Safe		
	Sgt Gibbon	......	Safe		
	Sgt Lodge	......	Safe		
	Sgt Abbot	......	Safe		

Took off tasked with escorting convoy HX93. The Sunderland was ordered to land at Invergordon and whilst doing so stalled and collapsed a float at 19:30 hrs. The aircraft turned turtle a quarter of a mile from the slipway and sank in 10 fathoms but without injury to the crew who had been landed earlier. Salvage was completed on the 27th of December 1940.

235 Sqn	Blenheim IV	Z5754	LA-B	**Op:**	**Escort**
	P/O J Coggins MBE DFM*	44458	+	Base:	Bircham Newton
	P/O N A Sadler	82732	+	T/o time:	15:35
	Sgt P R Prosser	755800	+		

Took off tasked with escorting gardening aircraft. Dived into the sea at 18:15 hrs on the return, off Brancaster, Norfolk. P/O Coggins MBE DFM*, and Sgt Prosser are listed on the Runnymede Memorial while P/O Sadler is buried locally in St Mary's Churchyard, Great Bircham.

16th December 1940

1 PRU	Spitfire I (PR) type ?	X4350	LY-	**Op:**	**Photo-Recce**
	F/O S J Millen DFC	41047	+	Base:	St Eval
				T/o time:	14:15

Failed to return from a PR sortie to Brest in this green Spitfire. Reportedly shot down by flak at Lannilis, Finistère. Some eight weeks earlier, on 29th October, F/O Millen flew the first operational sortie in one of the two prototype long-range 'bowser wing' Spitfire I (PR) type D conversions. The 5hr 25min flight in P9551 was the longest sortie to-date by the PRU, and had encompassed Stettin, Rostock, Emden, Cuxhaven and Berlin. F/O Millen, of Wellington, New Zealand, was awarded the DFC on 1st November 1940 and rests in Treflez Churchyard, Finistère.

248 Sqn	Blenheim IV	T1997	WR-	Duty:	Transit Flight
	Sgt E L Holmes	740063	Safe	Base:	Leuchars
				T/o time:	?

Set off on a flight to Dyce to pick up passengers. On landing the Blenheim collided with a truck on the runway and caught fire. The contributing factors to the accident were bad visibility and the decision to land on a runway out of the wind. Pilot incorrectly thought that the runway into wind was u/s, drifted to port, hit a contractors water tank and tarmac for construction.

17th December 1940

217 Sqn	Beaufort I	L9823	MW-L	Op:	Bordeaux
	F/Sgt Petch	. . . . .	Safe	Base:	St Eval
	Sgt Hayes	. . . . .	Safe	T/o time:	18:15
	Sgt H E Postill	546900	+		
	Sgt Penver	. . . . .	Safe		

Ditched into the Channel, out of fuel, 3 miles SE of The Needles, Isle of Wight at 01:15 hrs. The crew was picked up by an RAF high-speed launch but Sgt Postill's Mae West failed to keep him afloat and he is commemorated on the Runnymede Memorial.

217 Sqn	Beaufort I	L4463	MW-G	Op:	Bordeaux
	Sgt D A G Matthews	566240	+	Base:	St Eval
	Sgt J R Massey	590895	Evaded	T/o time:	23:00
	Sgt A H Hastie	974322	PoW		
	Sgt R Ayre	614211	PoW		

Shot down by flak near Vannes, France. Sgt Matthews rests in La Trinite-sur-Mer Communal Cemetery, Morbihan, France. Sgt Massey evaded but was killed on the 23rd May 1941 when Catalina AH560 crashed off Portugal on a ferry flight.

18th December 1940

22 Sqn	Beaufort I	L4516	OA-W	Op:	Wilhelmshaven
	Sgt D G How	742696	+	Base:	North Coates
	Sgt P V Renai	580978	+	T/o time:	20:10
	Sgt R G Hart	647852	+		
	Sgt L J Peachey	749539	+		

Stalled due to an engine failure shortly after take-off and crashed at Marshchapel, Lincolnshire. The Time Impact Mine exploded, setting the aircraft on fire and killing all the crew. Sgt Renai of Wellington, New Zealand, and the other crew members rest locally in St Nicholas Churchyard, North Cotes, Lincolnshire.

20th December 1940

206 Sqn	Hudson I	N7333	VX-E	Op:	Emro Patrol
	P/O R Ward	42471	+	Base:	Bircham Newton
	P/O K J Dobbie	79157	+	T/o time:	04:45
	Sgt G R Ellerington	627175	+		
	Sgt N G Riddell	616809	+		

Crashed at 05:00 hrs. P/O Ward, a Canadian from Toronto, rests locally in St Mary's Churchyard, Great Bircham, Norfolk; P/O Dobbie in Cadder Cemetery, Lanarkshire; Sgt Ellerington in All Saints Churchyard, Lund, Yorkshire, and Sgt Riddell in Amble West Cemetery, Northumberland.

217 Sqn	Beaufort I	L4474	MW-E	Op:	Lorient
	P/O N H Webb DFM	44594	+	Base:	St Eval
	Sgt C M Tiplady	745261	+	T/o time:	04:07
	Sgt W S Plant	620004	+		
	Sgt P Milligan	629402	+		

Lost without trace. All rest in Lanester Communal Cemetery, Morbihan, France.

21st December 1940

224 Sqn	Hudson I	N7222	QX-N	Op:	Stand Patrol
	F/O P J Jenkins MiD	40713	+	Base:	Leuchars
	P/O J C Dale	43284	+	T/o time: 07:10	
	Sgt R W Willis	552094	+		
	Sgt R Bracchi	550921	+		

Missing over the North Sea. All, including P/O Dale, an Australian from Victoria, and F/O Jenkins, from Sydney, Australia, are commemorated on the Runnymede Memorial.

236 Sqn	Blenheim IV	R3878	FA-Z	Op:	Brest Patrol
	S/Ldr G W Montagu	26241	+	Base:	St Eval
	Sgt D R Briggs	580535	+	T/o time: 14:55	
	P/O G H Hannan	79237	+		

Possibly shot down by Uffz Schmidt of 5./JG77 at 17:04 hrs off Brest. All are buried in Bayeux War Cemetery.

272 Sqn	Blenheim IV	L9415	XK-T	Op:	Convoy Escort
	Sgt Hobbs	.....	Interned	Base:	Aldergrove
	Sgt Ricketts	.....	Interned	T/o time: 12:55	
	Sgt Newport	.....	Interned		

Crashed about 10 miles inside the Irish border after the crew abandoned the aircraft by parachute. The crew were interned in Eire.

22nd December 1940

42 Sqn	Beaufort I	L9890	AW-L	Op:	Bombing Target
	F/Lt J A Richardson	37576	+	Base:	Wick
	Sgt B Drake	581325	+	T/o time: 02:20	
	Sgt R F Henry	627041	+		
	Sgt W R J Little	539889	+		

At 02:25 hrs a report was received from coast watchers that a violent explosion had been heard out at sea 3 miles E of Freswick Bay and it was thought to be either an aeroplane which had crashed or a mine which had gone off. There was a light SSE breeze and a moderate sea. At 03:30 hrs the motor lifeboat *City of Edinburgh* was launched and searched a wide area. She found nothing until 09:00 hrs when she came upon an open parachute, with harness attached, close to Duncansby Head. Nothing else was to be seen, and the lifeboat returned to her station at 12:00 hrs. Soon after daylight a further parachute, numerous small portions of clothing and pieces of aircraft later identified as from L9890 were found strewn along the beach where they had been washed ashore. It is presumed that the Beaufort suffered a petrol fire during take-off. F/Lt Richardson and his crew are commemorated on the Runnymede memorial.

24th December 1940

217 Sqn	Beaufort I	L9851	MW-	Duty:	Training
	P/O R A Robertson	76463	+	Base:	St Eval
				T/o time: 19:25	

Took off for solo local flying training. The aircraft is suspected to have stalled in a climbing turn after take-off and crashed from 700 feet in the vicinity of the water tower at Denzel Downs. The Court of Inquiry could not find any evidence of structural failure in the burned out wreckage. F/O Robertson was taken to Lambhill Cemetery, Glasgow, for burial.

26th December 1940

217 Sqn	Beaufort I	L9860	MW-F	Op:	Bordeaux
	P/O J H D Tilson	42030	+	Base:	St Eval
	Sgt J C Wild	751369	+	T/o time:	
	Sgt W B Miflin	550750	+		
	Sgt R A Bradshaw	905929	+		

Lost without trace. P/O Tilson and his crew all rest in Pornic War Cemetery, Loire-Atlantique, France.

27th December 1940

22 Sqn	**Beaufort I**	**N1118**	**OA-X**	**Op:**	**Rover Patrol**
	S/Ldr D V W Francis MiD**	37165	+	Base:	North Coates
	Sgt R J Farthing	564639	+	T/o time:	15:45
	Sgt J W Unett	638891	+		
	F/O E Pennington	77122	+		

Took off in the company with other squadron aircraft and set course for Holland. The flight made landfall on Texel at 16:55 hrs. Shortly afterwards S/Ldr 'Fanny' Francis, three times Mentioned in Despatches, was seen to bank sharply while low on the water having been shot down by the Sperrbrecher, SS *Templar*. The Beaufort had already dropped its torpedo which continued to run true to hit and damage the 6,727 ton vessel. Sgt Unett rests in Sage War Cemetery while S/Ldr Francis and the other crewmen are commemorated on the Runnymede Memorial.

210 Sqn	**Sunderland I**	**N9022**	**DA-B**	**Op:**	**Convoy Patrol**
	F/Lt I H Meggitt	40633	+	Base:	Oban
	F/O D A Stewart	. . . . .	Injured	T/o time:	11:56
	Sgt C C I Roberts	968757	+		
	Sgt A K Perkins	649616	+		
	Sgt N E Thomson RNZAF	40926	+		
	Sgt D Ogston	817057	+		
	Sgt L E Crawshaw	751624	+		
	LAC T A Kennedy	521902	+		
	AC1 J S Audsley	646551	+		
	S/Lt B F Leadbitter RN	–	+		

Crashed in a night landing, at 21:17 hrs, off Maiden Island, Oban Bay. The Sunderland landed safely but hit an underwater object which ripped open the hull and flipped the aircraft onto its back. The underwater object was thought to be a horse box from the SS *Breda*, sunk in Ardmucknish Bay four days earlier. F/Lt Meggitt, an Australian from Austinmer, rests locally in Pennyfuir Cemetery, Oban. The remaining crewmen including Sgt Thomson, a New Zealander from Taranaki, are commemorated on the Runnymede Memorial. S/Lt Leadbitter, attached to HMS *Victory*, has no known grave and is commemorated on the Portsmouth Naval Memorial.

220 Sqn	**Hudson II**	**T9373**	**NR-G**	**Op:**	**ASV Patrol**
	S/Ldr Rogenhagen	. . . . .	Injured	Base:	St Eval
	Sgt Lane	. . . . . .	Safe	T/o time:	13:00
	Sgt W E Callaghan	623929	+		
	Sgt J L Rees	751429	+		

Overstayed the prudent limit of endurance, ran out of fuel at night on the return and the crew abandoned by parachute 2-3 miles SE of Trevose Head. The Hudson finally crashed at 21:29 hrs near Towan Head, Newquay, Cornwall. S/Ldr Rogenhagen fractured an arm and a leg during bale-out. Those killed were considered to have landed in the sea and are commemorated on the Runnymede Memorial.

28th December 1940

42 Sqn	**Beaufort I**	**N1162**	**AW-G**	**Op:**	**Rover Patrol**
	F/Lt M R Baillon MiD	37147	+	Base:	Wick
	P/O L S Hill RCAF	J/2823	+	T/o time:	13:50
	P/O J H Gow	78671	+		
	Sgt C F Young	638694	+		

Set out in company with other squadron aircraft to torpedo a tanker off Trondheim. Last seen off Sumburgh, Shetland, on the return track and a log book and wreckage were later recovered off Kirkwall, Orkney. The crew, including P/O Hill from Calgary, are commemorated on the Runnymede Memorial.

53 Sqn	**Blenheim IV**	**L9043**	**PZ-O**	**Op:**	**Lorient**
	F/Lt J D Steuart-Richardson DFC 33465		+	Base:	Thorney Island
	Sgt J L Maguire	581234	+	T/o time:	06:00
	Sgt K W V Vowles	625038	+		

Stalled on take-off before crashing and blowing up. F/Lt Steuart-Richardson rests in Tonbridge Cemetery, Kent: Sgt Maguire in Manchester Southern Cemetery, Lancashire, and Sgt Vowles in Christ Church Churchyard, Downend, Gloucestershire.

Chapter 8

1st January 1941 to 5th March 1941

Shipping losses in late 1940 had exceeded anything the ship-building yards could replace and levels of imported war goods fell dramatically. In response to a request from the First Lord of the Admiralty, A V Alexander, for an additional 300 shore-based naval co-operation aircraft, the Defence Committee suggested handing Coastal Command over to the Royal Navy. Due to time constraints this was not actioned and Winston Churchill later added the proviso that the Navy must take operational control of the U-boat war. This all helped to bring the poor equipment levels of Coastal Command to the attention of those in power and resulted in the authorised formation of five ASV Mk.II-equipped Wellington squadrons and seven additional anti-shipping squadrons.

During December 1940 the U-boat activity off Portugal and West Africa increased, prompting Coastal Command to reform 95 Squadron (initially, using three Sunderlands of 210 Squadron) and to despatch it via Gibraltar to Sierra Leone at the end of January 1941. At the other end of Coastal Command's patrol area the formation of Iceland Area was actioned on the 1st of January 1941 and squadron deployment carried out a few weeks later.

Bad weather in the Atlantic during January 1941 and a temporary reduction in the number of operational submarines led to a drop in shipping losses. Most U-boat attacks occurred in the air cover gap in mid-Atlantic.

A re-organisation of Naval Commands took place on 7th February 1941 and 15 Group Headquarters moved to Liverpool to operate from the Combined Operations Room. No 15 Group was replaced at Plymouth by 19 Group to continue the SW Approaches and Biscay patrols.

Coastal Command concern over the effects of the German Capital Ships operating from the French Atlantic ports was justified when the *Admiral Hipper* broke out of Brest for a 14 day commerce raid in February 1941. The *Admiral Hipper* sank seven ships of a convoy in one day before returning to a protected anchorage underlining its effectiveness as a fighting unit if deployed correctly. The Admiralty pressed Bomber Command to take a more active role in the war at sea with attacks on ports, surface shipping, U-boats and U-boat bases and gained the backing of Churchill for the release of aircraft for the tasks.

In February the Atlantic weather improved and the presence of 67 new U-boats soon made their mark with 41 ships totalling 236,549 tons being sunk. As a result of its new strength, German Naval Command launched a massive campaign in March involving U-boats and surface raiders in a attempt to end the struggle with Britain within 60 days. To assist in combating this offensive, Coastal Command had a new weapon, the long-range Catalina flying-boat, the first example of which was delivered to 240 Sqn on 5th March 1941.

Both sides were now set for the Battle of the Atlantic.

1st January 1941

48 Sqn	Anson I	R3305	OY-	Op:	Convoy Patrol
	P/O J H Erskine	81034	+	Base:	Hooton Park
	Sgt J L Curry	748639	+	T/o time:	14:00
	Sgt W C Langdon	751603	+		
	Sgt W E Fennell	966641	+		

A wing hit the ground during a turn in bad visibility and the Anson crashed onto the beach at Hoylake, Cheshire at 17:46 hrs. P/O Erskine is buried in Berwick-Upon-Tweed Cemetery; Sgt Curry in St Mary Churchyard, Bucklesham, Suffolk; while Sgt Langdon was taken to Milford Haven Cemetery and Sgt Fennell to Rake Lane Cemetery, Wallasey, Cheshire.

206 Sqn	Hudson I	T9287	VX-	Duty:	Transit Flight
	F/O H E M Featherstone	41275	+	Base:	Bircham Newton
	P/O J B Allen	83260	+	T/o time:	?
	P/O R McK Mansell	81646	+		
	F/O D M G Kiralfy	70368	+		
	Sgt R A Plowright	550840	+		
	LAC K C G Gilder	639237	+		

| AC1 G A Meridew | 635301 | + |
| LAC W A Meller | 622156 | + |

Hit a barn with the port wing tip while low flying and crashed near Langham at 14:48 hrs. Those killed rest in various cemeteries in England.

4th January 1941

53 Sqn	Blenheim IV	R2773	PZ-V	Op:	Brest
	P/O P E Gibbs	85234	+	Base:	Thorney Island
	Sgt H S Wall	751254	+	T/o time:	15:30
	Sgt H G W Martin	744964	+		

Shot down by an Me109 during an attack on a destroyer in Rade Abri. Sgt Wall is buried in Greenbank Cemetery, Bristol, while Sgt Martin was taken to Canterbury Cemetery. P/O Gibbs is commemorated on the Runnymede Memorial.

7th January 1941

48 Sqn	Anson I	K8703	OY-	Op:	Convoy Escort
	F/O D M Brass	.....	Safe	Base:	Stornoway
				T/o time:	?

Overshot and hit a petrol pump on landing at Stornoway. This was an older type of Anson lacking flaps and the final landing was carried out after two overshoots.

209 Sqn	Lerwick I	L7262	WQ-Q	Duty:	?
	F/Lt D F Spotswood	37733	Safe	Base:	Stranraer
	Sgt D A Briggs	580000	Safe	T/o time:	11:00
	P/O G B Windeler	.....	Safe		
	Sgt W G Evans	530401	+		
	AC1 T Middlebrook	649212	+		

Dropped a wing on take-off, bounced and sank trapping two of the crew in the aircraft. Sgt Evans rests in Manchester Crematorium and AC1 Middlebrook is buried in Wednesbury Cemetery, Staffordshire. Four other individuals were reported as safe in addition to those listed above.

8th January 1941

233 Sqn	Hudson II	T9379	ZS-K	Op:	Convoy Escort
	P/O S C Stone	42540	+	Base:	Aldergrove
	P/O A R Quemby	42645	+	T/o time:	08:15
	Sgt D A Joseph	643237	+		
	Sgt G A Haddon	751070	+		

Took off for escort duty to SS *Kaaparen* but on the second circuit was seen to be flying at 500 feet with the landing lights on, whereupon it turned left and shallow dived into the ground 1½ miles from the aerodrome. Both P/O Stone and Sgt Joseph rest in St Catherine Church of Ireland Churchyard, Killead, County Antrim; P/O Quemby in Isleworth Cemetery, Heston and Isleworth, Middlesex; and Sgt Haddon in Gilroes Cemetery, Leicester.

9th January 1941

53 Sqn	Blenheim IV	V5370	PZ-S	Op:	Brest
	P/O J P Lucas	.....	Safe	Base:	Thorney Island
	Sgt G Gale	......	Safe	T/o time:	17:00
	Sgt H V Jackson	755742	+		

Took off to attack the *Admiral Hipper* in Brest dry dock. Crashed into the sea off Selsey Bill, near Wittering in Sussex, on the return leg at 22:00 hrs. A search by the Selsey lifeboat found only oil. Sgt Jackson is commemorated on the Runnymede Memorial.

10th January 1941

59 Sqn	Blenheim IV	T2217	TR-F	Op:	Brest
	P/O K C Cook	43096	+	Base:	Thorney Island
	Sgt D B C Smith	755260	+	T/o time:	00:30
	Sgt P E N Smith	973750	+		

Took off in company for an attack on the *Admiral Hipper* in Brest Harbour. Ran out of fuel while lost and crashed into the St George's Channel on the return from the target. The crew are commemorated on the Runnymede Memorial.

11th January 1941

224 Sqn	Hudson I	N7298	QX-O	Op:	Patrol
	P/O B L P Fox	42496	+	Base:	Leuchars
	Sgt K B Files	523740	+	T/o time:	01:17
	Sgt W R Martin	520434	+		
	P/O J McD S Wylie	43698	+		

Flew into high ground in bad visibility during a night flight over Kildare, Eire. Both Sgt Martin and P/O Wylie rest in Thornaby-on-Tees Cemetery; Sgt Files in St Mark Churchyard, Worsley, Lancashire and P/O Fox, an Australian from New South Wales, in St Mary Church Cemetery, Brancaster, Norfolk.

13th January 1941

612 Sqn	Whitley V	T4288	WL-	Duty:	?
	P/O G H M Riddell	. . . . .	Safe	Base:	Dyce
				Time:	?

Swung on take-off and hit two parked Blenheims. The Whitley was assessed as damaged beyond repair (DBR) and became a ground instructional airframe, serial 2579M.

15th January 1941

1 PRU	Spartan 7W-19	AX666		Duty:	Communications
	F/Lt M J B Young	. . . . .	Safe	Base:	?
				T/o time:	?

Made a heavy landing at 13:40 hrs on frozen ground at Montrose, Angus, and collapsed the u/c. *This aircraft was a former Iraqi-registered civilian aircraft (YI-SOF) that had been impressed into military service in August 1940, for use as a communications 'hack'. Deemed as damaged beyond repair in this accident it was reclassified as a ground instructional airframe with serial 2526M.*

22 Sqn	Beaufort I	W6489	OA-W	Op:	Gardening
	F/Lt J R Fishwick	33246	+	Base:	North Coates
	Sgt D S Craik RCAF	R/61304	+	T/o time:	18:10
	Sgt T Wareing	516730	+		
	Sgt A T Smith	755419	+		

Took off and set course for the River Weser Estuary. On return, aircraft 'S' of No 22 Squadron reported that at 19:15 hrs some 120 miles from base in position MFRC 3829 a brilliant white light was seen in the sky for ten minutes. It then faded gradually and appeared to lose height as it did so. The crew of S/22 think that it may have been an aircraft on fire. All, including Sgt Craik from Moosejaw, Saskatchewan, and F/Lt Fishwick from New Westminister, New Brunswick, Canada, are commemorated on the Runnymede Memorial. This had been this pilot's first operation with the squadron since being posted in as a replacement flight commander.

16th January 1941

220 Sqn	Hudson I	P5151	NR-B	Op:	Hornli Patrol
	P/O B J R George	44831	+	Base:	Thornaby
	Sgt A A Cross	741257	+	T/o time:	10:40
	Sgt J Chester	621389	+		
	Sgt F Hughes	553875	+		

Suffered an engine failure, lost height and ditched in the sea off Redcar at 11:14 hrs. The suspected location of ditching was in a minefield and was searched by naval vessels. All the crew are commemorated on the Runnymede Memorial.

17th January 1941

1 PRU	Spitfire I (PR) Type C	R6906	LY-	Op:	Reconnaissance
	F/Lt J S D Miles	28002	+	Base:	?

T/o time: ?

Shot down over Boulogne, France by Hptm H Ihlefeld of I/LG 2 at 15:50 hrs in an Me109. F/Lt Miles rests in Marquise Communal Cemetery, Pas-de-Calais.

217 Sqn	**Beaufort I**		L9862	**MW-H**	**Op:**	**Brest**
	F/O	Forward	. . . . .	Injured	Base:	St Eval
	Sgt	Rollo	. . . . .	Injured	T/o time:	18:19
	Sgt	Boddy	. . . . . .	Injured		
	Sgt	Martin	. . . . . .	Injured		

Took off along with six other aircraft of the squadron for an attack on the *Admiral Hipper* at Brest and the aerodrome at Vannes, but returned within two hours because of bad weather. On landing the aircraft was rounded out too high and dropped 50 feet onto the runway forcing the undercarriage up through the wings and shearing both engines off. All the crew were knocked unconscious and were found to have fractured spines when later examined in hospital.

22nd January 1941

22 Sqn	**Beaufort I**		N1151	**OA-T**	**Op:**	**Rover Patrol**
	F/O	D G G Coles	72509	+	Base:	North Coates
	P/O	V S Padgham	83739	+	T/o time:	10:30
	Sgt	H D F Hewett	623561	+		
	Sgt	E A Castle	967237	+		

Set course along with other squadron aircraft to Terschelling, Holland. N/22 reported that they were attacked at 11:15 hrs in position MFJK 0540. F/O Coles's Beaufort and one enemy aircraft disappeared into a cloud bank during the dogfight and were not seen again. The Beaufort was claimed by Fw Rudolf Mickel of 1./JG1 some 40 km (*c* 25 miles) NW of Terschelling. German radio later reported three Englishmen in the sea off Terschelling but F/O Coles and his crew were not recovered and are commemorated on the Runnymede Memorial.

220 Sqn	**Hudson II**		T9371	**NR-**	**Duty:**	**Ferry Flight**
	Sgt	C Smith	741069	Injured	Base:	Thornaby
	Sgt	L B Scase	745674	+	T/o time:	?
	Sgt	W Parfitt	626274	+		
	Sgt	T J McHugh	653675	Safe		

Took off for St Eval. At 11:30 hrs the Hudson flew into high ground at Ingleby Arncliffe, Yorkshire, in bad visibility. The Court of Inquiry ruled that the navigator was guilty of culpable negligence in setting a course without considering the obstacle caused by high ground. Sgt Smith was not free from blame as it was considered that he knew the hills were there and remembered them too late to avoid the crash. Sgt Scase rests in Hartshill Cemetery, and Sgt Parfitt in Longton Cemetery, both Stoke-On-Trent, Staffordshire.

23rd January 1941

502 Sqn	**Whitley V**		P5041	**YG-C**	**Op:**	**Convoy Escort**
	F/Lt	P L Billing	39297	+	Base:	Aldergrove
	F/O	A P B Holmes	90038	+	T/o time:	12:22
	Sgt	H Pilling	755384	+		
	Sgt	D J P Bradley	627135	+		
	Sgt	A R Hooker	754007	+		

Took off for escort duty to convoy HG50 and on the return crashed into hills near Campbeltown, Argyll. F/O Holmes rests in St Patrick Church of Ireland Churchyard, Drumbeg, County Antrim; F/Lt Billing in St Aidan Church of Ireland Churchyard, Glenavy, County Antrim; Sgt Pilling in Conisbrough Cemetery, Yorkshire; Sgt Bradley in Willesden New Cemetery, Middlesex and Sgt Hooker in Faversham Borough Cemetery, Kent.

24th January 1941

233 Sqn	**Hudson I**		P5123	**ZS-W**	**Op:**	**Convoy Escort**
	P/O	D Welply	. . . . .	Interned	Base:	Aldergrove
	P/O	Cowper	. . . . .	Interned	T/o time:	09:20
	Sgt	Todd	. . . . . .	Interned		
	P/O	Snow	. . . . .	Interned		

Force-landed due to fuel shortage at Sligo, Eire, on return from a convoy escort to HG50. The Hudson was interned and transferred to the Irish Air Corps on 13th April 1942..

502 Sqn	Whitley V	T4168	YG-E	Duty:	Search
	F/O L J Ward	41501	Interned	Base:	Aldergrove
	P/O E I C Johnson	41931	+	T/o time:	09:23
	Sgt J E Hogg	969800	+		
	Sgt C V Jefferson	816145	Interned		
	Sgt L Greenwood	553918	+		

Took off to search for tugs looking for bombed ships. Abandoned at 21:30 hrs when short of fuel and crashed into Lough Foyle. Both Sgt Greenwood and Sgt Hogg are commemorated on the Runnymede Memorial while P/O Johnson is buried in Rickmansworth Cemetery, Hertfordshire.

25th January 1941

217 Sqn	Anson I	L7994	MW-U		Ground Loss
				Base:	St Eval
	Damaged by a bomb blast in an air raid. Struck off charge.			Time:	21:25 hrs.

27th January 1941

224 Sqn	Hudson I	N7358	QX-H	Op:	Stand Patrol
	Sgt P R Lanchbery	741830	+	Base:	Leuchars
	Sgt C B Thomson	741812	+	T/o time:	?
	Sgt E A Perry	755035	+		
	Sgt H Mitchell	751210	+		

Shot down by Hptm R Kaldrack of III/ZG76 off Norway. All are commemorated on the Runnymede Memorial.

29th January 1941

236 Sqn	Blenheim IV	V5432	ND-A	Op:	Brest
	F/O Cotes-Preedy	. . . . .	Injured	Base:	St Eval
	Sgt Woodland	. . . . . .	Safe	T/o time:	07:40
	Sgt Shields	. . . . . .	Safe		

Took off for a Brest reconnaissance but suffered an engine failure and crashed through a tree into the side of a hill on St Columb Road after half a circuit. The Blenheim caught fire and Sgt Shields was pulled out by F/O Cotes-Preedy through the side of the aircraft after tearing away the fabric. F/O Cotes-Preedy was later found to have fractured his spine in the crash.

30th January 1941

248 Sqn	Blenheim IV	N6233	WR-N	Op:	Escort
	Sgt R J Houchin	518421	+	Base:	Dyce
	Sgt T W E Williams	911368	+	T/o time:	16:10
	Sgt J Kirkham	635832	+		

Took off to provide an escort to convoy EN64. Suffered an engine failure, stalled and dived into the ground at Newmarcham (sic), Lincolnshire, on the return. Sgt Houchin rests in Reading Cemetery, Sgt Williams in Trinity Cemetery, Broadhill Extension, Aberdeen and Sgt Kirkham in Burngreave Cemetery, Sheffield.

The point of impact, reported in official records as Newmarcham, is almost certainly incorrect, as no such named place can be located. Newham (Lincs) has been suggested as a possible alternative.

31st January 1941

1 PRU	Hornet Moth	BK837		Duty:	Training
	W/C G W Tuttle DFC	. . . . .	Safe	Base:	Benson
				T/o time:	11:00

Engine cut on take-off then the Moth stalled and crashed from 50 feet.

This Hornet Moth was another former civilian aircraft (ex-G-ADMP) impressed into RAF service as a wartime measure, and would have been used mainly for communications duties.

W/C Tuttle had assumed command of the Photographic Development Unit on 21st June 1940, just three days after the Unit was taken over by Coastal Command (16 Group). The PDU was redesignated as the Photographic Reconnaissance Unit (PRU) on 8th July 1940.

1st February 1941

217 Sqn	Beaufort I	L9835	MW-W	Op:	Brest
	F/Lt R A Oakley RAAF	215	+	Base:	St Eval
	Sgt A G Hayman	580515	+	T/o time:	14:55
	Sgt A J Croker	527080	+		
	Sgt K G Rowley	755531	+		

Took off to attack the *Admiral Hipper* in Brest Harbour. Reported an engine failure and D/F bearing which put the aircraft close to the coast of France, well off track. The Beaufort would have been fighting a 35 - 45 knot head-wind on one engine on the return leg. F/Lt Oakley, of Ashburton, Victoria, rests in Pihen-les-Guines Communal Cemetery, Pas de Calais while the others are commemorated on the Runnymede Memorial.

217 Sqn	Beaufort I	L9866	MW-J	Op:	Brest
	Sgt J B Rutherford	519262	+	Base:	St Eval
	Sgt T P O'Byrne	743014	+	T/o time:	14:57
	Sgt W S Browning	755933	+		
	Sgt J A D Wood	623845	+		

Took off to attack the *Admiral Hipper* in Brest Harbour. Possibly shot down at 17:00 hrs into the sea NW of Morlaix by Uffz Bochmann of II/JG 77. All are commemorated on the Runnymede Memorial.

2nd February 1941

59 Sqn	Blenheim IV	V5531	TR-N	Op:	St Omer
	P/O Trim	. . . . .	Safe	Base:	Manston
	P/O Blake	. . . . .	Safe	T/o time:	12:40
	Sgt Jones	. . . . . .	Safe		

Took off to attack St Omer Aerodrome. There was no cloud cover over France and on turning for home the Blenheim was attacked by three Me109s, one of which was claimed as shot down in flames. The remaining E/A continued the attack until Ramsgate when they retired, leaving the Blenheim badly damaged. On landing at Manston the aircraft caught fire.

4th February 1941

53 Sqn	Blenheim IV	Z5765	PZ-A	Op:	Brest
	P/O G F Marriott	84311	DoI	Base:	Thorney Island
	Sgt E L S Strudwick	743059	Injured	T/o time:	06:15
	Sgt G T Hadnam	755274	DoI		

Lost height during take-off and crashed. Both Sgt Strudwick and Sgt Hadnam died from their injuries and are buried in Durrington Cemetery, Worthing, and Hertford Road Cemetery, Enfield, Middlesex. The Blenheim caught fire during salvage operations and was destroyed.

53 Sqn	Blenheim IV	T2283	PZ-F	Op:	Brest
	P/O C P Morris	43108	+	Base:	Thorney Island
	Sgt G W F Ashwin	976524	+	T/o time:	06:21
	Sgt I R W Clark	977806	+		

Shot down by Uffz. R Schmidt of 5./JG 77 at 09:10 hrs into the sea NW of Morlaix during a raid on the cruiser *Admiral Hipper* in Brest. All are commemorated on the Runnymede Memorial.

53 Sqn	Blenheim IV	T1992	PZ-X	Op:	Cherbourg
	F/Lt B B St G Daly	25070	+	Base:	Thorney Island
	Sgt J L Jones	967660	+	T/o time:	18:42
	Sgt R H Trafford	552655	+		

Damaged by an Me109 near Brest and ditched off Ramsgate, Kent. Sgt Trafford, of Salt Spring Is, British Columbia, and the other crewmen, are commemorated on the Runnymede Memorial.

59 Sqn	Blenheim IV	.....?	TR-D	Op:	Cherbourg
	P/O D Custerson	83273	+	Base:	Thorney Island
	Sgt W Harker	749391	+	Time:	21:00
	Sgt Edgar	......	Safe		

Crashed on take-off and hit another aircraft on the edge of the aerodrome. P/O Custerson rests in St Andrew Churchyard, Cherry Hinton, Cambridgeshire and u/t observer Sgt Harker in Holy Trinity Churchyard, Seaton Carew, County Durham.

206 Sqn	Hudson I	T9331	VX-S	Op:	Emro Patrol
	P/O A R Blackett	42459	+	Base:	Bircham Newton
	P/O H W Noble	42425	+	T/o time:	04:20
	Sgt J T Kennett	751061	+		
	Sgt A Soppitt	654600	+		

Failed to return from a patrol between Emden and Rotterdam. All the crew are commemorated on the Runnymede Memorial.

502 Sqn	Whitley V	P5096	YG-	Op:	?
	F/Lt M G L Foster	.....	Safe	Base:	Wick
				T/o time:	07:15

Hit an air raid shelter on take-off and force-landed near Wick some 45 minutes later when an engine overheated due to coolant system damage incurred by a broken wheel.

7th February 1941

502 Sqn	Whitley V	T4223	YG-G	Op:	Escort Duty
	F/Lt G Henderson	90045	Injured	Base:	Aldergrove
	F/O R W G Holdsworth	74352	Injured	T/o time:	09:17
	Sgt R G Eaton	946965	Safe		
	Sgt R C Graham	653961	Injured		
	Sgt G Banner	810080	Injured		

Engine cut on an escort to convoy SC20 and the Whitley was ditched in position 5530N 1055W, 120 miles W of Malin Head, Ireland. The crew were picked up by HMS *Harvester*.

8th February 1941

269 Sqn	Hudson I	P5128	UA-H	Op:	Bert Patrol
	P/O E A Tingey	42450	+	Base:	Wick
	Sgt R W Baker	754446	+	T/o time:	10:07
	Sgt H D McNabb	628246	+		
	Sgt E Cottingham	935544	+		

Information was received through the Air Ministry that according to a German broadcast, this aircraft was shot down by Ltn Weyergand of 1.(Z)/JG 77 and that it crashed into the North Sea 35 km (c 21¾ miles) SW of Stavanger at 13:48 hrs, also that none of the crew could be rescued. All are commemorated on the Runnymede Memorial.

9th February 1941

42 Sqn	Beaufort I	L9832	AW-T	Op:	Special Striking Force
	S/Ldr A W D Millar	.....	Safe	Base:	Wick
	Sgt S Crocombe	744957	+	T/o time:	12:25
	Sgt W A Griffin	620429	+		
	Sgt C Bourne	971466	+		

Port engine stopped due to fuel starvation. Height could not be maintained and the aircraft was ditched about 20 miles from base. The dinghy blew away when released. S/Ldr Millar dived in and reached it but was unable to paddle back to the aircraft and although he shouted to the crew they failed to leave the aircraft. At 15:50 hrs the coastguard reported a British aeroplane in difficulties, and a few minutes later the news came that the aeroplane was down in the sea. Her position was given at 16 miles E of Wick. A south-west breeze was blowing, with a choppy sea. The motor lifeboat *City of Edinburgh* was launched at 16:10 hrs, and found an exhausted airman floating on a rubber dinghy. The lifeboat took him on board and then made a thorough search for the other members of the crew, but could not find them. She arrived back on station at 20:00 hrs. Those who died are commemorated on the Runnymede Memorial.

48 Sqn

Blenheim IV		Z5956	WR-V	Op:	Reconnaissance
S/Ldr J J E Coats	37157	+		Base:	Dyce
P/O D A P Warren	78259	+		T/o time:	07:12
Sgt A Douglas	974493	+			

Took off to carry out an operation to Kristiansand with the object to locate and report enemy warships, but crashed near Mandal, Norway. S/Ldr Coates and his crew rest locally in Mandal Churchyard, Norway.

10th February 1941

17 Sqn

Beaufort I		W6490	MW-S	Op:	Strike
F/O Livingstone	. . . . .	Safe		Base:	St Eval
Sgt Davis	. . . . . .	Safe		T/o time:	19:37
Sgt Beesley	. . . . . .	Safe			
Sgt Thompson	. . . . . .	Safe			

Took off in company to attack the power station at Cherbourg. On landing after the operation the port wheel appeared to stick slewing the aircraft to port. The starboard wheel went off the runway into a wet patch and collapsed causing a ground loop. All the crew escaped uninjured.

54 Sqn

Blenheim IV		N3528	QY-	Op:	Trondheim
F/O K I MacKenzie	42140	+		Base:	Sumburgh
Sgt J W B Craig	751594	+		T/o time:	?
AC2 H J Twinn	650673	+			

Failed to return. F/O MacKenzie and his crew are buried in Stavne Cemetery, Trondheim.

02 Sqn

Whitley V		T4320	YG-L	Op:	Convoy Escort
S/Ldr M J C Stanley	90035	Safe		Base:	Aldergrove
Sgt A W Wood	740518	Safe		T/o time:	06:30
Sgt J Matthews	625737	Safe			
Sgt Jones	. . . . . .	Safe			
Sgt P M Hollins	755300	Safe			

Took off to escort convoy WS6 but engine cut, lost height and belly-landed at 08:20 hrs, half a mile S of Ballintrae House, Port Ballintrae.

11th February 1941

2 Sqn

Beaufort I		N1109	OA-I	Op:	Gardening
F/O R C Greenlees	91106	+		Base:	North Coates
Sgt J A Jepson RCAF	R/53752	+		T/o time:	18:44
Sgt W Haywood	630520	+			
Sgt F W Smith	759075	+			

Took off and set course for the Borkum area. On return the Beaufort made landfall at Harwich and was plotted by Fighter Command as flying northwards. They were given D/F bearings and were last heard on W/T at 21:56 hrs when it was thought that F/O Greenlees was near the Wash but they were shot down at 22.00 hrs by Naval Flak (West Battery) and crashed into sea off Vlissingen. Sgt Jepson, an American, and the other crewmen are commemorated on the Runnymede Memorial.

06 Sqn

Hudson I		T9350	VX-J	Op:	Emro Patrol
P/O M A G Mason	42417	+		Base:	Bircham Newton
P/O J R Waterman	83731	+		T/o time:	21:03
Sgt J Wallace	638965	+			
Sgt A J Arnott	639142	+			

Ran out of fuel at night on the return leg and was abandoned in fog off the coast of Caithness at 01:13 hrs. P/O Mason, from Wellington, New Zealand, and his crew are all commemorated on the Runnymede Memorial.

06 Sqn

Hudson I		T9346	VX-K	Op:	Emro Patrol
Sgt R B Morris	741251	+		Base:	Bircham Newton
Sgt R Titchener	741126	+		T/o time:	21:20
Sgt T Beckett	751328	+			
Sgt L E Sawyer	620630	+			

Ran out of fuel at night and abandoned in fog 2 miles off Sarclet Head, Caithness. At 05:45 hrs information was received that a British aeroplane, some 20 miles due E, was making for Wick.

A few minutes later it was reported that she was down in the sea 2 miles SE of Sarclet Head. A fresh SE breeze was blowing, with a short swell. The motor lifeboat *City of Edinburgh* was launched at 06:20 hrs and searched without success until, about 11:00 hrs, she found the body of Sgt Titchener floating close to the cliffs at Whaligoe. The lifeboat returned with the body at 13:00 hrs. Sgt Titchener rests in All Hallows Churchyard, Bispham, nr Blackpool, while the other crewmen are commemorated on the Runnymede Memorial.

206 Sqn	Hudson I		T9289	VX-A	Op:	Emro Patrol
	Sgt	W A Bracher	745338	+	Base:	Bircham Newton
	Sgt	J Phillips	742921	+	T/o time:	21:20
	Sgt	J H Reed	627136	+		
	Sgt	B L Alpe	621140	+		

Ran out of fuel on the return leg and was abandoned over the sea at 01:13 hrs. Sgt Bracher rests in Canford Cemetery, Bristol, while the rest of his crew are commemorated on the Runnymede Memorial.

12th February 1941

217 Sqn	Beaufort I		N1173	MW-E	Op:	Rover Patrol
	F/Lt	A V Hunter	39318	PoW	Base:	St Eval
	Sgt	P H Clarke	745759	PoW	T/o time:	11:15
	Sgt	G D Holiday	627394	PoW		
	P/O	L B Barry	78668	PoW		
	F/O	J H Wybrant	79689	+		

Took off for a sweep of the Bay of Biscay. A D/F plot was obtained of an unknown aircraft about 50 miles W of Ushant. F/O Wybrant was a Pilot Instructor along as an observer from Group HQ and rests in Kerfautras Cemetery, Brest.

13th February 1941

233 Sqn	Hudson I		N7372	ZS-	Op:	Escort
	Sgt	R N R Wherrett	742504	Safe	Base:	Aldergrove
	Sgt	Johnston	......	Safe	T/o time:	06:31

Took off to escort the *Cymbula* and reached Inishtrahull where they encountered thick fog. The Hudson circled for 10 minutes then returned and overshot a landing at 08:45 hrs with the undercarriage folding on running into a soft patch of ground. The Hudson was deemed damaged beyond repair.

401 (Met) Flight	Gladiator II		N5620		Op:	Met Flight
	P/O	I R McDairmid	......	Safe	Base:	Mildenhall
					T/o time:	

Overshot in poor visibility, hit a tree and overturned at Beck Row, 09:10 hrs. DBR.

No 401 (Meteorological) Flight had been created on 4th February as a result of a redesignation of the RAF Meteorological Flight.

502 Sqn	Whitley V		T4276	YG-	Duty:	Transit Flight
	P/O	J S Dickson	90845	?	Base:	Wick
	Sgt	Buckley	......	Safe	T/o time:	?
	LAC	Douglas	......	Safe		
	LAC	Fraser	......	Safe		

Had an engine failure, lost height and crashed at 12:30 hrs in a forced landing on the Butt of Lewis, Hebrides.

14th February 1941

95 Sqn	Sunderland I		P9623	SE-E	Duty:	Ferry flight
	S/Ldr	Lombard	....	Interned	Base:	Mount Batten
	F/Lt	Evison	....	Interned	T/o time:	23:45
	F/O	Bowie	....	Interned		
	Sgt	Banfield	......	Interned		

Ran short of fuel and force-landed on a ferry flight to Gibraltar at Setubal and was interned in Portugal. The crew escaped with the help of the Royal Navy on 23rd March.

235 Sqn   **Blenheim IV**   **V5431**   **LA-T**   **Duty:** Training

P/O	Chamberlain	. . . . .	Injured	Base: Bircham Newton
P/O	E R Phillips	83293	+	T/o time: ?
Sgt	Burns	. . . . . .	Safe	

Flew into the ground during an overshoot at Langham and caught fire.
P/O Phillips rests in St Mary's Churchyard, Great Bircham, Norfolk.

235 Sqn   **Blenheim IV**   **Z5970**   **LA-L**   **Duty:** Training

Sgt	W Mason	745149	+	Base: Bircham Newton
Sgt	N M Stanger RNZAF	39943	+	T/o time: ?
Sgt	V C Pond	746722	+	

Flew into the ground and caught fire on return from a night Navex, 1 mile N of Great Croxton,
Norfolk at 21:50 hrs. Bad visibility and enemy activity were thought to have caused the accident.
Sgt Stanger, from Otago, New Zealand, rests in St Mark Churchyard, Bilton, Warwickshire;
Sgt Pond in Sutton Road Cemetery, Southend-on-Sea, Essex and Sgt Mason in York Cemetery.

15th February 1941

217 Sqn   **Beaufort I**   **L9807**   **MW-A**   **Op:** Brest

P/O	F A B Tams	43076	PoW	Base: St Eval
F/O	A H Stratford	76593	PoW	T/o time: 16:30
Sgt	C W D Cannon	550494	PoW	
Sgt	J F J Sheridan	905697	+	

Took off to attack the *Admiral Hipper* in Brest Harbour. Shot down by Me109s of JG77.
Sgt Sheridan rests in La Forest Churchyard, Finistère, France.

217 Sqn   **Beaufort I**   **L9794**   **MW-R**   **Op:** Brest

P/O	C G L Williams DFM	45542	+	Base: St Eval
Sgt	N V Pusey	580555	+	T/o time: 16:35
Sgt	H Cowling	526616	+	
Sgt	J Thompson	526413	+	

Took off to attack the *Admiral Hipper* in Brest Harbour. Shot down by Me109s of JG77.
All are commemorated on the Runnymede Memorial.

217 Sqn   **Beaufort I**   **W6493**   **MW-G**   **Op:** Brest

P/O	R W Gair	36171	+	Base: St Eval
Sgt	J R H Webster	958761	DoW	T/o time: 16:40
Sgt	A W R Beeden	552724	+	
Sgt	W N Abbott	903156	+	

Took off to attack the *Admiral Hipper* in Brest Harbour. Shot down by Me109s of JG77 and crashed
at Plougin, 14 km (c 8⁷⁄₁₀ miles) SW of Lannilis. Sgt Gair, from Wellington, New Zealand, and his
crew, including Sgt Webster who died from his wounds a few days later, rest in Lannilis
Communal Cemetery, Finistère, France.

16th February 1941

1 PRU   **Spitfire I(PR) Type C**   **P9561**   **LY-**   **Op:** Reconnaissance

P/O J D Chandler	79518	+	Base: ?
			T/o time: ?

Shot down by Ofw Hübner of II/JG 51 off Calais on an operation to Oostende.
P/O Chandler is commemorated on the Runnymede Memorial.

53 Sqn   **Blenheim IV**   **R3679**   **PZ-**   **Ground Loss**

Base: Bircham Newton
Time: 02:00 ?

Presumed destroyed in an air raid at 02:00 hrs.

17th February 1941

240 Sqn   **Stranraer I**   **K7293**   **BN-Z**   **Ground Loss**

Base: Stranraer
Time: ?

Sank in a gale at its moorings. Salvaged and sent to Scottish Aviation for repair but struck off
charge as being too badly damaged.

18th February 1941

612 Sqn	Whitley V		P5071	WL-	Duty:	?
	Sgt	Beere	......	Injured	Base:	Dyce
	Sgt	Milne	......	Injured	T/o time: ?	

Crashed on the approach to Dyce, Aberdeenshire, 10 minutes after take-off.
Both crewmen were taken to RN Kingseat with burns.

21st February 1941

236 Sqn	Blenheim IV		R2799	ND-Q	Op:	Patrol
	F/O	Lumsden	.....	Safe	Base:	St Eval
	Sgt	Snape	......	Injured	T/o time:	08:40
	Sgt	Tumbridge	......	Safe		

Crashed on take-off due to snow obscuring F/O Lumsden's vision. Stalled, struck the propellers
of one parked Blenheim, hit a hedge on the far side of the road and ended up in a field about 100
yards further on. The aircraft was completely wrecked, losing its starboard engine, starboard wing
and smashing in the nose. Sgt Snape was slightly injured and was taken to Truro Hospital.

22nd February 1941

209 Sqn	Lerwick I		L7263	WQ-L	Op:	Patrol
	W/C	J E M Bainbridge	05139	+	Base:	Stranraer
	P/O	R J Fyfe	44549	+	T/o time:	?
	F/O	R P Turner	74694	+		
	P/O	E F Cragg	78670	+		
	Sgt	F G Cross	568279	+		
	F/Sgt	M C Daniell	761087	+		
	Cpl	W C Davis	570228	+		
	F/Sgt	R L Dingle	754495	+		
	Sgt	T O Lewis	970474	+		
	LAC	A E McQuitty	911664	+		
	Sgt	J McI McDonald	621572	+		
	Sgt	A R Taylor	982555	+		
	Sgt	W E Tilley	516417	+		
	F/O	P T Anderson	84833	+		

Missing on patrol and possibly crashed in position 5340N 1240W. F/O Anderson was the station
Medical Officer and LAC McQuitty was from Dunedin, New Zealand. All are commemorated on
the Runnymede Memorial.

224 Sqn	Hudson I		T9315	QX-K	Op:	Escort
	P/O	J Wright	.....	Injured	Base:	Leuchars
	P/O	Holmes	.....	Injured	T/o time:	08:00
	Sgt	Purcell	......	Injured		
	Sgt	Brown	......	Injured		

Took off to provide an escort to the *Amsterdam*. Bounced on landing due to an error of judgement
at 10:05 hrs, suffered an engine failure on the attempted overshoot, dropped the port wing and
stalled into the ground at Leuchars, Fife.

235 Sqn	Blenheim IV		T1803	LA-D	Op:	Danish Sweep
	Sgt	D S Wallis	754744	+	Base:	Bircham Newton
	Sgt	R W Brookman RNZAF	40186	+	T/o time:	11:20
	Sgt	G C Pavitt	652166	+		

Took off in company with other squadron aircraft. Shot down about 20 miles from Borkum by
return fire from a He111 while on a sweep off Jutland, Denmark. All the crew including Sgt
Brookman, a New Zealander, from Auckland, are commemorated on the Runnymede Memorial.

612 Sqn	Whitley V		T4294	WL-	Duty:	Transit Flight
	P/O	A C Carter	.....	Safe	Base:	Dyce
	P/O	J B Hatchwell	.....	Injured	T/o time:	?

Took off for a flight to Wick. Flew into high ground in a snowstorm at Tannach Hill, Caithness.
The Whitley was destroyed by fire.

23rd February 1941

1 PRU	Spitfire I(PR) Type C	R6598	LY-	Op:	Reconnaissance
	F/Lt T M Lockyer	37193	PoW	Base:	Heston
				T/o time:	?

Engaged on an operation to Oostende. Possibly shot down by Ofw Staege of 2./LG 2.

59 Sqn	Blenheim IV	T2040	TR-X	Op:	Brest
	P/O W J Scafe	. . . . .	Injured	Base:	Manston
	P/O Bendry	. . . . .	Safe	T/o time:	17:07
	Sgt Taylor	. . . . . .	Safe		

Took off in company for an attack on the *Admiral Hipper* in Brest Harbour but failed to locate the target. On the return flight the wireless was unserviceable, the crew became lost and the Blenheim was abandoned at 21:25 hrs near Lamerton, Devon.

59 Sqn	Blenheim IV	V5394	TR-B	Op:	Brest
	P/O Wightman	. . . . .	Safe	Base:	Manston
	Sgt Crosher	. . . . . .	Safe	T/o time:	17:07
	Sgt Paterson	. . . . . .	Safe		

Took off for an attack on the *Admiral Hipper* in Brest Harbour. Unable to located the target due to cloud. Bombed flak positions but overshot the St Eval flare-path at 22:20 hrs on the return; swung and the u/c collapsed.

24th February 1941

236 Sqn	Blenheim IV	T1942	ND-J	Op:	Bust Patrol
	P/O Watters	. . . . .	Safe	Base:	St Eval
	Sgt Philip	. . . . . .	Safe	T/o time:	09:50
	Sgt Lawrence	. . . . . .	Safe		

Saw two enemy destroyers north of Cape Vierge. On the return an engine cut causing the Blenheim to overshoot, lose height and crash-land at 12:00 hrs. All the crew members suffered from bruises and shock.

321 Sqn	Anson I	N9535		Duty:	?
				Base:	Carew Cheriton

Ditched into the Bristol Channel. Date/Unit possibly suspect. T/o time: ?

500 Sqn	Anson I	R9698	MK-Y	Op:	Convoy Patrol
	P/O R Armstrong	. . . . .	Injured	Base:	Detling
	Sgt Gilman	. . . . . .	Injured	T/o time:	16:00
	Sgt C H Newton	812249	+		
	Sgt Smith	. . . . . .	Injured		

Took off to escort convoy Agent. Lost height on the approach to the flare-path on return and flew into the hillside at 20:00 hrs. Sgt Newton is buried in Palmerston Road Cemetery, Chatham, Kent.

25th February 1941

236 Sqn	Blenheim IV	V5450	ND-L	Op:	Bust
	P/O E A Alexander	88648	+	Base:	St Eval
	Sgt E K Lindsay	940172	+	T/o time:	14:55
	Sgt B M Mansfield	749519	+		

Believed shot down by Uffz. Esser of 4./JG 77 over the Channel at 17:13 hrs. All are commemorated on the Runnymede Memorial.

320 Sqn	Hudson I	T9364	NO-F	Op:	Convoy Escort
	Sgt VI J Brugman RNNAS	. . . . .	Injured	Base:	Carew Cheriton
	Ltz2 KMR M R Van Kooij RNNAS	. . . . .	+	Time:	07:14
	Res Sgt VI Sgt J Michels RNNAS	. . . . .	+		
	Kpl Telegr C J Rademaker RNNAS	. . . . .	+		
	Stoker 2e F Overdyk RNNAS	. . . . .	+		

Flew into a hangar on take-off. All those who died rest in the St Mary New Churchyard, Carew, Pembrokeshire. The aircraft had been individually named *Ypenburg*.

26th February 1941

240 Sqn	Stranraer I	K7299	BN-M	Duty:	?
	F/Lt V H Furlong	. . . . .		Base:	Stranraer
				T/o time:	?

Ran out of fuel due to head winds and ice forming on the ailerons and wing leading edge. Inaccurate D/F fixes were given leading to position uncertainty. At 20:15 hrs the Stranraer was ditched and drifted ashore 3½ hours later near Campbeltown, Argyll.

28th February 1941

254 Sqn	Blenheim IV	T1953	QY-	Duty:	?
	Sgt R S Hick	652673	+	Base:	Sumburgh
				T/o time:	?

Crashed and burned out on landing at Sumburgh. Sgt Hick rests in St Augustine Churchyard, Rumney, Monmouthshire.

3rd March 1941

224 Sqn	Hudson I	N7235	QX-A	Duty:	Training
	W/C R Neville-Clarke DFC	29063	+	Base:	Leuchars
	F/Lt E Ostlere	72064	+	T/o time:	12:00
	Sgt A C Davidson	966403	+		
	AC1 T E B Price	942179	+		
	AC1 Cordiner	552757	+		

Took off for a flight to Aldergrove but crashed near Loch Bradan, 2 miles W of Craigmalloch. W/C Neville-Clarke rests in St Peter Churchyard, Little Aston, Staffordshire; F/Lt Ostlere in Hayfield Cemetery, Kirkcaldy, Fife; Sgt Davidson in Carnmoney Cemetery, County Antrim; AC1 Price in St John's Westgate Cemetery, Newcastle-upon-Tyne and AC1 Cordiner in Dundee Eastern Necropolis.

254 Sqn	Blenheim IV	V5734	QY-	Duty:	?
	P/O T A Perry	. . . . .	Safe	Base:	Sumburgh
				T/o time:	?

Overshot during landing at Wick; swung and the u/c collapsed before the Blenheim caught fire at 15:10 hrs..

4th March 1941

248 Sqn	Blenheim IV	L9450	WR-H	Duty:	?
				Base:	?
	Struck off charge as burned out. No further details			Time:	?

254 Sqn	Blenheim IV	R3827	QY-O	Op:	?
	Sgt A W Tubbs	564445	+	Base:	Wick
	P/O R A Webb	83296	+	T/o time:	?
	Sgt Timoney	. . . . . .	Wounded		

Crashed on take-off. Sgt Tubbs rests in St Dunstan Churchyard, Monks Risborough, Buckinghamshire and P/O Webb is buried in St Nicholas Churchyard, North Stoneham, Hampshire.

5th March 1941

1 PRU	Spitfire I	L1055	LY-	Duty:	Training
	P/O E Kowalski PAF	. . . . .	Safe	Base:	Mount Farm
				Time:	10:35

Attempted to take-off in course pitch and failed to become airborne. Swung to avoid workmen.

224 Sqn	Hudson I	N7315	QX-Y	Duty:	Ferry Flight
	F/Lt R N Selley DFC	39689	+	Base:	Leuchars
	Sgt S L J Knight	740617	+	T/o time:	09:10
	Sgt W F Shaw	546061	+		
	AVM C D Breese CB AFC	51	+		

Took off for Sumburgh but suffered an engine failure, attempted to overshoot ¾ mile SW of Wick but spun into ground and caught fire. Sgt Knight rests in Ryecroft Cemetery, Walsall, Staffs and Sgt Shaw in Glasgow Crematorium. Air Vice-Marshal Breese was Air Officer Commanding 18 Group and his body was consigned to the deep with full Military and Naval Honours. F/Lt Selley rests in Warriston Crematorium, Edinburgh.

502 Sqn	Whitley V	P5010	YG-	Duty:	?
	P/O M Paterson	. . . . .	Safe	Base:	Limavady
	Sgt A W Morrisse	740776	Safe	T/o time:	?
	Sgt E D T Norman	581523	Safe		
	Sgt S A Smith	755334	Safe		
	Sgt R C Sawyer	943722	Safe		

Hit an obstruction on the runway during take-off and crash-landed on the foreshore of Lough Foyle at 08:25 hrs.

Chapter 9

6th March 1941 to 14th June 1941

On 6th of March Winston Churchill issued a directive giving the Battle of the Atlantic full priority and ordered Bomber Command to concentrate on naval targets. Nos 114, 18, 21, 107 and 139 Squadrons of 2 Group were tasked with attacking shipping in the North Sea while the heavy bombers attacked ports, thereby releasing Coastal Command units for operations in the North and South West.

The released Coastal Command Blenheim Squadrons re-armed with Beaufighters and a new dedicated strike force was created comprising four long-range Beaufighter squadrons, four Blenheim bomber squadrons and four Beaufort torpedo-bomber units. The operational debut of this strike force was delayed when 252 and 272 Squadrons were ordered to Middle East Command in late April and May.

Operation 'Channel Stop' started on 24th of April and utilised 101 Squadron flying from Manston. 'Channel Stop' was designed to close the Dover Straits to enemy shipping but the high losses incurred by 2 Group led to a temporary halt of the operation on the 9th of May.

As the initial moves in the German Offensive, the surface raiders *Scharnhorst* and *Gneisenau* slipped into the Atlantic and sank 22 ships totalling 115,600 tons, before using bad weather to enter Brest, and all without being seriously attacked. The appearance of these ships in a French port enabled Bomber Command to join the battle with an attack on the night of 30th/31st March using a force of 109 aircraft. Both the *Scharnhorst* and *Gneisenau* were to receive frequent attention from Bomber Command over the next four months.

In April, losses due to submarines rose to 43 vessels totalling 249,000 tons, despite surface forces having sunk five U-boats in March.

On 5th April *Gneisenau* was unexpectedly moved from dry dock to the inner harbour, thereby giving Coastal Command the chance of launching a torpedo attack by 22 Sqn from St Eval. Six aircraft were detailed three carrying mines to blow holes in torpedo nets which were expected to surround the ship and three with torpedos. The first to arrive was the torpedo Beaufort of F/O Campbell who circled in poor weather to await the rest of the force then, on finding no-one else in the mist, launched a one aircraft assault. The official citation of F/O Campbell's attack leading to the award of the Victoria Cross is given in the losses section of this chapter. The Beaufort was guided to a perfect torpedo drop position and a direct hit scored on the *Gneisenau* blew a 40 foot hole in the starboard side. F/O Campbell did not escape the hail of anti-aircraft fire surrounding the ship and the Beaufort crashed into the harbour with the loss of the full crew.

The *Gneisenau* returned to the dry dock for repair and the newly-formed 19 Group was tasked with keeping the *Scharnhorst* in Brest by continuous 'Stopper' Patrols. Meanwhile the *Bismarck* was ready for sea and on 20th May reports reached the Admiralty of the *Bismarck* and *Prinz Eugen* transiting the Kattegat to Bergen. Attacks on the ships at their moorings in Bergen were launched by Coastal Command Whitleys and Hudsons the next night. The strike force arrived to find the moorings empty: both ships had set sail a few hours before.

All available aircraft were committed to the hunt for the *Bismarck*. At midnight on the 24/25th May, after the *Bismarck* had sunk HMS *Hood*, FAA Swordfish attacked with torpedos, scoring a hit amidships and breaching some fuel tanks but the damaged vessel managed to elude the shadowing force. An extensive air search was ordered but nothing was found until ACM Bowhill, C-in-C Coastal Command, tasked two Catalina aircraft to fly much further south than the area suggested by the Admiralty. At 10:30 hrs on the 26th May the *Bismarck* was located by P/O Briggs' 209 Squadron crew, and the Royal Navy once again regained contact. A further Swordfish strike wrecked the *Bismarck*'s steering gear and she was finally sunk by torpedos from HMS *Dorsetshire*. The *Prinz Eugen* evaded all the search aircraft and reached Brest on the 1st of June, undamaged.

Allied shipping suffered total losses of 58 ships, 325,500 tons in May but almost 50% of these losses were due to six U-boats operating off Freetown in West Africa. A beefing up of Coastal Command operations in this area took place with 95 Sqn being supplemented with Hudsons of 200 Squadron in June 1941, even though all aircraft were badly needed for duties in the northern Atlantic.

Aircraft for convoy escort duties were reduced to a minimum and in May 1941 a concentrated effort was made to attack submarines in transit in the Iceland/Faeroes gap and Bay of Biscay area. It was thought that this method of attack would give a greater number of U-boat kills than those achieved by the convoy escort patrols.

The pressure on Coastal Command continued with reports on the 11th June of the *Lützow* and four destroyers making a transit through the Kattegat from the Baltic to the Atlantic. With the failure of the Whitley/Hudson strike on the *Bismarck* still fresh on his mind, ACM Bowhill committed an attack by two Beaufort squadrons without waiting for a position or course for the enemy ships. No 22 Squadron was sent to a position off Stavanger where they would head south and 42 Squadron was ordered to make for Lister then to head north. The operation was well underway when a Blenheim of 114 Squadron provided an accurate sighting report of the enemy force.

One of the 42 Squadron's Beauforts lost formation, tried to make Lister alone and after a fruitless search turned to make for base. Just after turning it flew over the *Lützow*'s wake and immediately launched a solo torpedo attack hitting the vessel amidships. Sgt Loviett's attack report brought all the remaining Beauforts to the scene but the smoke screen of the destroyer escort prevented any further attacks. The *Lützow* returned to Kiel and was dry-docked for six months, thereby preventing her taking any further part in the Battle of the Atlantic.

Coastal Command turned its attention to closing the Atlantic gap with the formation of 120 Squadron at Nutts Corner on the 2nd June 1941. The squadron would work up over the next few months with Consolidated Liberators. With an operational range of some 2,400 miles (nearly twice that of the Sunderland), and with its stable-mate the Catalina able to range for around 4,000 miles, Coastal Command had at last obtained the 'very long-range' aircraft capable of plugging 'the gap'. The introduction of these new types happened to coincide with the Germans deploying the new Mk.IX ocean-going U-boat into the Atlantic. Also under development by Coastal Command was a solution to the problems of attacking submarines at night involving a trainable searchlight attached to the aircraft. The use of the Leigh Light would severely hamper submarines that hitherto had used the cover of darkness to recharge batteries and to attack convoys on the surface.

7th March 1941

236 Sqn	Blenheim IV	T1812	ND-G	Op:	Patrol
	P/O Robb	. . . . .	Safe	Base:	St Eval
	Sgt Yates	. . . . . .	Safe	T/o time:	15:05
	Sgt Stewart	. . . . . .	Safe		

Took off for a patrol of the Tuskar - Smalls area. Suffered an engine failure in heavy ground mist and crashed in a forced landing 3 miles west of Truro, Cornwall. The crew were all slightly wounded in the crash at 19:40 hrs.

608 Sqn	Anson I	R9817	UL-Y	Duty:	Transit Flight
	Sgt R M Cutting	590946	+	Base:	Wick
	Sgt Frost	. . . . . .	Safe	T/o time:	07:50
	Sgt T A Edwards	970695	+		
	Sgt A C White	970692	+		

Left for a transit flight to Dyce but ditched at 08:40 hrs. At about 09:00, information was received that an aeroplane had crashed in the sea off Whinnyfold, and the coastguard sent out a motor boat from Cruden Bay. She found nothing, but a destroyer picked up one airman 3 miles off Collieston, Aberdeen. The Peterhead motor lifeboat also searched but without success.
Those who died are commemorated on the Runnymede Memorial.

8th March 1941

235 Sqn	Blenheim IV	V5896	LA-	Duty:	Transit Flight
	F/O Mackay	. . . . .		Base:	Bircham Newton
				T/o time:	?

Set off for a flight to St Eval but suffered an engine failure on take-off and belly-landed near the aerodrome.

269 Sqn	Hudson I	T9334	UA-Y	Op:	Escort I.S.
	Sgt N Child	539059	Safe	Base:	Wick
	Sgt J J H Deacon	745339	+	T/o time:	07:59
	Sgt W Dodds	974296	Safe		
	Sgt W R Catling	901844	+		

Experienced mechanical trouble and the crew were forced to make a parachute descent after abandoning the aircraft in position 6006N 0919W at 11:27 hrs. Sgt Child and Sgt Dodds were rescued by patrol vessel *Northern Chief*; Sgt Catling was picked up but found to have drowned and along with Sgt Deacon is commemorated on the Runnymede Memorial.

320 Sqn	**Hudson I**	T9356	NO-D	**Op:**	**Convoy Escort**
	F/O H C Prager RNNAS	. . . . .	Safe	Base:	Carew Cheriton
	P/O Oversynder RNNAS	. . . . .	Injured	T/o time:	17:55
	Cpl Tuurveld RNNAS	. . . . . .	Injured		
	A/B Mastbergen RNNAS	. . . . . .	Injured		
	A/B Longman RNNAS	. . . . . .	Injured		

Took off to escort convoy SL65BM but the undercarriage collapsed during the night landing at Carew Cheriton. The Hudson caught fire and was destroyed.

10th March 1941

272 Sqn	**Blenheim IV**	Z5733	XK-E	**Op:**	**Convoy Escort**
	Sgt P G V Chanler	745661	+	Base:	Aldergrove
	Sgt H K Pass	979685	+	T/o time:	13:35
	Sgt W A Newton	747993	+		

Took off tasked with a convoy escort. The weather became very bad and the flight was seen by another aircraft making a search but were soon out of visual range. They were plotted as on the northern coast of Ulster. Sgt Chanler, a Canadian from Toronto, and his crew are commemorated on the Runnymede Memorial. Sgt Chanler had just joined the squadron from OTU at Catfoss.

272 Sqn	**Blenheim IV**	Z5752	XK-L	**Op:**	**Convoy Escort**
	P/O A A L Van-Wayenberghe	81629	+	Base:	Aldergrove
	Sgt J R Thompson	755146	+	T/o time:	13:35
	Sgt D I McWatt	977821	+		

Took off tasked with a convoy escort. The weather became very bad and the flight was seen by another aircraft making a search but were soon out of visual range. They were plotted as on the northern coast of Ulster. P/O Van-Wayenberghe, a Belgian, and his crew are commemorated on the Runnymede Memorial.

11th March 1941

53 Sqn	**Blenheim IV**	P4850	PZ-V	**Op:**	**Brest**
	P/O D K Plumb	41734	+	Base:	St Eval
	Sgt R H S Maton	581235	+	T/o time:	05:13
	Sgt C MacL Calder	628106	+		

Took off as part of a ten aircraft strike and posted as missing from the attack on the *Admiral Hipper* in Brest Harbour. The crewmen are all commemorated on the Runnymede Memorial.

502 Sqn	**Whitley V**	P5045	YG-O	**Op:**	**Patrol**
	P/O E D Dear	82695	+	Base:	Aldergrove
	P/O W H Edwards	81033	+	T/o time:	16:58
	P/O D Midgley	. . . . .	Interned		
	Sgt S D S Goodlet	973901	+		
	Sgt R C Harkell	749495	Interned		

Crashed into Galway Bay, Eire, on the return from a patrol. Both P/O Dear and Sgt Goodlet are commemorated on the Runnymede Memorial while P/O Edwards rests in Shrewsbury General Cemetery, Shropshire.

502 Sqn	**Whitley V**	T4222	YG-H	**Op:**	**Convoy Escort**
	F/O J E Preston	33445	Safe	Base:	Limavady
	Sgt S E Esler	816082	Safe	T/o time:	17:05
	Sgt H H Green	915326	Safe		
	Sgt N Nava	810050	Safe		
	Sgt N M Williamson	973896	Safe		

Took off to escort convoy S466S. At 17:10 hrs F/O Preston set course for Tory Island but lost a propeller blade at 18:00 hrs and ditched at 18:30 hrs between Fanad Head and Malin Head. The crew took to the dinghy and were spotted by aircraft at 20:30 hrs and were finally rescued by SS *Glendalough* and landed at Ayr.

13th March 1941

22 Sqn	**Beaufort I**	L9798	OA-N	**Op:**	**Bombing**
	Sgt Pitman	. . . . . .	Safe	Base:	North Coates

Sgt	Morey	. . . . . .	Safe	T/o time: 19:56
Sgt	Brown	. . . . . .	Safe	
Sgt	G E Francis	. . . . . .	Injured	

Set off for a bombing operation and patrolled from the Frisian Islands to Rotersand. Sgt Pitman sighted four merchant vessels and attempted to attack but the bombs failed to drop. On the return journey attempts to jettison the bombs also failed. The Beaufort crashed at 01:57 hrs during a heavy landing at North Coates and fortunately the crew escaped safely.

14th March 1941

53 Sqn	Blenheim IV	V5399	PZ-	Op:	Brest
	P/O G R H Newton	43110	+	Base:	St Eval
	Sgt C Whitehill	581251	+	T/o time:	13:30
	Sgt J R Miller	642185	+		

Shot down by Oblt W Hoeckner of 6./JG 77 at 15:32 hrs while engaged on a daylight photo sortie to Brest. All rest in St Renan Churchyard, Finistere.

15th March 1941

53 Sqn	Blenheim IV	T2132	PZ-G	Op:	Brest
	P/O W H Leedam	43103	+	Base:	St Eval
	Sgt F P H Oatley	745081	+	T/o time:	01:49
	Sgt W E Williams DFM	645116	+		

Missing from an attack on the *Admiral Hipper* in Brest Harbour. P/O Leedam and his crew are commemorated on the Runnymede Memorial.

210 Sqn	Sunderland I	P9624	DA-	Op:	Convoy Escort
	F/O Butcher	. . . . .	Safe	Base:	Oban
	F/Sgt R Bette FAFL	30562	Safe	T/o time:	10:33
	F/Sgt Powell	. . . . . .	Safe		
	F/O F J Swain	82500	+		
	Sgt L Soden	620009	+		
	Sgt G G Prescott	572331	+		
	AC1 G Morris	639045	+		

Recalled at 15:00 hrs and at 21:37 hrs crashed on landing at Oban, Argyll. Sgt Soden rests in Chichester Cemetery, Sussex. The other crewmen are commemorated on the Runnymede Memorial.

16th March 1941

98 Sqn	Battle I	L5066		Duty:	Training
	Sgt H J Talbot	45946	Safe	Base:	Kaldadarnes
				T/o time:	?

Landed with u/c unlocked at Kaldadarnes, Iceland. Aircraft adjudged damaged beyond repair. See also 26th May 1941.

224 Sqn	Hudson I	N7369	QX-O	Op:	Escort
	P/O R P Drummond	. . . . .	Safe	Base:	Aldergrove
	P/O Pomeroy	. . . . .	Safe	T/o time:	10:43
	Sgt Rowlands	. . . . . .	Safe		
	Sgt McCusker	. . . . . .	Safe		

Took off to escort the *Sarpedon* but failed to meet the ship. At 11:22 hrs in position 5530N 0630W the Hudson encountered a thick mist and set course for base. Overshot the landing in bad visibility, ran through a hedge and the u/c collapsed.

17th March 1941

86 Sqn	Blenheim IV	V5464	BX-	Duty:	Training
	F/O B G Mace	33450	+	Base:	?
				T/o time:	?

Collided with Z5808 (below) and crashed.

86 Sqn	Blenheim IV	Z5808	BX-	Duty:	Training
	P/O J R Cresswell	89345	+	Base:	?
				T/o time:	?

Collided with V5464 (above) and caught fire.

The composition of crews of Blenheims V5464 and Z5808 is not known but included the following individuals:

Sgt	J S Wrightson	936191	+	(Obs)
Sgt	W R Loxton	965481	+	(Obs)
Sgt	B C Gilmore	970949	+	(WOp)
Sgt	F J Berry	751784	+	(WOp/Ag)

18th March 1941

59 Sqn	**Blenheim IV**		**V5533**	**TR-V**	**Op:**	**Pirate 2**
	P/O	Munro	. . . . .	Safe	Base:	Bircham Newton
	Sgt	Hunt	. . . . . .	Safe	T/o time:	17:30
	Sgt	Hales	. . . . . .	Safe		

The undercarriage collapsed at Marham following a heavy landing in mist on return from patrol. The landing caused a flare to catch fire which then ignited the bomb-load destroying the Blenheim.

19th March 1941

220 Sqn	**Hudson I**		**N7310**	**NR-L**	**Op:**	**Patrol**
	Sgt	R D Harris	741443	+	Base:	Wick
	Sgt	G E Towe	742440	+	T/o time:	05:55
	Sgt	H C Street	751912	+		
	Sgt	W Wood	751856	+		

Flew into hills in cloud at With Gill some 4½ miles NW of Tor Ness lighthouse, Hoy, Orkney. All rest in Lyness Royal Naval Cemetery, Orkney.

20th March 1941

22 Sqn	**Beaufort I**		**N1081**	**OA-U**	**Op:**	**Rover Patrol**
	F/O	F M Boycott	39963	+	Base:	North Coates
	P/O	S A Taylor	85695	+	T/o time:	11:40
	Sgt	A J Anthony	759275	+		
	Sgt	G W R Nesbitt	743084	+		

Took off along with other squadron aircraft and set course for Terschelling, Holland. At 13:50 hrs an unidentified SOS was heard by R/22. Although no trace of the Beaufort U/22 was found it is presumed that the aircraft was lost due to enemy action. All the crew are commemorated on the Runnymede Memorial.

206 Sqn	**Hudson IV**		**AE611**	**VX-**	**Op:**	**Convoy Escort**
	P/O	M K Warren	79560	+	Base:	Aldergrove
	P/O	R J Fuller	83722	+	T/o time:	05:15
	Sgt	C H Funnell	550862	+		
	Sgt	F L Holyoake	751825	+		

Climbed too steeply and dived into the ground after a night take-off. P/O Fuller is buried in Cambridge City Cemetery; Sgt Holyoake in Welford Road Cemetery, Leicester; Sgt Funnell in Norwich Cemetery, and P/O Warren in City of London Cemetery, Essex.

612 Sqn	**Whitley V**	**Z6471**	**WL-**	**Duty:**	**?**
				Base:	?
	Damaged beyond repair in an unknown accident.			Time:	?

21st March 1941

236 Sqn	**Blenheim IV**		**Z5755**	**ND-L**	**Op:**	**Escort**
	P/O	Barron	. . . . .	Safe	Base:	St Eval
	Sgt	Thornton	. . . . . .	Safe	T/o time:	17:40
	Sgt	H Sheard	638019	+		

Took off to escort convoy Scent. Abandoned at 20:45 hrs in bad weather on the return from patrol 1 mile SE of Boscastle, Cornwall. Sgt Sheard jumped first and is commemorated on the Runnymede Memorial.

240 Sqn	Catalina II	AM265	BN-A	Op:	Patrol
	F/O A E Whitworth	33555	+	Base:	Lough Erne
	F/O C P Davidson RCAF	J/3113	+	T/o time: ?	
	P/O H L Seward	84330	+		
	Sgt F R A Chalk	534048	+		
	Sgt H Dunbar	570770	+		
	Sgt R H Oldfield	940612	+		
	Sgt G H Slack	754693	+		
	Sgt H H Newbury	624214	+		

Crashed at Glengad Hill near Kinlough, Eire. P/O Seward rests in St Mary Churchyard, Appledram, Sussex and Sgt Newbury in the Sacred Heart R.C. Churchyard, Irvinestown. All the other crewmen, including F/O Davidson from Qualicum Beach, British Columbia, are buried in Irvinestown Church of Ireland Churchyard, County Fermanagh.

22nd March 1941

59 Sqn	Blenheim IV	T2433	TR-X	Op:	Emro Patrol
	P/O D W Date	86661	+	Base:	Bircham Newton
	P/O E P Moore	79752	+	T/o time: 03:15	
	Sgt B J O Watkins	633030	+		

Shot down at 07:42 hrs by Staffelkapitan Oblt P Stolte of 3./JG1 off Katwijk while on shipping patrol. All are commemorated on the Runnymede Memorial.

254 Sqn	Blenheim IV	L9406	QY-	Op:	?
	P/O J A Duff	86716	+	Base:	Sumburgh
	Sgt J K York	647004	+	T/o time: ?	

Lost off coast of Norway. Both rest in Rossebo Var Frelsers Cemetery, Haugesund, Norway.

612 Sqn	Whitley V	T4287	WL-	Duty:	Training
	Sgt R C Durbridge	754753	+	Base:	Dyce
	P/O W F Crockart	91231	+	T/o time: ?	
	Sgt B J Holden	650357	+		

Hit a house on the approach to Dyce and crashed onto the railway station at Stoneywood, Aberdeenshire. Sgt Holden, from Moate, Eire, rests in Kilcurley Catholic Cemetery, County Offaly, Eire; P/O Crockart locally in Dyce Old Churchyard and Sgt Durbridge in Stoke New Cemetery, Guildford, Surrey.

23rd March 1941

235 Sqn	Blenheim IV	L9404	LA-A	Op:	Pirate Patrol
	Sgt C R Evans	745506	+	Base:	Bircham Newton
	Sgt E H Harvey	970553	+	T/o time: 15:40	
	Sgt G S M MacLeod	553787	+		

Took off in company for an anti-shipping patrol. Sighted a convoy 14 km (c 8⁷⁄₁₀ miles) NW of the Maas lightship consisting of 3 coasters, 1 flak-ship and an E-boat and attacked with 40 lb GP bombs from 3,000 feet but without scoring any hits. The flight was immediately attacked by three Me109s and Sgt Evans who was lagging behind was shot down into the sea at 18:52 hrs by Uffz H Schubert of 3./JG1 . All the crew are commemorated on the Runnymede Memorial.

235 Sqn	Blenheim IV	Z6085	LA-D	Op:	Pirate Patrol
	P/O A W B Newman	87427	+	Base:	Bircham Newton
	Sgt H Willis	971577	+	T/o time: 15:40	
	Sgt V S Key	759103	+		

Took off in company for an anti-shipping patrol. Sighted a convoy 14 km (c 8⁷⁄₁₀ miles) NW of the Maas lightship consisting of 3 coasters, 1 flak-ship and an E-boat and attacked with 40 lb GP bombs from 3,000 feet but without scoring any hits. The flight was immediately attacked by three Me109s and Sgt Evans who was lagging behind was shot down into the sea. D/235 formated behind flight leader N/235 but was also attacked and went down with the port engine on fire off the Hoek van Holland. The Blenheim was claimed at 18:52 hrs by Oblt P Stolte of 3./JG1 operating from De Kooy. P/O Newman and his crew are commemorated on the Runnymede Memorial.

252 Sqn	Blenheim I	L8407	PN-	Duty:	Training
	F/O J W Blennerhassett	42044	Safe	Base:	Chivenor

Undershot during a night landing and hit a fence.   T/o time: ?

24th March 1941

209 Sqn	Lerwick I	L7252	WQ-	Duty:	Trials
	S/Ldr D K Banks	. . . . .	Safe	Base:	Pembroke Dock
				T/o time:	?

Took off for blind flying and Lorenz beam approach trials in almost zero visibility. Bounced on landing causing the starboard engine to shear from its mountings and slice into the aircraft fuselage. Sea water flooded into the hull and the Lerwick swung before finally sinking just off Pembroke Dock, Pembrokeshire. S/Ldr Banks was awarded a non-immediate AFC for this and subsequent Lerwick flights.

25th March 1941

22 Sqn	Beaufort I	W6486	OA-A	Op:	Rover Patrol
	S/Ldr F J Kelly	37188	+	Base:	North Coates
	P/O I MacLean RCAF	J/3115	+	T/o time:	10:40
	Sgt L A Arrighi	749492	+		
	Sgt E G Abraham	747928	+		

Shot down by flak off Terschelling, Holland. Sgt Arrighi rests in Vredenhof Cemetery on Schiermonnikoog while the remaining crewmen are commemorated on the Runnymede Memorial.

236 Sqn	Blenheim IV	T1806	ND-P	Duty:	Air Test
	P/O Chappell	. . . . .	Safe	Base:	Carew Cheriton
	Sgt J H R Dobbins	973306	+	T/o time:	06:00
	Sgt Lerway	. . . . . .	Safe		

Took off for a radio test in very bad weather. P/O Chappell was circling the aerodrome when he saw the runway suddenly clear and then stalled and crashed at Hays Brook Farm just short of the aerodrome while executing a tight turn. Sgt Dobbins rests in Cardiff Western Cemetery.

612 Sqn	Whitley V	T4290	WL-J	Duty:	Search
	P/O V D Emms	81337	+	Base:	Wick
	Sgt J Matthews	740784	+	T/o time:	20:15
	P/O A C Burton	89634	+		
	Sgt D Gunn	621074	+		
	Sgt D Henshaw	936323	+		
	Sgt L F Steele	817001	+		

Overshot the landing, lost height and ditched ¼ mile off Noss Head, Caithness at approximately 03:40 hrs on the 26th of March. No sign of the Whitley was found despite a search by the Wick lifeboat. All are commemorated on the Runnymede Memorial.

26th March 1941

59 Sqn	Blenheim IV	V6065	TR-A	Op:	Reconnaissance
	P/O L D Sandes DFC	42892	+	Base:	Thorney Island
	Sgt E K Robinson	751776	+	T/o time:	06:51
	Sgt G S Gates	751899	+		

Took off tasked with an operation to Brest. Flew into a hill near Little Bredy in fog on the return from the target at Winterbourne Abbas, Dorset, and caught fire. P/O Sandes is buried locally in Holy Trinity Churchyard, Warmwell, Dorset; Sgt Robinson in Blyth Cemetery, Northumberland and Sgt Gates was taken to Darlington North Cemetery, County Durham.

59 Sqn	Blenheim IV	V5648	TR-F	Op:	Dundee
	P/O P McMillan	88685	+	Base:	Thorney Island
	Sgt D C S Vane	910499	+	T/o time:	10:20
	Sgt W J Butler	751883	+		

Missing over the Channel. P/O McMillan, from Johannesburg, and Sgt Vane are both commemorated on the Runnymede Memorial while Sgt Butler rests in Dunkirk Town Cemetery.

27th March 1941

53 Sqn	Blenheim IV	T2332	PZ-O	Op:	Ushant
	P/O R N Philpott	87341	+	Base:	St Eval
	Sgt C A C Goad	745898	+	T/o time:	18:38
	Sgt F G Manning	755760	+		

Shot down by an Me1109 of JG77 during a shipping sweep off Ushant. P/O Phillpott, of Johannesburg, South Africa, rests in Perros-Guirec Communal Cemetery, Cotes-d'Armor, France; Sgt Goad in Guidel Communal Cemetery, Morbihan, France, while Sgt Manning is commemorated on the Runnymede Memorial.

53 Sqn	Blenheim IV	V5865	PZ-P	Op:	Ushant
	P/O J M Fothergill MC	43715	+	Base:	St Eval
	Sgt T P O'K T Coady	914505	+	T/o time:	18:38
	Sgt P R Parker	755738	+		

Shot down by an Me109 of JG77 off Ile de Batz, France. All are commemorated on the Runnymede Memorial.

30th March 1941

59 Sqn	Blenheim IV	V6064	TR-A	Op:	Tank
	P/O Griffith	. . . . .	Safe	Base:	Thorney Island
	Sgt Hunt	. . . . . .	Wounded	T/o time:	16:30
	Sgt Munt	. . . . . .	Wounded		

Took off to attack a tanker of about 6,000 tons and four smaller ships off Cap Griz Nes. Damaged by an Me109 off Calais, followed to the English coast. Crash-landed at Hawkinge, Kent.

252 Sqn	Blenheim IV	Z6254	PN-	Duty:	Training
	S/Lt V R Crane RN	–	Safe	Base:	Chivenor
				T/o time:	?

Engine would not idle after a night landing and the Blenheim ran off the runway and hit a truck.

31st March 1941

1 PRU	Spitfire I	X4029		Op:	Reconnaissance
	P/O J K Punshon	42724	+	Base:	?
				T/o time:	?

On an operation to Rotterdam, Holland. Possibly shot down NW of Calais at 11.35 hrs by Maj von Maltzahn of Stab/JG 53. P/O Punshon is commemorated on the Runnymede Memorial.

1st April 1941

235 Sqn	Blenheim IV	V5764	LA-	Duty:	Training
	P/O P H Blake	88677	+	Base:	Bircham Newton
	Sgt W Curry	945257	+	T/o time:	?

Stalled in a climbing turn and spun onto the beach near Hunstanton, Norfolk, and caught fire. P/O Blake is buried in St Mary's Churchyard, Great Bircham, Norfolk, and Sgt Curry in Hexham Cemetery, Northumberland.

235 Sqn	Blenheim IV	Z6022	LA-B	Op:	Roll
	P/O P A Annan	88675	Safe	Base:	Bircham Newton
	P/O O'Donnell	. . . . .	Safe	T/o time:	?
	Sgt Davies	. . . . . .	Safe		

Overturned during a forced landing on the beach while lost in bad weather at Snettisham, Norfolk, at 21:30 hrs. The crew spent the night in a beach hut.

2nd April 1941

220 Sqn	Hudson I	P5146	NR-X	Op:	Crossover Patrol
	P/O P H Milton	127851	PoW	Base:	Thornaby
	Sgt L H Houghton	964956	PoW	T/o time:	01:05
	Sgt R W Griffiths	938582	PoW		
	Sgt P L Burridge	901810	PoW		

Failed to return. The Hudson's last known position was 225° True from Longships.

4th April 1941

59 Sqn	**Blenheim IV**	**V5530**	**TR-H**	**Op:**	**Moon 1 Patrol**
	P/O R D Morton	84937	Safe	Base:	Thorney Island
	Sgt B R Flury	939502	Safe	T/o time:	22:30
	Sgt Searrott	......	Safe		

Took off for an anti-invasion patrol in the mid-channel. Tried to return to base but was diverted owing to fog. The W/T failed leaving the crew unable to get a homing beacon so the crew abandoned at 02:50 hrs leaving the Blenheim to crash at Combs, Suffolk. The aircraft had been shot at by British ground defences while over the Thames Estuary.

6th April 1941

22 Sqn	**Beaufort I**	**N1016**	**OA-X**	**Op:**	**Brest**
	F/O K Campbell vc	72446	+	Base:	St Eval
	Sgt J P Scott RCAF	R/63912	+	T/o time:	04:20
	Sgt W C Mulliss	746872	+		
	F/Sgt R W Hillman	643257	+		

Took off from St Eval as part of the torpedo wave of a two-force operation attacking the *Gneisanau* in Brest Harbour. F/O Campbell vc and his crew rest in Kerfautras Cemetery in Brest.

The London Gazette of 13th March 1942 gave the following account:
'Flying Officer Kenneth Campbell was the pilot of a Beaufort aircraft detailed to attack an enemy battle cruiser in Brest Harbour at first light on the morning of the 6th April, 1941. The ship was in a position protected by a stone mole bending round it, and rising ground behind on which stood batteries of guns.
  'Other batteries clustered thickly round the two arms of land which encircled the outer harbour, while three heavily armed anti-aircraft ships moored nearby guarded the cruiser. Even if an aircraft penetrated these formidable defences it would be almost impossible, after attacking at low level, to avoid crashing into the rising ground beyond. Knowing all this, Flying Officer Campbell ran the gauntlet of the defences and launched a torpedo at point-blank range, severely damaging the battle cruiser below water-line, so that she was obliged to return to the dock whence she had come only the day before. By pressing home the attack at close quarters in the face of withering fire, on a course fraught with extreme peril, this officer displayed valour of the highest order.'

22 Sqn	**Beaufort I**	**N1147**	**OA-V**	**Op:**	**Shipping Strike**
	F/O R Hicks	82956	PoW	Base:	St Eval
	Sgt R E Cree	746709	+	T/o time:	11:30
	Sgt J A Faill	635564	+		
	Sgt W C P Mitchell	900804	+		

Took off after the Brest attack and set course for the Gironde area. Sighted a convoy in position PSTK 4540 at 12:30 hrs and attacked a 3,000 ton ship. The flight was engaged by two Me110s and F/O Hicks was last seen off the Ile de Batz. See the accident to Beaufort L9856 on 16th October 1940 for another reference to Sgt Cree.

59 Sqn	**Blenheim IV**	**V5962**	**TR-J**	**Op:**	**Search**
	P/O M W Lishman	81934	+	Base:	Thorney Island
	P/O A W Martin	82720	+	T/o time:	10:30
	Sgt R Fitzpatrick	809113	+		

Missing off St Brieuc Bay, Brittany, France, after a message at 11:37 hrs stating 'Seven Escort Vessels double line astern steaming 240' which ended abruptly. Possibly shot down by Fw Bauer of II/JG 2 some 40 km (c 25 miles) N of Morlaix. The crew are commemorated on the Runnymede memorial.

107 Sqn	**Blenheim IV**	**V6023**	**OM-K**	**Op:**	**Convoy Escort**
	W/C W E Cameron	32072	+	Base:	Leuchars
	F/Sgt J H Spatchett	511016	+	T/o time:	12:00
	Sgt W J Howlett	550180	+		

Took off in company. While flying at 200 feet the Blenheim did a steep turn to starboard and crashed into the sea off Pittenweem, Fife. All are commemorated on the Runnymede Memorial.

272 Sqn	**Blenheim IV**	**L9252**	**XK-**	**Duty:**	**Transit Flight**
	Sgt G W Rouse	745335	Safe	Base:	Chivenor
				T/o time:	?

U/c collapsed on landing on soft ground and the Blenheim tipped up at Weston-Super-Mare, 15:30 hrs. The patch of soft ground had been marked after an aircraft of the training school had nosed over just before L9252 crashed.

7th April 1941

53 Sqn	Blenheim IV	T2398	PZ-E	Op:	Convoy Escort
	P/O E L E Nicholson	87340	+	Base:	St Eval
	P/O H A L Stone	87347	+	T/o time:	18:55
	Sgt P M Kinsey DFM	755740	+		

Failed to return from an escort to convoy Wheel.
The crew are commemorated on the Runnymede Memorial.

9th April 1941

53 Sqn	Blenheim IV	V5862	PZ-Y	Op:	Convoy Escort
	P/O I F Anderson	43082	+	Base:	St Eval
	Sgt H H Walker	754774	+	T/o time:	06:12
	Sgt E A J S Fabian	908487	+		

Took off with full nose trim and dived into ground out of control. P/O Anderson rests in
All Saints Churchyard, Wokingham, Berkshire; Sgt Fabian locally in St Eval Churchyard and
Sgt Walker is buried in St Mary the Less Churchyard, Chigwell, Essex.

86 Sqn	Blenheim IV	V6148	BX-G	Op:	Roll Patrol
	F/O M H Franklin	33423	+	Base:	Wattisham
	Sgt E S Jones	759235	+	T/o time:	15:33
	Sgt F C Sloane	755852	+		

Probably shot down by Uffz Schinabeck of I/JG 77 into the North Sea.
The crew are commemorated on the Runnymede Memorial.

254 Sqn	Blenheim IV	N3609	QY-H	Op:	?
	P/O J A Parry	84950	+	Base:	Sumburgh
	P/O C G Gibson	85023	+	T/o time:	?
	Sgt R K West	755094	+		

Damaged by Me110s of I(Z)/JG 77 off the coast of Norway and failed to return.
The crew are commemorated on the Runnymede Memorial.

10th April 1941

1 PRU	Spitfire I(PR) type C	P9307		Op:	Reconnaissance
	F/O L D Loasby	36242	+	Base:	St Eval
				T/o time:	07:50

Took off for an operation to Brest. Shot down north of Ile d'Ouessant at 09:22 hrs by
Ltn H Ulenberg of 2./JG26. F/O Loasby, from Wellington, New Zealand, is commemorated
on the Runnymede Memorial. This aircraft was painted in an overall green colour scheme.

1 PRU	Spitfire I (PR) type B	P9396		Op:	Reconnaissance
	P/O W K Manifould	81658	+	Base:	St Eval
				T/o time:	17:30

Took off tasked with a photo-operation to Brest. Shot down near Plouescat at 19:25 hrs by
Ltn H Ulenberg of 2./JG26. P/O Manifould is commemorated on the Runnymede Memorial.
This aircraft was believed to be painted in an overall green colour scheme.

221 Sqn	Wellington IC	R1049	DF-	Duty:	Training
	Sgt F H Butterworth	740122	+	Base:	Langham
	P/O P C Brown	85677	+	T/o time:	?
	Sgt E R Owen	975305	+		

Took off for night flying training at a satellite airfield. Intercepted (possibly by a Ju88) and both
aircraft opened fire simultaneously. The Wellington was set on fire in the air and crashed out
of control at Burnham Westgate, Norfolk. All three crew were killed. P/O Brown was buried
at Grantham Cemetery while Sgt Butterworth was taken to London for burial in Streatham
Cemetery. Sgt Owen rests in St Illtyd Churchyard, Pembrey, Carmarthenshire. Even though
the Squadron had been on operations since 23rd February, this was its first recorded loss since
reforming, the previous November. Tragically, a second loss was to follow only the next day.

11th April 1941

221 Sqn	Wellington VIII	W5653	DF-	Op:	Convoy Escort

F/O	A P Cattley	40888	+	Base:	Limavady
P/O	J L Montague	81359	+	T/o time:	05:55
Sgt	F K B Whalley	977309	+		
Sgt	B F Badman	976192	+		
Sgt	J W H Bateman	959540	+		
Sgt	F G Neil	976110	+		

On returning in bad weather, at 15:00 hrs, the Wellington flew into hill in cloud at Fort Lenah, Urris Hills, County Donegal, Eire. The crew rest in various cemeteries in England and Wales.

14th April 1941

1 PRU	**Blenheim IV**	**V5376**	**LY-**	**Op:**	**Reconnaissance**
	F/O J K Flynn	42462	+	Base:	Benson
	F/O W C Hall	78264	+	T/o time:	?
	F/Sgt R A Stephens	551633	+		

Damaged by flak over Vlissingen and then attacked by two Me109s. The Blenheim was finally shot down at 12:27 hrs by Oblt H Bennemann of Stab I/JG52 in an Me109 near Breskens. All rest in Vlissingen Northern Cemetery, Holland.

15th April 1941

233 Sqn	**Hudson III**	**T9432**	**ZS-B**	**Op:**	**Escort**
	Sgt D E Green	742597	+	Base:	Aldergrove
	Sgt F V N Lown	748548	+	T/o time:	13:40
	Sgt W A Rooks	759349	+		
	Sgt L A Aylott	747979	+		

Took off to escort convoy OB 309. Flew into Ben Lui, Perthshire, in bad visibility at night due to an error in navigation at 21:00 hrs. Sgt Lown rests in Hither Green Cemetery, Lewisham, London; Sgt Green in Milton Cemetery, Portsmouth; Sgt Rooks in Tiverton Cemetery, Devon; and Sgt Aylott in St John the Baptist Churchyard, Buckhurst Hill, Essex.

254 Sqn	**Blenheim IV**	**L8840**	**QY-P**	**Op:**	**Bert Patrol**
	F/Lt A E Hill	42125	+	Base:	Sumburgh
	P/O R H L Cressy	83294	+	T/o time:	05:52
	Sgt G J W Webb	759059	+		

Shot down by Lt Brandis of JG5 at 08:12 hrs and crashed at Storebo. All rest in Rossebo Var Frelsers Cemetery, Haugesund, Norway.

254 Sqn	**Blenheim IV**	**Z5953**	**QY-D**	**Op:**	**Stab Patrol**
	Sgt S C McAdam	740373	+	Base:	Sumburgh
	Sgt A N Forsyth	639587	+	T/o time:	06:16
	Sgt H Wood	945791	+		

Shot down by an Me110 and crashed into the North Sea 25 km (c 15½ miles) SW of Bergen. Sgt McAdam rests in Stavne Cemetery, Trondheim while the other members of the crew are commemorated on the Runnymede Memorial.

16th April 1941

53 Sqn	**Blenheim IV**	**V5518**	**PZ-H**	**Op:**	**Patrol**
	P/O R C L Reade	87055	+	Base:	St Eval
	Sgt J D O'Connell	913611	+	T/o time:	16:55
	Sgt R H W M Camm	1003424	Wounded		

An engine cut and the aircraft hit a wall during the forced landing at Longdowns, near Penryn, Cornwall, at 17:35 hrs. The Blenheim caught fire and was destroyed. P/O Reade is buried locally in St Eval Churchyard while Sgt O'Connell was taken to Lanherne Roman Catholic Cemetery, Cornwall.

59 Sqn	**Blenheim IV**	**V6174**	**TR-J**	**Op:**	**Rover Patrol**
	P/O Makgill	. . . . .	Safe	Base:	Thorney Island
	Sgt W H Johnson	900135	+	T/o time:	00:10
	Sgt Heenter	. . . . . .	Safe		

Lost height after a night take-off and crashed into sea. Sgt Johnson is buried locally in St Nicholas Churchyard, West Thorney.

252 Sqn	Beaufighter IC	T3238	PN-S	Op:	Patrol
P/O J G Lane	91008	+	Base:	Sumburgh
Sgt S Cross	506311	+	T/o time: 14:20

Took off for the squadron's first operational sortie. Shot down by Oblt Kriegl of III/ZG76 flying a Me110 off the coast of Norway in position 6045N 0445E at 17:11 hrs. The Beaufighter was seen to land on the sea and the crew to exit through the escape hatches before it sank. German news service reported that an Officer and a Sergeant had been picked up off the Norwegian coast. P/O Lane and Sgt Cross, from Victoria, Australia, are commemorated on the Runnymede Memorial.

17th April 1941

86 Sqn	Blenheim IV	V6145	BX-O	Duty:	Training
P/O J C Brice	. . . . .	Injured	Base:	Wattisham
			T/o time: ?

Flew into the ground at night during an attempted overshoot at Wattisham, 22:10 hrs, after turning onto the approach too soon. The aircraft was destroyed by fire.

107 Sqn	Blenheim IV	V5516	OM-	Op:	Escort
S/Ldr D R Briggs	. . . . .	Safe	Base:	Leuchars
P/O P E L Halls	. . . . .	Safe	T/o time: 18:45
Sgt V Johnson	936951	Safe

Took off for a convoy escort but on landing overshot the runway and crashed down the river bank at 21:15 hrs. Crew safe.

608 Sqn	Blenheim IV	V5526	UL-G	Op:	Convoy
P/O Reeve	. . . . .	Safe	Base:	Thornaby
P/O Bass	. . . . .	Safe	T/o time: ?
Sgt Bedford	. . . . . .	Safe

Suffered an engine failure on a convoy escort to Convoy FS65 and ditched 8 miles E of Tynemouth, Northumberland.

18th April 1941

53 Sqn	Blenheim IV	V6302	PZ-W	Op:	Patrol
P/O E W Thomas	86704	+	Base:	St Eval
Sgt D H Trotman	911534	+	T/o time: 06:00
Sgt S G Capel	906191	+

Shot down 70 km (c 43½ miles) W of Ile de Seine by Oblt Rysavy of II/JG26 at 09:48 hrs. Sgt Trotman rests in Kerfautras Cemetery, Brest, while both P/O Thomas and Sgt Capel are commemorated on the Runnymede Memorial.

107 Sqn	Blenheim IV	R3740	OM-L	Op:	Strike
Sgt J Hickingbotham	740338	+	Base:	Leuchars
Sgt R E Rowley	745434	+	T/o time: 09:40
Sgt D W Townsend	759109	+

Took off for a strike on an enemy convoy off Norway. Hit by fire from an armed escort vessel whilst making an attack and presumed to have crashed into the sea near the convoy. All the crew are commemorated on the Runnymede Memorial.

107 Sqn	Blenheim IV	R3873	OM-N	Op:	Strike
W/C A M A Birch	34101	+	Base:	Leuchars
P/O L B Hewitson	87418	+	T/o time: 10:35
Sgt H T W Montgomery	942725	+

Delayed due to engine problems for a strike on an enemy convoy off Norway. An SOS was heard from the aircraft on the return leg but it failed to return to base. It was W/C Birch's first operation with the squadron. All the crew are commemorated on the Runnymede Memorial.

114 Sqn	Blenheim IV	R3837	RT-T	Op:	Strike
W/C G R A Elsmie AFC	26133	+	Base:	Thornaby
Sgt C Jennings DFM	511537	+	T/o time: ?
Sgt M B Appleby	551671	+

Aircraft in Vic formation at 1,800 feet on course 035°. The flight dived to attack five vessels but was hit from astern by Me110s. Continued to bomb the vessels but both T/114 and A/114 were seen to fall into the sea in flames. All are commemorated on the Runnymede Memorial.

114 Sqn	Blenheim IV	V5494	RT-F	Op:	Strike
	F/Lt T H Myers	39893	+	Base:	Thornaby
	Sgt R E Williams	967873	+	T/o time:	?
	Sgt R R Mann	900288	+		

Aircraft in Vic formation at 1,800 feet on course 035°. The flight dived to attack five vessels but was hit from astern by Me110s. F/114 was seen to fall into the sea with the port engine on fire. Both F/Lt Myers from Ontario, Canada, and Sgt Williams are commemorated on the Runnymede Memorial, while Sgt Mann rests in Sola Churchyard, Norway.

114 Sqn	Blenheim IV	V5650	RT-A	Op:	Strike
	S/Ldr A S Q Robins	32179	+	Base:	Thornaby
	P/O M S Proudlock	42644	+	T/o time:	?
	Sgt S A du Plessis	905200	+		

Aircraft in Vic formation at 1,800 feet on course 035°. The flight dived to attack five vessels but was hit from astern by Me110s. Continued to bomb the vessels but both T/114 and A/114 were seen to fall into the sea in flames. All the crew, including Sgt du Plessis from Cape Province, South Africa, are commemorated on the Runnymede Memorial.

269 Sqn	Hudson III	T9462	UA-	Op:	Patrol
	F/O B F Fitzgibbon	. . . . .	Safe	Base:	Kaldadarnes
				T/o time:	?

Swung on landing in a cross-wind on the return from patrol and the u/c collapsed at Kaldadarnes, Iceland, 12:50 hrs.

500 Sqn	Blenheim IV	Z6050	MK-	Duty:	Training
	P/O J D Ready	42725	+	Base:	Detling
	P/O J A H Johnston	62025	+	T/o time:	?
	F/O H Jones	77344	+		
	Sgt A Shepherdson	971676	+		

Engine cut on take-off and the Blenheim then rolled, stalled and crashed onto the Maidstone to Sittingbourne road before catching fire. P/O Johnston rests in Kent County Crematorium; P/O Ready, a Canadian from Prince Edward Island, is buried in St Andrew Churchyard, Cherry Hinton, Cambridgeshire; Sgt Shepherdson in Hull Northern Cemetery; and F/O Jones in St Wilfred Churchyard, Honington, Lincolnshire.

19th April 1941

114 Sqn	Blenheim IV	R3806	RT-	Op:	?
	Sgt B Beardsley	939008	+	Base:	Thornaby
	Sgt L Fass	754442	+	T/o time:	
	Sgt L J Symes	975686	+		

Crashed on take-off and the bomb-load exploded. Sgt Fass rests in Linthorpe Cemetery, Middlesborough; Sgt Symes locally in Thornaby-on-Tees Cemetery; and Sgt Beardsley in West Norwood Crematorium, London.

210 Sqn	Catalina I	AH532	DA-	Op:	Convoy Escort
	F/Lt H F D Breese	33379	+	Base:	Lough Erne
	W/O C Bond	590299	+	T/o time:	21:15
	F/Sgt L S Dilnutt DFM	523495	+		
	F/Sgt A Tizzard	540427	+		
	Sgt A V McRae	755963	+		
	Sgt W H Blach	571761	+		
	Sgt H A Tann	901158	+		
	AC1 J F Woodward	652680	+		
	AC2 H V Norton	1063639	+		

Failed to return and believed to have crashed 250°, Stranraer. F/Sgt Tizzard rests in Knockanaman Graveyard, Innishmore, County Galway, Eire, and Sgt Tann in Cruit Island Catholic Cemetery, County Donegal, Eire. The remaining crewmen are commemorated on the Runnymede Memorial.

20th April 1941

224 Sqn	Hudson I	T9345	QX-G	Duty:	Transit Flight
	Sgt V D Hart	745683	+	Base:	Leuchars

Sgt	P G Akrill	754688	+		T/o time:	18:40
Sgt	J Eardley	936527	+			

Took off for Northern Ireland. Circled the aerodrome for 15 minutes after take-off at low height and speed. The engines are presumed to have lost power before the Hudson stalled in the circuit and crashed half a mile east of Leuchars, Fife. Sgt Akrill rests in Queensgate Cemetery, Beverley, Yorkshire; Sgt Hart in Gloucester Old Cemetery, and Sgt Eardley in St Mary Churchyard, Middleton, Yorkshire.

254 Sqn	Blenheim IV	T2135	QY-	Op:	Patrol
	Sgt D H Viney	968189	+	Base:	Sumburgh
	Sgt H A Morris	745283	+	T/o time:	?
	Sgt M D J Williams	911428	+		

Missing. The crew are commemorated on the Runnymede Memorial.

21st April 1941

206 Sqn	Hudson I	T9304	VX-C	Op:	Patrol A
	P/O R L Tanner	74692	+	Base:	St Eval
	Sgt G V Reeves	748689	+	T/o time:	20:41
	Sgt C T Handley	910738	+		
	Sgt F Allen	615122	+		

Lost sight of the airfield lights in haze and crashed at 03:35 hrs in an attempted forced landing at Providence Farm, Castleadinas, Pembrokeshire. P/O Tanner rests in St John's Crematorium, Woking, Surrey; Sgt Reeves in Nottingham Road Cemetery, Derby; Sgt Handley in Highgate Cemetery, London, and Sgt Allen in Southall Cemetery, Middlesex.

272 Sqn	Beaufighter IC	T3297	XK-	Duty:	Training
	Sgt R C Smith	565965	Safe	Base:	Chivenor
				T/o time:	16:10

Took off for local flying practice. Both engines cut due to fuel starvation on the approach and tried to glide with the u/c up but was belly-landed into the River Taw about 100 feet short of the boundary. The aircraft was damaged by water when overtaken by the tide. The Court of Inquiry stated that the accident was caused by the pilot failing to change tanks in time. It was salvaged and became a ground instruction airframe, serial 2599M.

22nd April 1941

82 Sqn	Blenheim IV	T2442	UX-F	Op:	Anti-Shipping
	Sgt Miller	. . . . . .	Safe	Base:	Lossiemouth
	Sgt Johnson	. . . . . .	Safe	T/o time:	10:23
	Sgt Newbon	. . . . . .	Safe		

Took off in company with 13 aircraft of the unit for a sweep off Norway.
Believed crashed near Embleton while trying to reach Acklington.

502 Sqn	Whitley V	T4278	YG-	Duty:	?
	F/O D B Hodgkinson	. . . .	Safe	Base:	?
				T/o time:	?

Hit a water wagon on landing in haze at Staverton, 17:55 hrs, ripping off the port main wheel.

23rd April 1941

204 Sqn	Sunderland I	N9023	KG-G	Op:	Convoy Escort
	F/Lt J D E Hughes DFC	. . . .	Injured	Base:	Reykjavik
	Sgt D W Helm	. . . . . .	Injured	T/o time:	20:15
	Cpl W Doddington	. . . . . .	Injured		
	Sgt W Cook	534591	DoI		
	AC1 A J T Copping	932621	DoI		
	Sgt H W Taylor	755791	+		

When on the return crashed into a mountain in fog at 05:45 hrs on the 24th, near Fragjadalsfjall, Iceland. The second pilot and Cpl Doddington walked to a local town for help. Sgt Taylor and both Sgt Cook and AC1 Copping who died of their injuries on the 26th rest in Fossvogur Cemetery, Reykjavik, Iceland. Ten airmen out of a crew of 13 were injured in the crash.

24th April 1941

22 Sqn	**Beaufort I**	**L9950**	**OA-L**	**Op:**	**Gardening**
	F/Sgt S I Sanders	741012	+	Base:	St Eval
	Sgt J H Smith RCAF	R/63906	+	T/o time:	?
	Sgt C L Ginnetta	746846	+		
	Sgt H Burton	751824	+		

Took off and set course for the Brest area but failed to return. F/Sgt Saunders and Sgt Smith, from Toronto, rest in cemeteries in Cornwall, while Sgt Ginnetta and Sgt Burton are buried in Leicestershire.

107 Sqn	**Blenheim IV**	**Z5795**	**OM-M**	**Op:**	**Stand Patrol**
	P/O C P H MacLaren	86640	+	Base:	Leuchars
	Sgt A J Hannah RNZAF	40738	+	T/o time:	18:00
	Sgt D S H King	751304	+		

Crashed near Kristiansand. P/O MacLaren rests in Kristiansand Civil Cemetery, Norway, while his crew are commemorated on the Runnymede Memorial.

248 Sqn	**Blenheim IV**	**L9452**	**WR-X**	**Op:**	**Interception Patrol**
	Sgt Graham	......	Safe	Base:	Dyce
	Sgt Bland	......	Safe	T/o time:	20:15
	Sgt Diamond	......	Safe		

Took off in company to intercept and engage enemy aircraft on route from Stavanger to attack a convoy. Undershot while landing at night in the rain and burned out.

612 Sqn	**Whitley V**	**T4321**	**WL-P**	**Duty:**	**Radar Beacon Trials**
	W/C J B Wallis	.....	Safe	Base:	Wick
	Crew		Safe	T/o time:	?

The Squadron's Commanding Officer took T4321 off into a roaring easterly wind to carry out trials of a new ASV from a range of approx 100 miles from Wick. An engine failed and the single-engine handling was so bad that a very skilful landing was necessary on North Rona, an extremely small island approx 40 miles NW of Cape Wrath. The crew vacated the aircraft and were rescued by RAF ASR launch from Kirkwall. This was the Wing Commander's second successful single-engine Whitley landing in the space of two months.

Due to the secret on-board equipment the aircraft was bodily salvaged, as photographs in the July 1988 *Flypast* Magazine revealed. The aircraft was subsequently repaired and went on to serve with 10 OTU, which is why this incident has not been included in the loss analysis tables.

25th April 1941

59 Sqn	**Blenheim IV**	**R3833**	**TR-D**	**Op:**	**Ijmuiden**
	P/O H Badland	86702	Safe	Base:	Thorney Island
	Sgt Cox	......	Injured	T/o time:	20:16
	Sgt R T Henderson	942398	Safe		

Took off for an attack on the E-boat base. Leader signalled that he was returning to base but the other two aircraft misunderstood and continued. Undershot landing at Langham, crashing through a hedge at 22:15 hrs.

612 Sqn	**Whitley V**	**T4296**	**WL-L**	**Duty:**	**?**
	F/O C C Watt	90546	+	Base:	Wick
	Sgt F J Milne	817033	+	T/o time:	?
	Sgt H E Smith	748709	+		
	Sgt L J G Lockwood	906101	+		
	Sgt W MacPherson	971383	+		
	Sgt A Maitland	817310	+		

While on the approach for a landing at Wick hit the Fever Hospital buildings and crashed at South Road, Wick. Sgt Maitland rests in Trinity Cemetery, Aberdeen; Sgt Milne in Springbank Cemetery, Aberdeen; Sgt Lockwood in St Paul Churchyard, Chippenham, Wiltshire; Sgt Smith in Chadwell Heath Cemetery, Dagenham, Essex; Sgt MacPherson in Kilsyth Cemetery, Stirlingshire, and F/O Watt in Longside New Churchyard, Aberdeenshire. Sadly, two of the hospital staff were also killed in the crash.

27th April 1941

22 Sqn	Beaufort I	X8917	OA-W	Op:	Gardening
	F/O I N W MacKie	70432	+	Base:	St Eval
	Sgt D W Arnold	751957	+	T/o time:	20:30
	Sgt J S Ramsay	968956	+		
	Sgt F Goodchild	624912	+		

Failed to return from a mining operation to the Brest area. All are commemorated on the Runnymede Memorial.

502 Sqn	Whitley V	Z6501	YG-S	Op:	Convoy Escort
	F/O J S Dickson	90845	Injured	Base:	Limavady
	P/O Carmichael	. . . . .	Injured	T/o time:	03:04
	Sgt O'Connell	. . . . . .	Injured		
	Sgt Dorney	. . . . . .	Injured		
	Sgt Redhead	. . . . . .	Injured		
	Sgt Wilson	. . . . . .	Injured		

Took off to escort convoy SC 28. At 03:15 hrs the Whitley flew over Eglington and its engines cut before crashing into a nearby hill at Glassa Kerin. A few hours later the second pilot telephoned operations to report that the aircraft had caught fire south of the Derry Road and that the bombs had exploded .

28th April 1941

10 (RAAF) Sqn	Sunderland I	T9075	RB-C	Op:	Crossover Patrol B
	F/O V A Hodgkinson	. . . . .	Safe	Base:	Pembroke Dock
	F/Sgt T A Egerton	1941	Safe	T/o time:	12:35
	F/O T G Joyce	513	+		
	Sgt J Bradbury RAF	938198	Safe		
	Cpl C O W Amos	3332	+		
	LAC N Raine	3683	+		
	Sgt C L Gehrig	3953	Safe		
	LAC R D Bell	207712	+		
	AC1 J C Francis	15774	+		
	Cpl F Hewitt	205727	+		
	Cpl L G Corcoran	4503	Safe		

The Sunderland had become lost, failed to receive bearings, then while circling a flame float to gauge wind direction, crashed in position 5249N 0501W at approx 03:30 hrs. The survivors all escaped from the wreckage and climbed onto the floating mainplane. At about 09:30 hrs on the 29th the airmen decided that the mainplane was sinking, boarded a dinghy that they had repaired and started paddling for land. The pigeon was freed but it was covered in oil and fell into the sea after flying for about 20 yards before being recovered and placed into the dinghy. At about 11:30 hrs the *Buziras* passed within 2 miles, sighted the dinghy and picked up the survivors 9 miles NNW of Bardsey Island. At about 18:00 on the 28th, the RAF. at Penrhos reported, through the coastguard, that an aeroplane was down in the sea 9 miles WNW of Bardsey Island. A moderate ENE wind was blowing, with a slight sea. The Porthdinllaen lifeboat was launched, aeroplanes went up, and by means of pre-arranged signals the coastguard called out the Bardsey Island motor boat. With a crew of five she searched throughout the night, but found nothing. F/O Joyce, LAC Bell and Cpl Hewitt are commemorated on the Runnymede Memorial while both AC1 Francis and Cpl Amos rest in St Mary Churchyard, Whicham, Cumbria, and LAC Raine in Pwllheli Borough Cemetery, Carnarvonshire.

59 Sqn	Blenheim IV	N3615	TR-E	Op:	Strike
	F/Lt A E R Fry DFC	70232	+	Base:	Thorney Island
	Sgt E Freeman	751931	+	T/o time:	10:18
	Sgt J F J Taylor	759097	+		

Took off for a sweep of the coast of Holland. Shot down at 12:20 hrs by flak-ship MFLA703 at 12:20 hrs off the Hoek van Holland. F/Lt Fry, from Somerset West, South Africa, and his crew are commemorated on the Runnymede Memorial.

59 Sqn	Blenheim IV	V5520	TR-F	Op:	Strike
	P/O S G Collier	82663	+	Base:	Thorney Island
	Sgt J Mingham	759032	+	T/o time:	10:18
	Sgt W Powell	809129	+		

Shot down by a flak-ship at 12:20 hrs during a convoy attack off the Hook of Holland. All rest in Hoek van Holland General Cemetery, Holland.

59 Sqn	**Blenheim IV**	**V5687**	**TR-H**	**Op:**	**Strike**
	P/O R D Morton	84937	PoW	**Base:**	Thorney Island
	Sgt B R Flury	939502	PoW	**T/o time:**	10:18
	Sgt J J Hulme	941305	+		

Shot down by a flak-ship at 12:20 hrs during a convoy attack off Hoek van Holland. Sgt Hulme was washed ashore on the 15th May 1941 near Bergen aan Zee and now rests in Bergen General Cemetery, Holland.

59 Sqn	**Blenheim IV**	**V6097**	**TR-A**	**Op:**	**Strike**
	P/O H Badland	86702	+	**Base:**	Thorney Island
	Sgt A H H Hazell	747835	+	**T/o time:**	10:18
	Sgt R T Henderson	942398	+		

Shot down by a flak-ship at 12:20 hrs during a convoy attack off Hoek van Holland. P/O Badland rests in Zeeweg General Cemetery, Rockanje; Sgt Henderson in Hoek van Holland General Cemetery, Holland; while Sgt Hazell is commemorated on the Runnymede Memorial.

114 Sqn	**Blenheim IV**	**V6022**	**RT-**	**Op:**	**Convoy Escort**
	P/O J G K Long	42374	+	**Base:**	Thornaby
	P/O N F Dawson	84729	+	**T/o time:**	?
	Sgt N F Taylor	755472	+		

Crashed on the return 2 miles from the flare-path. P/O Dawson rests in Writtle Road Cemetery, Chelmsford; Sgt Taylor in Cheltenham Cemetery, and P/O Long in Christ Church Churchyard, Downend, Gloucestershire.

269 Sqn	**Hudson III**	**T9456**	**UA-**	**Op:**	**?**
	Sgt S Myatt	758026	Safe	**Base:**	Kaldadarnes
				T/o time:	?

Undershot when landing , 14:00 hrs, at Kaldadarnes, Iceland and the u/c collapsed.
The Hudson was too badly damaged to continue in service and was reduced to spares.

29th April 1941

42 Sqn	**Beaufort I**	**W6527**	**AW-P**	**Op:**	**Strike**
	Sgt W Wilson	580305	Injured	**Base:**	Leuchars
	Sgt Chadwick	. . . . . .	Injured	**T/o time:**	18:36
	Sgt Michelin	. . . . . .	Safe		
	Sgt Thomas	. . . . . .	Safe		

Took off with two other aircraft for a strike. At 18:50 hrs the starboard engine lost power and the aircraft was unable to maintain height so they altered course for base. At 18:55 hrs the Beaufort was force-landed in the sea 200 yards off shore at Tentsmuir, Fife. Sgt Wilson and Chadwick sustained slight injuries but the dinghy was launched and pulled ashore in five feet of water. The aircraft was left high and dry at low tide.

82 Sqn	**Blenheim IV**	**V6451**	**UX-**	**Op:**	**Anti-Shipping**
	F/Lt R E Tallis DFC	84014	+	**Base:**	Lossiemouth
	Sgt D G Shayler	746878	+	**T/o time:**	13:43
	Sgt F E Davis	800559	+		

Presumed lost over the sea. F/Lt Tallis is buried in Sola Churchyard, Norway, while the others are commemorated on the Runnymede Memorial.

82 Sqn	**Blenheim IV**	**V6256**	**UX-W**	**Op:**	**Anti-Shipping**
	P/O D White	60809	+	**Base:**	Lossiemouth
	Sgt R G Hanson	754929	+	**T/o time:**	14:02
	Sgt W G Busby	751354	+		
	Cpl H E Hollis	912623	+		

Tasked to search for shipping off the coast of Norway. Lost without trace. All are commemorated on the Runnymede Memorial.

254 Sqn	**Blenheim IV**	**V5802**	**QY-**	**Op:**	**Rover**
	P/O C Tyler	85226	+	**Base:**	Sumburgh
	Sgt D M Syme	977804	+	**T/o time:**	?
	F/Sgt H F Bywaters	552640	+		

Lost without trace. All are commemorated on the Runnymede Memorial.

502 Sqn	Whitley V		Z6553	YG-E	Op:	Anti-Submarine Sweep
	S/Ldr	B G Corry	90033	Safe	Base:	Limavady
	P/O	G M Howard Jones	42229	Safe	T/o time:	19:38
	Sgt	Easton	......	Safe		
	Sgt	Banner	......	Safe		
	Sgt	Graham	......	Safe		

Suffered an engine failure at 00:01 hrs some 30 miles out. Lost height and then was abandoned and left to crash at Benevenagh near Lough Mevin, Eire at 04:00 hrs.

30th April 1941

269 Sqn	Hudson I		T9292	UA-P	Op:	Convoy Escort
	Sgt	N Child	539059	+	Base:	Wick
	Sgt	Marshall	......	Safe	T/o time:	17:36
	P/O	A J M Adolphus	65987	+		
	Sgt	A V Summers	906783	+		

While returning from Escort duties, encountered extremely bad weather. After several attempts to break cloud cover over the aerodrome and elsewhere, Sgt Child ordered the crew to abandon the aircraft. Sgt Adolphus and Sgt Summers were found drowned having landed in the sea off Brora, Sgt Marshall landed safely nearby, and Sgt Child was found dead near Brora, probably as a result of striking some part of the aircraft before pulling the rip-cord. The Hudson crashed approximately 1½ miles north of Brora. Sgt Child rests in Scholemoor Cemetery, Bradford; P/O Aldolphus is buried locally in Wick Cemetery and Sgt Summers in Hollybrook Cemetery, Southampton.

612 Sqn	Whitley V		P5070	WL-F	Op:	Patrol
	P/O	F L Arney	88854	DoI	Base:	Wick
	Sgt	H M Williams	742855	+	T/o time:	?
	Sgt	D J McPherson RNZAF	401213	+		
	Sgt	R F S Smith	755023	+		
	Sgt	A Skelhorn	755214	+		
	Sgt	J B McKenzie	817019	+		

Flew into Scaraben mountain near Dunbeith, Caithness, on the return from anti-submarine patrol. P/O Arney was found alive but died later after stating that his W/T had failed and did not hear the general recall due to bad weather. Sgt McKenzie rests in Grove Cemetery, Aberdeen; Sgt McPherson, from Wellington, New Zealand, locally in Wick Cemetery; Sgt Skelhorn in St Mary Churchyard Extension, Great Sankey, Lancashire; Sgt Smith in Hertford Road Cemetery, Enfield, Middlesex; Sgt Williams in Canford Cemetery, Bristol, and P/O Arney in Maidstone Cemetery, Kent.

1st May 1941

252 Sqn	Beaufighter IC		T3229	PN-	Duty:	Transit Flight
	S/Lt	R D B Hopkins RN	.....	Interned	Base:	St Eval
	Sgt	G Bell	523274	Interned	T/o time:	08:00

Missing on a flight to Gibraltar. Ditched off Lisbon, Portugal. Some sources suggest that this aircraft was recovered and found its way into the *Luftwaffe* as a war prize.

3rd May 1941

1 PRU	Spitfire I(PR) type C		R6805	LY-	Op:	Reconnaissance
	Sgt	P G Rose	748692	+	Base:	Benson
					T/o time:	?

Missing from an operation to the Ruhr and crashed at 13:15 hrs on land owned by Mr Spronck at Maireux-Soumagne, Belgium. Sgt Rose baled out but his parachute was damaged by the aircraft and he rests in Soumagne Communal Cemetery, Liege, Belgium.

1 PRU	Spitfire I(PR) type C		X4495	LY-	Op:	Reconnaissance
	F/O	W Panton DFC	43150	+	Base:	Benson
					T/o time:	15:10

Took off tasked for an operation to aerodromes in the Douain - Cambrai area, but possibly shot down by Hptm H Bretnütz of II/JG 53, south of Dungeness. F/O Panton is commemorated on the Runnymede Memorial.

269 Sqn	Hudson III	T9419	UA-	Op:	?
	Sgt R G Moreland	745299	Safe	Base:	Kaldadarnes
				T/o time:	?

Both engines cut and the Hudson was belly-landed in a marsh 3 miles E of Kaldadarnes, Iceland, at 04:30 hrs.

5th May 1941

86 Sqn	Blenheim IV	Z5809	BX-		Ground Loss
	Destroyed in an air raid at 00:21 hrs.			Base:	St Eval

86 Sqn	Blenheim IV	V5392	BX-F		Ground Loss
				Base:	Sydenham
	Destroyed in an air raid.			Time:	?

235 Sqn	Blenheim IV	Z5742	LA-A	Op:	Danish Sweep
	Sgt B L T Crawforth	742675	+	Base:	Bircham Newton
	Sgt C D Robertson	970095	+	T/o time:	08:30
	Sgt W K Blackford	944341	+		

Took off along with another squadron aircraft for a shipping sweep. Shot down by Me110s during an attack on a convoy off Borkum. Both Sgt Crawforth and Sgt Robertson rest in Sage War Cemetery, while Sgt Blackford is commemorated on the Runnymede Memorial.

6th May 1941

59 Sqn	Blenheim IV	. . . . . ?	TR-A	Op:	Emro Patrol
	F/Lt G T Palmer DFC	39333	+	Base:	Bircham Newton
	Sgt A D Whitson	746745	+	T/o time:	22:18
	F/Sgt C E A Dunlop DFM	625116	+		

Crashed into the North Sea. F/Lt Palmer rests in Sage War Cemetery, Germany, while both F/Sgt Dunlop and Sgt Whitson are commemorated on the Runnymede Memorial.

612 Sqn	Whitley V	T4280	WL-G	Op:	Sweep
	F/O H C Winter-Taylor	42733	Safe	Base:	Wick
				T/o time:	?

Engine cut on patrol near North Rona. F/O Winter-Taylor managed to reach Stornoway by using the emergency boost of the remaining Merlin but overshot the landing and ended up on the beach at Stornoway.

7th May 1941

86 Sqn	Blenheim IV	V5523	BX-U	Op:	Convoy Escort
	F/Lt T I Mathewson	. . . . .	Safe	Base:	Wattisham
	Sgt E J Martin	. . . . . .	Safe	T/o time:	07:35
	Sgt D Copes	. . . . . .	Safe		

Engine cut and the Blenheim was ditched off Harwich.

202 Sqn	Catalina I	AH554	TQ-		Ground Loss
	Catalina I	AH555	TQ-		Ground Loss
				Base:	Greenock
	Destroyed in an air raid.			Time:	?

240 Sqn	Catalina I	AH536	BN-	Duty:	?
	F/O P C Thomas	33552	+	Base:	Lough Erne
	P/O H H Hirst	78853	+	T/o time:	?
	F/Sgt W Peebles	755887	+		
	LAC H A Cottam	942733	+		
	Sgt J L Elwell	937611	+		
	P/O K B Fuller	88672	+		
	Sgt J S Hesk	570397	+		
	P/O D W Hockney	60779	+		
	LAC L R Holmes	622400	+		
	Sgt H E Wilson	908862	+		

Landed at 04:30 hrs without flares, crashed and sank at Lough Erne. LAC Holmes rests in St Woollos Cemetery, Monmouthshire while the rest of the crew are commemorated on the Runnymede Memorial.

9th May 1941

59 Sqn	Blenheim IV	T1874	TR-Y		Op:	Boulogne
	S/Ldr G C N Close GC	37383	+		Base:	Thorney Island
	F/O F G Roberts	80841	+		T/o time:	22:00
	Sgt G W Richards	911097	+			

Took off in company to attack Boulogne Harbour but failed to return. S/Ldr Close and his crew rest in Boulogne Eastern Cemetery.

S/Ldr Close had been awarded the Empire Gallantry Medal in 1937. He was duty pilot on the Miranshah aerodrome when an aircraft laden with bombs crashed and burst into flames. (The then) P/O Close, despite the explosion of a bomb and small arms ammunition, made persistent attempts to extinguish the flames and rescue the crew, until he was restrained by a superior officer.

The EGM was superseded by the George Cross when the latter award was instituted in September 1940, and at that time living recipients of the EGM were permitted to exchange their award for a George Cross.

10th May 1941

1 PRU	Spitfire I (PR) type D	P9552	LY-		Op:	Reconnaissance
	Sgt P A Mills	741481	+		Base:	Mount Farm
					T/o time:	10:10

Took off for an operation to Stettin and Swinemunde but failed to return.
Sgt Mills is commemorated on the Runnymede Memorial.

82 Sqn	Blenheim IV	V6070	UX-N			Ground Loss
	Blenheim IV	T2330	UX-			Ground Loss
					Base:	St Eval
	Both aircraft destroyed by enemy bombing.				Time:	?

11th May 1941

217 Sqn	Beaufort I	N1018	MW-K			Ground Loss
	Beaufort I	L9881	MW-			Ground Loss
	Both damaged beyond repair in an air raid at 00:01 hrs.				Base:	St Eval

12th May 1941

217 Sqn	Beaufort I	W6494	MW-F		Op:	St Nazaire
	Sgt D E R Elwood	745448	+		Base:	St Eval
	Sgt G T Hardwick	581334	+		T/o time:	?
	Sgt W Bennett	937589	PoW			
	Sgt G A D Ritchie	974516	PoW			

Took off (late on 11th or early on 12th – the date cannot be confirmed from sources) for an operation to identify why flak and balloons were increasing at St Nazaire. Upon return they were diverted to Boscombe Down by coded signal but this was unreadable as 217 Sqn did not carry decoders on operations. Plotted as over Boscombe but last heard very faintly at 04:06 hrs. Shot down by flak at Carpiquet, France. Both Sgt Hardwick and Sgt Elwood rest in Bayeux War Cemetery, Calvados, France.

221 Sqn	Wellington VIII	W5615	DF-		Op:	Anti-Submarine Patrol
	F/O J Robinson	91041	+		Base:	Limavady
	P/O R L Roberts-Brown	62247	+		T/o time:	02:00
	Sgt C J Wynn	581255	+			
	Sgt F L Boham	654488	+			
	Sgt N R Newey	944135	+			
	Sgt S G White	909277	+			

Crashed 20 minutes after take-off in Lough Foyle, 2 miles SW of Magilligan Point. Londonderry. P/O Roberts-Brown is buried in Billing Road Cemetery, Northampton, while the others are commemorated on the Runnymede Memorial.

500 Sqn	Anson I	W1828	MK-Q	Op:	Patrol
	Sgt V C Galt	. . . . . .	Safe	Base:	Detling
	P/O W Hollingsworth	. . . . .	Safe	T/o time:	?

Ditched 20 miles SE of Flamborough Head, Yorkshire, after the starboard engine failed. The aircraft had been flying at 200 feet when the power faded. No further details.

13th May 1941

82 Sqn	Blenheim IV	V6430	UX-	Op:	St Nazaire
	S/Ldr G S King	27107	+	Base:	Portreath
	Sgt J E Austen-Johnson	908839	+	T/o time:	08:07
	Sgt D Owen	640901	+		

Presumed crashed in the Channel off the coast of France. S/Ldr King and Sgt Austen-Johnson are buried in Escoublac-la-Baule War Cemetery, France, while Sgt Owen is commemorated on the Runnymede Memorial.

82 Sqn	Blenheim IV	V5997	UX-	Op:	St Nazaire
	Sgt F H Miller	. . . . . .	Interned	Base:	Portreath
	Sgt N J Ingram	. . . . . .	Interned	T/o time:	08:11
	Sgt W E W Whiteman	. . . . . .	Interned		

Force-landed in the target area.

1402 (Met) Flight	Gladiator II	N5590		Duty:	Training
	F/Lt W O V Bennett	70059	Safe	Base:	Aldergrove
				T/o time:	07:10

Took off for air-to-ground firing practice. Engine cut and crash-landed at Langford Lodge. Not repaired; struck off charge on 20th June 1942.

15th May 1941

269 Sqn	Hudson I	T9360	UA-	Duty:	?
	F/Sgt R Obee	562238	Injured	Base:	Wick
				T/o time:	04:15

Engine cut on take-off, swung off the runway, crashed and burned out. Crew slightly injured.

17th May 1941

206 Sqn	Hudson I	T9324	VX-	Op:	Pirate Patrol
	P/O L E H Cooper	84676	+	Base:	Bircham Newton
	P/O R J Tearle	84945	+	T/o time:	20:15
	Sgt A G Knight	639451	+		
	Sgt Pease	. . . . . .	Injured		
	Sgt Brown	. . . . . .	Injured		

Flew too low for accurate D/F bearings and attempted to force-land. Hit a boom on the beach 500 yards N of the Isle of Sheppy at 02:10 hrs while lost and was submerged for several hours either side of high tide. P/O Cooper rests in Doddington Road Cemetery, Wellingborough, Northamptonshire; Sgt Knight in Coed Bell Cemetery, Prestatyn, Flintshire, and P/O Tearle in Luton Church Burial Ground, Bedfordshire.

18th May 1941

272 Sqn	Beaufighter IC	T3302	XK-		?
	Sgt R F Tatnell	748556	+	Base:	Chivenor
				T/o time:	?

Dived into the ground after a night take-off. Sgt Tatnell rests in St Augustine Churchyard, Heanton Punchardon, Devon.

21st May 1941

233 Sqn	Hudson I	N7296	ZS-	Duty:	Training
	W/C E C Kidd DFC AFM	. . . . .	Safe	Base:	Nutts Corner
				T/o time:	04:00

Starboard brake seized causing the aircraft to swing, collapse the undercarriage and burst into flames.

236 Sqn	Blenheim IV	V5428	ND-F	Op:	Interception
	Sgt Lindley	. . . . . .	Safe	Base:	St Eval
	Sgt Fuller	. . . . . .	Safe	T/o time:	02:10
	Sgt Hale	. . . . . .	Safe		

Overshot on landing at 05:35 hrs in bad weather, swung to avoid other aircraft and the undercarriage leg collapsed. The Blenheim was deemed beyond repair.

404 Sqn	Blenheim I	L6595	EE-	Duty:	Training
	Sgt McLean	. . . . . .	Injured	Base:	Thorney Island
	Sgt McElman	. . . . . .	Injured	T/o time:	
	?	. . . . . .	Safe		

Lost height after take-off and crash-landed in a creek at the end of the runway.

22nd May 1941

252 Sqn	Beaufighter IC	T3235	BT-	Duty:	Ferry flight
	F/O J Holgate	. . . . .	Interned	Base:	Gibraltar
	F/O H Verity	. . . . .	Interned	T/o time:	10:00
	Sgt Barnett	. . . . . .	Interned		

On a flight from Gibraltar to St Eval forced landed in Eire and was interned.

252 Sqn	Beaufighter IC	T3249	BT-	Duty:	Ferry flight
	F/O S MacDonald	. . . . .	Safe	Base:	Gibraltar
	F/O G Lemar	. . . . .	Safe	T/o time:	10:00
	Sgt Booth	. . . . . .	Safe		

Ditched off Mousehole, Cornwall, short of fuel in bad weather on a ferry flight from Gibraltar to St Eval. The crew were picked up by a small coastal vessel and transferred to Truro Hospital after being landed.

23rd May 1941

217 Sqn	Beaufort I	N1040	MW-K	Op:	Anti-submarine Search
	Sgt Harper	. . . . . .	Injured	Base:	St Eval
	Sgt Scollin	. . . . . .	Injured	T/o time:	11:25
	Sgt Seth	. . . . . .	Injured		
	Sgt Wendle	. . . . . .	Injured		

Took off to search for a U-boat reported at La Rochelle. Located it and attacked with bombs and guns. Later the crew spotted a U-boat on the surface near the Ile d'Oleron and dropped a stick of four bombs. Another attack was made with the two remaining bombs but return fire had ripped open both leading wing edges. Sgt Harper made another run using machine-guns but a cannon shell tore open the starboard main tank and another exploded behind the observer's panel. Sgt Harper set course for home and reached the Bishop's Light before the fuel ran out. The starboard engine started to misfire and the Beaufort lost height. Damage had been done to the flaps and the undercarriage so they crash-landed in a field at Boscathnoe Lane, Heamoor, 2 miles N of Penzance, Cornwall.

24th May 1941

42 Sqn	Beaufort I	N1013	AW-G	Op:	Convoy Escort FS 98
	Sgt Morrison	. . . . . .	Safe	Base:	Leuchars
	Sgt Gawthorne	. . . . . .	Safe	T/o time:	14:05
	Sgt Harcourt	. . . . . .	Safe		
	Sgt Tyler	. . . . . .	Safe		

About 16:00 hrs the visibility deteriorated and the pilot decided to fly at 800 feet. At 16:27 hrs the starboard engine cut and although every effort was made to maintain height on the port engine, it was found to be impossible. At about 16:30 hrs the aircraft was forced to land in the sea 5 miles

E of Lindisfarne, Northumberland. Everybody got safely into the dinghy unhurt during the three minutes before the aircraft sank. At approximately 16:45 hrs a destroyer (whose lookout had seen the aircraft come down in the sea) picked up the crew.

114 Sqn	Blenheim IV	L9267	RT-K	Op:	Stand Patrol
	Sgt J McK McWilliam	971400	+	Base:	Leuchars
	P/O B A Godsmark	84024	+	T/o time:	?
	Sgt E D Maddison	974094	+		

Missing from patrol. All are commemorated on the Runnymede Memorial.
Possibly shot down by Oblt Carganico.

272 Sqn	Beaufighter IC	? T3317	XK-	Duty:	Transit Flight
	S/Ldr A W Fletcher	37280	?	Base:	Chivenor
	Sgt Ream	. . . . . .	Evaded	T/o time:	13:30
	Sgt Gallimore	. . . . . .	Evaded		

Ran out of fuel over Spain and made a forced landing in a cornfield and was interned by the Spanish Air Force. Sgt Ream only had time to burn his papers and destroy the IFF before being seized. He was held for a week until he was allowed to see Mr Lee the British Consul in Seville. Sgt Ream and Sgt Gallimore were given civilian clothes and smuggled aboard the SS *Aldergrove* which then sailed for Gibraltar.

25th May 1941

1 PRU	Spitfire I(PR) type C	R7070	LY-	Op:	Brest
	F/O R W Ayres DFC	40292	+	Base:	St Eval
				T/o time:	07:43

Believed ditched on return. Claimed as shot down by Ltn H Ulenberg of 2./JG26 at 09:01 hrs some 60 km (c 37¼ miles) N of Brest. F/O Ayres is commemorated on the Runnymede Memorial.

26th May 1941

53 Sqn	Blenheim IV	V6301	PZ-	Op:	Patrol
	W/C G W P Grant	29091	Safe	Base:	St Eval
				T/o time:	?

Hit a gunpost at St Eval when it undershot the landing on return from patrol in bad visibility at 11:30 hrs.

98 Sqn	Battle I	P2330		Duty:	Ferry Flight
	F/O A K Round	36201	+	Base:	Melgerdi
	F/Sgt R A Hopkins	751763	+	T/o time:	12:30
	F/Sgt K Garrett	620449	+		
	P/O H J Talbot	45946	+		

Picked up F/Sgt Garret and P/O Talbot but crashed into a mountain at Bakkasel. F/O Round, from Wellington, New Zealand, and the other airmen were initially commemorated on the Runnymede Memorial but an expedition recovered the crew's bodies in August 2000 and they now rest in Fossvogur Cemetery, Reykjavik, Iceland.

27th May 1941

236 Sqn	Blenheim IV	V5760	ND-R	Op:	?
	P/O P D W Chappell	. . . . .	Safe ?	Base:	Carew Cheriton
				T/o time:	2400

Flew into the ground while landing at Carew Cheriton in bad weather.
Date is suspect (26th or 27th or 28th ?) : accident happened at 24:00 hrs.

28th May 1941

235 Sqn	Blenheim IV	V5453	LA-O	Op:	Pirate Patrol
	Sgt H T Naughtin	754002	+	Base:	Bircham Newton
	Sgt R Oldroyd	937503	+	T/o time:	18:50
	Sgt S Gordon	939014	+		

Shot down between 20:55 hrs and 21:03 hrs by either Oblt P Stolte, Oblt K-H Leesmann or Ltn K Rung, of 2./JG52, operating from De Vlijt. The Blenheim crashed off Texel/Terschelling. All the Blenheim crew are commemorated on the Runnymede Memorial.

235 Sqn	Blenheim IV	Z5968	LA-V	Op:	Pirate Patrol
	P/O J O Fenton	81679	+	Base:	Bircham Newton
	Sgt R H Johnson	935948	+	T/o time:	18:50
	Sgt O J Dee	906581	+		

Shot down between 20:55 hrs and 21:03 hrs by either Oblt K-H Leesmann or Lt K Rung, both of 2./JG52 operating from De Vlijt. The Blenheim crashed off Texel/Terschelling. Both Sgt Johnson, who was washed ashore at Norderoog-Sand, and Sgt Dee were initially buried at Alte Kirche Friedhof on Pellworm Island but now rest in Hamburg Cemetery while P/O Fenton is commemorated on the Runnymede Memorial.

29th May 1941

59 Sqn	Blenheim IV	V6447	TR-R	Op:	Convoy Escort
	F/O J G R Sturrock	74691	+	Base:	Thorney Island
	Sgt N L Conrade	963798	+	T/o time:	09:25
	Sgt W A Smallbone	909986	+		

Failed to return. Sgt Conrade rests in Lodge Hill Cemetery, Birmingham, while the rest of the crew are commemorated on the Runnymede Memorial.

502 Sqn	Whitley V	T4142	YG-N	Op:	Convoy Escort
	F/O G A B Johnston	. . . . .	Safe	Base:	Limavady
	Sgt C K McPherson	816022	Safe	T/o time:	?
	P/O J Hutchison	. . . . .	Safe		
	Sgt J S Hare	943955	Safe		
	Sgt E E Laughton	755993	Safe		
	Sgt V D J Harris	694062	Safe		

Took off to escort convoy HG62. Ditched 22 miles SW of Barra.
The crew was picked up six hours later by the fishing vessel *River Doon*.

1st June 1941

220 Sqn	Hudson II	T9366	NR-R	Op:	Stab Patrol
	F/O J L Halstead	74350	+	Base:	Wick
	P/O T E Hampson	68726	+	T/o time:	09:15
	Sgt J Money	903251	+		
	Sgt R Fawcett	552816	+		

Shot down off Bergen by Oblt Brandis of Zerst/JG 77.
The crew is Commemorated on Runnymede Memorial.

2nd June 1941

22 Sqn	Beaufort I	X8921	OA-X	Op:	Rover Patrol
	F/O W D J McCaw	41397	PoW	Base:	North Coates
	Sgt F W O'Brien	516572	+	T/o time:	12:25
	Sgt I T C Edwards DFM	639611	+		
	Sgt P R Woodland	905872	PoW		

Took off in company with other aircraft of the squadron and set course for Terschelling, Holland. The flight sighted a convoy of 3 ships of 6,000 tons, 10 ships of 1,000 tons and 1 flak-ship, and then attacked with torpedos. Both F/O McCaw and F/Lt Gadd missed their targets and shadowed the convoy for seven minutes to take pictures and observe results. F/O McCaw was last seen at 14:00 hrs heading off while under attack by two Me110s. The Beaufort was forced to ditch 10 km (c 6¼ miles) W of Terschelling after being attacked by Uffz Becker of Erg/ZG76 flying from De Kooy. The dinghy failed to inflate due to damage so both F/O McCaw and Sgt Woodland clung to the wooden bomb bay doors of the aircraft. A Kriegsmarine vessel picked up both survivors and the bodies of the dead and landed them at Den Helder. Sgt O'Brien and Sgt Edwards were initially buried in Huisduinen Cemetery but now both rest in Bergen-op-Zoom War Cemetery, Holland.

3rd June 1941

59 Sqn	Blenheim IV	T2220	TR-J	Op:	Shipping Patrol
	P/O T D Kerr	44527	+	Base:	Thorney Island
	Sgt K P T Fletcher	956658	+	T/o time: 11:29	
	Sgt J Hine	990454	+		

Crashed near Lamballe, Cotes du Nord, after losing contact with C/59 on the outward flight. Both Sgt Fletcher and Sgt Hine are commemorated on the Runnymede Memorial, while P/O Kerr rests in Plurien Communal Cemetery, Cotes-d'Armor, France.

235 Sqn	Blenheim IV	Z6024	LA-Y	Duty:	Transit flight
	S/Ldr A G Wincott	. . . . .	Safe	Base:	Bircham Newton
	P/O W J Mason	. . . . .	Safe	T/o time: ?	
	Sgt K Campbell	. . . . . .	Safe		

Overshot during landing, swung on to soft ground and tipped up at Dyce, Aberdeenshire.

4th June 1941

21 Sqn	Blenheim IV	V6323	YH-	Duty:	Training
	Sgt E W Ashwood	904070	+	Base:	Lossiemouth
	Sgt W R Meaker	917235	+	T/o time: ?	
	Sgt P R Sutton	976352	+		

Took off for a Navex (Navigational Exercise). During the afternoon the Kinnaird Head coastguard reported a splash and the sound of an explosion bearing 360° from Kinnaird Head 2 miles distant, just after two British aeroplanes had disappeared into the mist, and the naval authorities asked the lifeboat to investigate.

At 17:40 hrs the motor lifeboat *John and Charles Kennedy* put out. A light SE wind was blowing, with a moderate sea. The lifeboat found a large patch of oil, a deflated rubber dinghy and three pieces of a Blenheim bomber, but no sign of any survivors. The crew is commemorated on the Runnymede Memorial.

612 Sqn	Whitley V	T4283	WL-		Ground Loss
				Base:	Wick
				Time:	19:24

Damaged beyond repair in an air raid by a Ju 88.

5th June 1941

612 Sqn	Whitley V	Z6720	WL-K	Duty:	?
	P/O Imber	. . . . .	Safe	Base:	Wick
	LAC Morrison	. . . . . .	Injured	Time:	?
	AC Wilkin	. . . . . .	Injured		

The Whitley burst a tyre on take-off, swung and hit a mound before catching fire.

6th June 1941

86 Sqn	Blenheim IV	V5646	BX-W	Op:	Convoy Escort
	P/O E W Evans	89347	Safe	Base:	North Coates
	?		. . . . . .	T/o time:	14:15

Suffered an engine failure on take-off and crash-landed.

8th June 1941

500 Sqn	Blenheim IV	V5689	MK-F	Duty:	Training
	F/O F W Hall-Jones RNZAF	2515	+	Base:	Bircham Newton
	P/O J M Johnston	63035	+	T/o time: ?	
	P/O A R P Shield	63037	+		

Flew into the ground in mist at Holme-next-the-Sea, Norfolk, at 16:35 hrs. F/O Hall-Jones, a New Zealander from Southland, is buried in St Mary's Churchyard, Great Bircham; P/O Johnston in Brookwood Military Cemetery, and P/O Shield rests in Handsworth Cemetery, Birmingham.

9th June 1941

1 PRU	Spitfire I(PR) Type C	X4496	LY-	Op:	Reconnaissance
	P/O I B Cooper	61289	+	Base:	Sumburgh
				T/o time:	11:35

Took off from Wick and flew to Sumburgh to refuel then set off for a photo-operation to Bergen, Stavanger and Kristiansand but crashed at Ockero. P/O Cooper, from Natal, South Africa, rests in Ockero Churchyard, Sweden.

254 Sqn	Blenheim IV	Z6025	QY-K	Duty:	?
	P/O C L H Werner	60759	+	Base:	Aldergrove
	Sgt R Shaw	916062	+	T/o time:	?
	Sgt J J E M O'Donnell	909566	+		

Lost control in cloud and dived into the ground 2 miles W of Garvagh, Londonderry. P/O Werner is buried in the St Catherine Church of Ireland Churchyard, Killead, County Antrim. Sgt Shaw, from Switzerland, is buried in Bournemouth North Cemetery, while Sgt O'Donnell rests in St Martin Churchyard Extension, Ruislip, Middlesex.

10th June 1941

204 Sqn	Sunderland I	N9047	KG-B		Ground Loss
				Base:	Reykjavik

The Sunderland alighted at Skerjafordur, near Rykjavik and was being refuelled. Approximately an hour later, at 17:23 hrs, SS *Manela* reported smoke coming from an aircraft at a mooring . Three minutes later the signaller reported the a/c on fire and flames and black smoke began billowing from above the mainplane. Within two and a half minutes the mainplane had broken and tipped over and at 17:30 hrs the aircraft was two-thirds under water, blazing furiously and sinking fast. Those of the crew still aboard had been rescued by a motor launch. Nobody was hurt. The aircraft was lying at moorings half a mile from the SS *Manela*. Overnight salvage work was begun and by the morning the four engines had been recovered. The fire had not reached them. Much gear was recovered on the 10th and by the 14th the mooring had been cleared of all wreckage.

217 Sqn	Beaufort I	W6530	MW-S	Duty:	Transit flight
	Sgt P F Holley	742265	+	Base:	Chivenor
	Sgt K J Whadcoat	957278	+	T/o time:	?
	Sgt P T Perrins	974123	+		
	Sgt C G J McIvor	615917	+		

Took off from St Eval on 9th June for a mining operation. Landed at Chivenor at 03:25 hrs on 10th June. Departed Chivenor for transit back to St Eval but crashed and blew up in Barnstaple Bay after an engine fire. Sgt Holley rests in St Mary Churchyard Extension, Flint, while the others are commemorated on the Runnymede Memorial.

11th June 1941

53 Sqn	Blenheim IV	V5933	PZ-U	Op:	Strike
	P/O N D MacLennan RCAF	J/3735	+	Base:	St Eval
	Sgt D C Taylor	754263	+	T/o time:	01:00
	Sgt W M Roberts	948880	+		

Flew into high ground in cloud on the return from an operation to St Nazaire at Brown Willy, Bodmin Moor, Cornwall. P/O MacLennan, a Canadian from Toronto, rests in St Eval Churchyard; Sgt Taylor was taken to Torrisholme Cemetery, Morecambe and Heysham; while Sgt Roberts is buried in Great Orme's Head Cemetery, Llandudno.

12th June 1941

22 Sqn	Beaufort I	W6521	OA-R	Op:	Shipping Strike
	S/Ldr E Culverwell	33235	+	Base:	Wick
	P/O A W Robson	88703	+	T/o time:	23:50
	Sgt B Kirkham	950127	+		
	Sgt E Shackleton	950261	+		

Failed to return from a shipping strike to Stavanger (search of the Norwegian coast for the Lützow). Believed shot down by Ltn Wienhusen off the Norwegian coast. S/Ldr 'Eddie' Culverwell and his crew are commemorated on the Runnymede Memorial.

206 Sqn	**Hudson IV**	**AE614**	**VX-J**	**Op:**	**Air Sea Rescue**
	P/O A F Sharp	88396	+	Base:	Bircham Newton
	P/O A L Gordon	89949	+	T/o time:	16:45
	Sgt K C Bisson	1164540	+		
	Sgt J A Oxley	950600	+		

Took off for its second sortie to search for a missing Wellington but was shot down into North Sea 120 km (c 74½ miles) W of Texel at 19.05 hrs by either Fw Metzler or at 21.15 hrs by Staffelkapitan Leesmann, both of I/JG52. All the crew are commemorated on the Runnymede Memorial.

235 Sqn	**Blenheim IV**	**T1955**	**LA-G**	**Op:**	**Stand 5**
	P/O M R Stephens	102074	+	Base:	Dyce
	Sgt J T Carmichael	759144	+	T/o time:	18:05
	Sgt W G Halliday	551729	+		

Shot down by a Me110 on a shipping patrol off coast of Norway. All are commemorated on the Runnymede Memorial.

248 Sqn	**Blenheim IV**	**T2121**	**WR-J**	**Op:**	**Stand Patrol**
	Sgt E L Holmes	740063	+	Base:	Dyce
	Sgt D E Richardson	976078	+	T/o time:	14:55
	Sgt J Till	552090	+		

Missing. Possibly the aircraft damaged by Me110 on shipping sweep off Denmark. All are commemorated on the Runnymede Memorial.

13th June 1941

22 Sqn	**Beaufort I**	**W6522**	**OA-K**	**Op:**	**Rotterdam**
	P/O J O H Willing	88691	+	Base:	North Coates
	P/O R L Blackmore RCAF	J/3273	+	T/o time:	00:44
	Sgt J Parsons	958806	+		
	Sgt H K Orme	979251	+		

Took off tasked with attacking the E-boat base at Rotterdam, but the Beaufort was shot down into the North Sea off the Hoek van Holland by flak. P/O Willing rests in Sage War Cemetery; P/O Blackmore and Sgt Parsons are buried locally in Noordwijk General Cemetery, Holland, while Sgt Orme was washed ashore on the beach at Hjerting on the 18th of August and is buried in Fourfelt Cemetery, Esbjerg, Denmark.

206 Sqn	**Hudson IV**	**AE612**	**VX-O**	**Duty:**	**Air Sea Rescue Search**
	P/O A F George	87392	+	Base:	Bircham Newton
	P/O S H Dale	87431	+	T/o time:	04:40
	Sgt E Johns	751751	+		
	Sgt R D Mills	751580	+		

Shot down into the North Sea 140 km (c 87 miles) W of Texel at 06.17 hrs by Oblt Leesmann of I/JG52. All the crew are commemorated on the Runnymede Memorial.

Chapter 10

15th June 1941 to 2nd September 1941

On the 15th of June 1941 Coastal Command acquired a new commander: Air Marshal Sir Philip B Joubert de la Ferté had taken over from Air Chief Marshal Sir Frederick W Bowhill. The tenacious Bowhill had been ideal as C-in-C for defending and building the Command during the early years but it was Joubert with his radio/radar background who would oversee the introduction of new technical weapons.

It was not all success for the new C-in-C, one of his first actions was to order suspension of work on the Leigh Light in favour of the Helmore Light. Although the Helmore Light was more powerful it could not be steered or dipped making it useless in the final stages of an attack. After two months the Helmore Light was dropped and the development on the Leigh Light re-started. By July just over half of Coastal Command aircraft were fitted with ASV Mk.I or Mk.II radar. Joubert was convinced that the Germans would soon develop a detector for the signals and believed the answer was in a new type of radar, so he pushed work on the centimetric ASV replacement to the front of the research list.

Coastal Command returned to the offensive in June by restarting Operation 'Channel Stop', single aircraft attacks on the European/Scandinavian coast and North Sea freelance patrols. No 2 Group also continued their attacks on shipping off the coast of Belgium and Holland. The Germans reacted by increasing convoy air cover and adding flak-ships. This led to losses of over 35% on aircraft on this type of strike. The intensity of sorties led to a new agreement between Bomber and Coastal Commands on areas of operation and the introduction of Fighter Command Hurricanes attacking flak-ships prior to shipping strikes.

The capital ships in Brest were subject to close watch by Coastal Command and on the 21st July photographs showed the *Scharnhorst* being made ready for sea. It was not until the following day that a further photo operation showed that the ship had sailed. Frantic searches were made until *Scharnhorst* was located in La Pallice on the 23rd July. That day both Coastal and Bomber Command launched raids on La Pallice. Two days later the *Scharnhorst* again sailed, not to the Atlantic but back to her mooring in Brest.

Barrier patrols across the U-boat transit routes helped to reduce U-boat shipping losses from 66 ships, 325,817 tons in June to 26 ships totalling 112,624 tons in July and 27 ships of 85,603 tons in August. The number of U-boats in service fell by one on the 27th August when the U-570 surrendered to S/Ldr Thompson of 269 Sqn after being depth charged earlier that day. The submarine was boarded 80 miles south of Iceland by an armed trawler and the prize was taken under tow. The U-570 was later returned to service as HMS *Graph* of the Royal Navy.

The transfer of badly needed aircraft from the North to the South Atlantic continued with the move of 204 Sqn and a detachment of 228 Sqn to Bathurst, in the Gambia. The increasing anti-submarine force in this region had an immediate reduction in sinkings during July/August. Elsewhere Coastal Command Squadrons were working up to becoming operational on the new Beaufighter and Liberator equipment, and first deliveries of the Mk.II Sunderland were imminent. On 13th July the Command took delivery of its first PR Mosquito, though it was September before operational flights were conducted. There was some adjustment of the PR assets on 15th August, when 3 Group Bomber Command's 3 PRU was absorbed into Coastal's 1 PRU at Benson. By September 1 PRU had a Unit Establishment of 37 Spitfires, 2 Marylands and 2 PR Mosquitos.

15th June 1941

22 Sqn	Beaufort I	X8920	OA-V	Op:	Shipping Strike
	P/O A W Camp	67036	+	Base:	North Coates
	Sgt W Myles	580974	+	T/o time:	10:40
	Sgt B J Conlon	553976	+		
	Sgt D G A Briers	755777	+		

Took off in company with other squadron aircraft for a Rover operation to the coast of Holland. Sighted and attacked a large convoy 30 km (c 18½ miles) NW of Texel. The flight leader, F/O Gibbs attacked from the landward side at 12:30 hrs and sank the 2,000 ton Danish ship *Hans Droge* but the other two aircraft failed to hit a vessel. P/O Camp is believed to have been shot down by a flak-ship 10 km (c 6¼ miles) W of Texel. All are commemorated on the Runnymede Memorial.

114 Sqn	Blenheim IV	V5887	RT-Q	Op:	Stand Patrol
	Sgt L C Dowse	907195	PoW	Base:	Leuchars
	P/O C F Starkey	88701	+	T/o time:	?
	Sgt F B Duffield	647048	PoW		

Shot down by Ltn R Glöckner of I/JG 77 off Norway at 13:19 hrs. P/O Starkey is commemorated on the Runnymede Memorial.

235 Sqn	Blenheim IV	V5452	LA-N	Op:	Bert Patrol
	F/Lt W B Goddard DFC	36126	+	Base:	Sumburgh
	Sgt A R Cain	755057	+	T/o time:	17:30
	F/Sgt H Smith	970743	+		

Shot down by Ltn Hartwein of I/JG 77 at 18:45 hrs off Norway on a shipping Sweep.
Sgt Cain is buried in Kviberg Cemetery, Sweden, while the other crewmen are commemorated on the Runnymede Memorial.

16th June 1941

59 Sqn	Blenheim IV	V6386	TR-G	Op:	Strike
	P/O P P Villa	87672	PoW	Base:	Detling
	Sgt J A Mortimer	754768	+	T/o time:	15:58
	Sgt S W McIntyre	747919	+		

Took off in company and met the fighter escort over Canterbury but failed to return. Thought to have been shot down by JG26. Both Sgt Mortimer and Sgt McIntyre are buried in Boulogne Eastern Cemetery.

59 Sqn	Blenheim IV	.....?	TR-Y	Op:	Strike
	P/O D E Kennedy	81358	PoW	Base:	Detling
	P/O P S E Briggs	79751	PoW	T/o time:	15:59
	Sgt C H Edgar	755720	PoW		

Took off in company for an operation to Boulogne but failed to return. Shot down by JG26.

17th June 1941

217 Sqn	Beaufort I	L9867	MW-	Duty:	Training
	F/O J A Eyre	43359	+	Base:	St Eval
				T/o time:	?

Took off for first solo circuits. Stalled in a forced landing after engine failure at Tompkins Garage near Padstow, Cornwall, at 15:43 hrs. F/O Eyre is buried in Urchfont Cemetery, Wiltshire.

220 Sqn	Hudson I	N7281	NR-Y	Duty:	Transit Flight
	P/O H B Ainsworth	78974	Safe	Base:	St Eval
				T/o time:	10:40

Took off for a flight to Thornaby. Engine cut and crashed in a forced landing at Newgale, Pembrokeshire, at 12:40 hrs. The aircraft was recovered but classed as damaged beyond economic repair.

18th June 1941

22 Sqn	Beaufort I	N1158	OA-P	Duty:	Transit Flight
	P/O D A Attewell	89077	+	Base:	Thorney Island
	Sgt G P Whicher RCAF	R/60108	+	T/o time:	?
	Sgt Towend	......	Injured		
	Sgt P McEwan	1355107	+		

Flew into a hill in bad visibility 2 miles SW of St Eval, Cornwall, at 12:15 hrs. P/O Attewell is buried in Holy Trinity Churchyard, Lenton, Nottinghamshire; Sgt Whicher rests in Lanherne Roman Catholic Cemetery, Cornwall and Sgt McEwan was taken to Urray New Parish Churchyard, Ross and Cromarty.

217 Sqn	Beaufort I	L9859	MW-W	Op:	Gardening
	Sgt A Gosden	916773	+	Base:	Thorney Island
	Sgt J D Norris	957339	+	T/o time:	22:50
	Sgt E Hollinghurst	922344	+		
	Sgt F Garbutt	992281	+		

Lost without trace off Brest, France. Sgt Gosden rests in Pornic War Cemetery, Loire-Atlantique, France; Sgt Hollinghurst in Ocean Communal Cemetery, Gironde, France. The remaining crewmen are commemorated on the Runnymede Memorial.

233 Sqn	Hudson III	T9447	ZS-	Duty:	Transit Flight
	F/O Winnicott	. . . . .	Safe	Base:	Limavady
	P/O Wilson	. . . . .	Safe	T/o time:	19:30
	P/O J G Haigh	. . . . .	Injured		

Engine cut on take-off from a forced landing the previous day, due to port engine failure and the Hudson was belly-landed 1 mile SW of Coleraine, Northern Ireland.

19th June 1941

59 Sqn	Blenheim IV	V5395	TR-N	Op:	Strike
	F/O Miles	. . . . .	Safe	Base:	Detling
	Sgt Lewis	. . . . . .	Safe	T/o time:	19:02
	Sgt Mikklesen	. . . . . .	Safe		

Attacked a convoy and reported a direct hit on a vessel but hit the sea avoiding flak off Etaples and crash-landed at Shoreham.

119 Sqn	Short S.26/M 'G' Class	X8274		Duty:	Transit Flight
	F/Sgt D F Meyrick	506585	+	Base:	Pembroke Dock
	Sgt H R Mason	365521	+	T/o time:	?
	Sgt A H S Waller	759038	+		
	P/O G H Bowes	77027	+		
	SGT W F Alexander	508826	+		
	F/Sgt C E Fowler	512994	+		
	P/O J Barry RAAF	400034	+		
	Capt P Michal FAFL	30415	+		
	LAC W T R Crago RAAF	205741	+		
	Brig Gen Tavener	. . . . .	PoW		
	P/O S G Long	70406	PoW		
	Sgt J E Hill	758249	PoW		
	Cpl L G Corcoran RAAF	4503	PoW		
	AC1 J Anderson	636035	PoW		

Ditched off Cape Finisterre and sank. All the commonwealth airmen killed are commemorated on the Runnymede Memorial. This was another former British civilian aircraft (ex-G-AFCJ) that had been impressed into military service. X8274 was named *Golden Fleece*.

21st June 1941

59 Sqn	Blenheim IV	V6387	TR-	Duty:	Training
	P/O R G W Beveridge	86337	Safe	Base:	?
				T/o time:	?

While on the approach to Thorney Island at 12:05 hrs the starboard engine caught fire. The Blenheim crash-landed and blew up at North Hayling, Hampshire.

217 Sqn	Beaufort I	W6528	MW-H	Op:	Rover Patrol
	P/O J Welsh	43122	+	Base:	St Eval
	Sgt W J P Wheat	982331	+	T/o time:	06:30
	Sgt H E C Young	755850	PoW		
	Sgt E Chesterman	901481	+		

Lost without trace. Sgt Wheat is commemorated on the Runnymede Memorial; P/O Welsh is buried in St Martin-de-Re Communal Cemetery, Charente-Maritime, France, and Sgt Chesterman in St Charles de Percy War Cemetery, Calvados, France.

22nd June 1941

221 Sqn	Wellington VIII	W5659	DF-	Op:	Anti-Submarine Patrol
	P/O A O Johnson	67596	+	Base:	Limavady
	Sgt J S Willis	580472	+	T/o time:	11:01
	Sgt K W Morgan	745208	+		
	Sgt W E Cass	970584	+		

| Sgt | A S Marshall | 978403 | + |
| Sgt | S A Smith | 626072 | + |

Took off on a routine patrol but failed to return or contact base. P/O Johnson and his crew are commemorated on the Runnymede Memorial.

23rd June 1941

48 Sqn	Anson I	K8771	OY-Q	Duty:	Training
	F/O R G R Fraser	41393	Safe	Base:	Sealand
				Time:	?

The Anson suffered a tailwheel collapse while taxying on hard ground after a slightly heavier landing than normal. The aircraft was designated a ground instruction airframe, serial 2634M.

53 Sqn	Blenheim IV	V5647	PZ-S	Op:	Convoy Escort
	P/O D M Bolton	61493	+	Base:	St Eval
	Sgt K E Corrie	918536	+	T/o time:	10:20
	Sgt G K Kircher	976992	+		

Shot down by Uffz K Rotte of 6./JG 2 off Pas-de-Calais at 12:46 hrs. All the crew are commemorated on the Runnymede Memorial.

53 Sqn	Blenheim IV	V6125	PZ-F	Op:	Bust Patrol
	P/O E Hewson	87400	PoW	Base:	St Eval
	Sgt A R Dawson	965676	PoW	T/o time:	18:00
	Sgt W G McCorkell	948299	PoW		

Crashed into the Channel. Sgt McCorkell was from South Rhodesia.

24th June 1941

10 (RAAF)	Sunderland I	P9603	RB-	Op:	Reconnaissance
Sqn	F/Lt T V Stokes	. . .	Injured	Base:	Mount Batten
	S/Ldr A N Hick	127	DoI	T/o time:	21:00
	F/O R B Scutts	836	DoI		
	Sgt S J Nichol	1874	Safe		
	Cpl J H Evans	4358	Safe		
	AC1 R M Draper	24175	Safe		
	Cpl L S Y Benham	2903	Safe		
	Cpl J M Lawrie	4571	Safe		
	LAC B F Minton	4632	Safe		
	Cpl E S Ingram	2154	Safe		
	AC1 T J Sheridan	22387	Safe		
	F/Lt Domville RAF	. . . . .	Injured		

On the return the Sunderland overshot the flare-path and hit the rocks off Popton Point, Milford Haven, Pembrokeshire, at 02:15 hrs. There was an air raid alert at Pembroke Dock when the Sunderland was trying to land and less than five minutes later the *Luftwaffe* was dropping mines into the estuary. S/Ldr Hick and F/O Scutts later died from their injuries and rest in Llanion Cemetery, Pembroke Dock, Pembrokeshire. F/Lt Domville was travelling as a passenger.

1403 (Met)	Blenheim IV	V5569	A	Op:	Met Flight
Flight	Sgt R F Culley	96007	Safe	Base:	Bircham Newton
	Sgt P H Thimblebee	963850	Safe	T/o time:	05:10
	F/Sgt Crowley	. . . . . .	Safe		

The Blenheim burst a tyre on landing, swung and then the u/c collapsed. See also 15th July 1941.

26th June 1941

53 Sqn	Blenheim IV	V6309	PZ-E	Op:	Bust Patrol
	P/O L J Francis	87435	+	Base:	St Eval
	Sgt R A Whitley	903706	+	T/o time:	07:55
	Sgt J St C Hopper	749412	+		

Shot down by St Fw Erwin Kley of 1./JG 2 at 09:13 hrs. Sgt Hopper rests in Bayeux War Cemetery, Calvados, France. The others are commemorated on the Runnymede Memorial.

| 53 Sqn | Blenheim IV | V6087 | PZ-O | Op: | C Patrol |

	P/O D T Herrick GM RNZAF	40974	DoI		Base:	St Eval
	Sgt G F Gahagan	957188	+		T/o time:	11:10
	Sgt G L Wells	946558	+			

Missing. P/O Herrick, from Wellington, New Zealand, died in the German Naval Hospital at Lorient and was buried on the 30th of June in Kerentrech Communal Cemetery, Lorient. Both Sgt Gahagan and Sgt Wells have no known graves and are commemorated on the Runnymede Memorial.

53 Sqn	**Blenheim IV**	**V6122**	**PZ-Y**		**Op:**	**C Patrol**
	P/O C E Greville-Heygate DFC	87396	+		Base:	St Eval
	P/O G Troup	87349	+		T/o time:	11:15
	Sgt C H Naylor	751140	+			

Failed to return. All are commemorated on the Runnymede Memorial.

500 Sqn	**Anson I**	**N9732**	**MK-V**		**Duty:**	**?**
	Sgt E W J Polden	754618	+		Base:	Bircham Newton
					T/o time:	?

Collided with Hurricane Z3391 and crashed 3 miles SW of Aylsham, Norfolk.
Sgt Polden is buried in All Saints Churchyard, Branksome Park, Dorset.

29th June 1941

22 Sqn	**Beaufort I**	**L9790**	**OA-G**		**Duty:**	**Training**
	F/Lt M J A ....?	40855	Safe		Base:	Thorney Island
					Time:	?

On take-off the Beaufort hit a bump then dropped a wing and tore an engine out in the resulting crash. The crew escaped without injury. Surname of pilot cannot be made out on the Form 1180.

30th June 1941

1 PRU	**Spitfire I(PR) type C**	**K9787**			**Op:**	**Reconnaissance**
	P/O S Bowes	44672	+		Base:	?
					T/o time:	14:45

Following trials work with the A&AEE and RAE, this, the very first production Spitfire I, was converted to PR standard. It took off for an operation to Le Havre and Cherbourg but failed to return. P/O Bowes is commemorated on the Runnymede Memorial.

59 Sqn	**Blenheim IV**	**V5863**	**TR-X**		**Op:**	**Wander Patrol**
	P/O J N Whitmore	44533	+		Base:	Detling
	Sgt D N Dulley	963822	+		T/o time:	02:26
	Sgt P A Truman	977753	+			

Hit a balloon cable on the return from the patrol to the coast of Holland and ditched off Dover, Kent. P/O Whitmore is buried in Folkestone New Cemetery while his crew are commemorated on the Runnymede Memorial.

608 Sqn	**Blenheim IV**	**Z5982**	**UL-U**		**Duty:**	**Air Sea Rescue Sortie**
	P/O Sir I W MacRobert	87425	+		Base:	Thornaby
	Sgt A P Best	937721	+		T/o time:	11:39
	Sgt H Hillwood	909044	+			
	F/O R K Keating MiD	76320	+			

Ditched while searching for a dinghy that had been reported approximately at 5325N 0230E. All are commemorated on the Runnymede Memorial. Sgt Best was a Canadian from Killam, Alberta, Canada, and F/O Keating was from New Zealand. Sir Iain MacRobert's mother later presented four Hurricanes and a Stirling to the Royal Air Force in memory of her son: one of the Hurricanes was named *Sir Iain*.

1st July 1941

206 Sqn	**Hudson IV**	**AE609**	**VX-U**		**Op:**	**Crossover Patrol**
	P/O J F Bendix	42737	+		Base:	St Eval
	P/O I M Strachan	87391	+		T/o time:	13:32
	Sgt D H Smith	755923	+			
	Sgt J F Smith	917550	+			

Failed to return from patrol. All are commemorated on the Runnymede Memorial.

209 Sqn	Catalina I	AH557	WQ-	Duty:	?
	S/Ldr B A Wood	33151	Safe	Base:	?
				T/o time:	?

On landing the bomb hatch blew open, filling the aircraft with sea water. Beached at Afiordur, Iceland, the aircraft was classed as damaged beyond repair. As a result it was recommended that a change be made to the hatch design on all new Catalinas.

2nd July 1941

248 Sqn	Blenheim IV	Z6171	WR-K	Op:	Pat (4)
	P/O R J Powell	84324	+	Base:	Bircham Newton
	Sgt H J Robinson	945707	+	T/o time:	09:55
	Sgt W G Sharratt	970532	+		

Took off at 08:35 hrs but returned early due to a u/s wireless set. Got off again at 09:55 but was intercepted at low level by Uffz F Metzler of 2./JG52 and shot down at 10:58 hrs, 80 km (c 49¾ miles) NW of Texel, Holland. The Blenheim's crew are commemorated on the Runnymede Memorial.

4th July 1941

114 Sqn	Blenheim IV	V6368	RT-X	Op:	Bergen
	Sgt N W Cook	565458	+	Base:	Leuchars
	Sgt W K Jenkins	968179	+	T/o time:	?
	Sgt B W F Bates	755299	+		

Took off in formation to attack the floating dock and shipping in Bergen Harbour. Both Sgt Cook and Sgt Bates rest locally in Mollendal Church Cemetery, Bergen, while Sgt Jenkins is commemorated on the Runnymede Memorial.

248 Sqn	Blenheim IV	T2078	WR-Q	Op:	Pirbo Patrol
	Sgt Easton	......	Injured	Base:	Bircham Newton
	Sgt R E Carter	970045	DoI	T/o time:	21:50
	Sgt Ferguson	......	Injured		

Flew into the ground at 01:10 hrs in bad visibility while trying to locate the flare-path at West Raynham, Massingham, Norfolk. Sgt Carter died of his injuries and rests in Ely Cemetery, Cambridgeshire.

5th July 1941

220 Sqn	Hudson I	R4059	NR-V	Op:	?
	Sgt J Hall	754778	Safe	Base:	Wick
				T/o time:	12:40

Swung on take-off and the port u/c collapsed before the Hudson caught fire and three depth charges blew up. The crew got safely clear after the crash.

235 Sqn	Blenheim IV	N3524	LA-O	Op:	North Bert Patrol
	P/O G E Botham	89344	+	Base:	Sumburgh
	P/O F McHardy	81410	+	T/o time:	10:10
	Sgt H J Ingram	925331	+		

Missing. Possibly shot down by Ltn Wienhusen. Both P/O Botham and Sgt Ingram are commemorated on the Runnymede Memorial while P/O McHardy rests in Stavne Cemetery, Trondheim, Norway.

7th July 1941

59 Sqn	Blenheim IV	Z7450	TR-O	Op:	Strike
	S/Ldr L Aitken	37492	+	Base:	Detling
	Sgt G T Wood	581057	+	T/o time:	15:03
	Sgt J H Brown	553432	+		

Shot down by flak from a destroyer off Gravelines and seen to dive into the sea with the starboard engine on fire. S/Ldr Aitken rests in Dunkirk Town Cemetery; Sgt Brown in Oostende New Communal Cemetery while Sgt Wood is commemorated on the Runnymede Memorial.

500 Sqn	Blenheim IV	Z6041	MK-Q	Duty:	Training
	F/O A Leeson	42065	+	Base:	Bircham Newton
	F/O R W V Smith	81035	+	T/o time: ?	
	Sgt C V Pearce	755745	+		

Took off for a practice QG. Shot down by an intruder at 02:00 hrs while landing at Docking, Norfolk. F/O Leeson rests in St Mary's Churchyard, Great Bircham; F/O Smith in Nottingham Southern Cemetery and Sgt Pearce is buried in Pinner New Cemetery, Harrow, Middlesex.

8th July 1941

42 Sqn	Beaufort I	W6541	AW-G	Duty:	Transit flight
	F/O A M Taylor	77612	Safe	Base:	Abbotsinch
				Time:	14:30

The Beaufort was taking off for a flight to Leuchars when the spectacle grip became detached from the control column and the aircraft was crash-landed straight ahead.

206 Sqn	Hudson IV	AE613	VX-B	Op:	Anti-Submarine Search
	P/O Kennan	. . . . .	Safe	Base:	St Eval
	Sgt Gibbs	. . . . . .	Safe	T/o time: 04:00	
	Sgt Livingstone	. . . . . .	Safe		
	Sgt Rowley	. . . . . .	Safe		

Starboard engine caught fire and the bomb-load was jettisoned. The Hudson failed to maintain height and the aircraft was ditched at 06:30 hrs, sinking in 1½ minutes. The next day its dinghy was sighted by M/206 and Sunderland T9047 of 10 (RAAF) Sqn carried out an unauthorised landing to pick up the crew. The Sunderland lost a float and ripped off an engine before attempting to taxy home but was eventually scuttled by destroyers L142 and L196 who picked up both crews. The Hudson may have been shot down by Staffelkapitan Oblt Leesmann of 2./JG52.

254 Sqn	Blenheim IV	T1941	QY-	Op:	?
	F/Sgt L E Larkin	564742	Safe	Base:	Aldergrove
				T/o time: ?	

Suffered an engine failure and ran into soft ground during a forced landing at Port Ellen, 20:45 hrs.

500 Sqn	Blenheim IV	Z6038	MK-	Duty:	Training
	Sgt J S Gray	900933	+	Base:	Bircham Newton
	Sgt A N F Glide	901291	+	T/o time: ?	

Overshot during landing from a Navex and hit a gun emplacement at Desford, before being destroyed by fire. Sgt Gray is buried in Streatham Park Cemetery, Surrey, and Sgt Glide in Arnos Vale Cemetery, Bristol.

9th July 1941

10 (RAAF) Sqn	Sunderland I	T9047	RB-L	Op:	Anti-Submarine Patrol
	F/O G R Thurstun	460	Safe	Base:	Pembroke Dock
	F/Lt Burrage	. . . . .	Safe	T/o time: 11:05	
	P/O H D White	. . . . .	Safe		

At 13:15 hrs Sunderland T9047 was diverted to a position where a dinghy with four British occupants had been sighted and given permission to land 'if sea permits'. At 14:45 hrs the dinghy containing survivors from Hudson AE613 VX-B of 206 Squadron was sighted some 160 miles W of Brest and, after inspecting the sea at low altitude, the captain decided it was safe to land. After touching down the aircraft ran for a short distance then struck a wave and was thrown into the air again. The throttles were opened but the aircraft landed on the bank of another wave, tearing the port engine from its mountings before being again thrown into the air this time breaking the port float struts on landing. The Sunderland launched a dinghy and two crewmen rowed over to the survivors and towed them back to the aircraft. At 16:30 hrs the Sunderland started to taxy towards the English coast on three engines. At 01:30 hrs the full crew and rescued survivors were picked up by HMS *Brocklesby* and after salvaging as much equipment as time allowed the aircraft was sunk by shell-fire in position 4815N 0845W.

254 Sqn	Blenheim IV	V5736	QY-	Op:	Convoy Escort
	Sgt G M Carnall	942213	+	Base:	Aldergrove
	Sgt A W Snashall	900931	+	T/o time: ?	

Damaged by Me110s and the engine cut causing the Blenheim to ditch. Sgt Carnall is commemorated on the Runnymede Memorial while Sgt Snashall rests in St John the Baptist Churchyard, Eltham, London.

11th July 1941

221 Sqn	Wellington VIII	W5631	DF-	Op:	Anti-Submarine Patrol
	F/O I C M Sanderson	77042	+	Base:	St Eval
	P/O R Edwards	84917	+	T/o time:	16:00
	P/O D H M Jack	88692	+		
	Sgt L P MacDowell	978205	+		
	Sgt V S Payne	975776	+		
	Sgt R G W Perkins	977815	+		

On returning F/O Sanderson was in W/T communication with base and was plotted in the vicinity of the Scilly Islands. Contact with the Wellington was lost and information was received that an aircraft had exploded in the air off the Islands. It was believed that F/O Sanderson was shot down by an enemy aircraft. A search by fighter aircraft from St Eval failed to find any trace of the Wellington. F/O Sanderson, from Argentina, rests in St Mary's Cemetery, Isles of Scilly, but his crew have no known graves and are commemorated on the Runnymede Memorial.

269 Sqn	Hudson III	T9452	UA-G	Op:	Convoy Escort
	Sgt J S C Edge	903825	+	Base:	Kaldadarnes
	P/O J P N Britton	68140	+	T/o time:	?
	Sgt J Campbell	759333	+		
	Sgt E G King	1153447	+		

Failed to return from escort to convoy OB343. All commemorated on the Runnymede Memorial.

15th July 1941

210 Sqn	Catalina I	AH533	DA-G	Op:	Patrol
	S/Ldr P S Hutchinson	34125	+	Base:	Helensburgh
	P/O E R Pinches	86644	+	T/o time:	21:20
	Sgt E C Graham	648550	+		
	LAC C A Kew	647323	+		
	AC1 R Fearnley	985827	+		
	Cpl T Simner-Jones	621755	+		
	Cpl J C Kinniard	1008386	+		
	AC J Kelly	......	Injured		

Intended to land at Oban but crashed and burned on high ground at the northern end of Jura. S/Ldr Hutchinson rests in Golders Green Crematorium, Middlesex; Sgt Graham in Christ Church Burial Ground, Swindon; LAC Kew in Gap Road Cemetery, Wimbledon, Surrey, and AC1 Fearnley in Warley Congregational Cemetery, Yorkshire. Both P/O Pinches and Cpl Simner-Jones are buried in Pennyfuir Cemetery, Oban while Cpl Kinniard rests in Allenvale Cemetery, Aberdeen. Small pieces of wreckage from this aircraft still lie in grid position NR687984.

1403 (Met) Flight	Blenheim IV	V5852	A	Op:	Met Flight
	Sgt R F Culley	960077	+	Base:	Bircham Newton
	Sgt L H Anderson	907274	+	T/o time:	05:15
	Sgt F Elliott	951775	+		

Failed to return. Both Sgt Anderson and Sgt Elliott are commemorated on the Runnymede Memorial while Sgt Cully rests in Tonder Cemetery,

16th July 1941

22 Sqn	Beaufort I	L9791	OA-O	Op:	Shipping Strike
	F/Sgt D Brett	742065	+	Base:	Thorney Island
	Sgt G A Todd	989694	+	T/o time:	03:05
	Sgt R E G Williams	915498	+		
	Sgt N A F Folkard	958778	+		

Crashed at 04:38 hrs at Jenners Hill near Beddingham, Sussex, in poor visibility after a number of D/F fixes had been passed. F/Sgt Brett rests locally in St Nicholas Churchyard, West Thorney; Sgt Todd is buried in Chevington Cemetery, Northumberland; Sgt Williams in Melksham Church Cemetery and Sgt Folkard was taken to Norwich Cemetery.

17th July 1941

86 Sqn	Beaufort I	AW205	BX-T	Op:	Gardening
	P/O W H Zillessen	89302	+	Base:	North Coates
	Sgt R Plume	981780	+	T/o time:	01:10

Sgt	W Buck	535188	PoW	
Sgt	L E Badland	1001641	+	

Lost off Schiermonnikoog, Holland. The Beaufort was presumed to have been shot down by enemy flak. Other aircraft of the flight reported accurate flak over the target and Borkum, then at 03:28 hrs a red glow was seen in sky, lasting a minute, which then appeared to break up. It was thought to be an aircraft in flames. P/O Zillessen rests in Sage War Cemetery while his crew are commemorated on the Runnymede Memorial.

502 Sqn

Whitley V		**Z6635**	**YG-Q**		**Op:**	**Convoy Escort**
W/C	D R Shore AFC	33015	Wounded		Base:	Limavady
F/O	A T Brock	70087	Safe		T/o time:	03:03
P/O	J D MacLeod	.....	Wounded			
Sgt	S Larmour	751541	Safe			
Sgt	B C Hanson	913503	Wounded			

Took off to escort convoy OB346. At 08:10 hrs the Whitley was involved in a dog fight with a Focke-Wulf Fw200. The Whitley was first to open fire but scored few hits with the front gun and the Fw200 returned fire hitting O/502 and causing the sea marker flares to ignite. At 08:15 hrs with the starboard engine overheating the combat was broken off and W/C Shore set course for base. The overheating continued, fuel pressure dropped and a fuel fire started around the engine. Height could not be maintained and the Whitley was ditched about 800 yards ahead of the leading convoy escort vessel at 08:25 hrs. As the crew was waiting in the dinghy to be picked up by HMS *Wescott* they saw that the aircraft had several bullet holes along the starboard side.

18th July 1941

217 Sqn

Beaufort I		**AW189**	**MW-X**		**Op:**	**Shipping Strike**
F/O	T F Kerr	41588	+		Base:	St Eval
Sgt	A D Scott RNZAF	401234	+		T/o time:	20:15
Sgt	A Windle	942630	+			
P/O	E C Whitehead	79200	+			

Took off along with other squadron aircraft for a shipping strike at St Nazaire, France. Last seen about 4 miles W of the harbour making a climbing turn to port and presumed shot down by flak. Sgt Scott, Sgt Windle and P/O Whitehead rest in Escoublac-la-Baule War Cemetery; F/O Kerr, a Canadian from Vancouver Island, in Pornic War Cemetery.

502 Sqn

Whitley V		**Z6634**	**YG-K**		**Op:**	**Convoy Escort**
F/O	E W Lindsay	.....	Safe		Base:	Limavady
Sgt	Bell	.....	Safe		T/o time:	17:34
P/O	A K Mearns	.....	Safe			
Sgt	P J Millington	......	Safe			
Sgt	Manning	......	Safe			
Sgt	Brown	......	Safe			

Took off to escort convoy OB346. On the return the Whitley was divereted to Aldergrove where due to fuel shortage it overshot the approach, ran across the Crumlin to Antrim Road and crashed into a line of trees at 04:35 hrs.

19th July 1941

220 Sqn

Hudson V		**AM533**	**NR-W**		**Op:**	**Bert Patrol**
F/O	F W F S Russell	42891	+		Base:	Wick
Sgt	D C A Laverack	748584	+		T/o time:	16:00
Sgt	B B Jackson	751797	+			
Sgt	J Boardman	553825	+			

Failed to return from an anti-shipping sortie. All are commemorated on the Runnymede Memorial.

254 Sqn

Blenheim IV		**T2120**	**QY-**		**Duty:**	**?**
P/O	W H King	88706	+		Base:	Aldergrove
Sgt	P E Neale	947874	+		T/o time:	11:35
Sgt	R E Lea	552844	+			
AC1	C H Hore	1301399	+		(non air-crew)	

The pilot had dived the aircraft to low level over the airfield, hit a telegraph pole and lost control. The aircraft crashed into the roof of the NAAFI building and the fuel tanks burst, setting the building on fire. Some of the wreckage was thrown in the direction of one of the 23 MU hangars and caused thirteen casualties, some fatal, among a party of the ground defence force who were drilling there. Some of the girls employed by NAAFI were trapped in the burning building and killed outright. Several others were injured. The station fire tender assisted by another from Nutts Corner managed to put the fire out. The three crew, six NAAFI girls and one airman were killed and a further ten airmen, four NAAFI girls and two civilian workers were injured. P/O King rests in All Saints Churchyard Extension, Sanderstead, Surrey; Sgt Lea is buried in SS. Peter and Paul Churchyard, Ormskirk, Lancashire, while both Sgt Neale and AC1 Hore were taken to Warwickshire for burial in St Michael Churchyard, Boldmere and Handsworth Cemetery, Birmingham respectively.

20th July 1941

86 Sqn	Beaufort I	AW208	BX-Y	Duty:	Training
	P/O S W Gooch	. . . . .	Safe	Base:	North Coates
				T/o time:	22:30

Crashed after an engine failure on take-off.

217 Sqn	Beaufort I	L9970	MW-B	Op:	Rover Patrol
	Sgt S W Jarvis	1252501	PoW	Base:	St Eval
	Sgt M Gillies RCAF	R/54575	PoW	T/o time:	12:55
	Sgt R S C T Griffin	928630	PoW		
	Sgt G Godwin	981765	PoW		

Lost without trace in the Bay of Biscay.

21st July 1941

1 PRU	Spitfire I (PR) type C	R6903	LY-	Op:	Reconnaissance
	F/O M F Suckling	42907	+	Base:	Benson
				T/o time:	10:00

Took off to carry out high level photo operation of the la Rochelle area but failed to return.
F/O Suckling is commemorated on the Runnymede Memorial.

86 Sqn	Beaufort I	W6533	BX-B	Op:	Gardening
	Sgt B A J Boyse	912229	+	Base:	North Coates
	Sgt A Pont	968128	+	T/o time:	02:10
	Sgt R J S Wicks	751165	+		
	Sgt C C Procter	990753	+		

Lost off Schiermonnikoog while on a mining operation.
Sgt Boyse and his crew are commemorated on the Runnymede Memorial.

23rd July 1941

22 Sqn	Beaufort I	L9891	OA-F	Duty:	Transit Flight
	P/O Rogers	. . . . .	Injured	Base:	St Eval
	Sgt Hills	. . . . . .	Injured	T/o time:	20:45
	Sgt J F McGee	952969	Safe		
	Sgt Hatherall	. . . . . .	Safe		
	+ 3 Passengers		Safe		

Following an engine failure, the aircraft crashed while making a forced landing on Bodmin Moor 1½ miles N of Altarnun, Cornwall, at 21:05 hrs . All were taken to Launceston Hospital.

24th July 1941

330 Sqn	Northrop N-3PB	F23	23	Duty:	Training
	Kpt H A Bugge RNorNAS	. . . . .	Safe	Base:	Reykjavik
				T/o time:	?

Night landing practice at Fossvogur. Turned over onto its nose and sank in 15 feet of water.
The aircraft was salvaged but declared damaged beyond repair.

Eighteen Northrop N-3PB single-engine twin-float seaplanes were supplied from Canada in mid-1941 for convoy escort and reconnaissance duties, crewed by the Norwegian personnel of this unit.
The N-3PBs of 330 Squadron remained in service until June 1943, although they were supplemented by Catalinas in July 1942, and by Sunderlands in February 1943.

25th July 1941

59 Sqn	Blenheim IV	V6313	TR-K	Op:	Habo Patrol
	P/O Richards	. . . . .	Safe	Base:	Detling
	Sgt Longworth	. . . . . .	Safe	T/o time:	22:38
	Sgt Major	. . . . .	Safe		

An engine cut at 23:15 hrs on the return from the patrol and the Blenheim hit a tree during the forced landing at Chart Sutton, Kent.

217 Sqn	Beaufort I	AW238	MW-X	Op:	Shipping Strike
	F/Lt A G Collings	137117	PoW	Base:	St Eval
	P/O W J Hunter	89835	PoW	T/o time:	05:30
	Sgt A J Appleby	949210	+		
	Sgt Taylor	. . . . . .	?		

Took off in company for an attack on the *Scharnhorst* which was thought to be making its way from La Pallice to Brest. Due to bad weather the flight did not make contact with the vessel but found and attacked a small convoy off Brest Harbour. The Beaufort was shot down by flak into the Bay of Biscay and Sgt Appleby is commemorated on the Runnymede Memorial.

500 Sqn	Blenheim IV	V5393	MK-	Duty:	Training
	Sgt P B Cunningham	903451	Safe	Base:	Docking
				T/o time:	16:10

The undercarriage was retracted prematurely on take-off causing the Blenheim to hit the ground and seize an engine before it crashed near Burnham Market, Norfolk. The Court of Inquiry noted that due to the undulating surface of the aerodrome it was common for aircraft to be thrown into the air in a stalled condition.

27th July 1941

1 PRU	Spitfire I (PR) type C	R6804	LY-	Op:	Reconnaissance
	P/O J K Charles-Jones	44661	+	Base:	?
				T/o time:	?

Missing from an operation to Trondheim. P/O Charles-Jones is commemorated on the Runnymede Memorial.

233 Sqn	Hudson V	AM541	ZS-N	Op:	Convoy Escort
	Sgt P F Downer	740354	Safe	Base:	Aldergrove
	Sgt Attwood	. . . . . .	Safe	T/o time:	16:38

Took off to escort convoy SL80. Met the convoy of two Destroyers, two Corvettes and ten merchant vessels at 18:20 hrs in position 5444N 1010W. When about to leave, the Hudson stalled while circling a Destroyer at 250 feet and crashed into the sea at 19:30 hrs, 70 miles SW of Tory Island. The crash was observed by both J/254 and O/254 and all of the crew were quickly picked up in position 5450N 1010W by HMS *Broke*.

29th July 1941

86 Sqn	Beaufort I	AW209	BX-	Duty:	Weather Test
	S/Ldr E L Wurtell	37220	Injured	Base:	North Coates
				T/o time:	?

Crashed in a forced landing with an engine on fire near Grimsby, Lincolnshire.

30th July 1941

22 Sqn	Beaufort I	W6470	OA-K	Op:	Torpedo Strike Force
	Sgt Pitman	. . . . . .	Safe	Base:	Manston
	Sgt Morey	. . . . . .	Safe	T/o time:	21:25
	Sgt Brown	. . . . . .	Safe		
	Sgt Bryan	. . . . . .	Safe		

Crashed on landing, 23:25 hrs, at Thorney Island due to heavy rain and very bad visibility obstructing the flare-path.

248 Sqn	Beaufighter IC	T4714	WR-	Duty:	Training
	Sgt R Cheshire	903399	Safe	Base:	Bircham Newton
				T/o time:	?

Undercarriage collapsed on landing at Bircham Newton at 17:00 hrs after formation training. The Beaufighter was classed as damaged beyond repair.

269 Sqn	Hudson III	V9056	UA-P	Duty:	Ferry
	Sgt H France-Cohen	741417	Safe	Base:	Reykjavik
				Time:	17:00

Swung on take-off, hit a packing case and caught fire. Crew safe. See also 5th August 1941.

330 Sqn	Northrop N-3PB	F24	GS-G	Duty:	Training
	Fen C C von Hanno RNorNAS	.....	+	Base:	Reykjavik
	Kvm O Batalden RNorNAS	.....	+	T/o time:	10:55
	Kvm A A Hansen RNorNAS	.....	+		

Took off for a Navex but failed to return.

407 (RCAF) Sqn	Hudson V	AM719	RR-	Duty:	Training
	Sgt G C Bingley	R/60964	+	Base:	North Coates
	P/O R E Buckolz	J/4538	+	T/o time:	?
	Cpl C Naylor RAF	570420	+		

Dived into the ground half a mile S of North Coates in clear weather. Sgt Bingley, from Edmonton, Alberta, and P/O Buckolz, an American from Rapid City, South Dakota, rest locally in St Nicholas Churchyard, North Cotes, while Cpl Naylor is buried in St Mary Churchyard, Deane, Lancashire.

31st July 1941

500 Sqn	Blenheim IV	Z6048	MK-	Duty:	Training
	P/O F G Tiller	.....	Safe	Base:	Bircham Newton
				T/o time:	?

Undershot making a turn at 01:00 hrs and hit a tree on the approach from night Navex at Langham.

1st August 1941

22 Sqn	Beaufort I	W6526	OA-T	Duty:	Transit flight
	Sgt H W Robinson	905788	Safe	Base:	Manston
	AC1 J Scarboro	1009196	+	T/o time:	?
	?	......	?		

Took off to return to Thorney Island after an Operational detachment. The crews had been cleared to practice low flying at every opportunity but misjudged height due to haze and glassy sea and struck the sea with the propellers. At 12:45 hrs the aeroplane was seen to crash into the sea about 1 mile from the coastguard look-out at Lade, Kent. Two rescue boats and a fishing boat with two men on board were close by and went to the spot. The fishing boat rescued one airman and the crash boats the other two. AC1 Scarboro rests in All Saints Churchyard, Toynton, Lincs.

2nd August 1941

22 Sqn	Beaufort I	X8919	OA-W	Op:	Rover Patrol
	F/O A P Culverwell AFC	81003	PoW	Base:	Manston
	Sgt H C Friend	754147	PoW	T/o time:	13:58
	Sgt R Tanfield	944327	PoW		
	F/Sgt W H Dulwich	751992	+		

Took off for a Rover patrol along with other squadron aircraft. Last seen when the formation lost contact near Oostende, Belgium, and was shot down 7 miles off Vlissingen at 15:25 hrs. F/Sgt Dulwich is commemorated on the Runnymede Memorial.

3rd August 1941

42 Sqn	Beaufort I	W6477	AW-O	Op:	Rover Patrol
	F/O K J Masters	41941	+	Base:	Leuchars
	Sgt R M Ramsden	952490	+	T/o time:	05:35
	Sgt L R Hutson	900279	+		
	F/Sgt G E Bolam	746909	+		

Course set for position BPZU 4000 but shot down while attacking a flak battery and crashed at 07:45 hrs near Agger, Denmark. All rest in Frederikshavn Cemetery, Denmark.

4th August 1941

220 Sqn	Hudson V	AM625	NR-R	Op:	South Bert Patrol
	Sgt E Ashworth	754706	+	Base:	Wick
	Sgt R L Viner	901044	+	T/o time:	?
	Sgt B Lloyd-Jones	625097	+		
	Sgt A H Rhodes	962178	+		

Failed to return. All are commemorated on the Runnymede Memorial.

5th August 1941

269 Sqn	Hudson III	V9055	UA-	Duty:	Convoy Escort
	Sgt H France-Cohen	741417	Safe	Base:	Kaldadarnes
				Time:	16:15

Swung on take-off and the u/c collapsed. Crew safe. See also 30th July 1941.

6th August 1941

86 Sqn	Beaufort I	X8928	BX-S	Duty:	?
	P/O G P Mandeville	64316	+	Base:	North Coates
				T/o time:	?

Spun into ground near Brough, Yorkshire. P/O Mandeville rests in St Catherine Churchyard, Leconfield, Yorkshire.

220 Sqn	Hudson V	AM583	NR-F	Op:	Bert Patrol
	F/O R S Jameson	81923	+	Base:	Thornaby
	P/O P K Clench	88391	+	T/o time:	21:20
	F/Sgt T J McHugh	653675	+		
	Sgt H O Cook	635563	+		

Airborne at Thornaby for a Bert Patrol and failed to return. F/O Jameson and his crew are commemorated on the Runnymede Memorial. Possibly shot down by Ltn Jakobi.

7th August 1941

220 Sqn	Hudson V	AM616	NR-	Duty:	?
	F/O Kendal	. . . . .	Injured	Base:	Stornoway
	P/O Nicholson	. . . . .	Injured	T/o time:	?
	P/O J A Rennie	61260	DoI		
	F/Sgt Smith	. . . . . .	Injured		
	F/Sgt Walshe	. . . . . .	Injured		

Collided with an Anson of 48 Squadron at the runway intersection shortly after becoming airborne. The Hudson had its tail cut off by the other aircraft and crashed in flames. P/O Rennie later died of his injuries and rests in Dunbar Cemetery, East Lothian.

500 Sqn	Blenheim IV	L4899	MK-E	Op:	Nomad Patrol
	P/O L Ward	45642	+	Base:	Bircham Newton
	Sgt W S Robinson	971021	+	T/o time:	22:00
	Sgt R L Burton	812221	+		

Took off for a shipping sweep off the Frisian Islands but crashed into the North Sea. All are commemorated on the Runnymede Memorial.

9th August 1941

404 (RCAF) Sqn	Blenheim IV	Z6178	EE-	Duty:	Training
	Sgt R K McKay	. . . . . .	Safe	Base:	Skitten
				T/o time:	?

Took off for single engine circuit and landing practice. Bounced on landing and engine cut causing the Blenheim to swing before the u/c collapsed. The aircraft was considered to have been damaged beyond repair.

10th August 1941

53 Sqn	Hudson V	AM672	PZ-P	Op:	Strike
	P/O A F Buck	87433	+	Base:	Bircham Newton
	Sgt L H Wood	755675	+	T/o time:	10:00
	F/Sgt T E Stepney	746831	+		
	F/Lt I P Magrath	76331	+		

Took off along with two other Hudsons for a patrol and sighted a ship of approx 7,000 to 8,000 tons escorted by five MTB's 30 km (c 18⅝ miles) north of Borkum. The flight attacked but the Hudson was shot down at 13:24 hrs by flak from the 6th Minesweeper Flotilla. The bodies of both Sgt Wood and P/O Buck were recovered N of Terschelling and were initially buried in Huisduinen but now rest in Bergen-Op-Zoom War Cemetery. F/Lt Magrath's body was washed ashore on 18th October and he is buried in Vredenhof Cemetery on Schiermonnikoog. F/Sgt Stepney is commemorated on the Runnymede Memorial.

320 Sqn	Hudson I	N7396	NO-V	Duty:	Training
	Res Sgt Vl i/o A M Ten Herkel RNNAS...	+		Base:	Leuchars
	Res Sgt Vl i/o W Hijkoop RNNAS	+		T/o time:	?

Crashed and burned while low flying 3 miles W of Dunino, Fife. The Court of Inquiry blamed an error of judgement by the pilot with over confidence and lack of type experience as the cause of the accident. Both airmen rest in Leuchars Cemetery.

11th August 1941

201 Sqn	Sunderland II	W3978	ZM-X	Op:	Anti-Submarine Patrol
	S/Ldr Fraser	.....	Safe	Base:	Sullom Voe
	F/O Champion	.....	Safe	T/o time:	19:06
	P/O Powell	.....	Safe		
	Sgt Briden	......	Safe		
	Sgt D T Owen	978468	+		
	Sgt Abbott	......	Safe		
	Sgt P J Butler	553258	+		
	Sgt Clark	......	Safe		
	Sgt H J Parkes	751667	+		
	LAC Walker	......	Safe		
	AC1 J W Cutchie	990955	+		
	AC1 W M Kinnish	966738	+		

Took off for a patrol of Nose 1 but flew into the water while landing at 22:21 hrs at Sullom Voe, Shetland. On landing the pilot switched on flap light and was blinded by green indicator lamp; both 1st and 2nd pilots leaned forward to cover the light with their hands and inadvertently one of the pilots may have pushed control column forward. Sgt Owen rests in Bebington Cemetery, Cheshire, AC1 Kinnish in Everton Cemetery, Liverpool, Sgt Parkes in St Giles Churchyard and Extension, Willenhall, Staffordshire, AC1 Cutchie locally in Lerwick New Cemetery, Shetland and Sgt Butler in Rothley Cemetery, Leicestershire. This was the unit's first loss of a Sunderland Mk.II.

217 Sqn	Beaufort I	L9972	MW-F	Op:	Shipping Search
	F/O E A Rance	79736	PoW	Base:	St Eval
	Sgt A G Wilson	982330	PoW	T/o time:	12:05
	Sgt A Chiplin	746770	+		
	Sgt S J Austin	746908	PoW		

Lost off St Nazaire, France. Last seen in position VCVU 3110 at 13:44 hrs.
Sgt Chiplin is commemorated on the Runnymede Memorial.

235 Sqn	Blenheim IV	P6908	LA-F	Op:	South Bert Patrol
	P/O W C Richards	102978	+	Base:	Sumburgh
	Sgt J C Mason	971264	+	T/o time:	10:20
	Sgt J D R H Archibald	1355114	+		

Missing from patrol. Possibly shot down by Ltn Jakobi.
All are commemorated on the Runnymede Memorial.

12th August 1941

407 (RCAF) Sqn	Hudson V	AM544	RR-W	Duty:	Training
	Sgt R Fraser	......	Safe	Base:	North Coates
	Sgt J W Creeden	......	Safe	T/o time:	?

Took off for night flying practice but undershot and crashed at Donna Nook, Lincolnshire.

13th August 1941

22 Sqn

Beaufort I	N1115	OA-U	Op:	Patrol
Sgt Griffiths	......	Safe	Base:	Manston
Sgt Tait	......	Safe	T/o time:	15:40
Sgt A L Brigstocke	977612	Safe		
Sgt Barry	......	Safe		

Detailed to patrol Oostende to IJmuiden. On landing at Manston the u/c leg collapsed and the Beaufort was struck off charge as beyond economic repair.

42 Sqn

Beaufort I	N1112	AW-J	Op:	Gardening
P/O J D E How	63788	+	Base:	Leuchars
F/Sgt C A L Powell	751317	+	T/o time:	00:35
F/Sgt N J Spicer	939324	+		
Sgt L G A Roberts	960195	+		

Lost into the North Sea, off Karmsund, Norway. P/O How and his crew are commemorated on the Runnymede Memorial.

42 Sqn

Beaufort I	AW200	AW-R	Op:	Karmsund
Sgt H G N Morison DFM	966010	+	Base:	Leuchars
Sgt H G Gibbon	745967	+	T/o time:	23:59
Sgt E R Harcourt	956665	+		
Sgt R MacNab	637612	+		
Sgt Tyler				

Tasked with a diversion operation for an FAA mining operation (codenamed Bottle). Set course for the Karmsund area but crashed into the sea off Valewag, Norway. Sgt Harcourt rests in Mollendal Church Cemetery, Bergen, Norway, while the others are commemorated on the Runnymede Memorial.

14th August 1941

143 Sqn

Beaufighter IF	T4648	HO-	Duty:	Training
Sgt S J Hobbs	742901	+	Base:	Dyce
Sgt A Handley	994082	+	T/o time:	?

Stalled on the approach then rolled and dived into the ground at Dyce, Aberdeenshire, before catching fire. Sgt Hobbs rests in Brookwood Military Cemetery, Surrey and Sgt Handley in Dewsbury Cemetery, Yorkshire.

15th August 1941

1 PRU

Spitfire I (PR)	.....?	LY-	Op:	Reconnaissance
F/O S H Dowse	86685	PoW	Base:	?
			T/o time:	07:35

Failed to return. No further details known.

500 Sqn

Blenheim IV	Z6036	MK-Y	Duty:	Air Sea Rescue Sortie
P/O C M Elgar	91234	+	Base:	Bircham Newton
Sgt J Halls	748358	+	T/o time:	10:30
Sgt D A Butterfield	748325	+		

Took off along with D/500 to search for a dinghy. Having located the dinghy with six occupants in position ZKHA 1942 at 11:10 hrs, Y/500 was left orbiting the dinghy while 'D'/500 went off in search of an ASR launch. When D/500 returned there was no sign of Y/500, only some wreckage about 100 yards NE of the dinghy. Z6036 was shot down at 14:30 hrs by Ofw Kornacker of 6./ZG76 flying from Leeuwarden. The crew is commemorated on the Runnymede Memorial.

16th August 1941

86 Sqn

Beaufort I	AW206	BX-	Duty:	Training
Sgt K M Dixon	......	Safe	Base:	North Coates
			T/o time:	?

Ditched 2 miles off North Coates.

206 Sqn

Hudson V	AM588	VX-E	Op:	Convoy Escort
P/O T L Hayston	87393	+	Base:	Aldergrove
Sgt Staite	......	Injured	T/o time:	03:30

Sgt	R E Ramsay	755620	DoI		
Sgt	Mann	......	Safe		

Failed to climb to a reasonable height after t/o and crashed 4 miles NE of Ladyhill, Co Antrim at 03:40 hrs. P/O Hayston is buried in St Bridget Churchyard, Bridekirk, Westmoreland. Sgt Ramsay died from his injuries a few days later and rests in St Nicholas Churchyard, Woodrising, Norfolk.

17th August 1941

22 Sqn	**Beaufort I**		**L9959**	**OA-D**	**Op:**	**Shipping Strike**
	Sgt	Buckmaster	......	Safe	Base:	Manston
	Sgt	E W Poole	745192	Safe	T/o time:	?
	P/O	Stevens	......	Safe		
	Sgt	S V Calvetti	755543	+		

Shortly after 18:00 hrs a Beaufort crashed into the sea between Kingsdown and Walmer, some 400 yards offshore. A fresh SW wind was blowing, with a choppy sea. The accident was seen by a man on his way to church, and he went at once to the beach, launched his 9 ft dinghy and rowed out accompanied by an unknown officer. They found three airmen in the sea, pulled two into the dinghy and, with the third airman made fast to her, returned to the shore. The fourth airman was lost. A motor boat had also put off, manned by the lifeboat coxswain, two men and a boy, but the dinghy had already rescued the men. Sgt Calvetti is buried in Nottingham Southern Cemetery.

22 Sqn	**Beaufort I**		**AW214**	**OA-G**	**Op:**	**Gardening**
	P/O	I G Mitchell	88667	+	Base:	Thorney Island
	P/O	H F Binns	89799	+	T/o time:	20:40
	Sgt	T Penrice	637107	+		
	Sgt	D A Campbell	974760	+		

Took off and set course for the Dewberry area off Boulogne but was shot down by flak (Abt. 31/XI) and crashed in the West Scheldt estuary. All the crew are commemorated on the Runnymede Memorial.

221 Sqn	**Wellington VIII**		**W5730**	**DF-**	**Op:**	**Crossover Patrol**
	F/Lt	C Cakebread	39854	+	Base:	St Eval
	Sgt	C J Fletcher	748046	+	T/o time:	08:25
	Sgt	J E Rees	759092	+		
	Sgt	D H Fugill	911372	+		
	Sgt	A E Earle	915593	+		
	Sgt	A E Cleary	639543	+		

Missing on patrol west of Ireland. Base tried unsuccessfully to contact the crew by W/T after the Wellington had been airborne for 3 hours. A Sunderland from RAF Mount Batten and patrols from St Eval searched for signs of wreckage during the day. Sgt Earle, from Newfoundland, and the other crew members were never found and are commemorated on the Runnymede Memorial.

18th August 1941

86 Sqn	**Beaufort I**		**W6471**	**BX-Z**	**Duty:**	**Training**
	Sgt P N Cowan RAAF		404171	+	Base:	North Coates
					T/o time:	?

Sgt Cowan rests in St Nicholas Churchyard, North Cotes, Lincolnshire. The Form 1180 records that the aircraft 'flew into high ground after take-off at Donna Nook, Lincolnshire', which is in itself odd, since the latter airfield is on the coast and the immediate surrounding terrain is quite flat. The nearest high ground, the Lincolnshire Wolds, approx 200 feet high, is some 7 miles away!

612 Sqn	**Whitley V**		**T4282**	**WL-E**	**Op:**	**Fate 1 Patrol**
	P/O	McRobbie	.....	Safe	Base:	Wick
	P/O	Ellis	.....	Safe	T/o time:	15:43
	Sgt	Johnstone	......	Safe		
	Sgt	Davies	......	Safe		
	Sgt	Pickering	......	Safe		
	Sgt	Mercer	......	Safe		

At 18:15 hrs the temperature of the staboard engine rose to 140° so they set course for Shetland, 100 miles away. At 18:50 hrs they jettisoned the bomb-load and at 19:16 hrs the starboard engine seized up and stopped. At 19:18 hrs the port engine began to fail so P/O McRobbie ditched 10 miles N of Muckle Flugga. The crew all safely transferred to the dinghy and they were picked up at 22:00 hrs some 20 miles N of the Shetlands by a RAF High-Speed Launch from Lerwick.

19th August 1941

22 Sqn	Beaufort I		AW211	OA-F	Op:	Gardening
	Sgt	P E Miller	960718	+	Base:	Thorney Island
	P/O	H E J Whiston RCAF	J/4696	+	T/o time:	19:40
	Sgt	K W S Ramsden	1051847	+		
	Sgt	A G Petty	958992	+		

Tasked with a mining operation to the Oysters area. On the return the Beaufort overshot and crashed into the Emsworth Channel at 23:05 hrs. Sgt Miller rests in SS Mary and Margaret Churchyard, Sprowston, Norfolk; Sgt Ramsden was cremated at Lawns Wood Crematorium, Leeds, while both P/O Whiston, from Montreal, and Sgt Petty are buried locally in St Nicholas Churchyard, West Thorney.

233 Sqn	Hudson III		T9442	ZS-	Op:	Stopper Patrol
	F/Sgt D J Muir		580184	+	Base:	St Eval
	Sgt	C G Burchardt	754231	+	T/o time:	00:45
	F/Sgt J M Wheatley		746837	+		
	Sgt	G E Buckley	973940	+		

Flew into a hill at 07:20 hrs on the return from a patrol some 3 miles S of Gefach Goch, Glamorganshire. The crew rest in various cemeteries in England and Scotland.

320 Sqn	Hudson III		T9413	NO-N	Op:	Stand Patrol
	F/O	C A Langelaar RNNAS	.....	+	Base:	Leuchars
	Sgt	J L Froweijn RNNAS	......	+	T/o time:	01:38
	P/O	J Peetoom RNNAS	......	+		
	Cpl	J G Uljee RNNAS	......	+		
	Stoker F A van der Hurk KM		......	+		

Failed to return from over the North Sea. The aircraft was named *Ockenburg*.

20th August 1941

1 PRU	Spitfire I PR type D	X4497	LY-	Op:	Reconnaissance
	?	.....		Base:	?
				T/o time:	?

Missing from a PR operation to Brest, France.

1 PRU	Spitfire I PR type E (PR.V)	X4491	LY-	Op:	Reconnaissance
	F/O C A S Greenhill	40906	PoW	Base:	Benson
				T/o time:	13:05

Took off tasked with a high level operation to the Brest area and was shot down from 30,000 feet into the Channel, 35 miles N of Brest, by three Me109s. A *Luftwaffe* flying-boat tried to land in the rough seas to rescue F/O Greenhill but this attempt had to be abandoned and he was finally picked up by an ocean-going tug.

21st August 1941

59 Sqn	Blenheim IV		R3631	TR-B	Op:	Habo Patrol
	P/O	W F W Foster	88477	+	Base:	Detling
	Sgt	J E Mylchreest	977614	+	T/o time:	14:55
	Sgt	G A Crowther	918137	+		

Missing off the Channel Ports. All are commemorated on the Runnymede Memorial.

201 Sqn	Sunderland II		W3982	ZM-	Op:	Anti-Submarine Patrol
	F/O	A G Evill	73043	+	Base:	Sullom Voe
	P/O	F W Selfe	61510	+	T/o time:	11:07
	Sgt	J M Simmons	937545	+		
	Sgt	L H Barraclough	958499	+		
	Sgt	J A C King	1150791	+		
	Sgt	D M V P Devereux	567519	+		
	Sgt	E O Adams	755269	+		
	Sgt	K E Newman	926329	+		
	Sgt	W P J Hancox	759140	+		
	F/Sgt E W W Gange		528264	+		
	LAC	T J Gordon	966724	+		
	LAC	J F Richard	629318	+		
	LAC	H Mills	702322	+		

Took off for a patrol of area Fate 3. Signalled that they had been attacked by an enemy aircraft and ditched NNW of the Shetlands. All are commemorated on the Runnymede Memorial.

217 Sqn	Beaufort I	N1041	MW-S	Op:	Rover Patrol
	P/O P F R Graham DFC	89363	+	Base:	St Eval
	P/O J A V Stockley	62677	+	T/o time:	14:45
	Sgt E A C Williams	926464	+		
	Sgt R Marshall	1304739	+		

Took off in company with one other aircraft but crashed into the sea off the coast of Loire-Atlantique. P/O Stockley rests in Escoublac-la-Baule War Cemetery, France, while the other crewmen are commemorated on the Runnymede Memorial.

22nd August 1941

119 Sqn	Short S.23/M 'C' Class	AX659	W	Duty:	Training
	F/O S J Rawlins	.....	Injured	Base:	Bowmore
				T/o time:	?

Suffered an engine failure and failed to maintain height on the remaining engines. It was affected by excessive drag due to the propeller on the failed engine being stuck in fine pitch, which stalled the starboard wing. F/O Rawlins could not prevent a bank to starboard and crashed at Bruichladdich on Islay at 18:15 hrs. AX659 was a former Imperial Airways 4-engined Empire flying-boat airliner, G-AETY, named *Clio*, which had been impressed for wartime service in July 1940.

23rd August 1941

235 Sqn	Blenheim IV	T1807	LA-N	Op:	A/A Patrol
	P/O P L Lander	88676	+	Base:	Dyce
	Sgt H Leake	915810	+	T/o time:	07:25
	Sgt G E R Latimer	745230	+		

Took off in company with other squadron aircraft for an escort to one Sunderland, two Catalinas and HMS *Rubis*. At 11:17 hrs the Blenheim stalled, dipped the starboard wing and dived into North Sea after engine failure at low altitude. Two people were thrown out and were presumed dead. The aircraft broke its back and disappeared within one minute. Sgt Leake rests in Frederikshavn Cemetery, Denmark while both P/O Lander and Sgt Latimer are commemorated on the Runnymede Memorial. The Commonwealth War Graves Commission records a date of death of 8th November 1941 for the crew.

413 (RCAF) Sqn	Catalina I	AH556	QL-	Duty:	Training
	F/O M A F Hirst RAF	76580	+	Base:	Stranraer
	F/O A L Fowler DFC RNZAF	42116	+	T/o time:	22:50
	Ens D A Eldred USN	.....	+		
	Sgt P J N Coady	R/70095	+		
	AC Muir RAF	1195496	Injured		
	AC1 P Q O'Brien RAF	575990	+		
	Sgt R B H Scroggs RAF	755904	Injured		

Took off for night flying practice, captained by instructor Pilot Ensign Eldred USN, but swung when leaving the water and crashed a few seconds later with full power on, and caught fire. Two of the crew survived, injured, but the other five died, including the 2nd pilot, Ensign Eldred, whose body was recovered from Loch Ryan on 10th September. Investigation revealed that the elevator trim had been set in the fully nose down position, and a recommendation made that illumination of this control should be provided in future for night operations. All those who died rest locally in the Glebe Cemetery, Stranraer, Wigtownshire.

502 Sqn	Whitley V	Z6500	YG-Q	Op:	Patrol
	F/O G D Sproule	41487	+	Base:	Limavady
	Sgt R Naylor	754349	+	T/o time:	?
	P/O J Matthews	104437	+		
	Sgt D H Jones	625737	+		
	Sgt S H Monk	943582	Injured		
	Sgt W H Bradshaw	751058	Injured		
	Lt D V Bevan RN	.....	+		

Crashed on the return from the patrol 1 mile W of Limavady. Sgt Naylor rests in All Saints Cemetery, Newcastle-Upon-Tyne; P/O Matthews in St Mary's Cemetery, Taunton, Somerset; Sgt Jones in Blaenwaun Chapelyard, St Dogmells, Cardiganshire, and F/O Sproule in St Michael Roman Catholic Churchyard, Belmont Abbey, Herefordshire.

24th August 1941

500 Sqn	Blenheim IV	Z6039	MK-Q	Op:	Nomad Patrol
	P/O G C M Fletcher	83995	+	Base:	Bircham Newton
	Sgt J E Mylrea RCAF	R/58213	+	T/o time:	10:30
	Sgt H Walton	105111	+		

Shot down at 13:05 hrs by flak from two HS-boats 10 miles off Hoek van Holland, Holland. Sgt Mylrea, an American from Los Angeles, and the other crew members are commemorated on the Runnymede Memorial.

26th August 1941

612 Sqn	Whitley V	Z6806	WL-W	Op:	Anti-Submarine Patrol
	F/O H C Winter-Taylor	42733	PoW	Base:	Wick
	Sgt R J Skuse	748628	PoW	T/o time:	08:15
	Sgt J H Kennedy	630077	PoW		
	Sgt Millar	......	?		
	Sgt J S Martin	998984	PoW		
	F/O Grocott	......	?		

At 13:15 hrs a faint repeated SOS signal was received, with no position and ending with the word 'landing'. The rough bearings taken gave the position as considerably East of the dead reckoning position. Searches were carried out but no trace of the Whitley was found. See also 6th May 1941.

27th August 1941

1 PRU	Spitfire I PR type D	X4493	LY-	Op:	Reconnaissance
	?	.....	+ (?)	Base:	?
				T/o time:	?

Missing from an operation to Kiel.

22 Sqn	Beaufort I	N1171	OA-H	Op:	Gardening
	F/Sgt H Menary DFM	748613	+	Base:	Thorney Island
	Sgt T S Royan RCAF	R/60002	+	T/o time:	19:00
	Sgt F S R Heard	914086	+		
	Sgt R P S Grenfell	900198	+		

Lost off Brest, France. The Beaufort signalled SOS at a time that suggested that it was on its return flight. Sgt Heard and Sgt Grenfell are commemorated on the Runnymede memorial while both F/Sgt Menary and Sgt Royan, from Calgary, rest in St Mary's Cemetery, Cornwall.

143 Sqn	Beaufighter IC	T3311	HO-	Duty:	?
	P/O J M Sayers	60312	+	Base:	Dyce
	Sgt A A Catton	971481	+	T/o time:	?

Lost height in a turn, hit a tree and crashed at Tillery, Aberdeenshire. Sgt Catton rests locally in Dyce Old Churchyard while P/O Sayers was taken to Cathcart Cemetery, Renfrewshire for burial.

209 Sqn	Catalina I	AH552	WQ-	Duty:	?
				Base:	Reykjavik
				Time:	?

Reason SoC unknown. Became an instructional airframe.

30th August 1941

22 Sqn	Beaufort I	X8939	OA-B	Duty:	Transit flight
	Sgt E W Poole	745192	Safe	Base:	Thorney Island
				T/o time:	06:25

Overshot at 09:00 hrs into a ditch on landing at too great a speed for the small aerodrome at Thornaby, Yorkshire. See also 17th Augusy 1941.

42 Sqn	Beaufort I	L9834	AW-V	Op:	Strike
	S/Ldr G S P Rooney DFC	39245	+	Base:	Leuchars
	Sgt L C Mansell RCAF	R/51633	+	T/o time:	02:10
	F/O C Grant	78749	+		
	F/Sgt R S Knott	551646	+		

Hit a hill two minutes after take-off and crashed at Craigfootie, Fife. S/L Rooney and Sgt Mansell, from Hamilton, Ontario, are both buried locally at Leuchars Cemetery; F/O Grant in Wellshill Cemetery, Perth, while F/Sgt Knott was taken to Milton Cemetery, Portsmouth.

320 Sqn	**Hudson II**	**T9380**	**NO-H**	**Op:**	**Shipping Strike**
	S/Lt S Hendrik-Jansen RNNAS	. . . . .	+	Base:	Leuchars
	Sgt J P J Bielfeldt RNNAS	12682	+	T/o time:	11:35
	Cpl H J Moll RNNAS	. . . . .	+		
	AB1 A A Recourt RNNAS	. . . . .	+		
	AB3 R Smidt RNNAS	. . . . .	+		

Named *Waalnaven*, this aircraft failed to return from an attack on a convoy off Kristiansand.

320 Sqn	**Hudson III**	**V9063**	**NO-M**	**Op:**	**Shipping Sweep**
	F/Lt W Bakker RNNAS	40595	PoW	Base:	Leuchars
	Lt K Deen KM	. . . . .	+	T/o time:	11:35
	Sgt C E van Huijstee RNNAS	11031	PoW		
	Seinermaat E H Chateau KM	. . . . .	+		
	Sgt H J Heeren RNNAS	. . . . .	+		

Completing a disastrous day for the Squadron, this Hudson, named *Islawreker*, was attacked by Me109s off the Norwegian coast. Damage was inflicted to the mainplanes and the Hudson was forced to ditch. All but Sgt Heeren managed to abandon the aircraft before it sank. F/Lt Bakker was picked up unconscious five hours later by the crew of a German Heinkel He59 rescue plane only to join Sgt Huijstee who was already on board.

320 Sqn	**Hudson III**	**V9065**	**NO-R**	**Op:**	**Shipping Sweep**
	F/O H C Prager RNNAS	. . . . .	+	Base:	Leuchars
	P/O J Weber RNNAS	. . . . .	+	T/o time:	11:35
	AB1 P J C H van der Linden RNNAS.		+		
	Vliegtuigmaker 3 K van Os RNNAS.		+		

This aircraft, named *Moesie*, failed to return from a sweep off Norway.

500 Sqn	**Blenheim IV**	**V5525**	**MK-B**	**Op:**	**Schiphol**
	Sgt D A Crosbie	968184	+	Base:	Bircham Newton
	Sgt D C Hyslop	968145	+	T/o time:	21:21
	Sgt A H Peek	902987	+		

Hit by flak at 23:37 hrs from ResFlakAbt/242 during a night attack and crashed at Amsterdame Bos. The aircraft was classified as having Dutch colours on the rudder by the German crash investigators but this was later found to be the RAF fin flash. All rest in Amsterdam New Eastern Cemetery.

500 Sqn	**Blenheim IV**	**Z6164**	**MK-V**	**Op:**	**Night Intruder**
	F/O I H N Terry	79737	+	Base:	Bircham Newton
	Sgt H D Poole	754015	+	T/o time:	21:21
	Sgt A C Scrivens	749499	+		

Crashed into the sea off Noordwijk during an operation to Soesterberg.
All are commemorated on the Runnymede Memorial.

31st August 1941

86 Sqn	**Beaufort I**	**AW213**	**BX-U**	**Duty:**	?
	Sgt T Kaye	1051935	+	Base:	North Coates
				Time:	?

Damaged in an undefined accident. Sgt Kaye is buried in Wellshill Cemetery, Perth.

1st September 1941

1 PRU	**Spitfire I PR type E**	**X4500**	**LY-**	**Op:**	**Reconnaissance**
	F/O C C Blair	77781	+	Base:	?
				T/o time:	?

Missing from a PR operation to Stavanger and Kirstiansand, Norway.
F/O Blair is commemorated on the Runnymede Memorial.

2nd September 1941

22 Sqn	**Beaufort I**	**AW218**	**OA-W**	**Op:**	**Shipping Strike**
	Sgt D McTavish	742641	+	Base:	Leuchars
	Sgt J R Durber	749320	+	T/o time:	13:45

Sgt   G A V Cope   751570   +
Sgt   G Waddilove   975061   +
Took off for an attack on shipping off Stavanger, Norway. During the attack Sgt McTavish was last seen with an engine on fire gliding down under control towards the sea in position ZNEF 5227. All the crew are commemorated on the Runnymede Memorial.

235 Sqn	Blenheim IV	L9261	LA-T	Op:	Trost Patrol
	F/Lt H M Hammond	37471	+	Base:	Sumburgh
	P/O W J Mason	60833	+	T/o time:	22:00
	Sgt G R Simpson	908869	+		

Flew into a hill in bad visibility at Hoxter Walls, Sandness, Shetland. F/Lt Hammond, a New Zealander from Wellington City, and the other crewmen rest locally in Lerwick New Cemetery, Shetland.

404 (RCAF) Sqn	Blenheim IV	L9394	EE-	Duty:	Training
	Sgt W E Dale	R/72360	+	Base:	Skitten
	Sgt E G Allen RAF	975744	+	T/o time:	?
	Cpl L W McKinlay RAF	567698	+		

Spun into the ground at 17:00 hrs, 1 mile E of Castletown, due to unknown causes. Sgt Dale from Ontario, and Cpl McKinlay are both buried in Wick Cemetery, while Sgt Allen rests in Penarth Cemetery, Glamorganshire.

608 Sqn	Hudson V	AM599	UL-H	Op:	North Hornli Patrol
	Sgt W C E Broomhead	936240	+	Base:	Thornaby
	Sgt B L Thomas	938213	+	T/o time:	11:09
	Sgt J M Christie	978672	+		
	Sgt G Law	1005490	+		

Failed to return from off Norway. All rest in Austad Churchyard, Flekkefjord, Norway.

Chapter 11

3rd September to 31st December 1941

On the 11th September, even though the USA was still not at war with Germany, President Roosevelt extended the United States battle against the U-boat from reporting locations to attacking them where found. Within a month the US Navy was escorting convoys almost two thirds of the way across the Atlantic, releasing Royal Navy ships for other duties. Despite the presence of the USN the increased number of operational U-boats led to heavy shipping losses in the mid-Atlantic gap. Three of the Liberators assigned to 120 Squadron for very long-range operations were re-assigned for Atlantic Ferry duties, postponing again the operational debut of the type. Also discussed but not actioned were proposals to transfer Coastal Whitley and Wellington resources to Bomber Command, but the Coastal Command C-in-C, Air Marshal Sir Philip Joubert de la Ferte, needed submarine sinkings to fight off these moves.

The Blenheim operations by Bomber Command proved too costly and 'Channel Stop' was transferred to Hurricane bombers of Fighter Command on the 9th of October. On the 25th of November, Bomber Command was released from anti-shipping operations with the exception of the Cherbourg section. Although the Beaufort torpedo-bomber force was increased with the formation of new squadrons, they were hindered by lack of experienced crews and the units transferred to mining operations.

Shipping losses in November were the lowest since the beginning of the war due mainly to 18 U-boats being transferred to the Mediterranean.

A large part of the Hudson force was diverted to Scottish and Channel bases to contain the *Tirpitz* in Trondheim as well as the *Scharnhorst*, *Gneisenau* and *Prinz Eugen* in Brest. Further aircraft were lost with the transfer of numerous crews and squadrons to the Middle and Far East commands.

The role of the United States in the war against Germany was to change dramatically in December with first the attack on Pearl Harbour by Japan on the 7th and then the declaration of War with Italy and Germany by America, on the 12th of December.

Coastal Command now had new allies in the shipping war but had also gained an additional war theatre to deplete its meagre resources.

4th September 1941

235 Sqn	Blenheim IV	R3909	LA-G	Op:	Stand Patrol
	F/O A E Cook	. . . . .	Safe	Base:	Dyce
	Sgt Ludlam	. . . . . .	Safe	T/o time:	23:35
	Sgt Godfrey	. . . . . .	Safe		

Hit a pole on a night approach in bad weather and crashed at 04:30 hrs on the return.

5th September 1941

48 Sqn	Anson I	W1769	OY-	Op:	Convoy Escort
	F/Sgt E F Howarth	741519	+	Base:	Stornoway
	Sgt F W Taylor	920733	+	T/o time:	
	Sgt R D Starkie-Bence	957734	+		
	Sgt J J Stritch	627347	+		

Hit a davit aboard HMS *Hebe* when the Anson dived low over the Sloop and crashed into sea in position 5804N 0613W. All are commemorated on the Runnymede Memorial.

6th September 1941

1402 (Met) Flight	Gladiator II	N5592		Op:	Met Flight
	F/Lt Bennett	. . . . .	Safe	Base:	Aldergrove
				T/o time:	?

Took off in early morning fog which was expected to clear. The Gladiator attempted to force-land when the fog persisted and hit the side of Lady Hill, County Antrim.

7th September 1941

86 Sqn	Beaufort I	W6542	BX-D	Duty:	Air Sea Rescue Sortie
	Sgt R A Dawes	1198393	+	Base:	North Coates
	Sgt S R Longhurst	1251534	+	T/o time: ?	
	Sgt W T Udale	1260382	+		
	Sgt E L Butt	1262088	+		

Crashed into the sea after an engine failure. Sgt Butt's body was recovered from the sea and he is buried in Nes General Cemetery on Ameland, Holland, while the rest of the crew are commemorated on the Runnymede Memorial.

608 Sqn	Hudson V	AM601	UL-N	Op:	Blocking Patrol
	Sgt Harrington	......	Injured	Base:	Thornaby
	Sgt Foster	......	Injured	T/o time: 19:30	
	Sgt Bennett	......	Injured		
	Sgt T R B Corrie	1254015	DoI		

Took off to cover convoy EC70. Overshot at 22:45 hrs during a night landing at Thornaby and crashed into the valley beyond the East/West runway. Sgt Corrie died during the night and rests in Thornaby-on-Tees Cemetery, Yorkshire.

10th September 1941

1 PRU	Spitfire I (PR) type D	R7039	LY-	Op:	Reconnaissance
	P/O G N Busbridge	87428	+	Base:	Benson
				T/o time: 09:50	

Missing on an operation to the France/Spain border in this, a 'bowser wing' Spitfire. P/O Busbridge is commemorated on the Runnymede Memorial.

22 Sqn	Beaufort I	X8930	OA-J	Op:	Rover Patrol
	Sgt Jennings	......	Safe	Base:	Leuchars
	Sgt Driscoll	......	Safe	T/o time: 10:45	
	Sgt Burgess	......	Wounded		
	Sgt Stacey	......	Wounded		

Tasked for a shipping strike off Kristiansand, Norway. The Beaufort was late in taking off and did not formate with the other a/c. Sgt Jennings continued alone and attacked the convoy in position ZNGB 0436 (approx.) and taking evasive action when jumped from astern by a Me109 flown by Ltn Widowitz. Sgt Burgess was hit in the first attack, Sgt Stacey went to the rear and got him out of the turret and continued firing before being also hit. Sgt Jennings managed to belly-land back at Leuchars at 16:11 hrs despite the tail trimmer being badly damaged and the W/T u/s.

143 Sqn	Beaufighter IC	T3323	HO-	Duty:	?
	F/Lt J G Lingard	.....	Safe	Base:	Dyce
				T/o time: ?	

Hit a wall at 04:45 hrs on a night approach and the u/c collapsed at Dyce, Aberdeenshire.

236 Sqn	Blenheim IV	T1811	ND-C	Op: Convoy Escort	
	P/O C B Pearson	66025	+	Base:	Carew Cheriton
	Sgt A K MacLean RCAF	R/54115	+	T/o time: 09:43	
	Sgt L H Winter	1154328	+		

Took off, in company with B/236 to escort a DC3 airliner, G-AGBD, but lost contact at 12:52 hrs on entering cloud off Hartland Point. The bodies of two of the crew were recovered: P/O Pearson rests in Hull Crematorium while Sgt MacLean, a Canadian from Ottawa, is buried in St Augustine Churchyard, Heanton Punchardon, Devon. Sgt Winter is commemorated on the Runnymede Memorial.

12th September 1941

254 Sqn	Blenheim IV	N3610	QY-	Duty:	Training
	Sgt A A McIntosh	970490	Safe	Base:	Aldergrove
				T/o time: ?	

A cowling became detached and struck the tailplane jamming the elevators. The Blenheim was belly-landed at Ballymaguire, County Tyrone.

13th September 1941

42 Sqn	Beaufort I	N1148	AW-U	Duty:	Training
	P/O A R Riefstahl	89801	+	Base:	Leuchars
				Time:	10:00

While carrying out solo circuits the Beaufort swung on opening the throttles after a bad landing and failed to gain enough height. The port wing struck the control tower, slewing the aircraft into the side of a hangar before it crashed in flames. Examination of the wreckage showed that the friction settings on the throttles had been incorrectly set allowing one engine to pick up before the other. P/O Riefstahl is commemorated in Dundee Crematorium, Angus, but his ashes were dropped into the North Sea on a Rover operation by the Squadron on 22nd September.

233 Sqn	Hudson V	AM548	ZS-D	Op:	Anti-Submarine Search
	P/O R O H Down	85251	PoW	Base:	St Eval
	F/O R T R Cowper	41988	PoW	T/o time:	12:20
	Failed to return.				

14th September 1941

53 Sqn	Hudson V	AM777	PZ-G	Op:	Anti-Submarine Sweep
	P/O T M Gay	. . . . .	Evaded	Base:	St Eval
	Sgt J M Powell	748711	PoW	T/o time:	13:50
	Sgt A H Graham	. . . . . .	Evaded		
	Sgt S Tyson	755464	PoW		
	Off course and crashed in France.				

15th September 1941

236 Sqn	Blenheim IV	V5567	ND-L	Op:	Convoy Escort
	Sgt Blackie	. . . . . .	Safe	Base:	Carew Cheriton
	Sgt McNicol	. . . . . .	Safe	T/o time:	16:42
	Sgt F E Richardson	755737	+		

Took off to escort convoy Camel. Due to bad weather and W/T failure the Blenheim ran out of fuel on return from the patrol at 23:20 hrs and was abandoned 1 mile NE of Bodorgan, Anglesey. Sgt Richardson's body was recovered from the sea at West Tarbet, Mull of Galloway and was cremated at Ipswich Crematorium.

16th September 1941

224 Sqn	Hudson V	AM539	QX-U	Duty:	?
	P/O H W Andrews	85639	Safe	Base:	Limavady
				Time:	14:45

Swung on take-off, ran off runway into soft ground, caught fire and the u/c collapsed. The Court of Inquiry pointed out that little damage would have been caused if the fire tender crew had been more experienced.

330 Sqn	Northrop N-3PB	F11	GS-B		Ground Loss
				Base:	Budareyri
				Time:	?

Totally wrecked at its mooring when three depth charges exploded. The fuselage was later salvaged but the engine was lost.

17th September 1941

22 Sqn	Beaufort I	W6491	OA-R	Duty:	Air Test
	Sgt S E Howroyd	935037	Injured	Base:	Thorney Island
				T/o time:	12:00

Force-landed after the starboard engine failed on take-off.

248 Sqn | Beaufighter IC | T3351 | WR-U | **Duty:** | **Air Test**
P/O S H Birtles | 87070 | + | **Base:** | Bircham Newton
AC1 W T Bourne | 652624 | + | T/o time:

Broke up near Bircham Newton, Norfolk. P/O Birtles rests in Scholemoor Cemetery, Bradford; AC1 Bourne in Nottingham Southern Cemetery.

18th September 1941

320 Sqn | Hudson II | T9381 | NO-R | **Op:** | **Strike**
Struck off charge. Details not known. | | | **Base:** | Leuchars

---

20th September 1941

254 Sqn | Blenheim IV | T2128 | QY-J | **Duty:** | **Training**
Sgt   K F V D Kuhle | 776036 | + | **Base:** | Aldergrove
Sgt   R Steel | 1054486 | + | T/o time: ?
AC2 T W Vickers | 1097025 | +

The Blenheim hit the water during a practice attack at Lough Neagh, 4 miles S of Randalstown. All, including Sgt Kuhle from Naivasha, Kenya, rest in St Catherine Church of Ireland Churchyard, Killead, County Antrim.

21st September 1941

236 Sqn | Blenheim IV | V5761 | ND-E | **Op:** | **Escort**
Sgt   Casley | ...... | Injured | **Base:** | Carew Cheriton
Sgt   Norton | ...... | Safe | T/o time: 09:50
Sgt   Langhorne | ...... | Safe

Took off for an escort to a DC3 airliner. At 11:15 hrs on the return the starboard engine cut, the Blenheim lost height and it was belly-landed 2½ miles SW of Carew Cheriton.

22nd September 1941

1 PRU | Spitfire I PR type E | X4385 | LY-B | **Op:** | **Reconnaissance**
F/Lt P Tomlinson | 39154 | PoW | **Base:** | Benson
| | | T/o time: 11:00

Took off on an operation to Hamburg but suffered engine failure and left u/c leg collapsed during taxying after landing on Deelen at 13.06 hrs.

209 Sqn | Catalina I | AH565 | WQ- | | **Ground Loss**
| | | **Base:** | Akranes
| | | Time: | ?

Wrecked in a gale at its base, Akranes, Iceland.

500 Sqn | Blenheim IV | V5684 | MK-S | **Op:** | **Shipping Patrol**
P/O S G Nicoll | 87458 | + | **Base:** | Bircham Newton
F/O R E M Hughes-Chamberlain | 42838 | + | T/o time: 09:35
Sgt J B Crees | 916495 | +

Took off in company with other aircraft but became separated in cloud. Crashed into the North Sea off the coast of Holland. All are commemorated on the Runnymede Memorial.

24th September 1941

206 Sqn | Hudson V | AM664 | VX-B | **Op:** | **Convoy Escort**
Sgt   F Dunn | 938241 | + | **Base:** | Aldergrove
Sgt   B Morgan | 965474 | + | T/o time: 06:00
Sgt   G O Linhart | 1006792 | +
Sgt   V C D Hayward | 906000 | +

Returned early due to aileron trouble. Carried out a steep turn while low to avoid trees and a house then stalled at 100 feet on the approach to Aldergrove at 09:05 hrs. Both Sgt Dunn and Sgt Linhart rest in St Catherine Church of Ireland Churchyard, Killead, County Antrim; Sgt Morgan in Glenavy Roman Catholic Churchyard, County Antrim and Sgt Hayward in Henley Road Cemetery, Reading.

26th September 1941

48 Sqn	Hudson III	V9104	OY-	Duty:	Training
	F/O C E Dewar	42814	+	Base:	Stornoway
	F/O K G Smith	81924	+	T/o time:	?
	Sgt A N Clethero	978003	+		
	F/Sgt F Hyde	6445	+		
	LAC W C Brooks	747121	+		
	F/Sgt L A Birkett	516511	+		

Took off on a Navex with three ground crew, F/Sgt Hyde, LAC Brooks and F/Sgt Birkett onboard. Stalled on the approach and spun into the ground at Odiham before catching fire and being destroyed at 17:40 hrs. The Court of Inquiry found that the pilot did a tight turn to avoid losing sight of the aerodrome. The crew are buried in various locations throughout England.

217 Sqn	Beaufort I	W6483	MW-A	Op:	Shipping Strike
	P/O J R Harrison	89822	+	Base:	St Eval
	P/O P F Opperman	100561	+	T/o time:	11:50
	Sgt H L Carter	1162321	+		
	Sgt D A Ryder	1255613	+		

Took off in company with other aircraft for an attack on an enemy merchant vessel. Hit the County Quarry, Tregouning Hill in bad visibility 3 miles NW of Helston, Cornwall. P/O Harrison is buried in St Giles the Abbot Churchyard, Farnborough, P/O Opperman in St Matthew Churchyard, Rowde, Wiltshire, Sgt Ryder rests in Enfield Crematorium, Middlesex and Sgt Carter in Hither Green Cemetery, Lewisham, London.

27th September 1941

612 Sqn	Whitley V	Z6735	WL-F	Op:	Anti-Submarine Sweep
	F/Sgt	Davies	......	Safe	Base:	Reykjavik
	Sgt	Dandy	......	Safe	T/o time:	09:30
	Sgt	Thorpe	......	Safe		
	Sgt	McKay	......	Safe		
	Sgt	Newman	......	Safe		
	Sgt	Thompson	......	Safe		

Took off for a sweep but found nothing of interest. On the return the Whitley aborted the approach, stalled and crash-landed at 18:50 hrs.

28th September 1941

217 Sqn	Beaufort I	W6501	MW-D	Op:	St Nazaire
	P/O W S P Griffiths	61267	+	Base:	St Eval
	Sgt S C E Sapwell RNZAF	401216	+	T/o time:	18:24
	Sgt E D Suggett	759265	+		
	Sgt J W Ball	940028	+		

Took off for a night strike and lost without trace. Both Sgt Sapwell, a New Zealander, and Sgt Ball are commemorated on the Runnymede Memorial, Sgt Suggett rests in Pornic War Cemetery and P/O Griffiths in La Gueriniere Communal Cemetery both in France.

500 Sqn	Blenheim IV	Z6163	MK-	Duty:	?
	?	.....		Base:	Bircham Newton
				T/o time:	?

Missing over Northern France.

29th September 1941

59 Sqn	Hudson V	AM867	TR-G	Duty:	Training
	S/Ldr P D Dear	39506	+	Base:	Thorney Island
	G/C H S Scroggs	03055	+	Time:	?
	AC2 A Gamston	1506002	+		

Swung on take-off and blew up. S/Ldr Dear is buried locally in St Nicholas Churchyard, West Thorney. Also killed were the station commander G/C Scroggs and AC2 Gamston of 415 Squadron.

30th September 1941

1 PRU	Spitfire I PR type D	R7043	LY-	Op:	Reconnaissance
	F/O J F Swift DFC	41080	+	Base:	Benson
				T/o time:	12:55

Failed to return from an operation to photograph Hamburg and Kiel at high level. F/O Swift, of Invercargill, Southland, New Zealand, was washed ashore and first buried at Wilhelmshaven but now rests in Sage War Cemetery, Germany.

2nd October 1941

489 (RNZAF)	Beaufort I	N1075	A	Duty:	Training
Sqn	P/O C E Horwood	66538	+	Base:	Leuchars
				T/o time:	12:30

Took off for solo training but crashed into the mouth of the River Eden on the approach. P/O Horwood's body was later recovered off Thornaby and he now rests in Thornaby-on-Tees Cemetery, Yorkshire.

3rd October 1941

59 Sqn	Hudson V	AM704	TR-D	Op:	Hach Patrol
	P/O C F Rogerson	89832	+	Base:	Thorney Island
	P/O R A Gee	89629	+	T/o time:	19:09
	F/Sgt M L Sharpe	633334	+		
	Sgt A S Riddell	946244	+		

Took off for a night patrol but failed to return after reporting three enemy patrol vessels about 6 miles W of Le Havre at 20:00 hrs. A Whitley in the same area reported that a Hudson had been hit by flak and crashed into the sea in flames. P/O Gee rests in Ste Marie Cemetery, Le Havre, while the others are all commemorated on the Runnymede Memorial.

612 Sqn	Whitley V	Z6486	WL-O	Op:	Sweep
	P/O Sladden	. . . . .	Safe	Base:	Reykjavik
				T/o time:	?

Took off for a sweep followed by return to Wick and was laden with spares and ground crew as passengers. After 50 minutes flying the port engine developed a fault and P/O Sladden made for Kaldadardnes. The port engine failed on the approach and the Whitley lost height, tried to land downwind, swung and the undercarriage collapsed.

4th October 1941

220 Sqn	Hudson III	V9066	NR-V	Op:	North Stab Patrol
	P/O V G Collins	84672	+	Base:	Wick
	Sgt K R McL Brown	527561	+	T/o time:	11:45
	Sgt L E Sexton	755619	+		
	Sgt F Harrison	1056673	+		

Failed to return from a sweep off Norway. All the crew are commemorated on the Runnymede Memorial.

5th October 1941

1 PRU	Spitfire I PR type D	R7033	LY-	Op:	Reconnaissance
	F/O F Ball	. . . . .	Safe	Base:	?
				T/o time:	13:30

Took off for an operation to Hannover during a cloud break. Windscreen iced up during the climb and encountered turbulence in cloud at 23,000 feet. The aircraft entered an uncontrollable dive near Bishops Stortford, Hertfordshire. During the dive F/O Ball blacked out then regained consciousness just as his harness straps broke and he was thrown clear as the aircraft broke up in mid-air. F/O Ball described how he was still in the seated position with his hands and feet on imaginary controls as he fell in mid-air before he pulled the parachute rip-cord.

6th October 1941

248 Sqn	Beaufighter IC	T4664	WR-	Op:	?
	Sgt P Mueller RAAF	400380	Injured	Base:	Bircham Newton
				T/o time:	?

Bounced on landing, stalled and overturned at Bircham Newton, Norfolk, 15:40 hrs. The Court of Inquiry recommended that the pilot be returned to an OTU for further training on the type as this was his third crash in 12 days.

10th October 1941

407 (RCAF) Sqn	Hudson V	AM586	RR-T	Op:	Holden Patrol
	P/O H F Hegarty	J/4536	+	Base:	North Coates
	F/O J W Renwick RAF	77537	+	T/o time:	20:25
	Sgt D S Mather	R/54288	+		
	Sgt C J F McCrum	R/54357	+		

Failed to return from anti-shipping sortie. All are commemorated on the Runnymede Memorial.

500 Sqn	Blenheim IV	V6171	MK-F	Op:	Nomad Patrol
	F/O C C G Webb	79738	+	Base:	Bircham Newton
	Sgt R C Roberts RCAF	R/56163	+	T/o time:	21:25
	Sgt R H Coomber	812107	+		

Crashed into the North Sea near Overstrand, 2 miles SE of Cromer, Norfolk. F/O Webb, a New Zealander from Canterbury, rests in Caister Cemetery, Great Yarmouth, Norfolk. Sgt Coomber and Sgt Roberts from St Lambert, Canada, are commemorated on the Runnymede Memorial.

11th October 1941

217 Sqn	Beaufort I	AW197	MW-E	Op:	Gardening
	Sgt K W Perry	918534	+	Base:	St Eval
	Sgt C C Thomsen RCAF	R/60289	+	T/o time:	18:41
	Sgt F J Gornall	1051580	PoW		
	Sgt C E Earl	923291	+		

Lost off Brest, France. All those killed including Sgt Thomsen, from Kerteminde, Denmark, are commemorated on the Runnymede Memorial.

13th October 1941

220 Sqn	Hudson V	AM636	NR-B	Op:	South Stab Patrol
	F/Lt A J C Simpson DFC	72349	+	Base:	Wick
	P/O P R Smith	61261	+	T/o time:	03:30
	Sgt A J K Parratt MiD	627223	+		
	Sgt P F Swain	751851	+		

Failed to return from anti-shipping sortie. Both F/Lt Simpson and F/Sgt Parratt rest in Stavne Cemetery, Trondheim, Sgt Swain in Mollendal Church Cemetery, Bergen, while P/O Smith is commemorated on the Runnymede Memorial.

14th October 1941

42 Sqn	Beaufort I	N1163	AW-N	Op:	Shipping Strike
	W/O J E Woodward	515054	+	Base:	Leuchars
	Sgt L T Powles	751356	+	T/o time:	15:25
	Sgt K P J Fullagar	903434	+		
	Sgt A R Credland	640148	+		

Came in too low and hit the sea off Sognal, Norway, while attacking a 2,000 ton vessel in position ZNGB 2400 at 17:45 hrs. W/O Woodward, Sgt Credland and Sgt Powles are commemorated on the Runnymede Memorial while Sgt Fullagar rests in Vanse Churchyard, Norway.

59 Sqn	Hudson III	V9116	TR-K	Duty:	Training
	P/O Bispham	.....	Safe	Base:	Thorney Island
	Sgt Sweeting	......	Injured	T/o time:	21:40

Flew into the ground on the edge of Emsworth Channel on a night take-off due to incorrect trimming. The Hudson caught fire and was destroyed.

16th October 1941

42 Sqn	Beaufort I	L9939	AW-W	Op:	Rover Patrol
	P/O G S Turner	107513	+	Base:	Leuchars
	F/O A E Snell RCAF	J/941	+	T/o time: 14:00	
	F/Sgt R L Robinson	650686	+		
	Sgt G G King	977633	+		

Lost without trace. F/O Snell from Ottawa, and the other crew members, are commemorated on the Runnymede Memorial.

59 Sqn	Hudson V	AM740	TR-O	Op:	Habo Patrol
	P/O M H Sherley-Price	62336	+	Base:	Thorney Island
	Sgt C E White	754875	+	T/o time: 18:50	
	Sgt H F Tomkins	755409	+		
	Sgt C H B Page	1162363	+		

Failed to return from a Le Havre to Boulogne patrol. All are commemorated on the Runnymede Memorial.

19th October 1941

220 Sqn	Hudson V	AM724	NR-W	Op:	South Stab Patrol
	F/Sgt W H R Smith	758003	+	Base:	Wick
	Sgt H Jones	965692	+	T/o time: ?	
	Sgt R S Feakins	744965	+		
	Sgt E J Diplock	955346	+		

Failed to return. All are commemorated on the Runnymede Memorial.

404 (RCAF) Sqn	Blenheim IV	Z5753	EE-	Op:	Convoy Escort
	Sgt I A M Barber	R/77034	+	Base:	Sumburgh
	Sgt E Gillam RAF	746755	+	T/o time: 15:50	
	Sgt J Shaw RAF	946427	+		

Returned from convoy escort in bad visibility but failed to land. The Blenheim was presumed to have ditched off Lerwick, Shetland. Sgt Barber, of Cornwall, Ontario, and the others are all commemorated on the Runnymede Memorial.

One published source, 'Canadian Squadrons in Coastal Command', suggests that Z5753 T/404 was damaged in an action against a Ju88, 50 miles E of Sumburgh on 18th December 1941, when being flown by W/C Woodruff. This conflict of information remains unresolved at this time.

502 Sqn	Whitley V	Z6502	YG-U	Op:	Anti-Submarine Sweep
	P/O D B Collie	. . . . .	Safe	Base:	Limavady
	Sgt R Bagley	900228	Safe	T/o time: 07:38	
	Sgt R C Sawyer	943722	Safe		
	Sgt S A Smith	755334	Safe		
	Sgt J B Murray RCAF	R/56178	Safe		
	Sgt J E Bacon	907761	Safe		

Took off with Sgt Bagley flying but suffered an engine failure at 50 feet. Nothing could be identified as causing the failure and he successfully avoided houses and trees to crash-land 2 miles SW of Limavady. The bomb-load could not be jettisoned because of the town and these exploded after the crash, destroying the aircraft.

20th October 1941

248 Sqn	Beaufighter IC	T4716	WR-	Duty:	Training
	Sgt Thwaites RAAF	400606	Safe	Base:	Bircham Newton
				T/o time: ?	

Undershot a night approach while on circuits and bumps and hit ground 500 yards SE of Docking 20:10 hrs.

608 Sqn	Hudson V	AM523	UL-F	Op:	Rover Patrol
	Sgt A Hendy	1250969	+	Base:	Thornaby
	Sgt S A Symons	924911	+	T/o time: 11:55	
	Sgt W P Wright	553835	+		
	Sgt W White	995408	+		

Took off in company with two other aircraft from the squadron. After failing to find any shipping the flight turned to attack the Thisted seaplane base. After dropping bombs on the slipway F/608 was seen to make a vertical bank and dropped out of sight. Shortly afterwards an aircraft was seen burning out on the ground. All rest in Frederikshavn Cemetery, Denmark.

22nd October 1941

330 Sqn	Northrop N-3PB	F15	GS-L	Duty:	Training
	Lt P Hektoen RNorNAS	. . . . .	Safe	Base:	Akureyri
				Time:	?

Crashed on second take-off when on the step, and sank. The aircraft was salvaged but was declared as damaged beyond repair (DBR).

413 (RCAF)	Catalina I	AH566	QL-	Op:	Tromso
Sqn	F/O C C Proby RAF	41321	+	Base:	Sullom Voe
	W/C R G Briese	C/147	+	T/o time:	02:34
	Sgt W H Martin RAF	979254	+		
	Sgt K C Lawry RAF	959601	+		
	Sgt R E Austin RAF	808407	+		
	P/O W J Hoover	J/4569	+		
	Sgt L J Harris RAF	808394	+		
	AC2 W Benson RAF	574560	+		
	AC1 T H Atkin RAF	1117675	+		
	AC1 A H Agus RAF	647396	+		

Failed to return from a special reconnaissance. W/C Briese rests in Stavne Cemetery, Trondheim, while the rest of the crew, including Sgt Austin of 419 Sqn, are all commemorated on the Runnymede Memorial.

500 Sqn	Blenheim IV	Z6047	MK-X	Duty:	Training
	Sgt C Hosford	1162828	Injured	Base:	Bircham Newton
	F/Sgt K H Elvidge	. . . . . .	Injured	T/o time:	?

While carrying out unauthorised low flying when on a W/T exercise, hit a tree 1½ miles from Benson, Oxfordshire, crashed and was destroyed by fire .

612 Sqn	Whitley V	T4329	WL-U	Op:	Anti-Submarine Patrol
	P/O D H Limbrey	. . . . .	Safe	Base:	St Eval
	Sgt Lindesey	. . . . . .	Safe	T/o time:	07:25
	Sgt Collins	. . . . . .	Safe		
	Sgt Belcher	. . . . . .	Safe		
	Sgt Turner	. . . . . .	Safe		
	Sgt McClay	. . . . . .	Safe		

Returning from the Bay of Biscay area when suffered starboard engine failure and was ditched 75 miles SW of the Scilly Isles at 10:55 hrs. The crew were sighted in their dinghy at 14:00 hrs by a Hudson and later a Sunderland from 10 (RAAF) Squadron landed and picked up the whole crew, landing them at Pembroke Dock at 20:00 hrs.

23rd October 1941

236 Sqn	Blenheim IV	V5728	ND-J	Op:	Escort
	Sgt Webster	. . . . .	Interned	Base:	Carew Cheriton
	Sgt D A Woodman RCAF	R/60047	DoI	T/o time:	09:10
	Sgt Brady	. . . . .	Interned		

Took off along with P/236 to escort convoy Child (SL 89). Last seen in position PXYS and signalled base at 10:51hrs of intention to return. Engine cut and the Blenheim was force-landed at Schull, County Cork, Eire. The crew was interned but Sgt Woodman, from Ontario, who was injured in the crash, died on the 24th and is buried in Goolds Hill Cemetery, Mallow, County Cork, Eire.

236 Sqn	Blenheim IV	Z6031	ND-V	Op:	Escort
	Sgt F M McCaffry RNZAF	40651	+	Base:	Carew Cheriton
	Sgt S W J Lamerton	922912	+	T/o time:	16:25
	Sgt Buck	. . . . .	Safe		

Took off along with P/236 to escort convoy Child. Flew into high ground at 22:30 hrs near Hayes Farm, Ridgeway Road, Pembrokeshire. Sgt McCaffry from Wellington, New Zealand, rests locally in St Mary New Churchyard, Carew, and Sgt Lamerton is buried in St Constantine Churchyard, Constantine, Cornwall.

24th October 1941

59 Sqn	Hudson V	AM862	TR-E	Op:	Focher Patrol
	F/Lt D A Buchan DFC	43092	+	Base:	Thorney Island
	Sgt P G Thompson	963185	+	T/o time: 18:33	
	Sgt R E French	975469	+		
	Sgt A Stringer	986905	+		

Dropped flares and was caught in a concentration of searchlights and flak while on a photo-recce operation to Cherbourg. All the crew are buried in Cherbourg Old Communal Cemetery, France.

502 Sqn	Whitley V	P5059	YG-D	Op:	Anti-Submarine Patrol
	P/O K Southan	. . . . .	Safe	Base:	Limavady
	F/Sgt R A Robinson	517228	Safe	T/o time: 05:37	
	Sgt I S Currie	969479	Safe		
	Sgt J Keery	816149	Safe		
	Sgt J McKerr	638338	Safe		
	Sgt P G Sharpe	551755	Safe		

At 10:00 hrs the port engine caught fire at 900 feet and all loose gear was jettisoned. P/O Southan set course for the SS *Athlone Castle* that they had sighted earlier but it was not found at the estimated position in the North Channel. At 12:15 hrs the Whitley was ditched in position 5605N 1053W, smashing in the nose as a result, but all the crew got safely into the dinghy and at 14:10 hrs they were spotted by C/502 and rescued by SS *Port Wyndham* at 18:30 hrs.

25th October 1941

500 Sqn	Blenheim IV	V5538	MK-X	Op:	Nomad Patrol
	P/O L W Brown	64305	+	Base:	Bircham Newton
	Sgt P A V Lyons	1153143	+	T/o time: 05:10	
	Sgt J K Mitchell	1051250	+		

Took off for an operation to the Den Haag area but crashed into the North Sea off the coast of Holland. All are commemorated on the Runnymede Memorial.

27th October 1941

53 Sqn	Hudson V	AM651	PZ-V	Op:	Anti-Submarine Sweep
	F/Lt J Bunce	. . . . .	Safe	Base:	St Eval
	Sgt F D King DFM	755231	+	T/o time: 05:30	
	Sgt W C Cleaver	. . . . .	Safe		
	Sgt E Leverington	1152021	+		

Hit by a night-fighter off the French coast, suffered an engine fire which later spread to the wing. At about 07:50 hrs the Hudson crashed into the sea a quarter of a mile east of Porthkerris beach in Falmouth Bay. A light northerly wind was blowing and the sea was calm. Three men who were at work in the St Keverne Quarry at once put out in a rowing boat. The Hudson had burst into flames and submerged very quickly, and they had to pull their boat through burning petrol on the surface of the sea. They succeeded in reaching the aeroplane, and rescued two of her crew of four. Sgt King and Sgt Leverington are commemorated on the Runnymede Memorial.

489 (RNZAF)	Beaufort I	N1106	O	Duty:	Training
Sqn	Sgt Rapp	. . . . .	Safe	Base:	Leuchars
				T/o time: ?	

Hit a stone wall after an engine failure and crashed east of St Andrews, Fife. All four crew escaped with slight injuries.

29th October 1941

1 PRU	Spitfire PR.IV	AA801	LY-	Duty:	Air Test
	P/O E R Hamer	100630	+	Base:	?
				T/o time: ?	

Camera test at 28,000 feet. Broke up in mid-air near Watchfield, Berkshire. The Court of Inquiry ruled that aileron flutter had caused the subsequent structural failure of the port wing. P/O Hamer rests in Darlington West Cemetery, County Durha.m

30th October 1941

86 Sqn	Beaufort I	X8925	BX-J	Duty:	Training
	Sgt M J Bell RAAF	402149	+	Base:	Abbotsinch
	P/O A G Thompson	117032	+	T/o time: ?	
	Sgt L G Staniland	1375445	+		
	AC1 K R E Dutton	553765	+		

Hit the sea while low flying during torpedo training off Ayr, Ayrshire. P/O Thompson rests in Kirkdale Cemetery, Liverpool, while Sgt Bell from New South Wales, Sgt Staniland and AC1 Dutton are commemorated on the Runnymede Memorial.

233 Sqn	Hudson V	AM573	ZS-	Op:	Anti-Submarine Patrol
	P/O H R Rowntree	85655	+	Base:	St Eval
	Sgt T Phillips	745399	+	T/o time:	21:15
	F/Sgt J Menzies	643471	+		
	Sgt J Walsh	645117	+		

Hit a balloon cable, damaging the port mainplane and crashed into Falmouth Harbour at 02:31 hrs. Sgt Phillips rests locally in Falmouth Cemetery, Cornwall, while the rest of the crew are commemorated on the Runnymede Memorial.

612 Sqn	Whitley VII	Z6961	WL-W	Op:	Convoy Escort
	F/O Downer	.....	Safe	Base:	Wick
	P/O Janssens de Verebeke	87706	Safe	T/o time:	08:40
	Sgt Smith	......	Safe		
	Sgt J Andrew	817097	+		
	Sgt Lord	......	Safe		
	Sgt Archer	......	Safe		

At 11:40 hrs met convoy ON 30 and fired the correct signal of the day. As the aircraft passed over the convoy it was hit by AA fire in the starboard engine. The Whitley was ditched at 11:45 hrs about 3 miles from the leading ships of the convoy and all but Sgt Andrew boarded the dinghy. It was assumed that he had been hit on the head by a wing and knocked out. The survivors were picked up by HMS *Ababis* and Sgt Andrew's body was recovered by the SS *Taranhi*. At 12:00 hrs the following day he was buried at sea and so is commemorated on the Runnymede Memorial.

31st October 1941

220 Sqn	Hudson V	AM618	NR-M	Op:	South Stab Patrol
	F/O G C H Birchall	42789	+	Base:	Wick
	P/O J P Croker	61239	+	T/o time:	16:06
	Sgt A McK Barr	701500	+		
	Sgt G L D Bailey	930437	+		

Failed to return after sending an SOS. All are commemorated on the Runnymede Memorial.

500 Sqn	Blenheim IV	V5537	MK-M	Op:	Shipping Sweep
	S/Ldr F C Phipps	36093	+	Base:	Bircham Newton
	Sgt T P Mowan	921870	+	T/o time:	22:00
	Sgt A A Miles	912232	+		

Crashed at 23:50 hrs, into the IJsselmeer, 4 miles W of Lemmer, after a convoy attack off the Frisians. Sgt Miles, from Penang, Malaya, and the other crewmen are commemorated on the Runnymede Memorial.

1st November 1941

404 (RCAF) Sqn	Blenheim IV	T1946	EE-	Duty:	?
	Sgt R F Leighton	R/74598	+	Base:	Sumburgh
	AC1 T A Gray RAF	1371299	+	T/o time: ?	
	AC2 T Clapperton RAF	1341877	+		

Collided with Blenheim Z6339 near Lerwick at 15:05 hrs. Sgt Leighton, from Duncan, British Columbia, rests locally in Lerwick New Cemetery, Shetland, while both AC2 Clapperton and AC1 Gray are buried at Edinburgh in Morningside Cemetery and Seafield Cemetery respectively.

404 (RCAF) Sqn	Blenheim IV	Z6339	EE-	Duty:	?
	P/O Inglis	.....	Injured	Base:	Sumburgh
	Cpl H E Holmes	......	Injured	T/o time: ?	

Collided with Blenheim T1946 near Lerwick at 15:05 hrs.

2nd November 1941

500 Sqn	Blenheim IV		Z7449	MK-Y	Op:	Strike
	P/O	Godfrey	. . . . .	?	Base:	Bircham Newton
	Sgt	Smith	. . . . . .	?	Time:	22:00
	Sgt	Glasscock	. . . . . .	?		

A bomb fell off on take-off and lifted the tail causing the Blenheim to nose in and blow up.

3rd November 1941

143 Sqn	Beaufighter IC		T3327	HO-	Op:	Faeroes Patrol
	Sgt	Cutten RNZAF	40756	Safe	Base:	Sumburgh
	Sgt	Burrows	. . . . . .	Safe	T/o time:	10:45

Swung on landing and hit a hangar at Sumburgh, 13:30 hrs.

235 Sqn	Blenheim IV		Z6144	LA-Y	Op:	South Stab Patrol
	P/O	H W Van Panhuys	65544	+	Base:	Dyce
	Sgt	L G Hillier	962181	+	T/o time:	16:39
	Sgt	H A Cook	1002345	+		

Missing from a patrol off Norway. Sgt Hillier rests in Mollendal Church Cemetery, Bergen, Norway, while both P/O Van Panhuys, Jonkheer from Holland, and Sgt Cook are commemorated on the Runnymede Memorial.

612 Sqn	Whitley V		T4325	WL-S	Op:	Anti-Submarine Patrol
	F/O	J Harrop	78526	+	Base:	St Eval
	Sgt	J H Watson	817073	+	T/o time:	20:55
	Sgt	R Broxap	981534	+		
	Sgt	F G Rae	817189	+		
	Sgt	B Clark	967467	+		
	F/O	H E P Williams	78870	+		

Took off for a creeping line ahead search in the Bay of Biscay but failed to return.
All are commemorated on the Runnymede Memorial.

4th November 1941

500 Sqn	Blenheim IV		Z5959	MK-X	Op:	Suivi
	P/O	W J Sipprell	43047	+	Base:	Bircham Newton
	Sgt	A T Hall RNZAF	402130	+	T/o time:	21:15
	Sgt	H R Davies	749575	+		

Took off for an attack on a convoy off Terschelling but crashed at 23:50 hrs into the IJsselmeer, 6 km (c 3¾ miles) W of Lemmer. P/O Sipprell from New Westminister, British Columbia;, Sgt Hall from Dunedin, New Zealand; and Sgt Davis are commemorated on the Runnymede Memorial. Sought by Beaufighters of 248 Squadron on Air Sea Rescue sorties, but failed to find any trace.

5th November 1941

22 Sqn	Beaufort I		AW202	OA-T	Op:	Rover Patrol
	P/O	P I Hall	88039	PoW	Base:	St Eval
	P/O	H L Powell	100633	+	T/o time:	03:39
	Sgt	J E Davis	1168513	+		
	Sgt	A Howard	943003	PoW		

Took off for a shipping patrol and crashed at St Trojan-les-Bains, France. P/O Powell and Sgt Davis are buried in St Trojan-les-Bains Communal Cemetery, Charente-Maritime.

404 (RCAF) Sqn	Blenheim IV		L9337	EE-	Op:	North Bert Patrol
	Sgt	J G Mackay	R/54293	+	Base:	Sumburgh
	Sgt	T E Hedefine RAF	986613	+	T/o time:	?
	Sgt	W J Pearce RAF	755517	+		

Missing off the coast of Norway. Sgt MacKay, from Ottawa, Ontario and his crew are all commemorated on the Runnymede Memorial.

407 (RCAF) Sqn	Hudson V		AE655	RR-R	Op:	Rover Patrol
	P/O	J F Codville	J/4543	+	Base:	North Coates
	Sgt	F T James	R/73092	+	T/o time:	17:06

Sgt	R L Armsby RAF	755284	+		
Sgt	G N Bryan	R/58294	+		

Shot down by Oblt Woltersdorf of 4./NJG1 operating from 'Aussenkommando' Wittmundhafen off Terschelling. P/O Codville, from Duncan, British Columbia, was washed ashore on Rottumeroog Island but now rests in Oldebroek General Cemetery, Gelderland, Holland, while the rest of the crew are commemorated on the Runnymede Memorial.

608 Sqn	Hudson V	AM657	UL-D	Op:	Shipping Strike
	W/C R S Darbyshire	24249	+	Base:	Thornaby
	P/O J D Berry	89341	+	T/o time:	20:01
	Sgt S R Mandall	755718	+		
	F/O G A Hoar	77922	+		

Took off in company but failed to return from a shipping strike off the Frisian Islands. All are commemorated on the Runnymede Memorial.

608 Sqn	Hudson V	AM642	UL-R	Op:	Shipping Strike
	Sgt G R Yeates RCAF	R/69759	+	Base:	Thornaby
	Sgt F J Hazlett RCAF	R/61076	+	T/o time:	21:17
	Sgt J Sansome	1166718	+		
	Sgt E W Elkington	1325097	+		

Failed to return from off Frisian Islands. Sgt Yeates and his crew are commemorated on the Runnymede Memorial.

6th November 1941

1401 Flight	Spitfire I (PR) type F	R6909	–	Duty:	?
	?	.....		Base:	?
	Damaged in undefined accident. SoC 15th January 1942.			Time:	?

7th November 1941

1401 Flight	Spitfire I (PR) type E (Mk.Vᴀ?)	P9550	–	Op:	Met Flight
	?	.....		Base:	?
	Missing. Circumstances yet to be determined.			T/o time:	?

10th November 1941

217 Sqn	Beaufort I	L9971	MW-	Duty:	Training
	Sgt P L Ankin	748362	+	Base:	Manston
	F/Sgt D R Wicks	581367	+	T/o time:	?
	Sgt C E Shield	959713	+		
	Sgt A A Smith	1152244	+		

Flew into the ground in cloud half a mile E of Manston, Kent. Sgt Ankin rests in Cambridge Crematorium, F/Sgt Wicks in Reading Cemetery; Sgt Shield in St Mary Churchyard, Belford, Northumberland and Sgt Smith in Stone Cemetery, Staffordshire.

413 (RCAF) Sqn	Catalina I	W8422	QL-		Ground Loss
	Catalina I	Z2141	QL-A		Ground Loss
				Base:	Sullom Voe
	Sank at their moorings during a gale.			Time:	?

12th November 1941

1 PRU	Spitfire PR.IV	AA782	LY-	Duty:	Training
	P/O W J F McEwan	77923	Safe	Base:	Wick
				T/o time:	12:15

Engine cut on take-off and force-landed into a field containing anti-glider obstruction poles. The pilot reported that he noticed a high engine temperature just before take-off.

14th November 1941

404 (RCAF) Sqn	Blenheim IV	P4845	EE-	Duty:	?
	P/O J G Dunlop	J/4754	+	Base:	?
				T/o time:	?

Overshot a forced landing and hit a wall while lost in bad visibility, 5 miles N of Dyce. P/O Dunlop, from Foam Lake, Saskatchewan, rests locally in Dyce Old Churchyard.

15th November 1941

217 Sqn	Beaufort I	AW236			?
	S/Ldr G C Halley	75362	+	Base:	?
	P/O C McLean	60787	+	T/o time:	?
	Sgt D L Heald	942529	+		
	Sgt F Childs	955494	+		

On loan to 217 Sqn from 5 OTU. Sgt Childs body was washed ashore 12th December 1941 at Bergen aan Zee and Sgt Heald a day later at Wijk aan Zee. Both are now buried in Bergen General Cemetery, Holland. The others are commemorated on the Runnymede Memorial.

16th November 1941

608 Sqn	Hudson V	AM883	UL-N	Op:	Stand Patrol
	F/Sgt R C Wood	520647	+	Base:	Thornaby
	Sgt R J Neville	905772	+	T/o time:	17:08
	Sgt L J Pain	755726	+		
	Sgt Shuidan	. . . . . .	Injured		

At 20:55 hrs N/608 was diverted to Kinloss. Flew into high ground at The Buck in bad weather 2 miles W of Lumsden, Aberdeenshire, 22:35 hrs. F/Sgt Wood rests in Dyce Old Churchyard; Sgt Pain in Earlsfield Cemetery, Wandsworth, London and Sgt Neville in Watling Street Cemetery, Dartford, Kent.

20th November 1941

59 Sqn	Hudson V	AM856	TR-	Duty:	Training
	P/O J F P Fitzgerald	. . . . .	Safe	Base:	?
				T/o time:	?

Overshot on landing at Roborough, 12:30 hrs.

21st November 1941

320 Sqn	Hudson III	T9440	NO-Q	Duty:	?
	?			Base:	?
				Time:	?

Damaged in circumstances yet to be determined. SoC on 29th November 1941.

23rd November 1941

86 Sqn	Beaufort I	X8927	BX-	Op:	Gardening
	Sgt N T Lawrence	935694	Safe	Base:	North Coates
				T/o time:	?

Crashed on landing at North Coates after an engine failure at 05:45 hrs caused the pilot to open up a throttle and mixture control instead of both throttles.

608 Sqn	Hudson V	AM715	UL-T	Op:	South Hornli Patrol
	Sgt R H MacMillan RCAF	R/78250	+	Base:	Thornaby
	Sgt G N Fullerton RCAF	R/58303	+	T/o time:	10:43
	Sgt J Short	923073	+		
	Sgt F G Simmonds	1153725	+		

Failed to return. Sgt MacMillan, a Canadian from Ontario, and his crew all rest in Frederikshavn Cemetery, Denmark.

24th November 1941

86 Sqn	Beaufort I	AW207	BX-H	Op:	Gardening
	P/O D Page	64320	PoW	Base:	North Coates
	F/O J Mc Paxton	81063	PoW	T/o time:	16:15
	Sgt J B Green	702081	PoW		
	Sgt J McCann	978471	PoW		

Took off for a mining operation in the Friese Gat between Ameland and Schiermonnikoog. On the run in for the mine drop the Beaufort was hit by flak and P/O Page altered course for Schiermonnikoog. The aircraft just missed crashing into the farm of De Kooi but came to earth at 18:15 hrs in a meadow just beyond. Wreckage was spread over an 80 metre area with one wing ripped off, both engines lost from their mountings and the mine thrown out but failing to explode. The crew were mostly uninjured with only Sgt McCann suffering a broken collar bone. The crew set fire to the aircraft before capture.

86 Sqn	Beaufort I	AW192	BX-T	Op:	Gardening
	P/O D R J Harper	61307	+	Base:	North Coates
	Sgt A P McGregor	917519	+	T/o time:	16:45
	Sgt A N Kennedy	971186	+		
	Sgt W T Large	1051844	+		

Shot down near Schiermonnikoog, Holland. Both P/O Harper and Sgt McGregor are commemorated on the Runnymede Memorial while Sgt Large was washed ashore on the 26th December 1941 at beach pole No 9 and rests locally in Vredenhof Cemetery on Schiermonnikoog and Sgt Kennedy in Mount Vernon Roman Catholic Cemetery, Edinburgh.

248 Sqn	Beaufighter IC	T3349	WR-	Duty:	?
	?	. . . . .		Base:	?
	Missing. No further details.			T/o time:	?

502 Sqn	Whitley VII	Z6967	YG-U	Op:	Convoy Escort
	F/O D B Collie	. . . . .	Safe	Base:	Limavady
	Sgt R Bagley	900228	Safe	T/o time:	08:41
	Sgt R C Sawyer	943722	Safe		
	Sgt S A Smith	755334	Safe		
	Sgt J B Murray RCAF	R/56178	Safe		
	Sgt J E Bacon	907761	Safe		

Convoy SC 54 was not met and at 14:02 hrs the Whitley was recalled to base. The crew became lost in the poor visibility and at 18:48 hrs they ran out of fuel and crash-landed at Presland, some 5 miles SE of Portrush, County Antrim.

25th November 1941

217 Sqn	Beaufort I	AW188	MW-Q	Op:	Gardening
	Sgt M Gill	1181624	+	Base:	Thorney Island
	Sgt N Boyd Orr	1053586	+	T/o time:	16:35
	Sgt J R Griffiths	1013752	+		
	Sgt J A Cronie	1057463	PoW		

Lost off Brest, France at 18:40 hrs. Both Sgt Gill and Sgt Griffiths rest in Kerfautras Cemetery, Brest, while Sgt Boyd Orr is commemorated on the Runnymede Memorial.

26th November 1941

22 Sqn	Beaufort I	L9793	OA-O	Op:	Gardening
	P/O R M Iliff	88041	PoW	Base:	St Eval
	Sgt H Smith	1061130	+	T/o time:	16:05
	Sgt A J Tonkin	922736	PoW		
	Sgt C G Meader	961018	PoW		

Tasked with mining in the Artichoke area off St Nazaire. Sgt Smith rests in Gavres Communal Cemetery, Morbihan.

28th November 1941

220 Sqn	Hudson V	AM799	NR-V	Op:	Varro
	F/O E W Tate DFC	83733	+	Base:	Wick
	Sgt C W Robinson	913652	+	T/o time:	12:46

	Sgt	P Shane	747833	+		
	Sgt	B R Edis	636262	+		

The Hudson suffered an engine failure during an attack on a ship near Stavanger, Norway. All are commemorated on the Runnymede Memorial.

221 Sqn	**Wellington VIII**		**T2988**	**DF-**	**Op:**	**Bear Patrol**
	F/O	J E Speak	78533	+	Base:	Reykjavik
	P/O	J B Gower	62321	+	T/o time:	14:20
	Sgt	G D Griffith	923993	+		
	Sgt	D J MacPherson	1305438	+		
	Sgt	K F Capper	975740	+		
	Sgt	J N Fergus	632337	+		

Last heard on W/T at 22:30 hrs on the return leg of the patrol. The Wellington and its crew were located by patrols of the 1st/5th West Yorks c 2,000 feet up the hillside at Hrafnkellsstadabotn, at the southern end of Kolgraffordur. All of the crew are buried in Fossvogur Cemetery, Reykjavik.

29th November 1941

42 Sqn	**Beaufort I**		**N1015**	**AW-F**	**Op:**	**Strike**
	Sgt	D B Heron	903482	+	Base:	Leuchars
	Sgt	A E Shaw RCAF	R/64712	+	T/o time:	13:45
	Sgt	D G Liveston	981109	+		
	Sgt	R Brown	1325003	+		

Took off in company with other squadron aircraft. Lost touch with the formation after reaching the English coast on the return leg. An SOS was received at 18:38 hrs and Sgt Heron was instructed to fly in the direction of searchlight beams, but the Beaufort was later known to have turned out to sea again from the Thames Estuary before crashing into high-tension cables near Rochester, Kent. The torpedo exploded destroying the aircraft. Both Sgt Heron and Sgt Shaw are buried in Gravesend Cemetery, while Sgt Liveston rests in Forfar Cemetery, Angus and Sgt Brown was taken to Polmont Churchyard, Stirlingshire.

42 Sqn	**Beaufort I**		**W6529**	**AW-J**	**Duty:**	**Air Test**
	P/O	H H Lawson	400204	+	Base:	Leuchars
	P/O	H L Russell	101579	+	T/o time:	15:00
	Sgt	B J Perrin	1375521	+		
	Sgt	T W Ogden	759141	+		

Flew into a hill at Pusk, Fife, in poor visibility at 150 feet. The accident was attributed to the pilot being concerned at losing sight of the aerodrome in cloud and so turned too sharply, stalling into the ground. Both P/O Lawson, an Australian and P/O Russell are buried locally in Leuchars Cemetery; Sgt Perrin was taken to Alperton Burial Ground, Wembley and Sgt Ogden rests in All Saints Churchyard Extension, Allesley, Warwickshire.

1st December 1941

407 (RCAF) Sqn	**Hudson V**		**AM778**	**RR-J**	**Op:**	**Strike 2**
	P/O	H N Fraser	J/4427	PoW	Base:	North Coates
	Sgt	G L Neeves RAF	904107	PoW	T/o time:	01:24
	F/Sgt	S Archer RAF	803473	PoW		
	Sgt	J Quinn RAF	759133	PoW		

Flew so low that the Hudson hit a ship's mast during the attack. The starboard engine caught fire and P/O Fraser was forced to ditch into the North Sea. The crew were picked up from their dinghy a few days later.

500 Sqn	**Hudson V**		**AM718**	**MK-A**	**Duty:**	**Air Test**
	P/O	A F N Ladefoged	66534	+	Base:	Bircham Newton
	Sgt	F A Mackey	1250635	+	T/o time:	?
	Sgt	F L Morgan	1154329	+		
	AC1	R Chadwick	1216942	+		
	AC1	H Sutcliffe	1139242	+		
	AC1	H A Lonergan RAAF	22201	+		

Crashed near Docking and caught fire. AC1 Chadwick, Sgt Morgan, AC1 Lonergan, from Thallon, Queensland, and P/O Ladefoged all rest locally in St Mary's Churchyard, Great Bircham, Norfolk, Sgt Mackey in Eltham Cemetery, Woolwich, London and AC1 Sutcliffe in Mossley Cemetery, Lancashire.

2nd December 1941

1 PRU	Spitfire I PR type D	R7040	LY-	Op:	Reconnaissance
	Sgt L Briggs	758051	+	Base:	?
				T/o time:	?

Took off for an operation to Brest but failed to return. Sgt Briggs is commemorated on the Runnymede Memorial.

22 Sqn	Beaufort I	AW221	OA-V	Op:	Nantes
	W/C J C Mayhew	33271	+	Base:	St Eval
	Sgt E W Walters	581544	+	T/o time:	15:33
	Sgt L H Fowler	751669	+		
	Sgt H Ashton	751288	+		

The formation made landfall at Ile Noirmontier and attacked Nantes at 18:25 hrs.
It was reported that two He115s were in the vicinity during the attack. W/C Mayhew, who was awarded the Norwegian War Cross with Sword, rests in Pont-Du-Cens Communal Cemetery, Nantes, along with his crew.

22 Sqn	Beaufort I	AW216	OA-P	Op:	Nantes
	F/Lt J R Noble	40843	+	Base:	St Eval
	P/O A J Dearden	63433	+	T/o time:	15:35
	Sgt W R Furzey	993605	+		
	Sgt J F McGee	952969	+		

The formation made landfall at Ile Noirmontier and attacked Nantes at 18:25 hrs.
It was reported that two He115s were in the vicinity during the attack.
Sgt McGee is commemorated on the Runnymede Memorial while the rest of the crew are buried in Quiberon Communal Cemetery, Morbihan.

320 Sqn	Hudson III	V9036	NO-O	Op:	Stand Patrol
	Cpl H W de Lijn RNNAS	.....	+	Base:	Leuchars
	P/O J D Dolman RNNAS	.....	+	T/o time:	16:45
	Sgt K van Tongeren RNNAS	......	+		
	Marinier 2 A Bom KMR	......	+		

Failed to return from the coast of Norway and crashed near Lista, Norway. All rest in Vestre Gravlund Dutch Field of Honour, Oslo, Norway. The aircraft was named *Makassar*.
Marinier 2 A Born was a serving member of the KMR (Royal Netherlands Marines).

3rd December 1941

201 Sqn	Sunderland II	W3988	ZM-P	Op:	Anti-Submarine Escort
	F/Lt J G Fleming DFC	.....	Interned	Base:	Castle Archdale
	P/O W S Emmett RNZAF	401377	+	T/o time:	06:30
	Sgt E W Jackson	999009	+		
	P/O E G Marker	101048	+		
	Sgt S J Epps	522263	+		
	Sgt M W G Fox	933498	+		
	Sgt J C Masterson	......	Interned		
	LAC F W Lea	904349	+		
	LAC A Doncaster	743595	+		
	LAC A P Walker MiD	972825	+		
	AC1 A E Bennett	1081395	+		

Lost the radio aids on a patrol then after two landing attempts crashed at Doonbeg, near Carrowmore Point, County Clare, Eire at 18:30 hrs. The crew all left the aircraft safely but were unable to keep the two dinghies together and row the 2 to 3 miles to the shore. F/Lt Fleming and Sgt Masterson drifted ashore unconscious supported by their Mae Wests. Sgt Epps, LAC Lea and Sgt Fox rest in Milltown Malbay Church of Ireland Churchyard while LAC Doncaster and AC1 Bennett are buried in Killard Church of Ireland Churchyard, in County Clare, Eire. P/O Emmett, a New Zealander, and the rest of the crew are commemorated on the Runnymede Memorial.

254 Sqn	Blenheim IV	Z6088	QY-	Duty:	Training
	Sgt M W Shand	912779	Injured	Base:	?
				T/o time:	?

Suffered an engine failure and the Blenheim crashed during a forced landing, some 2 miles S of Glenegedale, Islay, at 13:00 hrs. The Court of Inquiry recommended disciplinary action after it was found that the pilot had taken off with zero oil pressure.

4th December 1941

1 PRU	Mosquito I (PR)	W4055	LY-	Op:	Reconnaissance
	S/Ldr A L Taylor DFC**	39488	+	Base:	Wick
	Sgt S E Horsfall	921014	+	T/o time:	10:15

Missing from a PR operation to Trondheim, Norway. Shot down by Unteroffizier R Fenten of I/JG77 at 15:20 hrs near Stavanger at map reference Lg 49 433, 35 km (c 21¾ miles) W of Feistein. Both S/Ldr Taylor DFC and two bars, and Sgt Horsfall are commemorated on the Runnymede Memorial.

5th December 1941

10 (RAAF)	Sunderland I	T9072	RB-V	Duty:	Transit Flight
Sqn	S/Ldr E B Courtney	. . .	Safe	Base:	Oban
	P/O C W Steley	404554	Injured	T/o time:	09:25
	P/O G E Ferguson	404336	Injured		
	F/O S E Goddard	6059	Injured		
	Cpl S R Strang RAF	4677	Safe		
	Cpl W H Nelson	3929	Safe		
	LAC L Meredith	4292	Safe		
	LAC J P Lynch	19001	Safe		
	AC1 H J Webber	20003	+		
	AC2 P G Instance RAF	1375914	Safe		
	AC1 E W Lee	22137	Safe		
	W/C A X Richards	72	Safe		
	F/Lt S Thomson	1292	+		
	F/Lt R J Vaughan DFC RAF	41499	+		
	F/Lt W S Rae DFC RAF	36181	+		

Took off for a flight to Pembroke Dock to pick up the new OC and was flying at about 800 feet, 15 miles NW of Holyhead, Anglesey, at 11:21 hrs, when the port outer engine started to backfire. The engine cowling fractured sending the aircraft into a violent 45 degree bank and it hit the sea across the swell at 90 knots. The Sunderland broke up immediately and sank within five seconds. The survivors climbed onto the port mainplane where they were rescued by a boat from the MV *Kilkenny* at 12:15 hrs. F/Lt Vaughan and F/Lt Rae were from 4 OTU and were aboard to pick up a Sunderland from Pembroke for a ferry flight to Invergordon.

407 (RCAF)	Hudson V	AM556	RR-E	Op:	Shipping Strike
Sqn	Sgt S T C Thomson	R/68184	+	Base:	North Coates
	Sgt R J Fido RAF	913606	+	T/o time:	18:00
	Sgt G M Drennan	R/77371	+		
	Sgt J D Drennan	R/77465	+		

Shot down by naval flak and crashed into the North Sea 30 km west of Borkum Island. Sgt G M Drennan and Sgt J D Drennan were twin brothers from Lennoxville, Quebec. All the crewmen are commemorated on the Runnymede Memorial.

7th December 1941

1 PRU	Spitfire PR.IV	AA792		Op:	?
	F/Lt J B Hatchwell	91002	+	Base:	?
				T/o time:	?

Missing. F/Lt Hatchwell rests in St Cast Communal Cemetery, Cotes-du-Nord, France.

269 Sqn	Hudson III	T9416	UA-	Op:	Patrol
	F/Sgt E R Budgell	905997	+	Base:	Kaldadarnes
	F/O E E Stewart RNZAF	40244	+	T/o time:	?
	Sgt V S Lewis	755244	+		
	Sgt W Dodds	974296	+		

Flew into a hill in bad weather on return from a patrol 8 miles SW of Kaldadarnes, Iceland, at 16:45 hrs. F/O Stewart, from Southland, New Zealand, and the other crewmen rest in Fossvogur Cemetery, Reykjavik, Iceland.

8th December 1941

1404 Flt	Blenheim IV	Z7370		Op:	Met Flight

Sgt	L Watson	748600	+	Base:	St Eval
Sgt	A Hemming	923520	+	T/o time:	?
Sgt	A Bess	1172554	+		

Missing. No further details to hand.

9th December 1941

1 PRU	**Spitfire I PR type E**	**N3117**	**LY-**	**Op:**	**Reconnaissance**
	F/O J M H Sargent	43553	+	Base:	Benson
				T/o time:	11:05

Took off for a low level operation near Berck and failed to return. F/O Sargent is commemorated on the Runnymede Memorial. This a/c had been upgraded from a former light green PR type C.

22 Sqn	**Beaufort I**	**AW203**	**OA-A**	**Op:**	**Rover Patrol**
	F/O C L Jenkins	88040	+	Base:	St Eval
	Sgt F G Kipps	1164443	+	T/o time:	03:00
	Sgt T S Dickson	1023594	+		
	Sgt W A Hughes-Hughes	919475	+		

Took off for a patrol of the Bay of Biscay. A W/T message was received that early return was planned then no further messages were sent. The body of Sgt Dickson and parts of the aircraft were later washed up at Sennen Cove, Cornwall. Sgt Dickson is buried in Lambhill Cemetery, Glasgow and the rest of the crew are commemorated on the Runnymede Memorial.

42 Sqn	**Beaufort I**	**L9868**	**AW-S**	**Op:**	**Shipping Strike**
	P/O R Devenish-Meares RAAF	402156	+	Base:	Leuchars
	Sgt J Nash	777886	+	T/o time:	05:30
	Sgt A King	1014016	+		
	Sgt W A Nation	1375231	+		

Lost off Kristiansand. Sgt Nash, from Durban, South Africa, and the other crewmen are commemorated on the Runnymede Memorial.

217 Sqn	**Beaufort I**	**AW190**	**MW-K**	**Op:**	**Shipping Strike**
	P/O M Lee	89826	+	Base:	Manston
	Sgt J A Foster RCAF	R/58108	+	T/o time:	15:42
	Sgt H Carter	1311031	+		
	Sgt J A Chadaway	755149	+		

Took off in company with two other 217 Squadron Beauforts to attack a convoy sighted off Hoek van Holland earlier. At 16:39 hrs the flight found and attacked the convoy of one ship of 12,000 tons, five of between 1,000 and 2,000 tons and two flak-ships, positioned some 25 km (c 15½ miles) SW of Den Helder. F/Lt Finch attacked first and dropped three 500 lb bombs onto the *Madrid*. P/O Lee was next but was hit in the port engine which caught fire and the Beaufort crashed at 17:39 hrs just in front of the bow of the *Madrid*. P/O Aldridge was last to attack the *Madrid* but clipped one of the ship's masts with his aircraft's port wing. P/O Lee was washed ashore on Ameland and rests locally in Nes General Cemetery, while Sgt Chadaway, Sgt Carter and Sgt Foster, a Canadian from Vancouver, are commemorated on the Runnymede Memorial.

10th December 1941

120 Sqn	**Liberator I**	**AM926**	**OH-F**	**Duty:**	**Transit Flight**
	F/O J W Rae	42885	+	Base:	Dyce
	Sgt R W Magson	776060	+	T/o time:	?
	Sgt D Clark	964456	+		
	Sgt R H Dear	570241	+		
	Sgt D J Bartell	751348	+		

Took off for Nutts Corner. Crashed about 18:30 hrs at Tarmangie Hill, near Alva. F/O Rae rests in St Andrews Western Cemetery, Fife; Sgt Magson in Pickering Cemetery, Yorkshire and Sgt Bartell in Grandsable Cemetery, Grangemouth, Stirlingshire. Sgt Clark was taken to Dalston Road Cemetery, Carlisle and Sgt Dear is buried in All Saints Churchyard, Upper Clatford, Hampshire.

254 Sqn	**Blenheim IV**	**V5801**	**QY-P**	**Duty:**	**Transit Flight**
	W/C G C B Bernard-Smith	16025	+	Base:	Aldergrove
	Sgt W C F Harris	642560	+	T/o time:	?
	Sgt T K Sinclair	550691	+		
	Sgt A Stather	622756	+		

LAC   A Lovell   626261   +

Took off for a flight to Dyce but flew into high ground in cloud at Dykend, near Glenisla, Forfar, crashed and caught fire. Sgt Harris and W/C Bernard-Smith are buried locally in Sleepyhillock Cemetery, Montrose; Sgt Sinclair was taken to Bannockburn Parish Burial Ground, St Ninians, Stirlingshire; Sgt Stather rests in Fleetwood Borough Cemetery, Lancashire, while LAC Lovell is buried in Burslem Cemetery, Stoke-on-Trent.

11th December 1941

42 Sqn	Beaufort I	AW243	AW-O	Op:	Shipping Strike
	P/O O L S Philpot DFC	77131	PoW	Base:	Leuchars
	P/O G M Rackow	105191	PoW	T/o time:	09:50
	P/O E R Hester	46465	PoW		
	Sgt Smith	. . . . . .	?		

Tasked for a strike in position SJLE 0424. Took off and set course for Norway but failed to return. While a PoW his promotion became effective, so that it was as a F/O that Philpot escaped from Stalag Luft III, Sagan, on 29th October 1943, by means of a tunnel dug from under a wooden vaulting horse that had been carried into the middle of the compound each day. The story of his escape and subsequent return to the UK is described in detail in the book *The Wooden Horse* by Eric Williams.

404 (RCAF) Sqn	Blenheim IV	T1808	EE-N	Duty:	Training
	Sgt J V Ensom	R/71599	Safe	Base:	Sumburgh
				T/o time:	?

Starboard tyre burst on landing, the Blenheim swung into a sand dune and the u/c collapsed.

12th December 1941

22 Sqn	Beaufort I	N1085	OA-G	Op:	Donges
	Sgt I W Jones	950569	PoW	Base:	St Eval
	F/O A W Troup RCAF	J/4760	+	T/o time:	15:14
	Sgt C Guest	996840	PoW		
	Sgt A A Ferguson	1055942	PoW		

Crashed near Nantes, Loire-Atlantique. F/O Troup, a Canadian from Ontario, was initially buried in Soldiers Cemetery, La Gaudiniere, Nantes but now rests in Pont-Du-Cens Communal Cemetery, Nantes.

53 Sqn	Hudson IV	AE656	PZ-V	Op:	Anti-Submarine Patrol
	P/O C Thomas	64321	+	Base:	St Eval
	P/O F C Taylor	65520	+	T/o time:	06:23
	Sgt L Griffiths	943467	+		
	Sgt R Smith	945005	+		

Failed to return from a shipping strike off Brittany, France.
All are commemorated on the Runnymede Memorial.

14th December 1941

209 Sqn	Catalina I	AH530	WQ-T	Op:	Crossover Patrol
	F/Lt E A Jewiss DFC	44261	+	Base:	Pembroke Dock
	P/O F R Wellings RCAF	J/4890	+	T/o time:	04:45
	Sgt J P Taylor RCAF	R/61072	+		
	Sgt A Berry	812133	+		
	Sgt W W Stenning	917925	+		
	Sgt F F De Smidt	777609	+		
	Sgt H H Penrose	521238	+		
	Sgt S Napier	626781	+		
	Sgt H Greenwood	1002367	+		
	Sgt Rudge	. . . . . .	Safe		
	Sgt Tew	. . . . . .	Safe		

Took off for a 'Biscay 8' patrol but hit a drifter and crashed into the sea at 04:48 hrs, SW of Weare Point. F/Lt Jewiss rests in St John the Baptist Churchyard, Latton, Wiltshire; F/Sgt Taylor in St James Churchyard, Birstwith; Sgt Berry in Maidstone Cemetery, Kent, and the remaining crewmen are commemorated on the Runnymede Memorial.

15th December 1941

413 Sqn	Catalina I	AH569	QL-	Duty:	?
	Catalina I	W8419	QL-	Duty:	?
				Base:	?
	Damaged beyond repair. Reduced to spares.			Time:	?

16th December 1941

48 Sqn	Anson I	R3335	OY-D	Duty:	Transit Flight
	P/O G F Tredwell	64879	Injured	Base:	Stornoway
	P/O Sergeant	. . . . .	Injured	T/o time:	16:08

Suffered a starboard engine failure on take-off, stalled at 150 feet, was unable to maintain height and crashed into a garden at Anderson Road, Goathill, Stornoway. The conditions were very bad with limited visibility due to squalls.

407 (RCAF) Sqn	Hudson V	AM731	RR-H	Op:	Rover Patrol
	P/O L W Almquist	J/4339	+	Base:	North Coates
	P/O J A Bitcon	J/4751	+	T/o time:	?
	P/O P G Ford	J/6849	+		
	Sgt W Turley	R/77339	+		

Failed to return from a sortie off Terschelling. Both P/O Ford and Sgt Turley are rest in Holland at Vlieland General and Usquert General Cemeteries respectively. P/O Ford's body was washed ashore near breakwater No 14 on the 27th June 1942. The other crewmen are commemorated on the Runnymede Memorial.

20th December 1941

86 Sqn	Beaufort II	AW249	BX-	Duty:	Training
	F/Lt D E Shorman	41327	+	Base:	St Eval
	Sgt E G Forster	759029	+	T/o time:	?
	F/Sgt D Copes	651371	+		
	F/Sgt R E Howett	751101	Wounded		

Crashed into the sea off Cornwall after an engine failure. F/Sgt Howett was picked up from the sea some 2.5 hours after the crash, suffering from shock and exposure. After treatment at a hospital in St Ives he soon recovered. According to his statement the dinghy of the aircraft failed to open which resulted in the loss of the other three members of the crew. F/Sgt Copes rests in Colmonell Cemetery, Ayrshire, F/Lt Shorman, from Nairobi, Kenya, in Bournemouth East Cemetery, while F/Sgt Forster is commemorated on the Runnymede Memorial.

201 Sqn	Sunderland II	W3998	ZM-	Duty:	Transit Flight
	F/Lt D J Fletcher	41166	+	Base:	Mount Batten
	Sgt Booth	. . . . . .	Injured	T/o time:	04:20
	F/Sgt H F Mitchell	751120	+		
	P/O Ince	. . . . .	Injured		
	Sgt H L Southall	956331	+		
	Sgt Lodge	. . . . . .	Injured		
	Sgt Penny	. . . . . .	Injured		
	Cpl J H Martin	568015	+		
	AC1 R Cunningham	1127606	+		
	LAC J W Douglas	632860	+		
	AC1 K W Bennett	652800	+		
	LAC J H Wallace	967483	+		
	AC2 W Watson	1137037	+		
	AC2 J Robinson	1030192	+		
	LAC J B Hides	938541	+		

Posted to 202 Squadron at Gibraltar. Crashed on take-off 200 yards from the Breakwater Fort at Plymouth, Devon. F/Lt Fletcher is buried locally in Pennycomequick Cemetery, Plymouth; AC1 Cunningham in Knadgerhill Cemetery, Irvine, Ayrshire; F/Sgt Mitchell in St Mary Magdalene Churchyard, Great Burstead, Essex; AC2 Watson in Dalston Road Cemetery, Carlisle; AC2 Robinson in Blackburn Cemetery, Lancashire and Cpl Martin in St Teilo Churchyard, Bishopston, Glamorganshire. The remaining crewmen including LAC Douglas, a Canadian from New Westminster, British Columbia, are commemorated on the Runnymede Memorial.

21st December 1941

206 Sqn	Hudson V	AM837	VX-N	Op:	Donges
	P/O E D Rawes	63801	+	Base:	Chivenor
	F/Lt I W Terry RNZAF	40666	+	T/o time: 15:30	
	Sgt J W Durrant	633261	+		
	Sgt R L Watts	1210042	+		

Took off for a raid on an oil refinery but failed to return. All the crew, including P/O Rawes from Lisbon, Portugal, and F/Lt Terry, an Australian from Sydney, rest in Pont-Du-Cens Communal Cemetery, Nantes, France.

22nd December 1941

407 (RCAF) Sqn	Hudson V	AM728	RR-V	Op:	Rover Patrol
	W/O D Moss DFM	R/69580	+	Base:	North Coates
	Sgt J M Cluff	R/62262	+	T/o time:	
	Sgt M H McDonald RAF	1059781	+		
	Sgt S C Herbert RAF	909150	+		

Failed to return from an anti-shipping sortie off Texel. All are commemorated on the Runnymede Memorial.

23rd December 1941

10 (RAAF) Sqn	Sunderland I	P9605	RB-V	Op:	Anti-Submarine patrol
	F/Lt V A Hodgkinson RAAF	. . . . .	Safe	Base:	Pembroke Dock
				T/o time: ?	

It was holed below the waterline in an exchange of gunfire during an attack with depth charges and anti-submarine bombs on the 8,306 ton German tanker *Benno*, about 400 miles out in the North Atlantic and had to be beached upon return to base. The tanker sought sanctuary in Spain. This aircraft is not included in the loss analysis tables as it was eventually repaired and returned to service with 4 OTU, with whom it was ultimately struck off charge on 10th May 1944.

220 Sqn	Hudson V	AM678	NR-U	Op:	Middle Cup
	F/Sgt J W G Hall	754778	PoW	Base:	Wick
	P/O H D C Henderson	68778	+	T/o time: 11:54	
	Sgt H Hamer	970883	+		
	Sgt S J Price	923203	PoW		

Shot down by a Norwegian coastal flak battery at Vigdel and crashed about 300 yards from shore. The survivors and the bodies of the casualties were brought ashore by Norwegian fishermen. Both P/O Henderson and Sgt Hamer rest in Sola Churchyard, Norway.

240 Sqn	Catalina I	W8418	BN-	Op:	Convoy Escort
	P/O K A W Patterson	60112	Safe	Base:	?
	P/O A G W Debonnaire	63075	+	T/o time: 02:40	
	F/O V V Havlicek RCAF	J/3112	+		
	F/Sgt F R Lewis	529516	+		
	F/Sgt G E Jones	570782	+		
	Sgt Murphy	. . . . . .	?		
	Sgt Westby	. . . . . .	?		
	Sgt J S Gray	936555	+		
	Sgt Missett	. . . . . .	?		
	Sgt S Lockett	1051999	+		

A float dug in during a heavy landing at 20:00 hrs on return from patrol and the Catalina sank at Pembroke Dock, Pembrokeshire. F/O Havlicek, a Canadian, and his crew are commemorated on the Runnymede Memorial.

24th December 1941

254 Sqn	Blenheim IV	L9313	QY-	Duty:	Transit Flight
	F/Lt D M Poynter RNZAF	39933	+	Base:	Dyce
	P/O W R Constable	101504	+	T/o time: 14:15	
	AC2 T Broom	1105527	+		
	AC1 R F Watson	1175044	+		

Engine cut after take-off from Dyce, stalled and dived into the ground at Pitmedden Churchyard.

F/Lt Poynter, from Auckland, New Zealand, is buried locally in Dyce Old Churchyard;
P/O Constable rests in Crail Cemetery; AC2 Broom is buried in Philips Park Cemetery,
Manchester and AC1 Watson was taken to Northwood Cemetery, Middlesex.

25th December 1941

1 PRU	Spitfire I (PR) type E	X4538	LY-	Duty:	Training
	F/O A E Tilley	. . . . .	Safe	Base:	?
	Crashed on landing at Benson, 10:50 hrs.			T/o time:	?

224 Sqn	Hudson III	V9091	QX-B	Op:	Stepper Patrol
	P/O N A Mervyn-Smith	89382	Safe	Base:	St Eval
	Sgt R Mattison	. . . . . .	Safe	T/o time:	17:05
	Sgt H Clent	. . . . . .	Safe		
	Sgt H Flavell	. . . . . .	Safe		
	F/Sgt T Edgar	. . . . . .	Safe		

The radar failed at 18:53 hrs and the aircraft overshot on landing and hit a hedge at 22:16 hrs on
return to St Eval, Cornwall. The Hudson's nose was crushed, both engines were left hanging out
of the nacelles, the u/c was buckled and the port mainplane smashed.

224 Sqn	Hudson V	AM669	QX-F	Op:	Stepper Patrol
	S/Ldr C R Davies MiD	28147	+	Base:	St Eval
	Sgt T F Houldsworth	1000126	+	T/o time:	22:57
	F/Lt J H Higgleton	42968	+		
	Sgt A G Gooch	914261	+		
	Sgt J Roberts	646219	+		

Failed to return. Both S/Ldr Davies and Sgt Houldsworth rest in Bayeux War Cemetery, Calvados,
France, while the other crewmen are commemorated on the Runnymede Memorial.

612 Sqn	Whitley V	Z6810	WL-A	Duty:	Transit Flight
	P/O J F Catchpole	113327	+	Base:	Prestwick
	P/O P J Halliday	64913	+	T/o time:	?
	Sgt J H Taylor	947597	+		
	Sgt W H Lamond	972080	+		
	Sgt W Jamison	971731	+		
	Sgt J Wilson	1260082	+		
	F/Lt J Fiddes	89039	+		
	F/O E C Scholefield	63211	+		
	F/Lt F Spikins MiD	43569	+		

Presumed to have ditched between Prestwick and Reykjavik after being diverted back to Wick.
F/Lt Fiddes, the Medical Officer, F/O Scholefield, the Intelligence Officer and F/Lt Spikins, the
Torpedo Officer were passengers. All are commemorated on the Runnymede Memorial.

27th December 1941

235 Sqn	Beaufighter IC	T4765	LA-T	Op:	Archery
	P/O W H Hughes	60530	+	Base:	Dyce
	Sgt C F Myhill	916359	+	T/o time:	?

Shot down by an Me109 off coast of Norway. Both P/O Hughes and Sgt Myhill rest in Stavne
Cemetery, Trondheim, Norway.

236 Sqn	Beaufighter IC	T4825	ND-U	Op:	Archery
	P/O R A Baseby	89337	+	Base:	Sumburgh
	Sgt S D Gummery	1101219	+	T/o time:	10:30

Took off in company with two other Beaufighters to escort a convoy. Last seen breaking off after
attacking a He111, P/O Baseby's Beaufighter wobbling very badly before falling away. Both men
are commemorated on the Runnymede Memorial.

254 Sqn	Blenheim IV	Z6081	QY-	Op:	?
	F/O J W Roche RAAF	402191	+	Base:	Dyce
	P/O D A Halsall	62669	+	T/o time:	?
	Sgt F H Silk	634877	+		

Lost without trace. P/O Halsall rests in Stavne Cemetery, Trondheim while both F/O Roche and
Sgt Silk are commemorated on the Runnymede Memorial.

28th December 1941

1 PRU	Spitfire I(PR) type G	AA804	LY-	Op:	Reconnaissance
	P/O C P Hall MiD	50896	PoW	Base:	Benson
				T/o time:	10:40

Took off tasked with a high level operation to Dusseldorf and Essen but failed to return.
The engine cut and the Spitfire crashed SE of Bergen op Zoom, Holland, at 14:05 hrs.
P/O Hall was shot by the Gestapo on the 25th of March 1944 after taking part in the mass escape from Stalag Luft III, Sagan, and is buried at Poznan, Poland.

29th December 1941

42 Sqn	Beaufort I		L9874	AW-C	Op:	Rover
	P/O	Wood	. . . . .	Safe	Base:	Leuchars
	Sgt	Spark	. . . . . .	Safe	T/o time:	15:20
	Sgt	Bladen	. . . . . .	Safe		
	Sgt	Birchall	. . . . . .	Safe		

P/O Wood completed his task at 17:55 hrs in position FTTH 2200, and as nothing was seen he set course for base. At 19:50 hrs the Beaufort made landfall but could not identify its position. The pilot flew a southerly course using Lorenz beam but this failed after 5 minutes. At 19:15 hrs the IFF went u/s and the crew then had W/T failure. P/O Wood then tried R/T but could not be heard by a ground station. Still flying south he decided to crash-land owing to the thick fog coming up along with icing and petrol shortage. The bombs were jettisoned in a reservoir and the Beaufort crash-landed onto a road branching off the Kendal - Sedburgh trunk route at 21:15 hrs, 4 miles east of Kendal. No injuries were reported to the crew but the aircraft was badly damaged.

30th December 1941

1 PRU	Spitfire PR.IV	AA796	LY-	Op:	?
	S/Ldr T D Calnan	33228	PoW	Base:	?
	Missing.			T/o time:	?

235 Sqn	Beaufighter IC	. . . . .	LA-O	Base:	Dyce
				Time:	?

On the ground at Wick when struck by Beaufighter T3295 'LA-S' of 235 Squadron, piloted by Sgt Denley. Believed repaired and returned to service, so *not* included in loss analysis.

235 Sqn	Beaufighter IC		T3295	LA-S	Duty:	?
	Sgt	Denley			Base:	Dyce
					T/o time:	?

When landing at Wick struck Beaufighter T4725 'LA-O' of 235 Squadron and Hudson V AM880 of 608 Squadron. Repaired and returned to service with the unit, so *not* included in loss analysis.

235 Sqn	Beaufighter IC	T4725	LA-J	Duty:	?
				Base:	Dyce
				T/o time:	?

When landing at Wick ploughed into the wreckage of the previous accident involving Beaufighters 'LA-O' and 'LA-S' of 235 Squadron and Hudson V AM880 of 608 Squadron. DBR.

502 Sqn	Whitley VII		Z9372	YG-M	Op:	Shipping Search
	F/O	A Wood BEM	. . . . .	Safe	Base:	St Eval
	Sgt	R W Dix	. . . . . .	Safe	Time:	23:45
	F/O	P R Aitken	. . . . . .	Safe		
	Sgt	L E H Eullrich	. . . . . .	Safe		
	Sgt	H S Vince	. . . . . .	Safe		
	Sgt	H B Jordan	. . . . . .	Safe		

When flying at 500 feet hit an enemy MV and damaged the hydraulics. While at 100 feet trying to locate the St Eval runway in poor visibility the engine cut and the Whitley was crash-landed at 05:45 hrs. The enemy vessel was later shadowed by a Sunderland and sunk by the Royal Navy.

608 Sqn	Hudson V	AM880	UL-		Ground Loss
				Base:	?
				Time:	?

On the ground at Wick when struck by Beaufighters 'LA-S' and 'LA-J' of 235 Squadron as described above. Damaged beyond repair.

Royal Air Force
COASTAL COMMAND
LOSSES
of the Second World War

Appendices

Appendix A

Coastal Command Losses by Type 1939-1941

	Type	Op	Non-Op	Gnd
1939	Anson I	20	1	1
	Blenheim I	0	1	0
	Hudson I	6	5	0
	London II	2	0	1
	Stranraer I	0	1	0
	Sunderland I	3	1	0
	Totals	31	9	2
1940	Anson I	39	4	6
	Battle I	0	2	0
	Beaufort I	36	17	3
	Blenheim I	3	5	0
	Blenheim IV	113	27	12
	Botha I	1	1	0
	Fokker T-VIIIW	2	1	0
	Hudson I	81	11	3
	Hudson II	3	0	0
	Lerwick I	2	0	2
	London II	0	1	1
	Magister I	0	1	0
	Maryland I	0	1	0
	Master I	0	1	0
	Spitfire (PR)	11	2	0
	Stranraer I	0	0	3
	Sunderland I	13	0	4
	Tutor	0	1	0
	Vildebeest IV	0	1	0
	Whitley III	1	0	0
	Whitley V	4	1	0
	Totals	310	78	34

	Type	Op	Non-Op	Gnd
1941	Anson I	5	5	1
	Battle I	0	2	0
	Beaufighter I	5	13	0
	Beaufort I	73	20	2
	Beaufort II	0	1	0
	Blenheim I	0	2	0
	Blenheim IV	138	39	5
	Catalina I	6	7	5
	Catalina II	1	0	0
	Gladiator II	2	1	0
	Hornet Moth	0	1	0
	Hudson I	21	8	0
	Hudson II	4	1	0
	Hudson III	14	5	0
	Hudson IV	6	0	1
	Hudson V	34	5	1
	Lerwick I	1	3	1
	Liberator I	0	1	0
	Mosquito I (PR)	1	0	0
	Northrop N-3PB	0	3	1
	Spartan 7W-19	0	1	0
	Spitfire (PR)	29	5	0
	Stranraer I	0	1	1
	Sunderland I	5	2	1
	Sunderland II	3	1	0
	S.23/M 'C' Class	0	1	0
	S.26/M 'G' Class	0	1	0
	Wellington I	1	1	0
	Wellington VIII	5	0	0
	Whitley V	24	11	1
	Whitley VII	3	0	0
	Totals	381	141	20

Appendix B

Coastal Command Group Losses 1939-1941

Group	Type	Op	Non-Op	Gnd
1939				
15 Gp	Anson I	1	0	0
	Sunderland I	3	1	0
	Totals	4	1	0
16 Gp	Anson I	13	1	0
	Blenheim I	0	1	0
	Totals	13	2	0
18 Gp	Anson I	6	0	1
	Hudson I	6	5	0
	Hudson II	1	0	0
	London II	2	0	1
	Stranraer I	0	1	0
	Totals	15	6	2

Group	Type	Op	Non-Op	Gnd
1940				
15 Gp	Anson I	9	2	3
	Beaufort I	5	2	0
	Blenheim IV	2	0	0
	Fokker T-VIIIW	2	1	0
	Hudson I	2	3	1
	Lerwick I	1	0	0
	Stranraer I	0	0	3
	Sunderland I	7	0	3
	Whitley V	4	1	0
	Totals	32	9	10
16 Gp	Anson I	21	1	3
	Beaufort I	19	10	2
	Blenheim I	2	5	0
	Blenheim IV	95	20	10
	Hudson I	24	1	0
	Hudson II	1	0	0
	Hudson (PR)	2	0	0
	Magister I	0	1	0
	Maryland I	0	1	0
	Spitfire (PR)	11	3	0
	Tutor	0	1	0
	Vildebeest IV	0	1	0
	Whitley III	1	0	0
	Totals	176	44	15
18 Gp	Anson I	9	1	0
	Battle I	0	2	0
	Beaufort I	12	5	1
	Blenheim IV	16	8	2
	Botha I	1	1	0
	Hudson I	55	10	3
	Hudson II	2	0	0
	Lerwick I	1	0	0
	London II	0	1	0
	Magister I	0	1	0
	Sunderland I	6	0	1
	Totals	102	29	7

Group	Type	Op	Non-Op	Gnd
1941				
15 Gp	Anson I	0	2	1
	Beaufighter I	2	7	0
	Beaufort I	20	2	2
	Blenheim I	0	1	0
	Blenheim IV	2	1	0
	Catalina I	2	5	1
	Catalina II	1	0	0
	Gladiator II	1	1	0
	Hudson I	5	2	0
	Hudson II	3	0	0
	Hudson III	7	2	0
	Hudson V	7	1	0
	Lerwick I	1	3	1
	Liberator I	0	1	0
	Short S.23 'C' Class	0	1	0
	Short S.26 'G' Class	0	1	0
	Stranraer I	0	1	1
	Sunderland I	3	2	0
	Sunderland II	1	1	0
	Whitley V	15	3	0
	Whitley VII	2	0	0
	Totals	72	37	6
16 Gp	Anson I	5	2	0
	Beaufighter I	1	3	0
	Beaufort I	34	13	0
	Beaufort II	0	1	0
	Blenheim I	0	1	0
	Blenheim IV	97	36	0
	Gladiator II	1	0	0
	Hornet Moth	0	1	0
	Hudson I	6	0	0
	Hudson III	0	1	0
	Hudson IV	6	0	1
	Hudson V	12	3	0
	Mosquito (PR)	1	0	0
	Spartan 7W-19	0	1	0
	Spitfire I	3	2	0
	Spitfire (PR)	29	5	0
	Wellington IC	0	1	0
	Wellington VIII	5	0	0
	Totals	200	70	1

Group	Type	Op	Non-Op	Gnd
1941 continued				
18 Gp	Anson I	0	1	0
	Battle I	0	2	0
	Beaufighter I	1	3	0
	Beaufort I	13	5	0
	Blenheim IV	30	3	0
	Catalina I	3	2	2
	Hudson I	10	5	0
	Hudson II	7	2	0
	Hudson III	1	0	0
	Hudson V	15	1	1
	Northrop N-3PB	0	3	1
	Sunderland I	2	0	1
	Sunderland II	2	0	0
	Whitley V	9	8	1
	Whitley VII	1	0	0
	Totals	94	35	6
19 Gp	Beaufighter I	1	0	0
	Beaufort I	6	0	0
	Blenheim IV	9	1	0
	Catalina I	1	0	0
	Totals	17	1	0

Appendix C

Coastal Command Squadron Losses 1939-1941

Sqn	Type	Op	Non-Op	Gnd
1939				
22	Blenheim I	0	1	0
48	Anson I	6	1	0
201	London II	1	0	1
204	Sunderland I	2	0	0
206	Anson I	3	0	0
209	Stranraer I	0	1	0
210	Sunderland I	1	0	0
220	Anson I	1	0	0
	Hudson I	0	2	0
224	Hudson	4	2	0
228	Sunderland I	0	1	0
233	Anson I	1	0	1
	Hudson I	2	1	0
240	London II	1	0	0
269	Anson I	3	0	0
500	Anson I	4	0	0
502	Anson I	1	0	0
608	Anson I	1	0	0
	Totals	31	9	2

Sqn	Type	Op	Non-Op	Gnd
1940				
10 (RAAF)	Sunderland I	1	0	2
21	Blenheim IV	6	4	2
22	Beaufort I	19	10	2
	Maryland I	0	1	0
42	Vildebeest IV	0	1	0
	Beaufort I	12	5	1
	Anson I	0	1	0
48	Anson I	8	1	1
53	Blenheim IV	25	1	5
57	Blenheim IV	2	0	0
58	Whitley III	1	0	0
59	Blenheim IV	23	0	2
98	Battle I	0	2	0
201	Sunderland I	4	0	0
204	Sunderland I	4	0	1
206	Hudson I	24	1	0
	Anson I	0	0	1
	Hudson II	1	0	0
209	Lerwick I	2	0	2
210	Sunderland I	4	0	1
217	Anson I	6	1	1
	Beaufort I	5	2	0
220	Hudson I	13	3	2
	Hudson II	1	0	0

Sqn	Type	Op	Non-Op	Gnd
1940 continued				
224	Hudson I	22	4	0
233	Hudson I	12	1	0
	Hudson II	1	0	0
235	Blenheim I	0	1	0
	Blenheim IV	27	6	0
236	Blenheim I	3	4	0
	Blenheim IV	6	3	2
240	London II	0	1	1
	Stranraer I	0	0	3
248	Blenheim IV	8	5	0
	Magister I	0	1	0
254	Blenheim IV	14	8	1
269	Anson I	4	0	0
	Hudson I	8	2	1
272	Blenheim IV	2	0	0
320	Fokker T-VIIIW	2	1	0
	Anson I	0	1	0
321	Anson I	1	0	1
500	Tutor	0	1	0
	Anson I	13	0	1
502	Anson I	2	0	0
	Whitley V	4	1	0
608	Anson I	2	0	0
	Botha I	1	1	0
612	Anson I	3	0	0
PDU	Spitfire (PR)	1	0	0
PRU	Spitfire (PR)	8	3	0
PRU	Hudson (PR)	2	0	0
PRU	Magister	0	1	0
1 PRU	Spitfire (PR)	2	0	0
	Totals	310	78	34

Sqn	Type	Op	Non-Op	Gnd
1941				
10 (RAAF)	Sunderland I	3	1	0
21	Blenheim IV	0	1	0
22	Beaufort I	31	5	0
42	Beaufort I	13	3	0
48	Anson I	3	2	0
	Hudson III	0	1	0
53	Blenheim IV	21	0	1
	Hudson V	3	0	0
	Hudson IV	1	0	0
59	Blenheim IV	31	2	0
	Hudson III	0	1	0
	Hudson V	3	0	0
82	Blenheim IV	5	0	2
86	Blenheim IV	3	3	2
	Beaufort I	6	7	0
	Beaufort II	0	1	0
95	Sunderland I	0	1	0
98	Battle I	0	2	0
107	Blenheim IV	5	0	0
114	Blenheim IV	8	0	0
119	S.23/M 'C' Class	0	1	0
	S.26/M 'G' Class	0	1	0
120	Liberator I	0	1	0
143	Beaufighter I	1	3	0
201	Sunderland II	3	1	0
202	Catalina I	0	0	2
204	Sunderland I	1	0	1
206	Hudson I	6	1	0
	Hudson IV	5	0	1
	Hudson V	3	0	0
209	Lerwick I	1	3	1
	Catalina I	2	3	1
210	Sunderland I	1	0	0
	Catalina I	2	0	0
217	Beaufort I	23	3	2
	Anson I	0	0	1
220	Hudson I	4	1	0
	Hudson II	1	1	0
	Hudson V	8	1	0
	Hudson III	1	0	0
221	Wellington I	1	1	0
	Wellington VIII	5	0	0
224	Hudson I	4	3	0
	Hudson V	1	1	0
	Hudson III	1	0	0
233	Hudson II	1	0	0
	Hudson I	2	1	0
	Hudson III	2	1	0
	Hudson V	3	0	0
235	Blenheim IV	15	5	0
	Beaufighter I	1	1	0

Sqn	Type	Op	Non-Op	Gnd
1941 continued				
236	Blenheim IV	13	1	0
	Beaufighter I	1	0	0
240	Stranraer I	0	1	1
	Catalina I	1	1	0
	Catalina II	1	0	0
248	Blenheim IV	6	2	0
	Beaufighter I	1	3	0
252	Blenheim I	0	1	0
	Blenheim IV	0	1	0
	Beaufighter I	1	4	0
254	Blenheim IV	11	9	0
269	Hudson I	3	1	0
	Hudson III	6	1	0
272	Blenheim IV	2	1	0
	Beaufighter I	0	2	0
320	Hudson I	2	1	0
	Hudson III	4	1	0
	Hudson II	2	0	0
321	Anson I	0	1	0
330	N-3PB	0	3	1
404 (RCAF)	Blenheim I	0	1	0
	Blenheim IV	2	6	0
407 (RCAF)	Hudson V	6	2	0
413 (RCAF)	Catalina I	1	3	2
489	Beaufort I	0	2	0
500	Anson I	2	1	0
	Blenheim IV	11	8	0
	Hudson V	0	1	0
502	Whitley V	15	3	0
	Whitley VII	2	0	0
608	Anson I	0	1	0
	Blenheim IV	2	0	0
	Hudson V	7	0	1
612	Whitley V	9	8	1
	Whitley VII	1	0	0
401 Flt	Gladiator II	1	0	0
1401 Flt	Spitfire (PR)	1	1	0
1402 Flt	Gladiator II	1	1	0
1403 Flt	Blenheim IV	2	0	0
1404 Flt	Blenheim IV	1	0	0
1 PRU	Spartan 7W-19	0	1	0
	Hornet Moth	0	1	0
	Spitfire (PR)	28	4	0
	Blenheim IV	1	0	0
	Mosquito (PR)	1	0	0
	Totals	381	141	20

Appendix D

Prisoners of War 1939-1941

Details of airmen taken Prisoner of War are held in AIR20/2336 at the Public Record Office, Kew, Surrey, TW9 4DU.

The list is in alphabetical order as officers and airmen of the RAF, RAAF, RCAF, RNZAF and SAAF.

AIR20/2336 was compiled late in 1944 and is considered correct for that year. A few entries are included for 1945 but that list is incomplete. The location of the camp that an airman was incarcerated in during 1944 is denoted by a code which is explained in the adjacent column:

Code:		
	L1	Stalag Luft Barth Vogelsang
	L3	Stalag Luft Sagan and Belaria
	L6	Stalag Luft Heydekrug
	4B	Stalag Muhlberg-Elbe
	8C	Stalag Kr Spottau/Sagan
	11A	Stalag Altengrabow
	319	Stalag Cholm
	344	Stalag Lamsdorf
	357	Stalag Kopernikus
	383	Stalag Hohen Fels
	04C	Oflag Saalhaus Colditz

Camp	PoW No	Name	Unit	Svce No
1939				
L3	16	Edwards L H	206	31687
L3	22	Heaton-Nicols D G	224	27275
1940				
357	382	Pickering T	22	937061
L6	320	Brown E A	42	751798
L3	1285	Burns H F	42	41551
O4C	1267	Flinn F D	42	44120
L1	341	O'Malley F A	42	544944
L6	250	Robertson A M B	42	523060
L6	308	Shirley S W	42	516023
L3	1989	Smith F G L	42	29181
L6	214	Farrow A E	53	511965
L3	379	Panton A D	53	33331
L1	1219	George O F	210	619031
357	417	Ayre R	217	614211
357	433	Hastie A H	217	974322
344	11902	Steedman J B	217	973774
L3	340	Troward R E	217	42914
L6	452	Weston A R	217	940106
?	?	Wilson	217	?
L3	130	Rothwell T N C	224	41475
L3	172	Wood R C	224	41514
L3	81	Lancaster A O	235	755199
L3	584	Savill N A	235	41956
L3	61	Baird G M	248	42094
L3	423	Burton D L	248	40187
L3	69103	Wood S V	248	649800
L3	97	Hill A J	254	42004
L6	67	Brodie A M S	269	565699
L6	86	Hepburn J G	269	551354
L6	62	Lascelles E B	269	580224
344	26883	MacKenzie S	269	524386
L3	13034	MacKenzie J H	269	552160
L6	58	Napier A	269	614218
L6	155	Brockway J B S	500	78530
L6	178	Croft S R	500	632266

Camp	PoW No	Name	Unit	Svce No
1940 continued				
L6	144	Smith H W J	500	812199
L3	1290	Smalley J R T	PRU	39345
L6	233	Taylor-Gill J D T	PRU	590406
L3	624	Corbett A B	PRU	41666
L3	244	Dakeyne P L	PRU	39068
?	?	Rumsey A A	PRU	22246
?	?	Williams	PRU	?
?	?	Phillips	PRU	?
L6	328	Smith H W J	PRU	820009
1941				
L3	3670	Culverwell A P	22	81003
383	98	Ferguson A A	22	1055942
357	56	Friend H C	22	754147
L6	24753	Guest C	22	996840
L3	674	Hall P I	22	88039
L3	120	Hicks R	22	82956
L6	24460	Howard A	22	943003
L3	699	Iliff R M	22	88041
L6	24829	Jones I W	22	950569
L3	630	McCaw W D J	22	41397
383	103	Meader C G	22	961018
357	87	Tanfield R	22	944327
383	102	Tonkin A J	22	922736
8C	18288	Woodland P R	22	905872
L3	1426	Hester E R	42	46465
?	?	Philpot O L S	42	77131
L3	1436	Rackow G M	42	105191
L6	39250	Dawson A R	53	965676
L3	3724	Hewson E	53	87400
L6	39173	McCorkell W G	53	948299
L6	9626	Powell J M	53	748711
L6	9643	Tyson S	53	755464
L3	1354	Briggs P S E	59	79751
L6	39164	Edgar C H	59	755720
357	39228	Flury B R	59	939502
L3	3756	Kennedy D E	59	81358

Camp	PoW No	Name	Unit	Svce No
1941 continued				
L3	581	Morton R D	59	84937
L3	1365	Villa P P	59	87672
L3	538	Buck W	86	535188
383	73	Green J B	86	702081
383	79	McCann J	86	978471
L3	707	Page D	86	64320
L3	708	Paxton J Mc	86	81063
L6	39153	Dowse L C	114	907195
L6	39152	Duffield F B	114	647048
11A	140688	Anderson J	119	636035
357	9658	Corcoran L G	119	4503
357	39231	Hill J E	119	758249
L3	3707	Long S G	119	70406
L6	78	Austin S J	217	746908
L3	3642	Barry L B	217	78668
L6	39296	Bennett W	217	937589
357	489	Cannon C W D	217	550494
357	490	Clarke P H	217	745759
L3	1492	Collings A G	217	137117
L3	24802	Cronie J A	217	1057463
L6	39275	Gillies M	217	R/54575
L6	39270	Godwin G	217	981765
L6	24340	Gornall F J	217	1051580
L6	39269	Griffin R S C T	217	928630
L6	30	Holiday G D	217	627394
L3	467	Hunter A V	217	39318
L3	3367	Hunter W J	217	89835
L6	39274	Jarvis S W	217	1252501
L3	3727	Rance E A	217	79736

Camp	PoW No	Name	Unit	Svce No
L6	39330	Ritchie G A D	217	974516
L3	585	Stratford A H	217	76593
L3	586	Tams F A B	217	43076
L6	69	Wilson A G	217	982330
L6	24775	Young H E C	217	755850
344	24815	Burridge P L	220	901810?
?	Griffiths R W		220	938582
383	127	Hall J W G	220	745778
344	24845	Houghton L H	220	964956
L3	2277	Milton P H	220	127851
383	131	Price S J	220	923203
L3	3791	Cowper R T R	233	41988
L3	3782	Down R O H	233	85251
?	3789	Bakker W	320	40595
?	?	van Huijstee	320	11031
383	110	Archer S	407	803473
L3	696	Fraser H N	407	J/4427
L6	90086	Neeves G L	407	904107
383	113	Quinn J	407	759133
L6	9640	Kennedy J H	612	630077
L6	9646	Martin J S	612	998984
L6	9623	Skuse R J	612	748628
L3	3773	Winter-Taylor H C	612	42733
L3	4141	Calnan T D	1 PRU	33228
L3	39320	Dowse S H	1 PRU	86685
L3	3721	Greenhill C A S	1 PRU	40906
?	?	Hall C P	1 PRU	50896
L3	470	Lockyer T M	1 PRU	37193
L3	3805	Tomlinson P	1 PRU	39154

Appendix E

Escapers and Evaders 1939-1941

Due to the nature of Coastal Command operations there were few Evaders and Escapers compared to other Commands. This serves to draw attention to the exploits of the individuals who managed to evade capture and to the efforts of the escape organisations that assisted them.

Further details for each escape is held at the Public Record Office, Kew, London, in the Escape Reports, Class WO208. Internee details are in the same file

Date	Name	Unit
1939	No Escapers & Evaders	
11.06.40	Sgt A Sherwood	269 Sqn
11.08.40	P/O P J Coleman	53 Sqn
17.12.40	Sgt J R Massey	217 Sqn
24.05.41	Sgt A W Fletcher	272 Sqn
24.05.41	Sgt Gallimore	272 Sqn
24.05.41	Sgt Ream	272 Sqn
14.09.41	Sgt A H Graham	53 Sqn
14.09.41	P/O T M Gay	53 Sqn
11.12.41	F/O O L S Philpot DFC	42 Sqn

Appendix F

Internees 1939-1941

Within the same file as the Escape and Evasion Reports, W0208, are the reports of airmen interned in neutral countries. Two countries feature in the reports for this period: Portugal where the crashes were mainly of transit or ferry aircraft, and Eire, where the crashes were mainly of operational aircraft from Northern Ireland.

Date	Name	Country	Unit
1939	No Internees		
21.12.40	Sgt Hobbs	Eire	272 Sqn
21.12.40	Sgt Ricketts	Eire	272 Sqn
21.12.40	Sgt Newport	Eire	272 Sqn
24.01.41	P/O D Welply	Eire	233 Sqn
24.01.41	P/O Cowper	Eire	233 Sqn
24.01.41	Sgt Todd	Eire	233 Sqn
24.01.41	P/O Snow	Eire	233 Sqn
24.01.41	F/O L J Ward	Eire	502 Sqn
24.01.41	Sgt C V Jefferson	Eire	502 Sqn
14.02.41	S/Ldr Lombard	Portugal	95 Sqn
14.02.41	F/Lt Evison	Portugal	95 Sqn
14.02.41	F/O Bowie	Portugal	95 Sqn
14.02.41	Sgt Banfield	Portugal	95 Sqn
11.03.41	P/O D Midgley	Eire	502 Sqn
11.03.41	Sgt R C Harkell	Eire	502 Sqn
01.05.41	S/Lt R D B Hopkins RN	Portugal	252 Sqn
01.05.41	Sgt G Bell	Portugal	252 Sqn
13.05.41	Sgt F H Miller	Portugal	82 Sqn
13.05.41	Sgt N J Ingram	Portugal	82 Sqn
13.05.41	Sgt W E W Whiteman	Portugal	82 Sqn
22.05.41	F/O J Holgate	Portugal	252 Sqn
22.05.41	F/O H Verity	Portugal	252 Sqn
22.05.41	Sgt Barnett	Portugal	252 Sqn
23.10.41	Sgt Webster	Eire	236 Sqn
23.10.41	Sgt Brady	Eire	236 Sqn
03.12.41	F/Lt J G Fleming	Eire	201 Sqn
03.12.41	Sgt J C Masterson	Eire	201 Sqn

Appendix G

Coastal Command Flying Unit Bases 1939-1941

From the outset of the Second World War and to make the most of the meagre resources that were available to Coastal Command, units were required to change bases frequently, or several aircraft were detached from their parent units to other aerodromes on a regular basis. These complex positioning flights by Coastal Squadrons put great strain on servicing and clerical support staffs who were expected to maintain the high standards set by other RAF Home Commands.

As the war progressed the formation of new units (and their controlling groups) brought a greater number of bases into the action, and on occasions, depending upon the perceived threat at any time, additional units were borrowed from other Commands. Even with these additional assets, flexibility was still paramount.

This appendix attempts to provide a comprehensive listing of the complex positioning flights carried out by Coastal Command units as the various Group Headquarters did their utmost to counter the enemy threats.

Unit	Code	Base	Arrived	Comments
15 GROUP		Reformed as 15 (Reconnaissance) Group on 15th March 1939 at Lee-on-Solent. To Mount Wise Barracks, Plymouth, 6th June 1939. Headquarters to Egg Buckland Keep, 16th August 1941. To Derby House, Liverpool, early 1941; operational 14th February 1941.		
10 (RAAF) Sqn	RB	Pembroke Dock, Pembs	10 Oct 39	Placed under Coastal Command Control for war operations in European Theatre. (Had been in UK since Jul/Aug 39, albeit training under RAAF control.)
		Mount Batten, Devon	01 Apr 40	Sunderland I.
		Pembroke Dock, Pembs	14 Jul 40	Detachment. Left 18 Jul 40.
		Pembroke Dock, Pembs	27 Nov 40	Detachment. Left 30 Nov 40.
		Lough Erne, Co Fermanagh	06 Mar 41	Detachment.
22 Sqn	OA	Carew Cheriton, Pembs	09 Mar 40	Detachment from 16 Group. Beaufort I. Left Apr 40.
		St Eval, Cornwall	05 Nov 40	Detachment from 16 Group. Left 12 Nov 40.
42 Sqn	AW	Carew Cheriton, Pembs	23 Feb 40	Detachment from 16 Group. Vildebeest III/IV Left 30 Mar 40.
		St Eval, Cornwall	19 May 40	Detachment from 16 Group. Left 25 May 40.
		Abbotsinch, Renfrew	02 Oct 40	Detachment from 18 Group. Left 25 Oct 40.
48 Sqn	OY	St Eval, Cornwall	03 Sep 39	Detachment from 16 Group. Anson I. Left 17 Jul 40.
		Carew Cheriton, Pembs	11 Jul 40	Detachment from 16 Group. Left 31 Aug 40.
		Hooton Park, Cheshire	16 Jul 40	
		Aldergrove, Co Antrim	19 Jul 40	Detachment. Left 18 Nov 40.
		Sydenham, Co Down	18 Nov 40	Detachment. Left 02 Dec 40.
		Stornoway, Hebrides	02 Dec 40	Detachment.
		Stornoway, Hebrides	24 Jul 41	Squadron move to join Detachment. Hudson III/V, Sep 41. To 18 Group 20 Oct 41.
53 Sqn	PZ	Limavady, Londonderry	28 Aug 41	Detachment from 16 Group. Hudson V. Left 30 Aug 41.
		Limavady, Londonderry	17 Dec 41	From 19 Group.
59 Sqn	PJ	St Eval, Cornwall	17 Oct 40	Detachment from 16 Group. Left 18 Oct 40.
		St Eval, Cornwall	11 Nov 40	Detachment from 16 Group. Left 12 Nov 40.
		St Eval, Cornwall	14 Nov 40	Detachment from 16 Group. Left 15 Nov 40.
95 Sqn	SE	Pembroke Dock, Pembs	16 Jan 41	From 18 Group. Sunderland I. Moved to AHQ West Africa, Mar 41.
119 Sqn	–	Bowmore, Islay	13 Mar 41	Formed from G Flight. Short G/C Boat, Apr 41. Catalina Ib, Jun 41. To 19 Group 11 Aug 41.

120 Sqn	OH	Nutts Corner, Co Antrim	01 Jun 41	Re-formed. Liberator I, Jun 41. Liberator II, Nov 41.
143 Sqn	HO	Aldergrove, Co Antrim	15 Jun 41	Reformed. Crews from 252 Squadron. Beaufighter IC, Jun 41. To 18 Group 04 July 41.
201 Sqn	ZM	Aldergrove, Co Antrim	16 Dec 41	From 18 Group.
		Pembroke Dock, Pembs	01 Mar 40	Detachment (day of month arbitrary) from 18 Group. Re-equipping with Sunderland I. Left 23 Apr 40. Returned to 18 Group.
		Lough Erne, Co Fermanagh	09 Oct 41	From 18 Group. Sunderland III, Jan 42.
204 Sqn	KG	Mount Batten, Devon	03 Sep 39	*In situ.* Sunderland I. To 18 Group 02 Apr 40.
		Falmouth, Cornwall	01 Mar 40	Detachment. Left 26 Mar 40.
		Pembroke Dock, Pembs	01 Apr 40	Detachment. Left 26 Aug 41.
206 Sqn	VX	Carew Cheriton, Pembs	16 Sep 39	Detachment from 16 Group. Anson I. Left 10 Oct 39.
		Hooton Park, Cheshire	10 Oct 39	Detachment from 16 Group. Left 30 Nov 39.
		Aldergrove, Co Antrim	01 Apr 41	Detachment from 16 Group. Hudson I,II,III,IV. Left Jul 41.
		Stornoway, Hebrides	12 Aug 41	Detachment.
		Aldergrove, Co Antrim	12 Aug 41	From 19 Group. Hudson V, Oct 41.
209 Sqn	WQ	Falmouth, Cornwall	02 Oct 39	Detachment from 18 Group. Left 05 Nov 39.
		Pembroke Dock, Pembs	12 Jun 40	PBY-4, Nov 40.
		Stranraer, Wigtown	03 Jan 41	
		Lough Erne, Co Fermanagh	23 Mar 41	Catalina I, Apr 41. To AHQ Iceland 13 Jul 41.
210 Sqn	DA	Pembroke Dock, Pembs	03 Sep 39	*In situ.* Sunderland I. To 18 Group 18 Jul 40.
217 Sqn	MW	Warmwell, Dorset	03 Sep 39	*In situ.* Anson I.
		St Eval, Cornwall	02 Oct 39	Beaufort I, May 40. To 16 Group 29 Oct 41.
		Limavady, Londonderry	01 Mar 41	Detachment. Left 23 Mar 41.
220 Sqn	NR	St Eval, Cornwall	06 Nov 40	Detachment from 18 Group. Hudson I,III,VI. Left Apr 41.
221 Sqn	DF	Limavady, Londonderry	06 Mar 41	Detachment from 16 Group. Wellington IC.
		Limavady, Londonderry	02 May 41	Squadron move; to join Detachment. To AHQ Iceland 28 Sep 01.
		Limavady, Londonderry	05 Dec 41	From AHQ Iceland. To 16 Group 25 Dec 41.
224 Sqn	QA	Aldergrove, Co Antrim	13 Sep 39	Detachment from 18 Group. Hudson I Left 13 Dec 40.
		Aldergrove, Co Antrim	03 Mar 41	Detachment from 18 Group. Hudson I/III. Left 18 Mar 41.
		Limavady, Londonderry	29 Mar 41	Detachment from 18 Group.
		Limavady, Londonderry	15 Apr 41	Squadron move to join detachment. Hudson V, May 41. To 19 Group 20 Dec 41.
228 Sqn	DQ	Pembroke Dock, Pembroke	10 Sep 39	*In situ.* Sunderland I, PBY-4. To Middle East 10 Jun 40.
		Stranraer, Wigtown	09 Oct 41	Sunderland II, Nov 41.
233 Sqn		Aldergrove, Co Antrim	03 Aug 40	From 18 Group. Hudson I, Blenheim IV. To 18 Group 14 Sep 40.
		Aldergrove, Co Antrim	08 Dec 40	From 18 Group. Hudson III/V, Jan 41. To 19 Group 16 Aug 41.
235 Sqn	LA	St Eval, Cornwall	24 Dec 40	Detachment from 16 Group. Left 03 Jun 41.
		Aldergrove, Co Antrim	23 Mar 41	Detachment from 16 Group. Left 03 Jun 41.
236 Sqn	FA	Speke	23 Apr 40	From 16 Group. Equipping with Blenheim IV. To Fighter Command until 04 Jul 40.
		Filton, Bristol	25 May 40	To 16 Group 14 Jun 40.
		St Eval, Cornwall	30 Jul 40	Detachment from 16 Group.
		St Eval, Cornwall	07 Aug 40	Squadron move to join Detachment. To 19 Group 20 Mar 41.
		Aldergrove, Co Antrim	18 Sep 40	Detachment. Redesignated 272 Sqn 19 Nov 40.
		Aldergrove, Co Antrim	12 Jan 41	Detachment, Left 07 Feb 41.
		Aldergrove, Co Antrim	01 Mar 41	Detachment, Left 11 Mar 41.
240 Sqn	BN	Mount Batten, Devon	16 Sep 39	Detachment from 18 Group. Left 20 Sep 39.
		Falmouth, Cornwall	20 Sep 39	Detachment from 18 Group. Left Oct 39.
		Pembroke Dock, Pembs	27 May 40	From 18 Group. Stranraer I, Jun 40.
		Stranraer, Wigtown	30 Jul 40	Catalina I, Mar 41.
		Killadeas, Co Fermanagh	28 Mar 41	
		Lough Erne, Co Fermanagh	23 Aug 41	
252 Sqn	PN	Chivenor, Devon	01 Dec 40	From 16 Group. Blenheim IF/IVF, Dec 40. Beaufighter IC Dec 40.
		Aldergrove, Co Antrim	04 Apr 41	Disbanded into 143 Squadron, 15 Jun 41.

Unit	Code	Base	Arrived	Comments
254 Sqn	QY	Aldergrove, Co Antrim	07 Jan 41	Detachment (date arbitrary) from 18 Group. Blenheim IVF. Left May 41.
		Aldergrove, Co Antrim	29 May 41	From 18 Group.
272 Sqn	XK	Aldergrove, Co Antrim	19 Nov 40	Reformed from flights of 235 & 236 Squadron, Blenheim IVF, Nov 40. To 19 Group 03 Apr 41
		Sydenham, Co Down	03 Dec 40	Detachment. Left 07 Dec 40.
		Limavady, Londonderry	05 Jan 41	Detachment. Left 27 Jan 41.
320 Sqn	NO	Pembroke Dock, Pembs	01 Jun 40	Formed. Fokker T-VIIIW, Jun 40. Anson I, Aug 40. To 18 Group 01 Oct 40.
		Carew Cheriton, Pembs	30 Oct 40	Detachment from 18 Group. Left 18 Jan 41.
		Carew Cheriton, Pembs	18 Jan 41	Absorbed 321 Squadron 18 Jan 41. Hudson II, Mar 41. Hudson III, Jul 41, To 18 Group 20 Mar 41.
321 Sqn	–	Pembroke Dock, Pembs	01 Jun 40	Formed. Anson I.
		Carew Cheriton, Pembs	24 Jun 40	Combined with 320 Squadron, 18 Jan 41.
402 Met Flt	–	Aldergrove, Co Antrim	15 Jan 41	Formed from Aldergrove C Flight. Gladiator. Redesinated 1402 Flight 01 Mar 41.
404 Met Flt	–	St Eval, Cornwall	24 Dec 40	Formed. Blenheim IV. To 19 Group 01 Jan 41.
405 Met Flt	–	Aldergrove, Co Antrim	01 Nov 40	Formed. Blenheim IV. Redesignated 1405 Flight, 01 Mar 41.
413 (RCAF)	QL	Stranraer, Wigtown	01 Jul 41	Formed Catalina I, Jul 41. To 18 Group 04 Oct 41.
502 Sqn	YG	Aldergrove, Co Antrim	03 Sep 39	*In situ.* Anson I; Botha I, Aug 40; Whitley V, Sep 40.
		Hooton Park, Cheshire	01 Nov 39	Detachment (day of month arbitrary). Left 18 Jul 40.
		Limavady, Londonderry	27 Jan 41	Whitley VII, Nov 41. To 19 Group 26 Dec 41.
1402 Flight	–	Aldergrove, Co Antrim	11 Mar 41	Formed from re-designated 402 Flight. Gladiator. Spitfire, Sep 41.
1405 Flight	–	Aldergrove, Co Antrim	01 Mar 41	Formed from re-designated 405 Flight. Blenheim IV. Hudson III, Dec 41.
G Flight	–	Stranraer, Wigtown	26 Nov 40	From 18 Group. To 18 Group 24 Dec 40.

16 GROUP **Formed as a Reconnaissance Group at Wykeham Hall, Lee-on-Solent, 1st December 1936. Moved to Chatham 1st November 1938**

Unit	Code	Base	Arrived	Comments
1 GRU	–	Manston, Kent	19 Dec 39	Formed. Wellington, Mar 40. Left for Middle East, 18 May 40.
2 GRU	–	Bircham Newton, Norfolk	04 Mar 40	Formed. Wellington DWI. Left for Middle East 16 May 40.
3 GRU	–	Manston, Kent	22 Apr 40	Formed. Wellington DWI.
		Thorney Island, Sussex	24 May 40	Disbanded 26 Jul 40.
PDU	–	Heston, Middlesex	18 Jun 40	Ex-Fighter Command. Spitfire I (PR), Hudson plus hacks.
		Wick, Caithness	01 Jul 40	A Flt Detachment formed. Left 01 Oct 40.
		St Eval, Cornwall	01 Jul 40	B Flt Detachment formed. Left c.01 Oct 40. Redesignated PRU 8 Jul 1940.
PRU	LY	Heston, Middlesex	08 Jul 40	Former Photographic Development Unit.
		Wick, Caithness	01 Jul 40	A Flt Detachment formed. Left 01 Oct 40.
		St Eval, Cornwall	01 Jul 40	B Flt Detachment formed. Left c.01 Oct 40.
		Wick, Caithness	01 Oct 40	C Flt Detachment formed at Heston 24 Jul 40.
		St Eval, Cornwall	25 Jul 40	E Flt Detachment formed. PRU Redesignated 1PRU 16 Nov 40.
1 PRU	LY	Heston, Middlesex	16 Nov 40	Former Photographic Reconnaissance Unit. Spitfire 1 (PR), Hudson, Blenheim.
		Benson, Oxfordshire	27 Dec 40	Spitfire (PR). Mosquito I (PR) added 13 July 41. Absorbed 3 PRU, 15 Aug 41.
		Mount Farm, Oxfordshire	30 Dec 40	Satellite airfield. Used until 04 May 42. Disbanded into 540, 541, 542, 543 and 544 Squadrons, 19 Oct 42.

1 PRU		Wick, Caithness	16 Nov 41	C Flt Detachment. Left 07 Jan 41.
		St Eval, Cornwall	16 Nov 40	D Flt Detachment. Left c.Jan 41.
		St Eval, Cornwall	07 Jan 41	A Flt Detachment. Left 15 Apr 41. Returned Jul 41 until Oct 41.
		Wick, Caithness	09 Jan 41	B Flt Detachment. Left 16 Apr 41.
		St Eval, Cornwall	15 Apr 41	C Flt Detachment. Left c.15 Jul 41.
		Wick, Caithness	15 Apr 41	D Flt Detachment. Left 15 Jul 41 for Benson.
		Wick, Caithness	01 May 41	Mosquito Flt Detachment. Left Dec 41.
		Heston, Oxfordshire	18 Jun 41	G Flt Detachment formed. Spitfire 1(PR) and Maryland. Left 23 Jun 41.
		Gibraltar	24 Jun 41.	G Flt Marytland arrived Gibraltar this date.
		St Eval, Cornwall	01 Jul 41	A Flt Detachment. Left Oct 41.
		Wick, Caithness	15 Jul 41	E Flt Detachment. Left Oct 41.
		St Eval, Cornwall	01 Oct 41	B Flt Detachment.
		Leuchars, Fife	01 Oct 41	C Flt Detachment.
		Leuchars, Fife	01 Dec 41	Mosquito Flt Detachment.
22 Sqn	OA	Thorney Island, Sussex	03 Sep 39	*In situ.* Vildebeest I.,III, IV. Blenheim I. Beaufort I, Nov 39.
		Detling, Kent	04 Dec 39	Detachment. Left 10 Dec 39.
		North Coates, Lincolnshire	08 Apr 40	Maryland I, Aug 40.
		Bircham Newton, Norfolk	04 May 40	Detachment.
		Gosport, Hampshire	19 Jul 40	Detachment. Left 02 Aug 40.
		Thorney Island, Sussex	04 Sep 40	Detachment. Left 15 Dec 40.
		Thorney Island, Sussex	18 Mar 41	Detachment. Left 25 Mar 41.
		Thorney Island, Sussex	10 Jul 41	To 19 Group 28 Oct 41.
		Manston, Kent	29 Jul 41	Detachment from 19 Group. Left 28 Oct 41.
42 Sqn	AW	Bircham Newton, Norfolk	03 Sep 39	*In situ.* Vildebeest III/IV. Blenheim, Jan 40.
		Gosport, Hampshire	07 Apr 40	Beaufort I, Apr 40.
		Thorney Island, Sussex	17 Apr 40	To 18 Group 19 Jun 40.
		Thorney Island, Sussex	26 Sep 40	Detachment from 18 Group. Left 18 Oct 40.
		North Coates, Lincolnsire	05 Apr 41	Detachment from 18 Group. Left 13 May 41.
48 Sqn	OY	Thorney Island, Sussex	03 Sep 39	*In situ.* Anson I. Beaufort I, Jun 40. To 15 Group 16 Jul 40.
		Detling, Kent	03 Sep 39	Detachment. Left 24 Nov 39.
		Guernsey, Channel Islands	06 Sep 39	Detachment. Left 17 Jun 40.
		Bircham Newton, Norfolk	31 Mar 40	Detachment. Left 08 Jul 40.
		Detling, Kent	11 May 40	Detachment. Left 07 Jun 40.
53 Sqn	TE	Detling, Kent	03 Jul 40	Ex-Fighter Command.
		Bircham Newton, Norfolk	19 Sep 40	Detachment. Left 21 Sep 40.
		Manston, Kent	14 Nov 40	Detachment. Left 16 Nov 40.
		Thorney Island, Sussex	20 Nov 40	To 19 Group 20 Mar 41.
		Bircham Newton, Norfolk	08 Feb 41	Detachment. Left 23 Feb 41.
	PZ	Bircham Newton, Norfolk	03 Jul 41	From 19 Group. Hudson III/V, Jul 41.
58 Sqn	GE	Boscombe Down, Wiltshire	06 Oct 39	Ex-Bomber Command. To Bomber Command, 14 Feb 40.
59 Sqn	PJ	Thorney Island, Sussex	05 Jul 40	Ex-Fighter Command.
		Manston, Kent	01 Feb 41	Detachment. Left 01 Mar 41.
		Bircham Newton, Norfolk	01 Mar 41	Detachment. Left 02 Mar 41.
		Manston, Kent	05 Mar 41	Detachment. Left 15 Mar 41.
		Detling, Kent	02 Jun 41	Detachment. Left 04 Jun 41.
		Detling, Kent	11 Jun 41	Detachment.
		Detling, Kent	23 Jun 41	Squadron move to join Detachment.
		Thorney Island, Sussex	22 Jul 41	Hudson IIIa, Jul 41. Hudson V, Dec 41.
		Detling, Kent	22 Jul 41	Detachment. Left Aug 41.
		Bircham Newton, Norfolk	03 Oct 41	Detachment. Left 01 Jan 42.
82 Sqn	UX	Bodney, Norfolk	03 May 41	To Bomber Command Middle East 11 Jun 41.
86 Sqn	BX	Gosport, Hampshire	06 Dec 40	Formed. Blenheim IV, Dec 40. To 18 Group 02 Feb 41.
		Wattisham, Suffolk	03 Mar 41	From 18 Group.
		Ipswich, Suffolk	04 Mar 41	Detachment. Left 28 Mar 41.
		North Coates, Lincolnshire	12 May 41	Detachment. Left 01 Jun 41.
		North Coates, Lincolnshire	01 Jun 41	Beaufort I, Jun 41. Beaufort II, Dec 41.
98 Sqn	–	Gatwick, Sussex	01 Jul 40	Ex-Bomber Command. Battle I/ TTI. To 18 Group 27 Aug 40.
200 Sqn	–	Bircham Newton, Norfolk	25 May 41	Re-formed. Hudson IV, Jun 41. To 200 Group, 12 Jun 41.

Squadron	Code	Location	Date	Notes
206 Sqn	VX	Bircham Newton, Norfolk	03 Sep 39	*In situ.* Anson I.
				Hudson I, Mar 40. Hudson II, Apr 41.
				Hudson III, Apr 41. Hudson IV, Apr 41.
		Detling, Kent	03 Jun 40	Detachment. Left 10 Jun 40.
217 Sqn	MW	Thorney Island, Sussex	28 Oct 41	From 15 Group. Beaufort II, Oct 41.
		Manston, Kent	30 Oct 41	Detachment.
220 Sqn	NR	Bircham Newton, Norfolk	18 May 40	Detachment from 18 Group. Left 20 May 40.
		Bircham Newton, Norfolk	28 May 40	Detachment from 18 Group. Left 02 Jun 40.
		Detling, Kent	02 Jun 40	Detachment from 18 Group. Left 02 Jun 40.
221 Sqn	DF	Bircham Newton, Norfolk	21 Nov 40	Formed. Wellington IA, Nov 40, IC Dec 40.
				To 15 Group 02 May 41.
		Docking, Norfolk	25 Dec 41	From 15 Group. Wellington VIII, Jan 42.
224 Sqn	QA	Bircham Newton, Norfolk	28 Oct 39	Detachment from 18 Group. Left Nov 39.
		Bircham Newton, Norfolk	19 May 40	Detachment from 18 Group. Left 20 May 40.
233 Sqn	ZS	Bircham Newton, Norfolk	02 Dec 39	Detachment from 18 Group. Left 05 Jun 40.
		North Coates, Lincolnshire	18 May 40	Detachment from 18 Group. Left 19 May 40.
235 Sqn	LA	North Coates, Lincolnshire	27 Feb 40	Ex-Fighter Command.
				Blenheim IF. Blenheim IVF.
		Bircham Newton, Norfolk	25 Apr 40	
		Detling, Kent	26 May 40	
		Thorney Island, Sussex	10 Jun 40	
		Bircham Newton, Norfolk	24 Jun 40	To 18 Group 04 Jun 41.
		Thorney Island, Sussex	08 Aug 40	Detachment. Left 12 Jan 41.
		North Coates, Lincolnshire	09 Aug 40	Detachment. Left Sep 40.
236 Sqn	FA	North Coates, Lincolnshire	29 Feb 40	Ex-Fighter Command. Blenheim I.
				To 15 Group 23 Apr 40.
		Middle Wallop, Hampshire	14 Jun 40	From 15 Group.
		Thorney Island, Sussex	04 Jul 40	Blenheim IVF, Jul 40.
				To 15 Group 07 Aug 40.
		Detling, Kent	23 Jul 40	Detachment. Left 30 Jul 40.
		Bircham Newton, Norfolk	29 Jul 40	Detachment. Left 30 Jul 40.
		Bircham Newton, Norfolk	18 Dec 41	Detachment from 19 Group. Left 23 Dec 41.
248 Sqn	WR	North Coates, Lincolnshire	26 Feb 40	Ex-Fighter Command.
		Thorney Island, Sussex	08 Apr 40	
		Gosport, Hampshire	16 Apr 40	To Fighter Command, 22 May 40.
		Bircham Newton, Norfolk	03 Jun 41	Detachment from 18 Group.
		Bircham Newton, Norfolk	15 Jun 41	Squadron move to join Detachment.
				From 18 Group. Beaufighter IC, Jun 41.
252 Sqn	–	Bircham Newton, Norfolk	21 Nov 40	Reformed.
				To 15 Group 01 Dec 40.
254 Sqn	–	Bircham Newton, Norfolk	28 Jan 40	Ex-Fighter Command. Blenheim I/IVF.
				To 18 Group 23 Apr 40.
		Detling, Kent	29 May 40	Detachment from 18 Group. Left Jun 40.
279 Sqn	OS	Bircham Newton, Norfolk	16 Nov 41	Formed. Hudson III/V/VI, Nov 41.
280 Sqn	YF	Thorney Island, Sussex	10 Dec 41	Formed.
401 Flight	–	Mildenhall, Suffolk	04 Feb 41	Formed. Gladiator.
				Redesignated as 1401 Flight, 01 Mar 41.
403 Flight	–	Bircham Newton, Norfolk	01 Nov 40	Formed. Blenheim IV. Hudson Jan 42.
				Redesignated as 1403 Flight, 01 Mar 41.
404 (RCAF)	EE	Thorney Island, Sussex	01 May 41	Formed. Blenheim I/IV, May 41.
				To 18 Group 21 Jun 41.
407 (RCAF)	RR	Thorney Island, Sussex	08 May 41	Formed. Blenheim IV, May 41.
				Hudson I/III/V, Jun 41.
		North Coates, Lincolnshire	08 Jul 41	
415 (RCAF)	GX	Thorney Island, Sussex	20 Aug 41	Formed. Beaufort I, Blenheim IV.
				Hampden I, Jan 42.
		Detling, Kent	23 Dec 41	Detachment.
500 Sqn	MK	Detling, Kent	03 Sep 39	*In situ.* Anson I. Blenheim IV, Apr 41.
		Bircham Newton, Norfolk	30 May 41	Hudson III, Nov 41. Hudson V, Nov 41.
608 Sqn	UL	Bircham Newton, Norfolk	30 Jun 41	Detachment from 18 Group. Left Dec 41.
1401 Flight	TE	Mildenhall, Suffolk	01 Mar 41	Formed from 401 Flight. Blenheim IV.
		Bircham Newton, Norfolk	29 Oct 41	Gladiator, Hurricane.
				Absorbed 1403 Flight, 28 Oct 41.
1403 Flight	–	Bircham Newton, Norfolk	01 Mar 41	Formed from 403 Flight.
				Absorbed by 1401 Flight 28 Oct 41.

18 GROUP   Formed as a Reconnaissance Group 1st September 1938 at Lee-on-Solent.
Moved to Scotland 1st November, establishing an Ops Room at Donibristle and an
Administrative HQ at Pitreavie Castle. A combined HQ and underground Ops Room
in the grounds of Pitreavie Castle replaced that at Donibristle in February 1940 and
remained in use until Coastal Command was disbanded on 28th November 1969.

Unit	Code	Base	Arrived	Comments
10 (RAAF)	RB	Oban, Argyll	02 Aug 40	Detachment from 15 Group. Sunderland I. Left 15 Apr 41.
21 Sqn	YH	Lossiemouth, Moray	24 Jun 40	Ex-Bomber Command. Blenheim IV. To Bomber Command, 29 Oct 40.
		Lossiemouth, Moray	27 May 41	Detachment. Ex-Bomber Command. To Bomber Command, 14 Jun 41.
		Lossiemouth, Moray	07 Sep 41	Detachment. Ex-Bomber Command. To Bomber Command, 21 Sep 41.
22 Sqn	OA	Lossiemouth, Moray	01 May 40	Detachment from 16 Group. Beaufort I/II. Left 02 May 40.
		Wick, Caithness	12 Jun 40	Detachment from 16 Group. Left 18 Jun 40.
		Skitten, Caithness	22 May 41	Detachment from 16 Group. Left 30 May 41.
		Leuchars, Fife	01 Sep 41	Detachment.
42 Sqn	AW	Sumburgh, Shetlands	11 Jun 40	Detachment from 16 Group. Beaufort I/II. Left 18 Jun 40.
		Wick, Caithness	19 Jun 40	From 16 Group. Anson I, Aug 40.
		Leuchars, Fife	01 Mar 41	
		Wick, Caithness	14 Mar 41	Detachment.
		Sumburgh, Shetland	24 Jun 41	Detachment.
48 Sqn	OY	Port Ellen, Islay	01 Sep 40	Detachment from 15 Group. Anson I. Left 24 Jul 41.
		Skitten, Caithness	20 Oct 41	From 15 Group.
51 Sqn	MH	Kinloss, Moray	24 Nov 39	Ex-Bomber Command. Whitley V. To Bomber Command, 06 Dec 39.
57 Sqn	DX ?	Lossiemouth, Moray	24 Jun 40	Ex-Bomber Command. Blenheim IV. To Bomber Command, 13 Aug 40.
82 Sqn	UX	Lossiemouth, Moray	18 Apr 41	Ex-Bomber Command. Blenheim IV. To 16 Group 03 May 41.
86 Sqn	BX	Leuchars, Fife	02 Feb 41	From 16 Group. Blenheim IV. To 16 Group, 03 Mar 41.
		Leuchars, Fife	12 Sep 41	Detachment from 16 Group. Beaufort I. Left 13 Sep 41.
95 Sqn	SE	Oban, Argyll	15 Jan 41	Formed from a flight of 210 Squadron. Sunderland I, Jan 41. To 15 Group 16 Jan 41.
98 Sqn	–	Kaldadarnes, Iceland	27 Aug 40	From 16 Group. Battle I,.Tiger Moth. Hurricane Ia, Jun 41. To AHQ Iceland 19 Mar 41
		Melgerdi, Iceland	12 Sep 40	Detachment. Left 17 Sep 40.
102 Sqn	DY	Prestwick, Ayrshire	01 Sep 40	Ex Bomber Command. Whitley V. To Bomber Command 10 Oct 40.
107 Sqn	OM	Leuchars, Fife	03 Mar 41	Ex-Bomber Command. Blenheim IV. To Bomber Command, 11 May 41.
114 Sqn	FD	Thornaby, Yorkshire	02 Mar 41	Ex-Bomber Command. Blenheim IV.
		Leuchars, Fife	13 May 41	To Bomber Command, 19 Jul 41.
143 Sqn	HO	Thornaby, Yorkshire	05 Jul 41	From 15 Group. Beaufighter I.
		Dyce, Aberdeenshire	19 Jul 41	
		Sumburgh, Shetlands	23 Sep 41	
		Dyce, Aberdeenshire	05 Dec 41	Blenheim IVF, Dec 41. To 15 Group 16 Dec 41.
201 Sqn	VQ	Sullom Voe, Shetlands	03 Sep 39	In situ. London II. Stranraer, Sep 39.
		Invergordon, Ross & Cromarty	06 Nov 39	Sunderland I, Apr 40.
		Sullom Voe, Shetlands	06 Nov 39	Detachment.
	ZM	Sullom Voe, Shetlands	26 May 40	Squadron move to join Detachment. Sunderland II, May 41. To 15 Group 09 Oct 41.
		Invergordon, Ross & Cromarty	26 May 40	Detachment. Left Sep 41.
204 Sqn	KG	Sullom Voe, Shetlands	02 Apr 40	From 15 Group. To AHQ Iceland 03 Apr 41.
		Reykjavik, Iceland	14 Jun 40	Detachment. Left 20 Jun 40.
		Oban, Argyll	27 Jun 40	Detachment. Left 09 Jul 41.

		Reykjavik, Iceland	09 Nov 40	Detachment. Left 19 Nov 40.
206 Sqn	VX	Wick, Caithness	16 Nov 41	Detachment from 15 Group. Hudsons.
209 Sqn	WQ	Invergordon, Ross & Cromarty	03 Sep 39	*In situ.* Stranraer I.
		Sullom Voe, Shetlands	16 Sep 39	Detachment. Left 10 Oct 39.
		Oban, Argyll	07 Oct 39	Lerwick I, Dec 39. To 15 Group 12 Jun 40.
210 Sqn	DA	Invergordon, Ross & Cromarty	01 Oct 39	Detachment from 15 Group. Sunderland I. Left 08 Nov 39.
		Oban, Argyll	16 Nov 39	Detachment from 15 Group. Left 17 Jul 40.
		Invergordon, Ross & Cromarty	23 Nov 39	Detachment from 15 Group. Left Jun 40.
		Sullom Voe, Shetlands	30 Nov 39	Detachment from 15 Group. Left 06 Dec 39.
		Sullom Voe, Shetlands	09 Apr 40	Detachment from 15 Group. Left Jun 40.
		Oban, Argyll	18 Jul 40	From 15 Group. Catalina I/Ib, Apr 41.
220 Sqn	NR	Thornaby, Yorkshire	03 Sep 39	*In situ.* Anson I. Hudson I, III, IV Sep 39.
		Wick, Caithness	30 Apr 40	Detachment. Left 05 May 40.
		Wick, Caithness	28 Apr 41	Fortress I, Dec 41. To 18 Group 09 Jan 42.
224 Sqn	QA	Leuchars, Fife	03 Sep 39	*In situ.* Hudson I. Hudson III, Mar 41. To 19 Group 15 Apr 41.
		Thornaby, Yorkshire	05 Sep 39	Detachment. Left Apr 41.
		Wick, Caithness	14 Oct 39	Detachment. Left Apr 41.
228 Sqn	DQ	Invergordon, Ross & Cromarty	23 Oct 39	Detachment from 15 Group. Left 10 Jun 40.
233 Sqn	EY/ZS	Leuchars, Fife	03 Sep 39	*In situ.* Anson I, Hudson I. Blenheim IV (for 'D' Flight) Oct 39. To 15 Group, Aug 40.
		Wick, Caithness	21 Mar 40	Detachment. Left Apr 40.
		Leuchars, Fife	14 Sep 40	From 15 Group. To 15 Group 08 Dec 40.
235 Sqn	LA	Dyce, Aberdeenshire	04 Jun 41	From 16 Group. Blenheim IVF. Beaufighter IC, Dec 41.
		Sumburgh, Shetlands	09 Jun 41	Detachment. Left 30 Oct 41.
236 Sqn	FA	Sumburgh, Shetlands	23 Dec 41	Detachment from 19 Group. Blenheim IVF. Left 29 Dec 41.
240 Sqn	BN	Invergordon, Ross & Cromarty	03 Sep 39	*In situ.* Lerwick I, London II.
		Sullom Voe, Shetlands	09 Sep 39	Detachment.
		Sullom Voe, Shetlands	04 Nov 39	Squadron move to join Detachment.
		Invergordon, Ross & Cromarty	12 Feb 40	
		Sullom Voe, Shetlands	12 Feb 40	Detachment.
		Sullom Voe, Shetlands	17 Apr 40	Squadron move to join Detachment. To 15 Group 27 May 40.
		Oban, Argyll	19 Jul 40	Detachment from 15 Group. Stranraer I, Jun 40. Left Sep 40.
248 Sqn	WR	Dyce, Aberdeenshire	21 Jun 40	Ex-Fighter Command. Blenheim IVF.
		Sumburgh, Shetlands	14 Jul 40	
		Wick, Caithness	13 Dec 40	Detachment. Left 03 Jun 41.
		Dyce, Aberdeenshire	06 Jan 41	To 16 Group 15 June 41.
252 Sqn	PN	Sumburgh, Shetlands	16 Apr 41	Detachment from 15 Group. Left May 41.
254 Sqn	QY	Lossiemouth, Moray	20 Mar 40	Detachment from 16 Group. Blenheim IVF. Left 23 Apr 40.
		Hatston, Orkneys	23 Apr 40	From 16 Group.
		Sumburgh, Shetlands	17 May 40	
		Dyce, Aberdeenshire	02 Aug 40	
		Sumburgh, Shetlands	07 Jan 41	To 15 Group 29 May 41.
		Dyce, Aberdeenshire	07 Jan 41	Date arbitrary. Detachment from 15 Group. Left May 41.
		Sumburgh, Shetlands	10 Dec 41	Detachment from 15 Group.
		Wick, Caithness	10 Dec 41	Detachment from 15 Group.
		Dyce, Aberdeenshire	10 Dec 41	From 15 Group.
269 Sqn	UA	Montrose, Angus	03 Sep 39	*In situ.* Anson I.
		Wick, Caithness	10 Oct 39	Hudson I, Mar 40. To AHQ Iceland 11 Mar 41.
		Sumburgh, Shetlands	10 Jun 40	Detachment. Left 11 Jun 40.
272 Sqn	XK	Sumburgh, Shetlands	03 Apr 41	Detachment from 19 Group. Beaufighter IC, Apr-Jul 41. Left May 41.
320 Sqn	NO	Leuchars, Fife	01 Oct 40	From 15 Group. Hudson I, Oct 40. To 15 Group 18 Jan 41.
		Leuchars, Fife	20 Mar 41	From 15 Group.
404 (RCAF) Sqn	EE	Castletown, Caithness	21 Jun 41	From 16 Group. Blenheim IVF.
		Skitten, Caithness	27 Jul 41	
		Dyce, Aberdeenshire	09 Oct 41	

		Sumburgh, Shetlands	09 Oct 41	Detachment.
		Sumburgh, Shetlands	06 Dec 41	Squadron move to join Detachment.
		Dyce, Aberdeenshire	06 Dec 41	Detachment.
413 (RCAF) Sqn	QL	Sullom Voe, Shetlands	04 Oct 41	From 15 Group. Catalina I. Left for Far East 01 Mar 42.
489 (RNZAF) Sqn	–	Leuchars, Fife	12 Aug 41	Formed. Beaufort I, Aug 41. Blenheim IVF, Jan 42.
502 Sqn	YG	Wick, Caithness	01 Jan 41	Detachment from 15 Group (date arbitrary). Whitley V. Left Dec 41.
608 Sqn	UL	Thornaby, Yorkshire	03 Sep 39	*In situ.* Anson I. Botha I, Jun 40. Blenheim I, Feb 41. Blenheim IV May 41. Hudson V, Jul 41. Hudson III, Aug 41.
		Dyce, Aberdeenshire	03 Sep 39	Detachment (date arbitrary). Left Dec 41.
612 Sqn	WL	Dyce, Aberdeenshire	03 Sep 39	*In situ.* Hector I. Anson I. Hudson, Mar 40. Whitley V, Nov 40.
		Wick, Caithness	10 Feb 41	Detachment. Left 31 Mar 41.
		Wick, Caithness	31 Mar 41	Whitley VII, May 41. To AHQ Iceland 15 Dec 41.
1406 Flight	–	Wick, Caithness	09 May 41	Formed as a Met Flight. Spitfire.
1408 Flight	–	Wick, Caithness	03 Dec 41	Formed. Hudson III. Hampden I (?).
G Flight	–	Helensburgh, Argyll & Bute	21 Sep 40	Formed. Short 'G' Class flying-boats. To 15 Group 26 Nov 40.
		Bowmore, Islay	24 Dec 40	From 15 Group. Redesignated as 119 Squadron 13 Mar 41.

19 GROUP   **Formed at Mount Wise, Plymouth in January 1941. Took over control of South-West approaches from an Ops Room in Egg Buckland Keep on 7th February. The Ops staff, along with Naval staff of C-in-C Plymouth moved into a new Combined Area HQ below Mount Wise on 10th January 1942., remaining there for the duration of the war.**

Unit	Code	Base	Arrived	Comments
10 (RAAF)	RB	Pembroke Dock, Pembs	14 Feb 41	Detachment.
22 Sqn	OA	St Eval, Cornwall	29 Mar 41	Detachment from 16 Group. Beaufort I. Left 08 May 41
		St Eval, Cornwall	23 Jul 41	Detachment from 16 Group. Left 23 Jul 41.
		St Eval, Cornwall	28 Oct 41	From 16 Group. Beaufort II, Nov 41.
53 Sqn	TE	St Eval, Cornwall	20 Mar 41	From 16 Group. Blenheim IV. To 16 Group 03 Jul 41.
	PZ	St Eval, Cornwall	30 Aug 41	Detachment. Hudson V. Left 03 Sep 41.
		St Eval, Cornwall	13 Sep 41	Detachment.
		St Eval, Cornwall	20 Oct 41	Squadron move to join Detachment. To 15 Group 17 Dec 41.
59 Sqn	PJ	St Eval, Cornwall	19 Feb 41	Detachment from 16 Group. Blenheim IV. Left 01 Mar 41.
82 Sqn	UX	St Eval, Cornwall	10 May 41	Detachment from 16 Group. Blenheim IV. Left 11 May 41.
		Portreath, Cornwall	13 May 41	Detachment from 16 Group. Left 11 Jun 41.
86 Sqn	BX	St Eval, Cornwall	13 Dec 41	Detachment from 16 Group. Beaufort I. Left 10 Jan 42.
119 Sqn		Pembroke Dock, Pembs	14 Jun 41	Detachment. Short S.23M/26M.
		Pembroke Dock, Pembs	11 Aug 41	Squadron move to join Detachment. Non-operational until April 1942.
204 Sqn	KG	Pembroke Dock, Pembs	10 Aug 41	From 200 Group. Left for W.Africa, 28 Aug 41.
206 Sqn	VX	St Eval, Cornwall	01 Apr 41	Detachment from 16 Group. Hudson I/II/III/IV. To 15 Group 12 Aug 41.
		St Eval, Cornwall	12 Aug 41	Detachment from 15 Group.
		Chivenor, Devon	11 Dec 41	Detachment from 15 Group.
209 Sqn	WQ	Pembroke Dock	10 Oct 41	From AHQ Iceland. Catalina Ib.
217 Sqn	MW	Carew Cheriton, Pembs	29 Aug 41	Detachment from 15 Group. Left 28 Oct 41.
		St Eval, Cornwall	28 Oct 41	Detachment from 15 Group.
221 Sqn	DF	St Eval, Cornwall	04 Apr 41	Detachment from 15 Group. Wellington IC. Left 02 May 41.

		St Eval, Cornwall	26 May 41	Detachment from 15 Group. Left 28 Sep 41.
224 Sqn	QA	St Eval, Cornwall	20 Dec 41	From 15 Group. Hudson V.
233 Sqn	ZS	St Eval, Cornwall	16 Aug 41	From 15 Group. Hudson III/V.
236 Sqn	FA	Carew Cheriton, Pembs	20 Mar 41	From 15 Group. Blenheim IVF. Beaufighter IC, Oct 41.
		St Eval, Cornwall	20 Mar 41	Detachment. Left 07 Sep 41.
		Portreath, Cornwall	09 Dec 41	Detachment. Left 15 Dec 41.
248 Sqn	WR	Carew Cheriton, Pembs	16 Sep 41	Detachment from 16 Group. Beaufighter IC.
		St Eval, Cornwall	29 Sep 41	Detachment from 16 Group.
		Portreath, Cornwall	13 Oct 41	Detachment from 16 Group.
252 Sqn	PN	Chivenor, Devon	24 May 41	Detachment from 15 Group. Beaufighter I. Left 15 Jun 41.
254 Sqn	QY	Carew Cheriton, Pembs	29 May 41	Detachment from 15 Group (date arbitrary). Beaufighter IVF. Left Dec 41.
272 Sqn	XK	Chivenor, Devon	03 Apr 41	From 15 Group. Beaufighter IC, Apr 41. To Middle East 24 May 41.
500 Sqn	MK	Carew Cheriton, Pembs	28 Aug 41	Detachment from 16 Group. Blenheim IV.
502 Sqn	YG	Chivenor, Devon	28 Nov 41	Detachment from 15 Group. Whitley V. Left 11 Dec 41.
		St Eval, Cornwall	11 Dec 41	Detachment. Left 26 Dec 41.
		St Eval, Cornwall	26 Dec 41	Squadron move to join Detachment.
612 Sqn	WL	St Eval, Cornwall	20 Oct 41	Detachment from 18 Group. Left 04 Nov 41.
404 Flight	–	St Eval, Cornwall	01 Jan 41	From 15 Group. Hudson. Ventura. Redesignated as 1404 Flight 01 Mar 41.
1404 Flight	–	St Eval, Cornwall	01 Mar 41	Formed from 404 Flight. Hudson. Ventura.

GROUP POOL

206 Sqn	VX	Silloth, Cumberland	30 Nov 39	Detachment from 16 Group. Anson I. Left May 40.
320 Sqn	NO	Silloth, Cumberland	18 Jan 41	Detachment from 15 Group. Anson I. Left Apr 42.

AHQ ICELAND **Work commenced on a base in Iceland under 18 Group, in August 1940**
AHQ Iceland formed 19th March 1941 to control Nos 30 and 100 Wings.
Area Combined HQ formed at Mentaskolinn, nr Reykjavik in June 1940.
No 100 Wing ceased Ops from Iceland in July 1944, and disbanded in July 1945.

Unit	Code	Base	Arrived	Comments
22 Sqn	OA	Kaldadarnes	22 May 41	Detachment from 16 Group. Beaufort I. Left 30 May 41.
98 Sqn	–	Kaldadarnes	19 Mar 41	*In situ*. From 18 Group. Battle I. Hurricane Ia added, Jun 41.
		Melgerdi	19 Apr 41	Detachment. Left 26 Apr 41. Redesignated as 1423 Flight 15 Jul 41.
201 Sqn	ZM	Reykjavik	18 Mar 41	Detachment from 18 Group. Sunderland I/II. Left 16 Apr 41.
		Reykjavik	12 May 41	Detachment from 18 Group. Sunderland I/II. Left 02 Jun 41.
204 Sqn	KG	Reykjavik	03 Apr 41	Sunderland II, Jun 41. To 200 Group 15 Jul 41.
209 Sqn	WQ	Reykjavik	13 Jul 41	From 15 Group. Catalina Ib. To 19 Group 10 Oct 41.
210 Sqn	DA	Reykjavik	24 May 41	Detachment from 18 Group. Catalina I. Left 28 May 41.
		Reykjavik	26 Jun 41	Detachment from 18 Group. Left 14 Jul 41.
		Reykjavik	11 Aug 41	Detachment from 18 Group. Left 15 Aug 41.
221 Sqn	DF	Reykjavik	11 Aug 41	Detachment from 15 Group. Wellington IC. Left 13 Aug 41.
		Reykjavik	28 Sep 41	Squadron move from 15 Group to join Detachment. To 15 Group 05 Dec 41.

240 Sqn	BN	Reykjavik	13 May 41	Detachment from 15 Group. Catalina I. Left 28 May 41.
		Reykjavik	04 Jul 41	Detachment from 15 Group. Left 31 Jul 41.
		Reykjavik	12 Sep 41	Detachment from 15 Group. Left 21 Sep 41.
269 Sqn	UA	Reykjavik	11 Mar 41	From 18 Group. Hudson I/II.
		Kaldadarnes	12 Apr 41	Hudson III. May 41.
		Kaldadarnes	01 Jun 41	Squadron move to join detachment.
		Reykjavik	12 Dec 41	Detachment.
330 Sqn	GS	Reykjavik	25 Apr 41	Formed. Northrop N-3PB, May 41.
		Akureyri	20 Jul 41	Detachment.
		Budareyri	11 Sep 41	Detachment.
502 Sqn	YG	Reykjavik	24 Aug 41	Detachment from 15 Group. Whitley V. Left 30 Aug 41.
612 Sqn	WL	Reykjavik	12 Sep 41	Detachment from 18 Group. Whitley V/VII. Left 03 Oct 41.
		Reykjavik	15 Dec 41	From 18 Group. Whitley V/VII.
1407 (Met) Flt		Reykjavik	02 Oct 41	Formed. Hudson III/IIIa received Apr 42.
1423 (Fighter) Flight		Kaldadarnes	10 Jun 41	Formed from Hurricane Flt of 98 Squadron.
		Reykjavik	26 Jul 41	Hurricane Ia. Ceased operations 03 Dec 41. To 13 Group (Ouston, UK) 19 Dec 41.

200 GROUP

Formed 25th September 1939 with Headquarters in the Bristol Hotel, Gibraltar. Covered part of RAF Mediterranean Area in control of 202 Squadron. Taken over by Coastal Command 12th August 1940 with responsibility for all flying boats and maritime landplanes based on Gibraltar. Disbanded 21st December 1941 and immediately reformed as Air Headquarters (AHQ) Gibraltar.

Unit	Code	Base	Arrived	Comments
1 PRU	LY	North Front	24 Jun 41	'G' Flight. Spitfire I (PR) Type D. Maryland I.
10 (RAAF) Sqn	RB	New Camp	08 Jul 40	Detachment from 15 Group. Sunderland I. Left 07 Aug 40.
200 Sqn	–	North Front	12 Jun 41	From 16 Group. Hudson IV. To West Africa 18 Jun 41.
202 Sqn	TQ	New Camp	25 Sep 39	*In situ* since 10 Sep 39. London II. Absorbed Swordfish I floatplanes of 3 CAACU, Sep 40. Catalina Ib, Apr 41, Catalina II May 41. Sunderland I/II Dec 41.
204 Sqn	KG	New Camp	14 Jul 41	From AHQ Iceland. Sunderland II. To 19 Group 10 Aug 41.
233 Sqn	ZS	North Front	1 Dec 41	Detachment from 15 Group. Hudson I/III,V.

AHQ GIBRALTAR

Formed 21st December 1941 from 200 Group. Operated from premises in Cathedral Sq. An Area Combined HQ was formed with the Royal Navy at the Tower in the Dockyard early in 1942. The Flying-boat Station was known as RAF New Camp after 1st May 42.

Unit	Code	Base	Arrived	Comments
1 PRU	LY	North Front	*In situ*	'G' Flight. From 200 Group. Spitfire I (PR) Type D, Maryland.
202 Sqn	TQ	New Camp	*In situ*	From 200 Group. Sunderland I/II. Sunderland III, Mar 42.
233 Sqn	ZS	North Front	*In situ*	From 200 Group. Hudson I/III/V.

Appendix H

Coastal Command Bases 1939

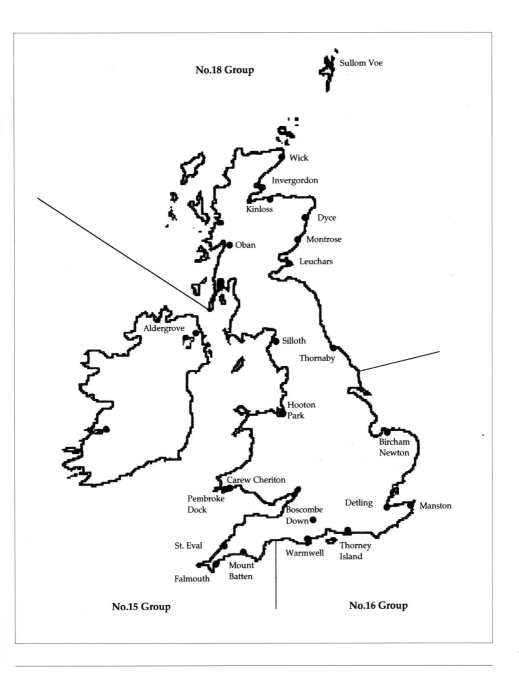

Appendix I

Coastal Command Bases 1940

Appendix J

Coastal Command Bases 1941

(Groups as at February 1941)

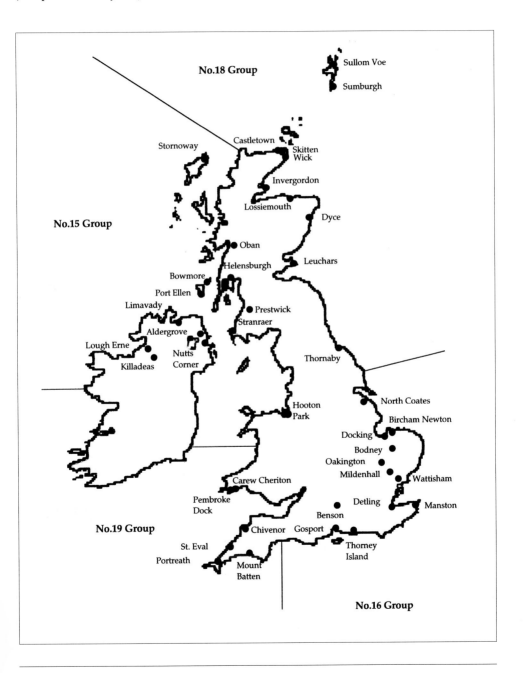

Appendix K

Coastal Command Aircraft

A Representative Selection of the Aircraft Types used by Coastal Command, 1939-1941.

The intention here is to provide a visual reminder of the majority of the different types of aircraft employed by the flying units under the control of Coastal Command during the period covered by this volume, and at the same time to provide some details about the aircraft concerned that should complement any comments that appear in the introductions to the various chapters. Many of the types of aircraft involved will have suffered losses where the circumstances are described in the main chapters of the book.

This is a representative selection, therefore not every type mentioned elsewhere is featured. Any omissions will hopefully be included in future planned volumes of this work.

The Cheetah-engined Avro 652A Anson was in front-line use with ten of Coastal Command's operational squadrons at the start of the Second World War. No 321 Squadron Mk.I N9742 has had its triangular unit badge (forward of the tailplane fin-flash) blocked-out by the wartime censor. N9742 ditched off Holyhead, Anglesey, on 29th November 1940. *P.H.T. Green collection*

No 269 Squadron Avro Anson Mk.I N9673 'UA-J' hit an obstruction when attempting to take-off from Wick on 21st March 1940. A total of 8,138 Ansons were built in the UK and a further 2,882 in Canada. Most were employed as trainers and light transport aircraft by the RAF as well as several overseas users. Ansons eventually retired from the RAF in 1968. *P.H.T. Green collection*

Armstrong Whitworth AW.38 Whitley Mk.Is and Mk.Vs, either detached from or passed on by Bomber Command, were the first of the type to serve with Coastal Command. The General Reconnaissance Mk.VII, represented by Z6633 of 612 Squadron, entered service at the end of 1941 and featured ASV Mk.II radar, a crew of six and extra tankage. *P.H.T. Green collection*

The Avro 621 Tutor, which first flew in 1929, was designed as a successor to the Avro 504 basic trainer. Of the 400 or so built, approx 200 were still on RAF strength at the outset of the Second World War. Most of these became station or squadron hacks. K6100, delivered to the RAF in 1935, served with a number of units until struck off charge in June 1944. *P.H.T. Green collection*

The Blackburn B-26 Botha Mk.I general reconnaissance/torpedo-bomber entered Coastal Command service with 608 Squadron in June 1940 ('UL-A' being an example). They proved to be seriously underpowered and by February 1941 had been withdrawn from front-line use. No 502 Squadron also had a few on charge from August to November 1940. *R Hayward via Andrew Thomas*

This extremely murky shot of a Bristol Blenheim Mk.1F was probably typical of an early morning scene on a Second World War coastal airfield. It shows the first Blenheim delivered to 235 Squadron at RAF Manston in February 1940, following the hasty transfer of four of Fighter Command's squadrons to reinforce Coastal Command, early in 1940. *P.H.T. Green collection*

The Bristol 149 Blenheim Mk.IV superseded the Mk.I in 1939 and was to serve with 13 Coastal Command squadrons – ten in the Mk.IVF fighter role and with three as bombers. L8793 was one of the latter variant, and was photographed in mid-1940 at RAF Odiham. It was reputedly coded 'TR-J' by the time it crashed into the sea on 25th September 1940. *P.H.T. Green collection*

Bristol Blenheim Mk.IV L9394 'WR-O' of 248 Squadron was photogaphed in 1940 and clearly shows the lengthened nose to provide space for a navigator / radio operator, and the ventral gun tray. Over 3,100 examples of this Mark were produced. L9394 was serving with 404 (RCAF) Squadron when it spun into the ground on 2nd September 1941. *P.H.T. Green collection*

Following a prolonged and problematical introduction into servce, the Bristol 152 Beaufort Mk.I superseded the elderly Vildebeest biplane and became Coastal Command's standard torpedo-bomber from 1940 to 1943. L9834's career came to an untimely end when it flew into a hill following a night take-off from Leuchars, on 30th August 1941. *P.H.T. Green collection*

No 22 Squadron was the first front-line Coastal Command unit to receive the Beaufort, in November 1940, although it was to be the following April before their first operational sortie. Mk.I X8930 'OA-J' was found to have 309 bullet holes in it, following a shipping strike off Kristiansand and a subsequent belly-landing at Leuchars, 10th September 1941. *P.H.T. Green collection*

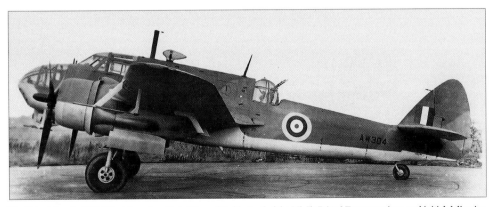

The Bristol Beaufort Mk.II had American Twin Wasps fitted instead of the Mk.I's Bristol Taurus engines, and initial deliveries went to 217 Squadron at Thorney Island, Sussex, in November 1941. Production of this variant, which began with AW244, totalled 415. AW304 is seen here after emerging from the Bristol Aeroplane Company factory at Filton. *P.H.T. Green collection*

The first deliveries of the very capable Consolidated Catalina Mk.I flying-boat (equivalent to the US Navy's PBY-5) went to 240 Squadron in March 1941. The enemy was not the only threat, as 413 Squadron lost two of their charges on 10th November 1941 (including Z2141) when they sank at their Sullom Voe moorings during a gale. *P.H.T. Green collection*

The arrival of the Catalinas helped to close the notorious Atlantic 'gap', and a small batch of Mk.IIs was delivered almost concurrently with the first Mk.Is. Catalina Mk.II AM267, photographed in 1941, served with 240 Squadron and later with Nos 4 and 131 (Coastal) Operational Training Units, surviving only to be struck off charge in October 1944. *P.H.T. Green collection*

The Consolidated Liberator Mk.I was the second of the very long-range aircraft acquired from the USA in a bid to close the mid-Atlantic 'gap', where enemy U-boats had hitherto escaped attention from the shore-based aircraft. The first RAF unit to be declared operational on the type was 120 Squadron, based at Nutts Corner near Belfast, Northern Ireland. *P.H.T. Green collection*

The DH.82A Tiger Moth elementary trainer was introduced into RAF service in February 1932. Over 7,000 were built world-wide and the Mk.II remained in RAF service for over 15 years. They were also employed as 'hack' communications aircraft by many units during the Second World War. This representative image features a 182 Squadron machine. *P.H.T. Green collection*

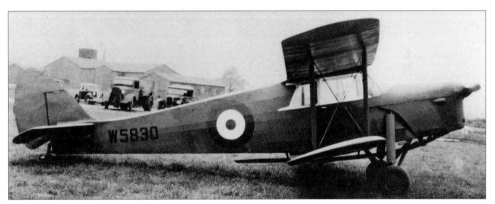

Over 60 UK civil DH.87B Hornet Moths were impressed into the RAF for wartime military service for communications duties and to equip six Coastal Patrol Flights in Coastal Command who undertook off-shore radar calibration flights in 1940. W5830, the former G-ADKE; served with a variety of units prior to being struck off charge on 13th July 1945. *P.H.T. Green collection*

Although near obsolete, the Fairey Battle equipped an entire Bomber Command group at the start of the Second World War. Coastal Command only had the use of 98 Squadron in Iceland, where L5343 crashed on 13th September 1940. L5343, seen here at St Athan in 1990, following restoration, went to the RAF Museum where it is now on display. *P.H.T. Green collection*

Lockheed Hudsons were just reaching Coastal Command squadrons at the outbreak of war, though by early 1942 had completely superseded the shorter-range Anson. No 269 Squadron Mk.III, T9465, delivered in June 1941, bears the legend 'Presented by Lockheed-Vega Employees'. It later passed to 161 Squadron and was DBR at Blida on 21st July 1943. *P.H.T. Green collection*

Eighteen Northrop N-3PB seaplanes were delivered to Iceland from Canada for 330 Squadron, a unit manned by Norwegian naval personnel that was operating from near Reykjavik, from mid-1941 onwards. The N-3PBs were used on reconnaissance and convoy escort duties and were eventually supplemented by Catalinas and later still by Sunderlands. *P.H.T. Green collection*

The Saro Lerwick, second of the new monoplane flying-boats, after the Sunderland, failed to come up to expectation and only 21 were constructed. Trials were conducted by 240 Squadron from June 1939 and 209 squadron was obliged to use them operationally until April 1941, at which point they were passed to 4 (Coastal) OTU. 'TA-S' is L7257. *P.H.T. Green collection*

Introduced into RAF service in 1936, only 31 Saro A27 Londons were built, including a prototype, ten Mk.Is and the balance of Mk.IIs. K5910, 'BN-L' of 240 Squadron, was a Mk.II; and was photographed over the North Sea in mid-May 1940. Londons remained in front-line use with 202 Squadron, in Gibraltar, until around the middle of 1941. *P.H.T. Green collection*

When war was declared, 29 of the original 31 Saro A27 Londons were still on RAF strength and at the time two were in fact patrolling over the North Sea. K9686 was a 240 Squadron Mk.II, this latter variant being identifiable by Pegasus X engines, round cowlings and four-blade airscrews. It was photographed in 1939, *en route* for the Shetlands. *P.H.T. Green collection*

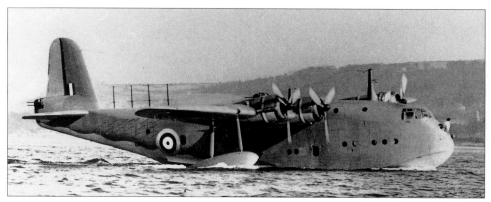

Two of Imperial Airways' famous Short S.26/M 'C' Class flying-boat airliners were impressed for wartime military service in July 1940, to replace two S.30s lost in Norway. AX659 was formerly G-AETY *Clio*, and after conversion was sent to 119 Squadron at Bowmore. AX659 crashed on Islay on 22nd August 1941 after a failed engine had stuck in fine pitch. *P.H.T. Green collection*

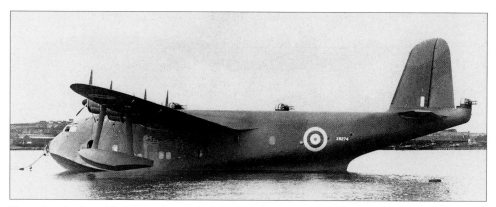

Three enlarged variants of the S.23 were impressed in July 1940, before they could be operated by Imperial Airways and then converted for military use, as the S.26/M 'G' Class. X8274, ex- G-AFCJ *Golden Fleece*, went to G Flight (later 119 Squadron). The tail turret had been faired-in, similar to AX659 above, before X8274 was lost on 20th June 1941. *P.H.T. Green collection*

Designed as a military development of the 'C' Class Empire flying-boat, the Short S.25 Sunderland Mk.I entered service with the RAF in mid-1938. L2165, 'B' of 210 Squadron, possibly photographed just before the onset of war, lacks the unit's later 'DA' code-letter prefix and camouflage. L2165 crashed at Milford Haven, early on 18th September 1939. *P.H.T. Green collection*

In Great Britain converting onto Sunderlands when war broke out, the detachment of 10 Squadron of the Royal Australian Air Force was ordered to stay put and join the fray. Short Sunderland Mk.I N9048 'RB-B' is seen here at Mount Batten in 1940. It was hangared and under maintenance there when destroyed in an air raid on 28th November 1940. *P.H.T. Green collection*

Spitfire Mk.I X4492 was one of 20 or so converted to PR Type C status, with F.24 cameras in the wings and an extra fuel tank in the rear fuselage. It served with the PRU/1 PRU and at some stage was modified further, eventually to the interim long-range Type F (PR.VI) variant, before being passed on to serve with 140 Squadron and later still the RCAF. *P.H.T. Green collection*

The Vickers Vildebeest design dates from 1928. Around 200 were built, of which approx 100 were still in use at the start of the war, when they were the sole first-line torpedo-bombers available to Coastal Command. The Perseus-engined Mk.IVs went into service with 42 Squadron in March 1937. This view was taken just five days before war was declared. *P.H.T. Green collection*

Another victim of extremely bad weather – Supermarine Stranraer K7290 'BN-X', which sank at its moorings on 21st November 1940 – again at Stranraer. This provides a rare view of the keel of the last of a long line of biplane flying-boats designed by R J Mitchell (creator of the Spitfire). Only 24 Stranraers were built in Britain; others were built in Canada. *P.H.T. Green collection*

No 240 Squadron lost their fair share of Supermarine Type 304 Stranraers while at their moorings. K7301 sank in a gale on 21st August 1940 – at Stranraer ! *P.H.T. Green collection*

The unusual-looking degaussing system fitted to the Vickers Wellington DWI Mk.Is was designed to combat the magnetic mine menace in the early days of war. *P.H.T. Green collection*

Coastal Command embraced the Vickers Wellington in November 1940, when 221 Squadron reformed at Bircham Newton with Mk.ICs. W5674 'DF-D' is seen here after conversion to GR.VIII standard in mid-1941. It displays the ASV Mk.II aerials atop the fuselage and under the wings but like the majority of this mark, it is not fitted with a Leigh light. *P.H.T. Green collection*

RAF FIGHTER COMMAND LOSSES OF THE SECOND WORLD WAR

Norman Franks

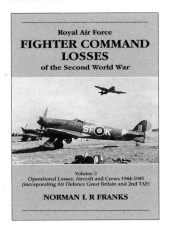

ROYAL AIR FORCE BOMBER COMMAND LOSSES of the SECOND WORLD WAR

W R Chorley

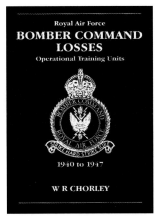

We hope you enjoyed this book . . .

Midland Publishing titles are edited and designed by an experienced and enthusiastic team of specialists.

Further titles are in preparation and we always welcome ideas from authors or readers for books they would like to see published.

In addition, our associate company, Midland Counties Publications, offers an exceptionally wide range of aviation, military, naval and transport books and videos for sale by mail-order around the world.

For a copy of the appropriate catalogue, or to order further copies of this book, and any of the titles mentioned on this or the following page, please write, telephone, fax or e-mail to:

Midland Counties Publications
4 Watling Drive,
Hinckley, Leics,
LE10 3EY,
England

Tel: (+44) 01455 254 450
Fax: (+44) 01455 233 737
e-mail: midlandbooks@compuserve.com
www.midlandcountiessuperstore.com

Following the Battle of France and the retreat through Dunkirk, Britain stood alone awaiting the inevitable onslaught from Germany. At the forefront of the UK's defence was Fighter Command and it was their Hurricanes, Spitfires, Blenheims and Defiants that became the world-famed 'Few' that managed to repulse the Luftwaffe in 'The Battle of Britain' during the summer of 1940.

Germany's failure to overcome the RAF and lthe decision to attack Russia, allowed Britain to consolidate, rebuild, go on the offensive, and after D-day, battle across Europe to the bitter end..

Between 1939-45 Fighter Command, ADGB and 2nd TAF lost over 5,000 aircrew. This work examines on a day-to-day basis the sacrifices made by these men during the desperate years of the war. The reasons and circumstances for the losses are given as crucial campaigns are enacted.

Available in 234 x 156mm sbk format:

Volume 1: 1939-41
Details 1,000 aircraft losses; 168pp
40 b/w pics 1 85780 055 9 **£12.95**

Volume 2: 1942-43
Details 1,800+ aircraft losses; 156pp
53 b/w pics 1 85780 075 3 **£12.95**

Volume 3: 1944-45
Details c.2,450 acft losses; 200pp
83 b/w pics 1 85780 093 1 **£14.95**

This highly acclaimed series identifies, on a day-by-day basis, the individual aircraft, crews and circumstances of each of the 10,000+ aircraft lost in the European Theatre of operations during the Second World War.

Appendices include loss totals by squadron and aircraft type each year; Group loss totals; Squadron bases, bomber OTU losses by unit and type, PoWs, escapers and evaders etc.

Available in 234 x 156mm sbk format:

Volume 2: 1941
Details 1,515 aircraft losses; 224pp
0 904597 87 3 **£12.95**

Volume 3: 1942
Details 2,035 aircraft losses; 318pp
0 904597 89 X **£15.95**

Volume 7: Operational Training Units 1940-1947
Details 2,400 aircraft losses; 384pp
1 85780 132 6 **£18.99**

Volume 8: Heavy Conversion Units & Flights 1940-1947
To be published in October; c280pp
1 85780 034 6 c**£16.99**

Please note that volumes 1, 4, 5 and 6 are currently out of print.

BRITISH SECRET PROJECTS – JET FIGHTERS SINCE 1950

Tony Buttler

A huge number of fighter projects have been drawn by British companies over the last 50 years, in particular prior to the 1957 White Paper, but with few turned into hardware, little has been published about these fascinating 'might-have-beens'. One reason was that all military brochures remained classified once a competition winner had been chosen. This work makes extensive use of previously unpublished primary source material, much recently declassified. It gives an insight into a secret world where the public had little idea of what was going on, while at the same time presenting a coherent nationwide picture of fighter development and evolution. Particular emphasis is placed on tender design competitions and some of the events which led to certain aircraft either being cancelled or produced. Some of the many and varied types included are the Hawker P.1103/P.1136/P.1121 series, and the Fairey 'Delta III' (shown in the Keith Woodcock cover painting). The book includes many illustrations plus specially commissioned renditions of 'might-have-been' types in contemporary markings.

Hbk, 282 x 213 mm, 176 pages
130 b/w photos; 140 three-views, and an 8-page colour section
1 85780 095 8 **£24.95**

BRITISH SECRET PROJECTS JET BOMBERS SINCE 1949

Tony Buttler

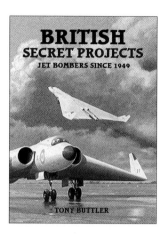

This long-awaited title forms a natural successor to the author's successful volume on fighters. The design and development of the British bomber since World War Two is covered in similar depth and again the emphasis is placed on the tender design competitions between projects from different companies. Extensive reference has been made to recently declassified archives in national and industry collections which allows many little-known projects to be brought together within a full narrative of bomber development. The design backgrounds to the V-Bomber programme, Canberra, Buccaneer, Avro 730, TSR.2, Harrier, Jaguar and Tornado are revealed in more detail than has probably ever been published before, but attention is also given to anti-submarine types and stillborn programmes such as the RAF's first requirement for a low-level bomber and the AFVG. Includes many previously unpublished illustrations plus specially commissioned renditions of 'might-have-been' types in contemporary markings. Keith Woodcock's cover painting shows how the Avro 698 might have looked in service had it not become the Vulcan.

Hbk, 282 x 213 mm, 224 pages
160 b/w photos; many three-views, and 9 pages of colour
1 85780 130 X **£24.99**

BRITISH AIRFIELD BUILDINGS
Vol.2:The Expansion & Inter-War Periods

Graham Buchan Innes

Airfield buildings are a constant source of fascination to enthusiasts and historians who welcomed Graham Innes' first genuinely pocket-sized and affordable volume *British Airfield Buildings of the Second World War*.

This second volume primarily focuses on the expansion period 1935-1939 when the government belatedly responded to the rise of Hitler and the threat he posed to Britain's inadequate air defences, but includes a handful of First World War and post First World War buildings as well as some wartime temporary designs for comparison. The majority of photographs are in colour, and as with the first volume provide an illustration of a surviving example of the building, highlighting details and other styles of similar building.

A wide variety of buildings are shown, including hangars, barrack blocks, maintenance buildings, guard houses, mess buildings, down to the humble latrines. A valuable and convenient reference.

Sbk 184 x 120mm, 128 pages
261 colour photographs
1 85780 101 6
£8.95